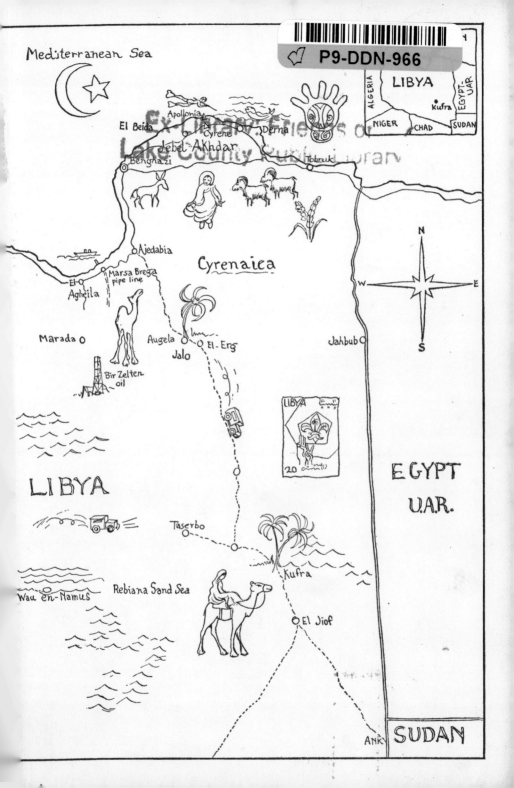

BY AGNES NEWTON KEITH

Children of Allah

The Medina el Kadima, Tripoli

Children of Allah

by AGNES NEWTON KEITH

sketches by the author

An Atlantic Monthly Press Book

LITTLE, BROWN AND COMPANY · BOSTON · TORONTO

ATLANTIC–LITTLE, BROWN BOOKS
ARE PUBLISHED BY
LITTLE, BROWN AND COMPANY
IN ASSOCIATION WITH
THE ATLANTIC MONTHLY PRESS

*Published simultaneously in Canada
by Little, Brown & Company (Canada) Limited*

PRINTED IN THE UNITED STATES OF AMERICA

For H. G. K.
"Vous estes ma morte et ma vye"
Anonymous

Author's Note

BORN to an arid and denuded land, Libyans all their lives are ruled by sea and Sahara, by coming of rain or of drought, by sandstorm or flood, by harvesting of cereals, or by famine for their flocks; and now in the century of Sahara wealth, by the flowing of oil from their sands.

They feast all night and fast from the dawn for one month every year, and pray towards Mecca five times daily, and murmur the ninety-nine beautiful names of Allah in submission to his will. They drive Alfa-Romeos, Jaguars, camels, and donkeys, some have Louis Quinze furniture while some live in black tents and caves, they go to Rome for holidays, they hide their wives in sheets and veils, they win university scholarships, and many can't sign their names.

This is the story of a proud Islamic people struggling for a modern life in a new Kingdom in a Stone Age land. The action and events in *Children of Allah* are true. However, the names used in the Libyan world are, in some cases, fictitious ones.

The choice of the defining Arabic article l, il, el, al depends on the sound following it, which depends on the voice and pronunciation of the person speaking, and the part of the country he comes from. It cannot be authentically standardized. But I find that most maps and many writers use el for all place names, and al for persons' names. I aim at this. Place names may be correctly used both with el and without any article.

Agnes Newton Keith
August 1965

Contents

I

City of Allah

1. City of Allah

THERE were screaming babies and airsick mothers, embarrassed fathers who tried to disown them, and worried fathers who hovered over their sick ones, urging glasses of livid Orange Crush and soft caramels on them until they were sick again. The original color of skins was problematical, as most passengers were slightly green. An Arabian nightmare! I thought.

"I am afraid we Middle Easterners are not very good travelers!" Mr. Abou Babba whispered apologetically to Harry and me. We had nothing to add to the statement.

Before landing, I made an attempt to approach the "Ladies," but found the toilet afloat. Harry had been right when he said that Middle East airlines should supply the passengers with rubber boots.

The plane was circling now over Idris Airport, and mothers begin to tidy up, wipe babies' faces, plug mouths with pacifiers, collect soiled napkins and sucked oranges, abandon airsickness bags to the aisles, and look as if they hoped to live to land. The air in the plane is very hot, and overly sweet with strong Cairo perfumes, fruit peelings, and aroma of babies. Husbands are gathering up paper bundles, string bags, wicker baskets bulging with fruit and sugar goodies, and cartons of ex-Customs cigarettes. Several mothers are wrapping themselves from top to toe in white sheets which cover the face and head, while babies subdue their screams to whimpers, and fathers resolve never to do it again.

A gentle bounce, and we're down on Libyan soil at last.

We had met Mr. Abou Babba in the Rome airport waiting for the same plane. Like Harry, he was going to Libya as a technical expert with the Food and Agriculture Organization (FAO) of the United Nations. Only Mr. Abou Babba had been there before, and he knew everything. He was a Jordanian, an Arab, and a Moslem. I didn't think he looked like an Arab, dressed in his smart business suit — but I didn't know then what an Arab looked like.

The first thing Harry had asked him was, "What is the country really like?"

"Desert!"

What would a forestry expert do in the desert, I wondered. Plant trees, I suppose. I used to think that forestry went with forests; it had in Borneo and the Philippines. But perhaps the fewer trees there were in a country, the more an expert was needed.

"Libya is a very strict Moslem country," Mr. Abou Babba continued. "Do you know the ways of Islam?"

"Yes," said Harry, "I almost made the pilgrimage to Mecca once myself."

Mr. Abou Babba raised his eyebrows in surprise, then said proudly, "I am myself a Hajji, and also my wife has made the pilgrimage."

I was very impressed. "I didn't know that a woman could make the journey," I said.

"Oh, yes, if she is strong. My wife is stronger than I am. Is that not usual in women, Mrs. Keith?"

"Well, we live longer." I looked at Mr. Abou Babba with increased interest to try to connect this seemingly Westernized man with the simple, white-robed pilgrims I had read of.

"Are there many UN experts in Libya?" Harry wanted to know.

Mr. Abou Babba giggled. "Let me tell you. When you drive out on the Libyan desert and stop your car, there is not a living thing in sight. Then three things happen: first an Arab appears, then a fly, then an expert!" This story amused them both for some time.

Our new friend had distributed a few more scattered facts about the country: strong Libyan tea promotes ulcers, don't drink tap water, be careful of fleas (they are carried in baracans). Libyan women must cover their faces and live in seclusion. The King is a saint. The first queen is very good and very beautiful and much younger than the King, but unfortunately, she has had no children. Also the second queen has still no heir. Shalhi's assassination last year frightened the royal family. Revolution? Not while the King lives . . .

The hostess opened the plane door, and the air from an oven burst in. I could feel sand gritting in my teeth.

"Oh, dear, it's a ghibli day!" Mr. Abou Babba leaned across the aisle and looked apprehensively out into the yellow air. "Tut-tut! I do hope you are dressed for the heat, Mrs. Keith!"

It was September 1955, and Harry and I had just come down from London via Rome, still wearing our Harris tweeds.

That word "ghibli" I remembered from the United Nations post report, which is an account of conditions in a country to which a UN member is going for a new assignment. "Ghibli — a blast of hot, dry air off the Sahara, a powerful, sand-laden wind which sometimes buries entire villages in sand, and blows from one to nine days at a time. It is also called sirocco, and khamsin." They could call it what they liked, but *I* had never felt anything like it for making a tweed suit scratch.

As we left the plane there was no sky visible, only a fevered, tawny coloring all about us. The three-minute walk across the tarmac to the Immigration Office taught me more about the Sahara than the post report could. The air was desiccated and scorching, and the sand whipped my face, and I wanted to cover my nose,

mouth and eyes completely. In fact, I needed the very thing that a
Libyan near me, bent down against the wind, was staggering along
in, a voluminous, once-white, wool blanket which draped about him
and was wrapped entirely over his face. A baracan, Mr. Abou Babba
said. The several sheet-wrapped ladies, now quite blinded by their
coverings, were being led along by the neat little Egyptian hostess.

The Immigration Office was the size of a closet, and all forty passengers pressed in, with the exception of the veiled ladies, who had
suddenly vanished from sight as if wafted to Paradise or sucked down
a drain, leaving their husbands to deal with the officials. If smuggling
went on here, it could be ideally handled under those sheets, I
thought.

Three young Libyan officials stood behind the desk collecting passports and declarations, and scrutinizing them upside down. I looked
with interest at the three young men, hoping to find a clue to the
Libyan bloodstream; perhaps I did, as one was black, one was white,
and the other was tan.

The usual number of people had no visas, or had expired passports,
or an Israeli visa — the possession of which excludes entry in an
Arab country — or no vaccination, or something wrong. Harry and
I had everything perfect — but the official could not find our passports. He agreed that we had handed them to him, his hands were
crammed full of passports, many in Arabic, but ours he could not
find.

"They are gone!" he sobbed, dry-eyed. "Your passports I cannot
find! Where are they? Who has them? They are lost! Lost! But it is
not my fault! It is not my fault!" He looked down at his hands
accusingly, with an expression which said that they had played a
mean trick on him, and he shuffled through the passports again. He
needed somebody to comfort him, but it didn't seem to be us.

Now Mr. Abou Babba, who has already been successfully admitted on his Arabic credentials, takes up our case in Arabic with the
young official, who wrings his hands tearlessly and invokes Allah.
Mr. Abou Babba pats him on the shoulder and says, "Malesh!" — my
first meeting with the outstanding Libyan phrase of "Never mind."

"Ask the official to let you look at the passports, Harry," I whisper. "I'm sure he can't read English!"

"He'll find ours after the others take their passports," says Harry calmly. Then to the sad young man, "They'll turn up. You go ahead with the rest."

I look at Harry with admiration and say, "I'm afraid you're getting old, dear!"

Now Mr. Abou Babba tells us goodbye, says quite unnecessarily, "Keep calm," says he hopes they'll find our passports, if Allah wills! Shakes hands with the officials, and disappears from sight. I didn't realize then how very important Mr. Abou Babba and "his kind" were as a bridge between "our kind" and the Libyans. He had two worlds at his command, the East and the West.

We balance on the edge of a very small table, feeling hot and dry, and longing for a drink of water. "Don't drink tap water!" Probably wasn't a tap here anyway. All the other passengers have left the office now, and I can see through the open door that they are being embraced, kissed, munched on, and nibbled by waiting Arabic friends. All are men, and are clad in baracans, or very old khaki uniforms. The ladies are by now at home in the harem, I suppose.

And now our young man comes to us in triumph with two passports, one green and one blue, and says contentedly, "You see? They are not lost at all! Praise be to Allah!"

Although there was no one waiting to kiss us and munch us after we escaped from the Immigration Office, Jimmy Taylor, the representative of the Food and Agriculture Organization of the United Nations, was there with a closed car, more necessary by far than kisses, to convey us to Tripoli, twenty miles from the airport.

As we drove along the macadam road I pressed my nose against the window and saw a countryside which was not desert, nor was it green and fertile. Could this be the Italian-cultivated oasis area surrounding Tripoli of which I had read? There was nothing green in sight in the ghibli. There were stretches of dust-covered olive orchards and gray-powdered almond trees, and peanut plants bent low under the weight of sand, and through the yellow air I saw an occasional white stone house. After half an hour's travel we entered a long avenue bordered on both sides by stately eucalyptus trees, a sight which I learned to appreciate more after I had lived longer in Libya. This day they were just tall, dusty trees to me.

But not to Harry. "Planted by the Italians," he said admiringly. "They must have planted every tree in Tripolitania!"

We entered a maze of city streets, mostly narrow and twisting, but clean and white and tidy except for the sandy air.

"The cleanest city in the Middle East!" said Jimmy Taylor, in the proud tone of a man who has just finished sweeping the streets himself. This attitude I soon came to understand, for everyone in the city, stranger or Libyan, took tremendous pride in its cleanliness and beauty.

There were no tall buildings, but the skyline was pierced by the crescent-topped minarets of many mosques, and the high, domed tombs of holy men. The few figures on the streets were mostly men, scurrying alone, heads down against the wind, clad in old remnants of discarded World War II khaki uniforms or in the blanket baracans that I had seen at the airport. The occasional woman visible was wrapped from top to toe, including head and face, in her white sheet, which was also a baracan. This was gripped in the wearer's mouth, I saw, in such manner as to expose only one eye, and this only for emergency. The white-sheeted women is the first sight one never forgets from the Tripoli streets. It was going to be a contrast to our last post in the Philippines, where the women took a vital part in the life of the nation, as well as the family.

Soon we turned into a broad, palm-tree-lined boulevard running parallel to the sea, though one could scarcely see the water through the gusts of sand. "The breeze from the Mediterranean is cool and clean," said the post report, but this day the Mediterranean was drowned in the Sahara.

Now we entered a crescent-shaped drive, and in a moment had arrived at the Del Mehari (Racing Camel) Hotel. I had just one wish: a glass of cold water, whether from the tap, the bathtub or the shower. While we were unloading our various belongings, a strong, metallic voice suddenly rang out from a loudspeaker above our heads, echoing and re-echoing in Arabic across the city — the muezzin in the minaret was calling the Moslems to prayer.

It was sunset. The Mediterranean lay before us like a saffron sea, with the sun dropping into it like a ripe, red African orange in a golden haze. As I looked at Harry, his face, too, was a tawny yellow, and mine was, I knew, if I could see it. Tripoli, the golden, was here to stay in our tweeds, our skins and our memories.

The next day the Sahara was retreating but the yellow dust still hung in the air. The Racing Camel chambermaid was horrified when she found our window open in the morning and yellow stucco dust on us and everything. So was I, but it takes time to learn not to throw open a window.

"I know what they mean when they say that the desert never stops moving," Harry said, as he brushed the Sahara out of his hair, shook it out of his trousers, and wiped it off his shoes. "I am now thoroughly convinced of the need for sand fixation!"

"Yes, indeed. But do hurry. I can't get out of bed to dress until you leave for breakfast; the room's too small!" I looked gloomily towards the window which presumably looked towards the sea which presumably existed, when the dust settled.

The day after that, however, belonged exclusively to the Mediterranean, with layer on layer of clear sapphire-blue sea rippling placidly before us under a breeze that was cool and clean. Never on European shores had I seen the equal in color and translucence of Mare Nostrum under the African sky. From that second glimpse on I was a worshipper at its sun-kissed, blinding-blue shrine.

I was often to remember that post report on Libya. "Hotels third class, restaurants bad, housing poor, insufficient and costly. Bring your own drugs. Libya is classified by the United States Embassy as a hardship post!"

How could I have fallen so deeply in love with this country of Allah, this hardship post? But Allah is great!

I had no misgivings about going to Africa for the first time. Harry likes to say that I am an optimist right up to the moment when I fall through the hole in the floor; Harry is inclined to see the hole before the floor is in sight. Our characters supplement each other, as do our eyes; I am farsighted and he is nearsighted, but together we do quite well.

I am American by birth, by choice, and by exhaustive footwork during thirty years of living abroad, and signing my name in Ameri-

can consulates to remain American. I first went to Asia, to British
North Borneo, in 1934, as the bride of a young English conservator
of forests in that country, the youngest conservator in the British
Empire.

I wrote my book *Land Below the Wind* about a glamorous, beautiful, tropical jungle country, North Borneo, which is now called
Sabah and is the center of Indonesian ambition and guerrilla warfare.

It was a gay, happy book, as my pen friends say when they suggest that I write another "just like it." I, also, would like to write
another *Land Below the Wind* — but I shall never be a bride again in
Borneo! One cannot go on indefinitely being young, carefree, just
married, astonished by many things and delighted by all, and seeing
the great wide world for the first time. I now approach life with a
little more caution, despite Harry's view of me. I am a little less
certain of the ultimate triumph of right, being less sure now what is
right. But all in all, I live the life that I like best with the person
whom I love most.

My husband, Harry, was born of English parents in New Zealand,
went to school in England, and came to the United States where we
first met when he was a blond, blue-eyed, fourteen-year-old boy.
After his service in the United States Navy in the First World War,
he went to the University of California, where I registered the following year. I loved him, but he said co-eds were expensive, and he
had no money. In time, adorned with a wedding ring, I went with
him to Borneo, where we lived happily until the Second World War
when Harry and I and our two-year-old son, George, were taken
captive by the Japanese. For three and a half years we survived as
best we could in Japanese prison camps, an endurance which I have
described in my book *Three Came Home*.

We have two children: Jean, married, with four young offspring,
and George, now in the United States Marines. Both are tired of
being in Mamma's books, especially George, whose nursery was a
Japanese prison camp.

Harry is now an internationally known and experienced expert in
tropical forestry, and has been working with the Food and Agriculture Organization of the United Nations for twelve years as a technical expert. Each country we live in has won my heart; each time I

have said goodbye with sorrow. For this reason I went to Libya intending not to get emotionally involved — with what success this book will tell.

For thirty years our lives have been cast in underdeveloped countries. Primitive people are often more colorful than highly developed ones, and easier to write about — at least, they complain less if they think you malign them. But when we were assigned to Libya I soon found that though the country itself was underdeveloped, the word primitive could not be applied to the people, the majority of whom came from one of the earliest of civilized peoples.

I did not expect ever to really feel at home in Libya, for our assignment was for only one year, although in the end it stretched out to almost nine. A year would never be time, I thought, to know and make friends with a strange, Middle Eastern people who were . . . what? African? Arab? Semitic? I didn't know, except that they were Moslems.

I knew that historically North Africa had once been the granary of the Roman Empire, with many magnificent cities built by African slaves. Now the cities lay in ruins, the slaves were dead or free, and the Romans lived in Rome. This left me with everything to learn about modern Libya.

When we arrived in Libya in 1955, the kingdom was not yet four years old, the youngest independent country in the world. Libya was a special charge of the United Nations, who had more or less assembled her as a nation, and were now making her technical development program the United Nations' greatest single care. And with good reason. For Libya, with a population at the time of about one million people, had only sixteen persons with the equivalent of a university education when she gained her independence on December 24, 1951.

Four-fifths of the 700,000-square-mile land area of the new kingdom was absolute desert. Of the other fifth, only a narrow coastal strip and a small plateau were arable. Nobody has yet settled the problem of how the Romans fed their Empire from this!

The Racing Camel Hotel was a sprawling, one-and-a-half-story building, with its bedrooms laid out around five separate garden courtyards with running fountains, jasmine, and bougainvillea. The hotel had been built in Mussolini's time, when Libya was an Italian colony. It was a "strength through joy" project in conjunction with the Mellaha racecourse in Tripoli. Even the Fascisti needed fun, and here the overworked assistant dictators came to relax on weekends from Italy, bringing with them their lady friends, who apparently arrived with very little luggage, but liked a big double bed.

For the bed was the main feature of each tiny bedroom, and a huge metal bedspring supported on two wooden sawhorses almost filled the room. Our luggage was stacked ceiling-high along one wall, and we had to take turns getting out of bed to dress. A small bathroom with two doors without keys served our room and a stranger's, the room being small enough so that one could sit on the tub or the toilet and hold on to the other door.

My first reaction was that the Racing Camel was comparatively unbearable, considering the fact that we had to pay to live in it. However, we had no choice, as a desert film was being made by a movie company, and the better hotel, the third-class one, was filled with actors. And time soon dulled our senses to aesthetic values, smells and costs.

By the time we left the Racing Camel we were almost nostalgic for the smell of stale beer and whiskey with our morning coffee, for this was the aroma left over from the night before in the bar where breakfast was served. One feature, however, which brought us unfailing pleasure was the homeward flight at sunset of the sparrows who nested in hundreds in the huge old bougainvillea vines which filled the courtyards with a cerise-flowered canopy and evening twitterings.

We lived here seven weeks while I was searching the city for a house. As our new car had been misplaced in the Customs, my searching took place in four-wheel, horse-drawn gharries. The horses were the originals of Rosa Bonheur's horse portraits, and now in their age they were constantly falling down, or sitting down, in the streets. Once down, they took a rest, and the driver had to appeal to the passerby to help lift the horse to his feet and fit him back into the gharry shafts. Tenderhearted Westerners suffered a great deal for these horses. But when one looked at the emaciated, ragged, depressed Libyans who drove them, one suffered for them, too. The colored feathers and jingle bells with which horses and gharries were festooned added a sad, mad, macabre touch. Meanwhile, I helped the gharry trade considerably, but I found no vacant house.

I discovered, however, the fascination of Tripoli's sidewalk cafés, which thrive in summer shade and flourish in winter sun. In every little space where a man can sit in a spindle-legged chair with a drink nearby, man sits — while woman flits. At midday, dusk and every evening, and all day long on Fridays, Saturdays and Sundays, all three of which are holidays for some faith here, the polyglot population of Moslems, Jews, Catholics, Protestants and undenominated foreigners willingly gives its small change for coffee, tea and a ring-side seat to watch the greatest show on earth — the passing female form. This is the type of social life, time-spending but inexpensive, in which the true Mediterranean basks. It is a life which depends for its very being on soft breezes and warm South Mediterranean character, and it is a tribute to the fact that Italians still greatly predominate in the foreign population.

But sidewalk cafés are a pastime and not a full-time occupation. When at last our Vauxhall emerged from the Customs shed, and Harry left for the neighboring province of Cyrenaica to be away a week, I felt that fate had spoken. I determined to find a house and be in it by his return.

First I tried Garden City, where the upper classes lived on paved roads under street lights. The houses here had been built in Italian times for Italian occupation; they had the charm and easy elegance of Italian architecture, with well-established gardens, and gaudy, brilliant flower heads peeking over high stone garden walls. But these were already occupied by embassies and consulates, and ex-British military administrators who were now advising the new government, and British and American top brass, and other better folk of which we were not. Once convinced of the failure of my mission, I took off on a new scent.

I hastened to the wrong side of the railroad tracks, about two miles west of Tripoli on the Tunis highway, to a tiny Arab village, Gargaresh. I had heard of a young English bachelor here who was leaving Tripoli and wished to sublease his villa. Occupancy of his house, I found, included buying his furniture and employing the

Arab houseboy, as well as paying the lease. I was prepared for this, but not for the extensive limestone cave which undermined most of the back garden area and was the home of a large Arab family who came and went via this garden. As a newcomer to an Arab land, I decided against it.

Adjacent to Gargaresh towards Tripoli, a small suburb known as Giorgimpopoli was just developing. This was patronized mostly by American families from Wheelus Field, the largest American Air Force base outside of the United States. Some ten small new stone villas were scattered about on old Italian farmland, most of which was still covered with barley and olive trees. One of these villas was occupied by a friend of ours who had decided to move back to the city. The lease could be had by paying the rent, buying the furniture, and hiring the houseboy, Abdullah, with it. I took it with a grateful Thanks be to Allah! — whose name I was soon using.

The streets had no names, the houses had no numbers, it was dusty in summer and boggy in winter, the lights went out with each wind, and we cooked with bottled gas. The only clue to where you lived was your own sense of direction, and a plan drawn up for your friends. It was considered quite daring to live so far out of the city then, and people used to say, "Aren't you afraid?"

The only danger we encountered was a plague of locusts, who came in hordes, and in one hour one afternoon ate the farm crops and our garden, despite the fact that we all stood outdoors and banged on tins to frighten them away. A hailstorm shortly after broke our motorcar headlights and dented the hood. But we were never successfully robbed, pilfered or molested.

It was while house-hunting that I began to learn something of the city of Tripoli, which is two cities and two separate living centers, a European one and a Middle Eastern medina. The Medina el Kadima extends along the sea front northwest of new Tripoli, and although this hidden city was once completely walled against all invaders, now only long segments of tall, crumbling walls remain.

The entrance to the medina from modern Tripoli is through two impressive gates, one of which leads directly to the suk, or the bazaar, where business is always as usual. The other cuts through the thick walls of the old Barbary Coast castle, which was Turkish before that time, and Spanish before that, and Byzantine before that, and so on, back in time. Here the American sailors from the foundered frigate *Philadelphia* were imprisoned in 1803.

To a newcomer like myself, the medina at first seemed a secret, ambiguous Libyan enclave behind great walls and massive closed doors. Its narrow streets were passable only to pedestrians and bicycles, and filled with toddling children, fierce-eyed boys, one-eyed old men, and seldom a woman. Here was hidden an unknown populace in a battered, history-filled city, whose beginnings went back to 700 B.C. As a Western stranger, I both loved the medina and was uneasy in it.

It was not until we had acquired some kind Libyan friends who took us into their own homes in the medina, walking with us down its narrow ways, opening its closed doors to us, introducing us to the women in the shaded interior courtyards, and finally taking us up the little twisting stairways which lead high onto the roofs, where one emerges to become part of magic skyline, and from which one surveys all the other rooftops of the medina, fluttering gaily with women in baracans — it was only then that we felt at home.

The suk is different, although it, too, moves at an Oriental pace. Business is its being, and attracting tourists is its living, and anyone with cash can feel at home. But don't rush things — the merchant is happier if you show interest in getting your money's worth. There wasn't much to be had, though, in 1955, only some poor-quality sleeping baracans and high-carat gold jewelry in pawn.

2. Hammet

HAMMET was the first Libyan I was conscious of as a man. When we met that first day at Hescian I saw a tallish, widish, handsome Arab whom Salem introduced as Hammet ———, who though his clothes were shabby was an obvious aristocrat. Even then I noticed his hands which were small, smooth and beautiful, with long, tapered fingers, and his mouth, full-lipped under a small black moustache, set in a broad, shining face.

Salem, who is in the Libyan Forest Department and is Hammet's current brother-in-law, was hoping to find a job for Hammet with FAO, so he introduced him to us as speaking English. This proved to be two phrases, "Pardon me?" and "Yes," both of which he used with good results through our first meeting. As Salem was ostensibly showing Harry through the Forest Department nursery at Hescian, he and Salem walked together while inspecting the thousands of seedlings and saplings of many varieties, and Hammet and I followed, engaged in a spirited conversation.

I, "It is a beautiful nursery!"

"Yes," with a sweet smile.

"Who takes care of all the trees?"

"Yes," another smile.

"Is there enough water all the year?"

"Pardon me?"

"Water? Is there always water? Or does the well go dry?"

"Yes," with a look of doubt.

"Then how do they keep the trees alive?"

"Pardon me?"

"If the water dries up, how can they water the saplings?"

"Yes?" the same sweet smile.

Salem looks back over his shoulder and speaks in Arabic to Hammet, who makes a lengthy response. Then Salem says to me, "Hammet says to please excuse him, his English not yet perfect."

"Yes, certainly, Salem. Please tell him his English is very good."

Later when we are having Arab tea brewed and stewed by a forest guard, and served in the little Hescian office, Salem introduces the idea of Hammet as a candidate for the FAO work with Harry. As Salem knows, Harry has decided to find a young, intelligent Libyan who speaks enough English to work with him, and to train him as his assistant in Libya. Although Harry has been advised to take an Italian, who would be easier to train, he has decided that in an independent Libyan state, Libyans themselves must be trained as fast as possible. However, at this time in Libya English-speaking Tripolinos were limited. Salem, who has trained at the British Forestry College in English-speaking (then) Cyprus, speaks out to Harry as we sit at tea, "Hammet likes to work with you for FAO."

"Has he any forestry training?"

"No, but he is very smart."

"Has he any training in administration?"

"No, but he has friends in government. His family is a very good family. One time Libyan kings all from his family. Hammet know everybody."

Hammet smiles sweetly through the dialogue, his little finger extended daintily beyond his tea glass, his wide, ingenuous eyes watching Harry.

"He doesn't seem to speak much English."

"He soon learn when he talk to you."

Harry thought this was probably true, as most Arabs learn languages easily, as a part of their cosmopolitan heritage.

"You wish to work with me for FAO?" Harry asks Hammet.

Hammet smiles gently, "Pardon me?"

Salem hastily interprets the question in Arabic for Hammet, who answers to Harry, "Yes."

"You tell him, Salem, that I shall want him to go with me *every* place, you understand? To the desert, to Cyrenaica, to Sirte, to see

government officials, and out on trips. I want him to learn everything possible that he can from me, so that when I finish in Libya, he
can continue."

Salem interprets fully, and Hammet nods and smiles.

"How much salary do you want?" Harry asks.

A serious confab in Arabic ensues between Hammet and Salem.
Then Salem names a sum to Harry, which Harry replies to by saying, "Salem, what Hammet asks is more than the government pays
you, and you are a trained man! Tell Hammet I will pay him just
half of that amount."

Another confab, and then Salem says, "Hammet says it is very
small sum for him and wife and family to live. But Hammet will take
the work because he sees you are a very good man, and you will be
like his father to him, and he will be your son."

And during eight and a half years, it was so.

The Arabs are far from being a primitive people, I soon discovered; yet they are not European, nor Western, nor Asian. I was just
beginning to build up a picture for myself of a Libyan when Hammet came into our lives. Yet he was not typical, for elegance and
grace are not typical of Libyans; rather hospitality and warmth are.

Salem, who is completely unlike Hammet, is more orthodox. Salem is a bruiser, a brute-force type, who goes at everything like a
weight-lifter, including, I imagine, the delicate business of impreg-
nating his wife, who is constantly pregnant. But he *is* a force, and
handsome in a dark, sulky way, his eyes always burning, his skin
shining, and his expression one of absolute determination in making
even the slightest decision. He has strong feelings on all subjects, and
I cannot imagine him hiding them.

Hammet is another individual entirely; a descendant of true Turks
almost three hundred years ago when the Pashas ruled Libya, today
he is a Libyan, but still seems reminiscent of the atmosphere of Constantinople. He is named after his ancestor Hammet the Great, who
in 1714 made himself sovereign of Tripoli in an outstanding way: he
arranged the strangling of three hundred Turks, one by one without
any confusion, as they entered his banquet hall for a feast. No Turkish soldiers were found in the city next day — no live ones, that is.

It is hard to explain our friend Hammet, who has qualities of gentleness, delicacy, and feminine fastidiousness, and at the same time is fiercely, incorrigibly masculine. He has a thin, brown skin which tans quickly, and through which his blushes show easily, and wide-set, ingenuous brown eyes which quite conceal his noningenuous thoughts. He is frankly emotional yet calculating, cunning yet generous, careful but lavish, loving and faithless. He is a true friend, and a doubtful husband. His capacity to love is great, but it has not yet been dedicated to anyone except himself — unless, perhaps, to my husband.

Karamanli Mosque

3. Those Who Looked Across the Lake

THE NAME Libya once referred to the whole of North Africa, except Egypt.

The original Libyan belonged to one of two indigenous tribal groups: one group was Mediterranean and of white blood, and the other was of black African stock. The Berber of today comes from the Mediterranean group, and the Fezzani, the desert dweller, is of the Negroid group.

The Libyan, because of his advantageous location on the shores of Mare Nostrum, has, for all his historical life, been the host to invaders who looked across the lake to sunny African shores. He has by turns both profited and lost. When one conqueror builds cities, the next one tears them down; when one economy brings prosperity, the next economy exploits it; when one occupier rewards intelligence, the following one prohibits education; when one age is golden, the next is apt to be brass. It seems impossible to say whether man advances, or just runs as fast as he can to stay where he is.

Recorded history first commenced here about seven hundred years before Christ, when Libya experienced a period of Phoenician coastal settlement, entirely for purposes of Mediterranean commerce. A triumvirate of cities was established — Oea, Leptis Magna and Sabratha. Oea flourishes today as the city of Tripoli, also as the home of Oea beer; Leptis Magna and Sabratha exist as historic ruins. The name of the modern province of Tripolitania means Triple Cities.

Then began a Roman period which commenced one hundred fifty years before Christ, and lasted for six hundred years. At the beginning of the Roman episode, the Greeks were colonizing the adjacent territory of Cyrenaica. The antagonism between these two different

colonizing influences continues today in the spirit of suppressed hostility which exists between Tripolitania and Cyrenaica.

The results of Roman occupation were here to stay in Libya. Half-buried cities are now being excavated; distorted, ageless olive trees still survive from the original Roman orchards, and still bear olives; remains of old stone olive presses are everywhere; remnants of dams and roads continue to mark the most advantageous sites for new dams and roads. There are systems of Roman water cisterns which are not beyond reclaiming for use today. Ancient Rome was the greatest African builder in history, ably, if not willingly, assisted by African slave labor.

But what one man builds, the next destroys, and in A.D. 450 the Vandals did their best to wipe out what the Romans had created. Less than a hundred years later, however, the Byzantine Emperor Justinian, who inherited the Roman Empire, put the Vandals to flight and started rebuilding in the Roman tradition.

Again a hundred years passed, and in A.D. 643 the Arab invaders, from their base in Egypt, spread over the hills and plains of Libya as well as the coastal towns. They were the first people to reach far inland from the sea, and they settled down to stay for five hundred years. This period includes a second Arab invasion which introduced two tribes, the Beni Suleim and the Beni Hilal, who maintain their identity today.

In 1145 the Norman dukes of Sicily, just across the lake, developed a desire for the port of Tripoli, occupied it, and managed to keep their handsome banners flying there for fifteen years. They, in turn, were supplanted again by the Arabs, who kept their footing until 1510, when the Spanish in their turn looked across the lake, and longed for the African port. They took Tripoli, and ravaged it, and after that lost interest. Twenty years later they signed over Tripoli, along with the island of Malta, to the Knights of Malta.

In 1551 the Turkish Navy seized Tripoli to reclaim the land for Islam. A Turkish government was set up under a system of Pashas, who were mostly adventurers, appointed by Constantinople for personal and Turkish gain.

Hammet Pasha Karamanli, a Turkish cavalry officer, seized Tripoli for himself in 1714. The Karamanlis successfully held it for one

hundred twenty years as a princedom exclusively for Karamanlis. Karamanli is the name that Libyans think of today as meaning family power, political acumen, quick wit, and ability to make money.

During the Karamanli regime the Barbary Coast pirates supplied the income for the state by plundering Mediterranean merchant shipping. Being quite without conscience or prudish prejudices, they not only took material riches of all sorts, but captured white passengers whom they sold as slaves, and if a female was young and attractive they kept her for their own harems, or sold or lent her to the Pasha. The Pashas made an added income by collecting tribute from the United States and other countries for supposed immunity from pirate raids.

I think this was the date when the habit of shouting "Yank, go home!" in front of American consulates was initiated, the specific event being when Yussef Karamanli, then Pasha of Tripoli, chopped down the American flagpole in the Tripoli consulate in 1801. Today such things have become routine, but at the time it was rather badly thought of.

A patriotic American citizen, William Eaton, who was American consul in Tunis, viewed insults to the flag seriously, and he started his own expedition against Yussef Karamanli. After a killing march from Egypt in which Eaton and Hammet Karamanli, deposed brother of Yussef and Eaton's own candidate for the Tripoli job, and seven US Marines and two sailors led four hundred Arabs and mercenaries across the desert, they captured Derna, a small Libyan village near the eastern border. Here William Eaton himself heard "Yank, go home!" — but this time the order came from the US government, who had meanwhile, in 1805, signed a treaty of peace with Yussef! So the Yanks went home, but the stirring Marine Corps song "Shores of Tripoli" remains.

To go back two years before the peace treaty, we find that the United States had lost patience with being blackmailed and sent a squadron of ships to bombard Tripoli and to blockade the pirates. But the pirates knew their sea too well, and the US frigate *Philadelphia*, while in pursuit of a pirate ship, was lured onto a notorious reef near Tripoli, and grounded. Helpless on the wounded ship, the captain and his three hundred men were taken prisoner and incarcerated

in the old Castello on the sea, the very building which today houses the Tripolitania Museum. Here the prisoners existed, in chains and half starving, until after the peace treaty of 1805, when they were ransomed by the United States for sixty thousand dollars.

Now the enterprising pirates, working in their home waters, soon refloated the *Philadelphia*, and prepared to send her out again under the red crescent flag. But another patriotic American, Lieutenant Stephen Decatur, commander of the USS *Enterprise*, in Libyan waters, learned of the planned insult to the United States of sending their own ship against them. Decatur, using the ketch *Intrepid*, which itself had been captured from the pirates, stole into Tripoli harbor after dark on February 15, 1804, and set fire to the salvaged *Philadelphia*, which shortly exploded, sinking with its guards on board. Decatur and his men all returned safely.

However, all was still not well — except for the pirates who continued to furnish their harems with ladies, and to scourge the sea. Six months after sinking the *Philadelphia*, the same ketch, now the USS *Intrepid*, loaded with one hundred barrels of gunpowder, crept secretly into the harbor of Tripoli after dusk on September 4, 1804. She was manned by a volunteer crew, and the plan was to light a slow fuse to fire the *Intrepid* herself and then set her adrift landward in the hope that she would set fire to the ships of the pirate fleet which sheltered in port. The men of the *Intrepid* planned to escape from her in a small boat, and make their way back to the American vessels which were blockading the mouth of the harbor.

What went wrong no one can say, but suddenly a roar shattered the starlit night, and flames scorched the rippling sea, and the *Intrepid* and all her men went down together, while the pirate ships rocked peacefully on lurid African waters in the port of Tripoli. What the imprisoned Americans in the Castello must have felt as they listened and shuddered at the fireworks outside, one must imagine.

Today in Tripoli there is a plot of dedicated soil which every American visits. In a small Protestant graveyard facing the sea lie what are believed to be the remains of five American sailors, members of the volunteer crew of the *Intrepid*. Every year on American Memorial Day wreaths are placed here, and a service is held.

Looking back, one sees the nineteenth century in Africa as a century of individual violences and personal brutalities, of human rights habitually violated with little protest. This age reeks of stories of small and lurid unpleasantness which are somehow less forgettable than the mass murder of the twentieth century.

With the ultimate subduing of pirate activity, the Karamanli princedom was left without revenue. In the attempt to raise revenue, the state imposed heavier taxes on the people, and this created rebellions. Finally in 1835, in order to hold the country for Islam, Turkey reasserted her dominion, and placed Tripolitania under the rule of Pashas again.

In 1911 Italy looked across the lake, and decided that she, too, wanted a southern shore in the African sun. She landed a force in Italy to fight the local Turks, and found to her surprise that this involved fighting the Libyans, too. It was not until the outbreak of the Balkan War in 1912, when Turkey found herself too busy in Europe to defend Libya, and consequently renounced her claims to Tripolitania, that the Italians could really move in.

The Italians, like the Romans, left their mark. Forests were planted, orchards were started, agricultural land was developed, roads were built and colonial farmers were settled, and farms were planted. The only drawback to the scheme was that it was all done to develop Libya for the Italians, and the Libyans had no place in it. The farmers did their own farming and used Italian labor, not Libyan. A handsome city with fine buildings and nice homes was built for the Italians. Many schools were built and education was revered and made available — for the Italians. It was old style colonialism with few pretenses at altruism, and with a single object, to benefit the colonizing nation.

And yet, inexplicably enough, it established what is today a perfect example of love-hate relationship. Resenting though the Libyan does his memory of second-class citizenship under the Italians, the educated Libyan today reveres the educated Italian and his Italian culture and ways more than those of any other nation. He goes to Italy for his holiday, for his medical care, for his clothes, for his home furnishings — and his wife knows that her rivals are there.

The country remained nominally Italian until January 1943, when the Allied forces under Field Marshal Montgomery entered Tripoli, and placed it under British military administration. All through the Second World War this desert country was fought back and forth across by German, Italian, Arab and Allied forces. Two things were left behind: myriads of discarded, outworn khaki uniforms which for a long while clothed the majority of Libyans, and a country honeycombed with deadly, unexploded land mines and bombs which still take Libyan lives weekly.

In 1958 the latest invasion begins, that of the oil age. This brings Western contacts, modern techniques, big business, artisan employment, clerical needs, and riches beyond Libyan dreams. Is it to be a golden age, or a brass one? It depends on the Libyan.

4. Abdullah

ABDULLAH our houseboy had a mother, a wife, and four small daughters whose existence, he believed, represented the will of Allah. Abdullah himself, however, was solely responsible for the existence of his motorcycle, which he loved accordingly, feeding it better than he fed his family, and spending more time and money on it. He had bought it the American credit way, a system to which he took naturally, with ten dollars down and a hundred promised. Libyan finances have always been based on credit, and every Libyan family regularly spends more than it earns, but now that everyone knows that wealthy Americans do the same, the system is seen to be the road to riches.

Abdullah had been passed on to me by my friend, Abdullah's departing mistress, with the recommendation that although he was not very industrious, he was absolutely honest and clean, and he could make a good soufflé! I soon found that the thing I liked best about him was that he always went home promptly at five, as that was as long as I could stand him about the house. He was tall and handsome, and so full of libido and carnal possibilities that one could not be unconscious of his presence. His waves of sexuality permeated closed doors and hung on the air like vapors, and I often wondered how it was that he was devoted only to his motorcycle.

My first realization of how much he loved this vehicle came to me

via the purchase of bottled gas. In Giorgimpopoli we cooked with
this imported fuel for which we paid the equivalent of six dollars a
bottle, and I always paid cash. The gas was delivered in a motorcycle
sidecar by Bruno, a dashing, fierce-eyed young Sicilian, on behalf of
his buccaneering papa who controlled the Italian agency for distributing the gas. One evening after Abdullah had left for home our
doorbell rang, and Harry answered it to find Bruno facing him, eagle-
eyed and indignant.

"I want my money!" he shouted.

"Money for what?" asked Harry curiously, never having seen
Bruno before.

"Money for gas. Three bottles you no pay. I want my money!"

"What about this, Agnes?" Harry asked, as I arrived at the door.

"I don't owe him anything. I always pay cash for gas!" I said
equally indignant.

"Well, who do you pay? This brute here?"

"I don't know, come to think of it. Abdullah always buys it. I give
Abdullah the money."

Meanwhile Bruno, whom I took to be at least twenty-two at the
time, and who later proved to be fifteen, snorted when I said Abdullah, and said, furiously, "Abdullah! Abdullah! He buy motorcycle.
He no pay for your gas. He buy petrol for motorcycle. Now I want
my money!"

"You come tomorrow morning when Abdullah is here, and if he
hasn't paid you, I'll pay you then," I promised, as my portrait of
"absolutely honest" Abdullah began to come into a clearer focus.
After a prolonged dirty look Bruno said, "O.K.," and left.

"I'd hate to meet him on a dark night," said Harry. "Abdullah
. . . absolutely honest! Have you tried him with a soufflé?"

The next morning I said to Abdullah, "That Sicilian boy who delivers gas says you haven't paid him for three bottles. He's coming
today for the money."

"Who?"

"You know who — Bruno, I think, is his name."

"Oh, Bruno."

"Why didn't you pay him when I gave you the money?"

"Bruno?"

"Yes, Bruno!"

"Oh, Bruno. I paid him."

"Then why did he come here and shout for money?"

"Maybe he no understand you."

"He understands if he gets paid or not!"

"Maybe you no understand Bruno!"

Just then the doorbell peals, and enter Bruno. A violent, loud, explosive conversation takes place in Arabic and Italian, neither of which I understand at this time. Then six dollars is handed to Bruno, and Abdullah's tone becomes slightly placating, as he promises, no doubt, to pay the other twelve dollars soon. To my surprise, Bruno leaves with a moderately pleasant expression and without appealing to me to give him the rest of the money.

"Bruno very good boy," says Abdullah patronizingly to me. "You see? He just not understand."

I didn't see, and I gave up trying. Perhaps it came down to live and let live, and the Sicilian lad knew he had to live with his independent Arab neighbors.

"So you have a motorcycle?" I say to Abdullah.

His heavy, handsome face lights up as he answers ardently, "Yes, Signora, and it is a real one, not just a motor bike, like some boys'. It was very costly, but it is very good."

"But you never ride it to work here. I see you always come on a bicycle."

"I rent that bicycle, Signora, then the bike wears out. My motorcycle I save for Sundays and holidays. It costs very much to buy the petrol. On Sundays I go with my friends in the Motorcycle Club to Zavia, Zuara, Zliten, Jefren, Garian, many places. It is very educational to travel."

"Yes," I agree, "it is. I myself am learning something every day! Meanwhile, when are you going to pay Bruno his money?"

"Perhaps, Signora, if you could advance my salary . . . ?"

I saw my mistake too late.

The next Sunday when Harry and I were rounding a blind bend in the Tripoli to Homs road, our little Vauxhall was overtaken and roared past by a bevy of motorcycle boys. The last one of these wore the familiar black and orange turtleneck sweater which Abdullah used for best, and waved one arm frantically at us as he cleared us by an inch. His postilion passenger in Arab green turned around and waved, too, with a disregard for balance which almost upset them.

"There goes your gas money, Ma," said Harry.

"I suppose he's got to have *some* fun," I said doubtfully.

On Monday Abdullah reminded me that he had passed us in our "little Vauxhall" when he was out with the boys of his Club.

"You boys were going too fast for that road," I suggested.

"Yes, Signora, and our motorcycles can go even faster still!" he said proudly.

A few weeks later "the Club" swept past us again, this time on the Tunisia coast road. All members of the Club appeared to recognize our poor little vehicle, and more arms waved madly as daring young men endangered themselves by twisting and veering for our admiration.

"Not a crash helmet among them," said Harry. "Better not let Abdullah get too far ahead with his salary advances!"

"I wonder why Barbara said he was so honest and reliable."

"She's a kind-hearted type, and wanted to get him a job before she left!"

"Perhaps he *can* make a soufflé!"

Monday, Tuesday and Wednesday Abdullah didn't turn up for work. On Thursday I asked Hammet, on whom I was already beginning to lean, to go with me to find his house in the old city, and see what had gone wrong. I remembered the corner on top of the hill overlooking the harbor, where I had left Abdullah several times when I had driven him home. It was just beyond the little flag-draped Marabut's tomb which stood so engagingly in the middle of the main road. Just here, we stopped the car, and Hammet got out to inquire for Abdullah's house from the mob of Arab youngsters who instantly appeared. I saw his face grow suddenly grave, and after a couple of minutes' talk he turned back to me and said, "The house is just down there, but Abdullah was killed in an accident on his motorcycle last Sunday."

"Oh!" I was shocked, yet not surprised. Then, as Hammet got back in the car, "Shouldn't you go to the house and see if there is anything we can do?"

"No, is better not. Is all women crying now. By and by, they want something, they very quick come to you and ask."

And this was true. Ten days later a delegation arrived before my front gate. When I heard the wailing outside, and saw three baracan-shrouded women, four children, and a young man waiting in formation before my front gate I had a feeling of panic. Up to this moment I had felt rather badly done by, for Abdullah had died owing me six weeks' work on a six weeks' salary advance. But when I saw the line-up of bereaved relatives and realized that my emotions were about to be played on, I knew I was going to end up worse off still.

When I opened the gate, the young man explained in English that he was the brother of Abdullah's wife, and introduced the wife, the wife's sister, Abdullah's mother, and his four children, all of whom had come to call on me and thank me for my kindness to the departed Abdullah, he said. On the strength of this genteel gambit, we entered the house.

When baracans were lowered, I saw that the wife looked as old as the mother, neither of whom seemed to have any kinship with the virile, sizzling Abdullah, and I began to see why he had taken to his motorcycle. I hastily brought out lemon soda pop, cookies and sweets, and then we all sat down and stared at each other, wondering who would start, and where to begin. Finally the brother came out with his salient point: Abdullah had told them that I had not paid him his salary for the last four weeks! Now Abdullah was dead, and they needed money badly, and they hoped it wouldn't inconvenience me to pay them the salary that I owed him.

My calm departed, and I corrected their misapprehensions. Abdullah it was who owed *me* six weeks' services for salary advances, I told them heatedly. This was the signal for everybody to start crying in earnest. Fortunately, at this moment Harry arrived, as the room was growing damp, and I hadn't an idea what I should do, but I didn't feel obligated to support Abdullah's family when he himself hadn't. As Harry entered the room I had hopes that the ladies would hurry home, or at least submerge in their baracans when faced with a man. Instead, their only move was to squirm in their chairs, and it became obvious that (a) Harry wasn't young enough to disturb them, (b) he was a foreigner, and (c) where money was concerned, the ladies were prepared to breach tradition.

I introduced the delegation, and explained the situation to Harry, who showed no surprise. He repeated my statement that Abdullah had received a large advance, and we owed them nothing. He said, however, that we would discuss the matter with a Libyan friend, who would call on the family later. Finally, as everyone seemed to have adhered to his chair, and I guessed that only cash would unglue them, and as after all they had paid bus fares to come out, and as they were poor and they all looked utterly miserable, and the kids were messy, dirty, sad and pathetic, and we were incomparably more fortunate than they, and probably could afford to give them something . . .

"Do you plan to get another boy to take Abdullah's place?" Harry asked me later that evening.

"Not unless he's an orphan, unmarried, and hates motorcycles."

"Hammet knows a nice youngster he thinks we ought to try."

"Well, I don't know — It is really a relief not to have that sizzling body around! The only reason I want *anybody* in the house is that it is a way to get to know Libyans. There are so few doors open to me here."

The next night Harry, who never delays, came home and said, "Well, I've got you a boy!"

"Without my seeing him!" I gasped. "Or interviewing him! Or knowing if I want him? Has he worked for Europeans before? Why did you hire him, what's good about him?"

"He looked so cheerful, that's why I took him. Hammet says he's a nice boy, and he and Salem guaranteed him. Salem's mother helped raise the kid."

"But what can he do besides look cheerful?"

"You can teach him, can't you? Anyway, he can't make a soufflé, and that's one recommendation!"

And this was my first introduction to "my son, Mohamed."

5. Mohamed

THE NEXT morning Mohamed arrived. When I asked him his age, he said he thought he was fifteen, maybe sixteen years, for Libyans, I have found, are never very certain of their ages. This was the same age as our son George, who was sixteen, I told him, and from that moment on George became a matter of deep interest to Mohamed.

I pointed to his photograph on the table, and Mohamed went over and studied it carefully. Then he said, "He comes to Libya, maybe?"

"Yes, this summer for his holiday."

"Good. He will be my friend." I liked the straightforward approach, but I wondered how much housework a combination of Mohamed plus George would be good for.

Mohamed was a nice-looking, cleanly polished boy, with an attractive air of youthful gaiety and insouciance, which was evidently what had sold him to Harry. He wore skin-tight blue jeans, which inevitably meant a profitable association with the American Air Force base at Wheelus Field. He had been a golf caddy there, he said, but the work was irregular. He had, however, picked up GI English of a useful but doubtfully respectable type. He had a modest manner, and an embarrassed way of giggling, which was a relief to me after the unshakable poise of our former steaming sheik. Mohamed had never worked in a house before, he could not cook, he did not have a motorcycle, not even a bicycle. But perhaps, he said, with a very engaging smile, perhaps he would buy one soon to ride to work!

"It is better you come here by bus, Mohamed," I said firmly. "I will pay your bus fare."

But Mohamed was back at the table looking at George's photograph again. "He go to school now?"

"Yes, in Canada."

"I like to go to school, too."

"Perhaps you can go to night school in Tripoli."

After another long look at George, he says enthusiastically, "George is very good boy!"

"Well, sometimes."

"George will be my brother when he comes. How many boys you got, Missus?"

"Only one boy, and one girl."

"My mother had six boys and three girls."

"Oh, very fortunate," I said rather doubtfully.

"All dead now but me," he said blithely.

"Oh, Mohamed!"

"Yes, all dead. My mother knows very much about babies, I think."

It seemed more likely to me that she didn't know much about babies, if they had all died.

Mohamed said he would start work today, right now. I showed him the small bathroom with toilet, handbasin and washtub, and said that this would be his own to use, and he could change to his work clothes in here. He was delighted, and immediately closed the door, and for the next half hour I heard water flowing steadily from all the water fixtures. He emerged wearing the same clothes, but with his face even more polished, and his curly, black hair soaking wet and plastered down, having apparently had a bath in the washtub.

From this day on, Mohamed's first act on entering our home was to go to his little bathroom and perform complete ablutions, which included shaving as soon as his whiskers had appeared, and in due time included reading Arabic comics on the toilet. He bathed again every afternoon before leaving for home.

This lust for cleanliness at first surprised me, but now with more experience here, I would defy anyone to call the Libyans other than clean, when they have the opportunity to get water. What is difficult for North Americans to understand is the fact that in a semi-desert land, water is not a casual necessity but a true luxury. Many city dwellings, even, have no running water, and at best have only a central village tap from which a number of homes draw water.

In the small pre-desert villages water is limited, and in the desert itself it is almost nonexistent. Only the scattered oases are blest with plenty. In time to come in Libya I was to see Libyans show greater appreciation of water, and take more trouble to utilize it, despite uncomfortable circumstances, than the average foreigner. As well as ritual washing five times a day before saying his prayers, no Libyan will touch food without washing his hands, nor go to bed without washing his feet. I have seen my Libyan friends in the desert wash their feet in icy water, and then let them dry in the air, sooner than get into their cots dirty, or soil the towel they use for their faces by drying their feet with it.

"Well, what do you think of Mohamed?" Harry asked that night.

"He's a charmer, and a nice kid, and intelligent, and I like him. But as to housework, he knows nothing! He's never even been inside a European house before."

"He can learn, if he's intelligent."

"Yes, if he wants to. But boys and young men just naturally don't like doing women's jobs."

"Well, try him, anyway. He needs the money. Hammet tells me that his mother's blind and his father's an alcoholic, and their only income comes from Mohamed."

"Oh, I'll try him, all right — I don't think I can get rid of him! He's already adopted George as his brother. That's something I like about Mohamed, he isn't servile, or abject. He's as good as anybody, and I like him for it. He calls me Missus, but I will end up Mom, I expect!"

"Better keep him in his place, and don't let him walk on you."

"But where is his place? He'll never be a servant, I can tell you that now."

The first lesson the next day was bed-making. A Western bed with mattress and bedding and sheets was a mystery to Mohamed, who, like most Libyans, slept on a woven mat on the floor, rolled up in his baracan with his head covered. I myself am a meticulous bed maker, and love to see corners neatly folded, covers straight and pillows in line. Mohamed admired my work, but could not emulate it, and although in time he was able to cover the bed with covers, he

never saw any obligatory relationship between the length of the bed
and the longer dimensions of sheets and blankets.

Washing the tile floor by sluicing buckets of water on it he took
to naturally, but forgot to sweep the dirt up first, unless reminded
daily. Corners were ignored as not existing, and dust accumulated
under furniture, until I moved the furniture. Then Mohamed would
rebuke me gently with, "I no can see dirt because your table is on
top."

Mohamed usually did the marketing when he passed through the
city on his way to our suburban house. If I asked him for five
pounds of the best potatoes he proudly brought me ten pounds of
the worst for the same price, and I had to throw out three-quarters.
This was his principle about all food purchases. Three pounds of
cheap stew beef, which included two pounds of bone, fat and muscle, was to him the best possible buy. This was reasonable for a Libyan shopper, as Libyans use meat chiefly as a stew, which they generally like as fat as possible so it provides large quantities of greasy
gravy to swab up with bread.

As Mohamed always had his midday meal at our house he had a
personal interest in our diet and always purchased our meat from the
Moslem butcher, as unless it had been ritually slaughtered with a

prayer from the Koran he could not eat it. Unfortunately, the Arab butchers cut meat as if they tore it apart with their teeth, and a mess of fresh meat looked as if cannibals had been interrupted in the middle of a feast.

In time, I decided to go to market myself and give Mohamed money to buy his own favorite tidbits separately. At first, I found it difficult to get accustomed to seeing whole carcasses hanging before me, and to have to pinpoint the exact gland, gut or slab which I wanted. In fact, seeing the animal whole almost turned me into a vegetarian. Now, after eight years of choosing my own special piece of meat, I find the supermarket cellophane packets of sterile chops, steaks and roasts tasteless and uninteresting.

Mohamed learned to wash the sheets and towels, the tableware, and Harry's Palm Beach suits and shirts, but was never equal to my things. His washing was passable but his ironing was painful, and he suffered with each stroke of the iron. Soon he began to store away unironed shirts in his bathroom, hoping for some painless solution. On his day off I formed the habit of cleaning his bathroom, and relocating lost garments. There was never a hint of dishonesty in his action, it was just that he hoped in time Allah would offer some solution to ironing those shirts other than having Mohamed iron them. Sometimes Allah did, and I ironed them; other times Allah shook his head, and Mohamed had to.

Now Mohamed started teaching me Arabic phrases, polite greetings and farewells, and the responses to these gracious expressions of thanks and appreciation, requests to bring coffee, cigarettes and food, requests for the costs of market foods, and questions as to what one was doing. We would sit chatting in English and Arabic for an hour over coffee, and Mohamed was at his best. He was lazy physically but liked using his mind; in fact his English was improving more rapidly than I was learning Arabic.

As his vocabulary grew, he became tremendously proud of his English but still quite innocently used a number of disreputable phrases of gutter English which he had heard the GIs use. I was horrified when he first dropped these words, and I explained to him that no decent man used these words before a woman, and that English-speaking people would misjudge him by them. But Mohamed insisted that I was quite wrong because, he said, the soldiers used them all the time! Maybe to each other, I said, but not to women. But Mohamed never really believed me, and I had a long struggle to make him stop using them in my home. I could visualize that his generation of Arabic youngsters in Tripoli who learned English from the GIs would provide some shocks if they ever went abroad.

When we first moved into our little villa in Giorgimpopoli we were well out in the country, surrounded by farm acres, olive trees, barley and vegetables. But very soon the farm acres were stripped and sold and subdivided, and now we were rapidly being surrounded by more limestone brick villas, Italian and Arab owned, which rented at high prices to American Air Force families from Wheelus Field.

When at the end of our first year in Libya the government asked FAO to extend Harry's assignment here, I was delighted that we were comfortably settled in Giorgimpopoli. As the old-timer here, I found myself filling the position among my neighbors of Venerable Lady who knows everything, or so they thought! After many years of living abroad I had become fairly self-sufficient in resolving my own problems, having learned from Harry that in every decision one can only be (a) right, or (b) wrong, and the two are often quite close, and in any case any decision is probably better than none.

My new neighbors soon came to me for advice about the details of local living. Should they wear shorts out here in Giorgimpopoli? No, I said! But they always did. Should they use a bikini? Yes, but only when bathing from their own Wheelus beach. So they came to visit me, while Mohamed's eyes bulged, clad in bikinis! Were the Libyans clean? Those I knew certainly were. Was it safe to eat lettuce? No, but I always did. Would I trust an Arab boy to baby-sit? I would wish to know the boy first. Was it safe to go to the Old City? No place safer. And finally, where did I think that Mustapha went to when he disappeared for two months (during the halfa harvesting season, I note!) and he *said* he was doing "military service" (there is no compulsory military service!).

My neighbors all envied me my Mohamed, and his six months of loyal and devoted service to me. They didn't keep a "boy" longer than two weeks, themselves. What they didn't know yet was that in six months of devoted service, one only gets about two weeks of real work. They also envied me Mohamed's ability to speak English, and all about me used him freely as an interpreter, on my time. As interpreting was tastier to Mohamed than dish-washing, I didn't get my house chores done until my neighbors had had their morning instructions relayed in Arabic to their less gifted Libyan domestics. Naturally there were certain modest perquisites which accrued to Mohamed from my Wheelus base employed friends, outstandingly, tax-free cigarettes. Unfortunately, we of the UN had no perquisites, and nothing free of tax.

When Harry came to Libya he brought with him a modest but sufficient tool kit. Mohamed was delighted when he discovered this, and immediately made himself acquainted with the tools. Before long he had maimed, mutilated, or broken every tool by reason of the superhuman strength which he exerted to do the most minute repair job. Now a prong is missing from the hammer, the head shoots off, the screwdrivers are blunted, the knives are dull, the saw is chipped, and the drill doesn't drill. Large nails are used where tacks would be suitable, and tacks are used where screws are needed.

This lack of ability to use instruments handily runs throughout our neighborhood among all the Libyan boys, and I suspect that it goes through all walks of Libyan life. Libyan mechanics are said to be death to motors, and many Libyan drivers are death, period. Hammet is the exception, as he is a very skillful driver. With boys like Mohamed, one can realize that they and their forbears have had few possessions, and no opportunity to learn how to use modern implements. They feel instinctively they must expend the same large amount of physical energy over the machine that they would use to achieve their end by hand.

They have little sense of thrift or husbandry, because they have had little to husband. A pair of my shears came apart the other day, and I asked Mohamed to take them to the city to be mended. He said he didn't know any place to mend them, that I had better throw them away! I said, certainly not! You take them to the same place where you would take your own to get them mended. He said, my scissors break, I throw away! And I realize that he would — if he had any, but he probably never had a pair of shears.

Nevertheless, our tool kit, wounded though it is, is a great source of satisfaction to Mohamed, as it supplies him with something to lend to people. And if I suggest that it is possible for others beside the Keiths to purchase tools in Tripoli, he gives me a look of deep rebuke for my selfishness. And again I realize that a Libyan has few personal rights over anything he owns, and if a friend asks for anything from him, he is obligated to give or lend it. A boy buys a bicycle; a friend borrows it, and breaks it. Well, that's the will of Allah! says the friend. This is one of the first laws of Libyan life: what's yours is also that of your family and your friends.

I find that "my son, Mohamed," for Missus has changed to Mom, has never been outside of Tripoli, of which city his birthplace, Suk el Juma, is a suburb. The Fezzan, where the black Libyans come from, is less familiar to Mohamed than is the United States, whose open-handed servicemen indirectly and illegally supply him with blue jeans and smokes. Cyrenaica, the province where the Bedawi never fully surrendered to Italian occupation, is more foreign to him and less sympathetic than the England he hears about from Tommies who give him a lift in their jeeps. He has a more clear mental picture of the USA than of the Sahara. This condition is found in most Libyans, and is symptomatic of the attitudes of the three provinces which have been forcibly molded into a sovereign state. Tripolitania despises Cyrenaica; Cyrenaica distrusts Tripolitania; they both despise and distrust the Fezzan. Or so it seemed to me then.

6. Brothers

THE LITTLE airport was bustling and self-important under the midnight marvel of the African sky. The landing strip rests on the extreme edge of Tripoli's cultivated acres, south of which lie the great stretches of pre-desert, and the nighttime skies here are adorned with blazing stars which hang from indigo depths and mix confusedly with the homing lights of airplanes. It is a most advantageous place from which to see the night. Nevertheless, when blinking green and red lights of the London plane finally sorted themselves out from the stars and settled gently on the runway, I sighed with relief; he was on land again.

The passengers climbed off the plane and streamed across the field, and I could not see *him*.

"He isn't there, Harry! He's missed the plane!"

"Of course he's there; I see him. With his overcoat thrown over one shoulder."

"George? That man! But he's grown so tall!"

George saw us then, and gave us the properly casual nod and wave. His once round, boyish face was replaced now by a thin, more mature one, but as he came close to the barrier I saw that his gray-blue eyes were the same, and his beige skin was smooth and fine.

Children are illusive creatures, never being the same for any length of time. Old phases of them are constantly dying, while new phases are coming to life. Each time one says goodbye to a child, one says goodbye forever, for when one meets again, a new child will have been born. I know this to be a fact, but it still shocks me.

Even in adults there is a limited marvel of perpetual rebirth which makes it advisable to hold no grudges. What one did yesterday, one might not do tomorrow. Yet each act of life builds on us like barnacles, and constantly changes the structure which is visible to the world. That footstep cast in cement for the hall of fame may be all that's left of a reputation, for a reputation can never be cast in cement.

Tonight, this is a new George I see.

Next morning I find one thing about George that has not changed: he still likes to lie in bed and sleep.

Mohamed arrived unusually early in his anxiety to see George in the flesh. "Let him sleep," I said. "We were late last night." So Mohamed tiptoed around the house with loudly squeaking boots.

"Why don't you go barefoot in the house the way you always do?" I asked.

Mohamed looked sheepish, then said, "But George wears shoes?"

"To travel in, certainly, but I'm sure he'll go barefoot here."

"George wears blue jeans?"

"I'm not sure, but I think his school in Canada doesn't allow them. But he has old khaki slacks with him."

"Is George married?"

"Heavens no! He couldn't support a wife!" Mohamed looked thoughtful.

Very shortly I heard the voices of Mohamed and George. There was obviously no problem in understanding each other. Soon I heard delighted laughter from Mohamed, and deep chuckles from George. I guessed Mohamed was sitting on the side of the bed, and I knew from the confidential tones of George's voice that he was relating one of his fabulous tales, true or false. Soon Mohamed passed my open door, and called in virtuously, "I am taking George his coffee."

"In bed?"

"He likes it in bed. George is very good boy!" There were two coffee cups on the tray.

One thing I knew I could rely on about George, he was no snob, and he had no artificial prejudices. Mohamed was Mohamed was Mohamed, and as far as George was concerned, I could be the mother of both without any ill feeling. It was almost midday, and a day lost to housework, but gained, I hoped, in something else.

In a few minutes I heard a tremendous squeaking of springs which meant that George was jumping from bed. Then, "Ma, has Pa got a bathing suit?"

"Yes, those batik trunks in the bottom drawer in the chest in your room. Didn't you bring one of your own?"

"I'm lending mine to Mohamed. He's taking me swimming down to the beach where he bathes." This time Mohamed really tiptoes past my door!

"Be sure to get back by two o'clock, so you'll be here when Pa comes home. And be careful! The bathing here is very treacherous. If you go in that little cove at Kilo Five with Mohamed, don't swim out beyond the breakers."

"Ma, I'm a strong swimmer, now!"

"Those are just the very swimmers who get drowned!"

I saw that I should never be able to get over giving advice to George, seeing him in my mind's eye drowned, run over, injured in a motor accident, burned in a plane crash . . . All the fates which only the "will of Allah" could protect him from, I was constantly reaching out to push away.

They got home, though, but late; dripping, laughing, splashing sand and water all over the place. Before he left for home that afternoon Mohamed confided to me, "George swim very good," and I knew George had been showing off, no doubt far out beyond the breakers.

"Did he meet some of your friends?"

"Yes, I tell them this is my brother!" says Mohamed proudly. I didn't ask for details, but I wondered.

Later I asked George, "When Mohamed said you were his brother, what did the boys say?"

"Well, they looked at me and said, 'You're very white, aren't you?' I said, 'Of course, I've been living in England where there's no sun. I'm going to Oxford there. I won a scholarship!'"

I laughed at the obvious (to one who knew George) joke of his winning a scholarship, and said, "In your imagination!"

George ignored this with dignity.

"How did you like Mohamed?"

"Fine. He's a swell kid. Did you know that he's got to get married soon? He doesn't want to, but his mother wants him to have some children."

"Mohamed is just your age, George, and he hasn't a bean! How can he get married?"

"He says he has to; he has to do what his mother tells him! That's the Arab civilization, Ma. The old folks tell them what to do."

"Not much like our Western one, is it? To do what your mother tells you?"

George grinned. "In the West a fellow has to keep his independence!"

"What do you want to do tomorrow? This weekend we thought we'd go to the Roman ruins at Sabratha."

"Well, Ma, just so it isn't a cathedral. I can't take any more of those after Paris and London!"

"Sabratha is entirely different; it's the loveliest, most alluring ruin I know. Anyway, there is a marvelous bathing cove there. We'll go in the Land Rover and take sandwiches and make a day of it."

"And take Mohamed?"

"Yes."

"O.K. then for Saturday. But tomorrow Mohamed is going to take me to see an Arab movie made in Egypt."

"Who does my housework tomorrow?"

"The house looks swell to me!"

"Exactly. That's because *I* did the work today!"

"We can go in the afternoon when Mohamed has finished work and is ready to go home."

"Well, I'll drive you to town."

"No, we'll go by bus, Mohamed says. Say Ma, did you know that Mohamed wants to buy himself a bicycle so he can ride out here?"

"Of course, I knew. Every houseboy in Giorgimpopoli wants to. And every employer is supposed to advance cash for the bike, and the bike disintegrates before it's paid for. Don't encourage Mohamed along that line."

"He says he could get here earlier with a bike."

"I don't want him earlier, *or* later. I just like to catch a glimpse of him occasionally!"

George gave me a rebuking look, and said, "You know, Ma, Mohamed is awful fond of you!"

"Good! But no bicycle."

So we went to Sabratha, of all ruins my favorite because of its
pure physical loveliness. No place in all this world may its equal be
had for hot African sunlight, cerulean sky and crashing blue sea as a
background for golden limestone relics of centuries past! I have
often left antique sites with sore feet, aching head and breaking
back, as well perhaps as mental exhilaration and historical awe, but
seldom indeed can sheer emotional enjoyment subdue my aches as a
ruins viewer. Sabratha alone does this.

Two thousand years ago this was a famous Roman city, and before that it was the site of a Phoenician trading settlement. Yet today
one finds in the museum perfectly preserved one of the most beautiful Justinian mosaics in the world. On the site itself, many-styled,
bleaching temple columns and whitening Roman statues mark the
layout of the ancient city and the sculptural talents of its early citizens, and the remnants of a crumbling, magnificent Roman amphi-
theater stand golden and upright against the blazing African sky.
These are archeological facts of historical importance, but they cannot dim or rival this quiescent city's beguiling beauty.

We drive through an avenue of dark green crypress trees and approach golden sandstone columns which we have seen from a distance outlined against the sky. We hear frothy breakers crash on
once Roman shores, where saffron sands now offer their warmth for
the outspread nets of local fishermen and the huge iron anchors of
their tuna traps. The smell of salt, seaweed and rotting fish is strong
in the air, and life is all about us as if the ruined city still were filled
with living men. As perhaps it is, for no city loses completely the
poltergeists of its inhabitants, and ghosts are happiest in African sun.
Nor does a city ever die whose shores are touched by a central sea
which binds it to other living shores.

Today on the sands of Sabratha families are picnicking with glee-
ful ease, and among the Roman statues laughing Italian couples add
their living heads to headless figures to be photographed. Nearby in
the Forum, teen-age bodies twist frenziedly to the strains of Italian
harmonicas under the blind gaze of Roman busts. High in the top

rows of the ancient theater loving couples twine together in a manner as old as new, sublimely unconscious of the best view in Sabratha, where the golden arches of the stage frame the sapphire sea.

To George and Mohamed, who have never been here before, the scene is immensely gayer and more entertaining than they had expected. I had heard George telling Mohamed before we came that ruins were supposed to be educational, and that he and Mohamed ought to see Sabratha even if it wasn't much fun. Anyway, Ma had promised they could also have a swim!

Now that we were well amongst the ruins and all enjoying them, Mohamed developed a slightly proprietary air which took into account that they were *his* Libyan ruins, and he led the chase, over all obstacles, to the top of the theater, back to the stage, behind every statue, and into every excavation, with boyish agility, meanwhile distributing pieces of misinformation.

"You see this temple, George? Is very old, maybe one hundred years!"

"More like nineteen hundred years, Mohamed," says Harry.

"Yes, maybe. And this very big house here is old, too?"

"Yes, that big house is the Basilica of Justinian, and probably thirteen hundred years old. The mosaic in the museum was taken from this basilica."

"Yes, yes, just the same mosaic we have in Karamanli Mosque in Tripoli."

"Not quite the same. The Sabratha mosaic was laid eleven hundred years before your Karamanli Mosque was built!"

"Yes, maybe."

There were others besides George and Mohamed who dodged among the pillars with extreme agility, and these were the illegal teen-age salesmen of contraband antiquities, raggedly dressed, barefooted, audacious Arab youngsters who spent their time dredging the sand for relics to sell. Themselves always belligerently pursued by the less nimble unformed guards, they never ceased to pursue the visitors with early Roman coins, cracked pieces of possibly Roman crockery, tidbits of maybe mosaic, and cracklings of shard. Bargaining madly with George and Mohamed, who were determined to acquire souvenirs, yet disappearing like wraiths as a guard approached, and reappearing each time we halted, the young brigands accompanied us all the way until bargains had been struck.

Sabratha has lived many lives, and died many deaths. First built by the Phoenicians, later dominated by Carthaginians, then mutilated by the Numidians, it was finally rebuilt by the Romans to become one of the three great centers, Sabratha, Leptis Magna and Oea, now Tripoli, for trading in gold, ivory and slaves which were brought to the African coast by caravan from Lake Chad. In time destroyed by the Vandals, Sabratha was rebuilt by the Byzantines, laid waste and turned into a fortress under the Arabs, permitted to crumble and bleed to death under the Turks, and once more rediscovered, uncovered and partially restored under the Italian occupation of the present century.

Mare Nostrum is ringed with the relics of great cities and civilizations whose glories have passed, yet whose tenacious capacity for living and loving survives. Today, Sabratha awaits the vital touch to spring again to life. The secret is not oil, nor cash, nor gifts, nor advice, nor sweating foreign experts, nor Arab Leagues, nor Nasser, but human effort. What made Rome great was the Romans; only the Libyans will make Libya great again.

"Yes," gloats George, as we sit by the sea on an ancient stone ramp and eat our sandwiches, "these are sure enough Roman coins! Do you think those boys really found them here on this site?"

"Why not? Sabratha is an authentic Roman site, and an early Phoenician one before that," says Harry. "What have you got there, Mohamed?"

Mohamed exhibits a broken fragment of what might once have been a tiny terra-cotta oil lamp. "It's Roman, too," he says proudly.

"More likely Greek, I think. How much did they soak you for that?"

"I pay ten piastres." *

Harry laughs and shakes his head. "You boys were really investing! And it's all illegal, too. These kids in the ruins have no business collecting stuff from the site or selling it. Everything here belongs to the Libyan State. That's you, Mohamed."

"Then is O.K. I take my lamp," says Mohamed reasonably.

"Sabratha is still being excavated, as you can see. That's what the little dump carts are for. I'm not sure if they sift it all on site and then carry away the discarded sand, or carry it all away for sifting."

A long discussion ensues, and I can see that both boys are fascinated in spite of themselves by the historical and archeological facts of the place. I as usual can only sit enthralled by the warm golden sand, the copper-colored columns against the cobalt sky and the crashing whitecaps on the cobalt sea.

All summer, it interested me to watch secretly these two young adolescents finding so much in common in their lives which were in reality so different. Both lived in the never-never land of their imaginations; Mohamed with his many ambitions which would probably never come true, and George in his fabulous dreams which were equally far from reality. What twist of circumstances would ultimately chain them to earth? What acts of living must in time open their eyes? It was sad to think these things — but ultimately life has to be reconciled to fact, I suppose.

* About thirty cents.

The Sabratha visit had an incredible postscript. Two years later when George was spending the summer with us in Benghazi, he met again the boy who sold him the coins at Sabratha. Here in Benghazi the boy, Ali, was trying to make a living shining shoes, and he was usually to be found in front of the Vienna restaurant. A number of times that summer he and George met and exchanged friendly gossip. He told George that he knew our red Vauxhall and me by sight.

The following year we moved back to Tripoli. I parked my car in the city one day and the same Libyan boy, now a young man, ran after me on the street and asked, "Where is George now?"

I told him that George was at school in Canada. He nodded his head approvingly and said, "Good. George is my friend. I like George." He himself now had a good job, he said, with an import firm connected with oil drilling machinery.

A few days later I parked my car in the same place, and Ali hurried up to me. He placed a little tissue paper packet in my hand and said earnestly, "Here are some Roman coins for George. He liked Roman coins. Please send them to him from me."

7. Ruins in the Sun

ABOUT NOW George became absorbed in learning to dive with an aqualung, and discovering the underwater world. In these days the Underwater Explorers Club in Tripoli was exactly what the name implied, and only the few who wanted to explore the sea belonged. The high, jutting rocks of the club's sea frontage arose directly from deep sea, and the lack of bathing beach and shallow water discouraged children.

A handsome former Guards officer and an expert in aqualung diving, Simon, the club owner and manager, seemed to belong to a day that was past, when every officer was first of all a gentleman, and generally a handsome one. One felt that he maintained the club for his own good pleasure, as a place to loll, drink, gossip, escape from domesticity, and most of all to dive from, which he did superlatively well. A familiar sight now was Simon and George, both tall, thin, brown, dripping and shivering, emerging from the Mediterranean with the faraway look of men who have returned from another world.

George, enthralled by the depths, was not enthusiastic about visiting more ruins, but Harry and I wanted him to see something beside the tourist attractions of Tripoli. We planned to drive to Cyrenaica, with Cyrene, the ancient Greek city on a hilltop, as our goal. So we headed east along the coast road which follows the sea until we arrived at Sirte, about two hundred eighty-five miles east of Tripoli. Sirte was at this time known as the taking-off point for a Sahara trip, as it marks the place where the true desert comes almost to the Mediterranean shore. Just here on the Gulf of Sirte there is a lonely little wooden shingle which sticks up at the edge of the coast road and points south, saying simply TO THE SAHARA. There is something about

this little sign which one never forgets, especially when one looks
for the road south to the Sahara, and finds only a few diverging
vehicle tracks fading away on the sand.

We slept the night at Sirte, at the little bugless (a fact worth not-
ing) rest house, and ate spaghetti in the nearby kitchen-restaurant
where an Italian family has for years produced an edible meal for
passersby of every race and religion. It is noteworthy that five years
later, with the discovery of oil in Libya, a traveler would have to
reserve accommodations weeks ahead at this same little rest house.
The spaghetti kitchen, I hope, made its fortune.

This coast and the desert of Libya were fought back and forth
across by our Allied forces in the Second World War, and heavily
mined by both sides. Even now the sand is lethal in many areas, and a
week never passes without one's reading in the papers that some
shepherd boy, or wandering child, has been injured by an old bomb.

The next morning we went to the lonely Sahara signpost and then
detoured south in our new Land Rover following the vehicle tracks
for some kilometers. We wanted to observe the differences between
true desert and pre-desert, a difference which appeared to my non-
technical mind to be that pre-desert may have many arid varieties of
desert growth, but true desert has sand, gravel, pebbles, stones and
rock, but no growth. Or, looking at it from a different angle, Profes-
sor Emeberger the ecologist says, "The true desert is where there
are no fleas and no flies."

The phrase "sand sea" is a perfect pictorial description of real desert, and as one stares across the shimmering sand waves one feels
that shrubs and trees would be as out of place here as on the sea.

Back on the coast road again, we hurried eastward for a hundred
miles until we came in sight of the incongruous type of thing for
which I love Libya. Here, completely isolated on blazing desert
sand, stands a white stone arch some hundred feet high, under which
the rough road passes. Italian-built, the arch stands out from great
distances, golden in the sunrise, or black against the setting sun, a
towering, shining symbol of a people who think no place too out-
landish in which to create a monument of beauty and splendor, even
though nothing could be less expedient or appropriate to the hard
day's travel.

This polished arch was erected in 1937 to mark the completion of the Sirtic highway to connect Benghazi with Tripoli. Its splendid elegance, its utter uselessness, its perfect unsuitability and inaptness to the scene make it beloved to all travelers, and utterly unforgettable. The arch is generally considered as marking roughly the boundary between the provinces of Tripolitania and Cyrenaica, although the exact entry to Cyrenaica is at el Agheila.

Another and more dramatic event that is also commemorated by the arch is the fifth-century accomplishment of the brothers Philaeni, two champion Greek foot runners who set out from Carthage, Tunisia, on foot and raced furiously eastward to meet two fleet foot runners from Cyrene who were racing westward. The spot where the rival racers met was to be accepted as the frontier between east and west Libya. They met; they had a riotous row, with each side claiming that the other side had cheated. Finally the brothers Philaeni agreed to be buried alive to establish the boundary, proving just what I can't imagine, except that there were no lions around to be fed.

Yet the arch is not the real burial site of the Philaeni, assuming that the Philaeni were real, for their grave sites lie in a Roman ruin fifteen miles from the arch. Nevertheless, the suitably flamboyant arch is dedicated, in Latin, jointly to the city of Rome — "You never see, Oh Sun, anything greater than the City of Rome" — and to the Philaeni. Life-size bronzed statues of the brothers, lying comfortably down to rest at last, are placed recumbent high overhead in two niches on the opposing sides of the arch. Altogether, this arch found in the middle of the desert is something for a tired desert traveler to marvel at — even if in the circumstances he might prefer a cold beer.

The Philaeni Arch was destined to become something quite different again the year following, when in 1957 the Latin inscription was expunged by the Libyan Government, and a new Arabic inscription was embossed in its place:

To commemorate the glory of Rome, the tyrants a monument have built, but the Almighty, their collapse had destined.

> What had Rome to do with people who are originally
> Arabs; who by the teaching of the Best of Crea-
> tion [i.e., the Prophet] have abided, and have
> benefitted.
> This country, when the call "Allah is Great" echoes
> on its horizons, shall be protected by the guid-
> ance of Islam.

We arrived in Benghazi, the second capital of Libya, by dusk. The original city on this site was Euhesperides, a Greek-founded city dating four centuries before Christ. Two centuries later it was re-named Berenice, after a Ptolemaic queen, and sixteen centuries later it became Benghazi, renamed this time after Sidi Ghazi, a saintly Moslem.

As modern Benghazi was almost entirely destroyed by Allied bombing in the Second World War, it is not surprising that, com-pared to Tripoli, I found it unattractive. What remained to our view was a rustic Bedawi village with little style, and none of Tripoli's cosmopolitan flare. I did not know then that Benghazi would soon be our future home. And if anyone had told me so, I would have com-plained loudly and never have believed that I could come to love it as I did.

In these days the real point in going to Benghazi (that hole! Tripo-linos said) was to visit Cyrene, or Shahat, the lyrical Greek ruins which nestled in the Green Mountain two thousand feet above the sea, and a hundred and fifty miles by road from Benghazi. Motorists affect to hasten through Benghazi streets and past the salt flats with eyes averted, and only begin to enjoy things when the road com-mences to zigzag up towards the Jebel Akhdar.

Then gray shrubs give way to green acres, and wheat and barley fields stretch before us, and the only farmland in Libya opens out. This is centered around el Merj, called Barca in Greek times and Barce in recent Italian years, a tiny city but an important farm center — one which was to be almost entirely destroyed a few years later in an earthquake. Beyond Barce we pass the ruins of Ptolemais, a huge, ancient city not far from the main highway, but as our time and appetite for ruins are limited, we do not turn off.

Dried up riverbeds and streams in Libya are called wadis, and because of the lack of reforestation and water catchment areas, the principal wadis, almost without exception, flood at the first rainfall, dashing the priceless rainwater down into the sea in soil-laden torrents. Nothing is more shocking than to watch the surging, silt-laden mouths of these wadis as they empty the priceless long-term wealths of Libya, soil and water, into the Mediterranean. The great wadis are awesome in their violent design with brutal, sheer, limestone sides, entirely without greenery of any sort, no ferns, no vines, no shaded nooks, no soft moss underfoot, no birds nor fluttering life, only a tortured, waterless waterbed.

There is one great wadi which defies this cruel description, Wadi el Kuf, which divides eastern and western Cyrenaica, and which we cross on the way to Cyrene. As its original handsome Italian concrete bridge was destroyed in the war, we still, eighteen years later, cross by the Bailey bridge left by the British forces. Wadi el Kuf is seldom completely dry, and its craggy sides are covered with shrubs and trees, birds flit about and bees hum, and it invites one to stop and picnic. Even in prehistoric times this seems to have been a coveted spot, and caves from which prehistoric remains have been taken are found along its course.

To be honest about inconsistent wadis, I must mention another exception. When one travels in semi-desert any rill, tiny valley or depression becomes a wadi for whatever moisture there may be, whether from the air or in the soil. When all the scene about is arid, thirsty, desiccated, one may still sometimes find in the small wadi bottom, where moisture collects, scraps of leafy vegetation, a patch of tended emerald green barley or blue-green wheat.

As I remember these small wadis, these patches of green pigment in the scorched landscape, these life givers to shepherds and nomads, I know again that it is useless to generalize about this inconsistent, ambivalent, paradoxical desert land of Libya which flowers when one expects it to wither, flows when one says it is arid, and blossoms where buds are not seen.

In 1964, Beida became the summer capital of Libya, where the King opens parliament. But Beida when I first saw it was no more than a place to drive by for non-Moslem visitors. It had a few ruins, as what part of Libya has not? But its chief significance was religious; here was the tomb of the "best friend" of the Prophet, here the first Senusi Zawiya, or convent, had been established, and here later was opened the Religious Institute for Senusiyan Moslem teaching. King Idris had a summer palace here.

But none of these things made el Beida more than a roadside name until a few years later, when King Idris decided that Beida should become a permanent capital of Libya. He probably had two reasons in mind: that the religious influence in Libya would be strengthened by propinquity with Moslem monuments, and that foreign influences would be lessened in a capital city isolated from the seaports. This partially ignored the fact that any capital city must by its very nature be the center of foreign influences, when twenty-nine different foreign countries are represented here. Certainly, the idea of isolation was very unpopular with most Libyan government personnel.

With the King's goal in mind, tremendous sums of foreign aid money were soon being spent for the construction of government buildings, apartments, duplexes, and villas for government employees and others, and hotel accommodations and shops. Later, when oil revenues came in sight, large Libyan funds were allocated for the same purpose. The fact that Beida lacked the water resources for a large city was ignored. Foreign embassies moved into temporary quarters, while they bargained for permanent sites.

But at the time of this trip this expansion was still a thing of the future, and we had only Cyrene in mind as we flew by the little signpost pointing left to Beida. Much of the beauty of Cyrene depends on the weather in which one views it, and although I read in the tourist guide that "Cyrene is above all humidity and dampness," it was undoubtedly dripping with rain and shrouded in mist when we arrived there at five P.M. When we stopped overnight at Benghazi we had acquired two young girl friends of George's age to accompany us, and as we were planning to stay several nights at the large, deserted, marble-halled Cyrene Hotel, a stone's throw from the ruins, we decided to save ancient Greece for the next day when the sun might shine.

As it did. As the mist rose in the morning, and the sun worked its way through to blaze on the hilltop, one of the loveliest sights of

Libya opened before us. The classic Greek columns of Cyrene were outlined against the grassy slopes of the former Acropolis hill; myriad wild flowers crept among the cracks of the crumbling Roman baths; the rock-cut Greek tombs faced towards the morning sea where thousands of feet below us the Mediterranean lay, blue and smooth and smiling.

Harry went off with the provincial forest officer to visit plantations, while the girls and George and I went to work immediately on the ruins, uphill and down, through glass and rubble and rolling stones and centipedes, during several hours and over some acres. We went to the Sanctuary, the Temple and Fountain of Apollo, the Baths, the Triumphal Arch, the Agora-Forum, the Acropolis, the tomb of Battus, then we stumbled breathlessly upwards to the hill-top Temple and the Temple of Zeus, and finally, at the girls' tireless request, we made a return visit to the Fountain. I recognized then that one of the virtues of my favorite ruin, Sabratha, was its being on sea level.

Cyrene has a Greek framework, though most of the buildings must have been reconstructed in Roman times, thanks to natural catastrophes and the short life of the soft Cyrene limestone. Although less than a quarter of the area of the original city has been excavated, it is still a several days' job to get the scattered layout in mind, a thing I never really did. The girls were incredible, however, as girls often are at sixteen years, terrifyingly agile both physically and mentally, and far outstripping their young friend George, for the more he is pushed, the slower he moves. A few years later might find the girls cultivating a few frailties, perhaps even admiring a boyfriend's strength — but not today.

When we got back to Apollo's Fountain, George said he'd had it! He'd seen all the ruins he intended to see! And he sat firmly down among the crumbling archeological treasures and removed a shoe, in search of a blister, he said — but in protest, I suspect, against the girls' insatiable enthusiasm.

Naturally Pam and Jane said they were not tired at all! But they sat down long enough for Pam, the youngest, smallest and swiftest, and a guidebook on legs, to produce the story of the founding of Cyrene, which came about, as we all vaguely knew, as the result of a search for Greek living space. Meanwhile, George found his blister, and even Jane seemed content to relax.

"Seven centuries before Christ," Pam began conscientiously, "the Greek island of Thera was suffering with a seven-year drought . . ."

"And chronic overpopulation!" inserts Jane, from the same guidebook, which she read when George, no doubt, was reading his mystery thriller.

"The island leaders," continues Pam, "decided to go to the Oracle of Apollo at Delphi, who was famous for giving good advice."

"Advice about what?" asks George.

"Oh, politics, and love lives, and all of that," says Jane.

"Look, who's telling this? Anyway, the Oracle gave them advice; he told them to leave their island and go to Libya and establish a new Greek colony there. So they did."

"You didn't tell about Apollo!" complains Jane.

"Give me time! You see, this Greek God, Apollo, developed a terrific case on this Greek nymph, Kyrene, who was really something special in nymphs!" For the first time, George looks interested. "So Apollo goes to Cheiron, the Centaur, and tells him he's in love with Kyrene, and he asks the Centaur what to do."

"Didn't Apollo know what to do?" suggests George.

"I mean, Apollo wanted to know what was *advisable*," says Pam, anxious to do her Greeks justice.

"So the Centaur told Apollo for him and Kyrene to go ahead and have fun!" Jane hustles Pam. "And they did have fun!"

"And then Apollo married Kyrene, and brought her to Libya, up here to Cyrene, which is really the same name as Kyrene," ends Pam triumphantly.

"Don't forget about Kyrene's specialty of strangling old lions with her bare hands," I add, from the same guidebook, "and searching for silphium, the wonder, cure-all plant which had disappeared."

"I thought Kyrene discovered the Fountain of Apollo," says George, surprising everybody including himself.

"Well," concedes Pam, "Kyrene made a torrent of water gush out of the cavern's mouth, like it does today. That was where the visiting nymphs all went to bathe nude with Kyrene."

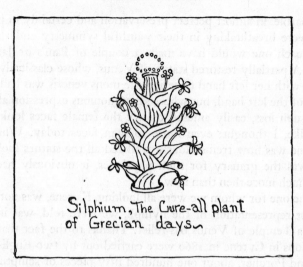

Silphium, The Cure-all plant
of Grecian days

"Any of them around now?" asks George.

Twenty-five hundred years ago Kyrene located the waters of Apollo — and the torrent still gushes. I think such a continuing water source must mean that although civilizations rise, and tumble, Cyrene as a city site will never die. Almost beside us, as we sit here in the crumbling ruins, now prospers the small, quiet village of Shahat, where thirsty Libyans today quench their thirst and their water needs from the ancient fountain sources, a part of which are now diverted to supply the village aqueduct.

There was no difficulty in getting the girls to the museum on the hilltop that afternoon. They knew just what archeological finds to look for, what sculpture to admire, and where to find both. They were not only frankly intelligent, but they had that wonderful feminine asset of liking to please.

George, however, would have much preferred to be, literally, at the bottom of the sea with an aqualung. He also was intelligent, but he had that wonderful masculine asset of liking to please himself.

The finest sculptural pieces from Cyrene have now been installed in the museum, for the sake of their preservation, and there were several pieces which pleased us all. The Three Graces, in glowing white marble, in almost perfect preservation and certainly in perfect shape, were breathtaking in their youthful symmetry and rhythm, though each one would have made a couple of Pam's or Jane's in weight. A partially restored statue of Venus, whose classically modest pose with her left hand covering the mons veneris was balked by the loss of the left hand, but whose sanctimonious expression allowed for no such loss, easily amused us. All the female faces looked exactly alike, I thought; even more so than faces today. What also struck me was how tremendously well fed all the statues looked; if Libya was the granary for such physiques, it obviously had produced much more then than now.

But the one for whom we were all looking, Kyrene, was not there. The best representation of the nymph, we were told, was in London, in a Temple of Venus bas-relief. Thanks to the fact that early excavations in Cyrene in 1860 were carried out by two Englishmen, Smith and Porcher, about one hundred fifty pieces of sculpture had been transported to the British Museum, where the Mediterraneans, in their warm country nudity and scant summer drapes, must be freezing. However, we found photographs of the Kyrene bas-relief with the nymph in breezy draperies, bare-legged and bare-handed, squeezing the final breath out of a poor, toothless, old mannish-looking lion with a long curly mane like a judge's wig. Kyrene herself is being crowned by a smug-looking Goddess of Libya for her deed, though I would have thought that her gift of water divining was more worthy of crowning, and of more local use.

The Cyrene Museum, which verges on and overlooks the ruins, has in its library the finest and rarest collection extant of literature, reference books and articles on Libya and North Africa, dating from the first printed references known to date. The learned and erudite curator of the museum, Richard Goodchild, is also the Director of Antiquities for Cyrenaica.

Fortunately, the history-conscious Italian occupiers of Libya were alive to the value of its antiquities, and they carried on excavations here from 1913 until the beginning of the Second World War. After Libya became independent and since 1954, the Cyrenaican Department of Antiquities has continued this work, aided by archeological grants and missions from Italy, the United States, and other countries.

One of the most interesting aspects of Libyan ruins is that they are still in the process of being excavated. Pieces of shard, mosaic, coins, beads, tiny figurines and broken lamps may still be found on site, where they seem incomparably more vital than after they have been cleaned, polished, catalogued and placed under glass in museums.

At dinner in the huge, chill, almost empty hotel overlooking the ruins, Pam and Jane and George were in good spirits and bickering pleasantly over everything they had seen. The girls ordered chicken, George had lamb, and Harry and I had steak, all of which tasted exactly alike, but the pale, white Cyrene wine made by an Italian winery, for which the vineyards are famous, was good. Only Harry, after a day looking at Jebel Akhdar macchia forests, was out of sorts and depressed. He had returned to the hotel just before dinner, escorted by two Land Rovers full of what appeared to be forest guards.

"Were those all Cyrenaican Forest Department officers?" I asked.

"Yes," said Harry glumly. "They've got a huge staff of forest guards and forest watchmen — every one of them a hero of the Resistance! And they know bugger-all about trees — except how to cut them down!"

"The *forest guards* cut down trees?"

"As good as. The Forest Department is now giving licenses to cut down the trees in the natural forests to sell for firewood. Then, with the firewood revenue, they are going to build roads! That gives employment both for tree-cutting and for road-building, so the Director tells me. Well, he's a nomad himself and a Bedawi, and he's happiest in a desert! He simply refuses to understand that there just won't *be* any firewood in a few years' time, if they don't guard the forests."

"Are they doing any replanting?"

"Almost none. Heroes of the Resistance prefer office jobs!"

"Can't you get your ideas over to any of them?"

"I just don't know! All they can say is, Our people want firewood! Our people are hungry! They have to be employed!"

"Why don't they hire them to plant trees, instead of cutting them down?"

"They haven't seedlings at present. The Cyrenaican nurseries are so badly run that very few seedlings survive. I must say that compared to the young men I have been working with in Tripolitania, the Cyrenaicans are hopeless. When the Tripolinos were learning from the Italians, the Cyrenaicans were shooting at them! And all they can do now is talk about it!"

In ancient days the road to Apollonia (now Susa), the port for Cyrene, was chiseled into solid rock, and the 2000-foot ascent and descent between seaport and city must have been tortuous. Today, for Harry, George and me and the girls, the ten-mile drive to the ancient seaport via the modern Italian-built highway is only a matter of minutes. The view of the blue-green Mediterranean opens before us as we descend, the glowing perfection of the weather exhilarates us, and a magic element is added to the relics of ancient life which are flung about us on every hillside and valley.

Here it is easy to forget the limitations and frustrations of past centuries, and think only of how satisfying it must have been to live one's life out on one of these glorious Greek or Roman sites, in a city without any traffic, without skyscrapers or apartment houses, without TVs and radios to spread alarms from all the world. To know only one's own problem, and the dissonance of one's own family and city, to feel loyalty only to one's own small group, to watch by the sapphire sea for the monthly ship which bring news and tradewares and departs again with grain and olive oil, and then to watch again. And if the barbarians came, they came unheralded, unpredicted, without bargaining, without dread anticipations and threats. And when one died, one died once only, without being made a coward of by threats and fears.

In Grecian days, Apollonia must have been perfectly situated on the edge of a small harbor, entered by a narrow, deep-water channel. Today, due to the subsidence of the land probably from earthquakes, about half the area of the former city lies under water, where it forms a thrilling challenge to underwater bathers. This was where George immediately wanted to be, down among the temples and tombs which quiver under deep curtains of quiet water, inhabited only by scuttling crabs, fluttering sea anemones and swaying squid.

"You see, Ma," he said reproachfully, looking longingly down into the liquid depths, "I could learn just as much Libyan history down there as in that museum! And enjoy myself, too."

"I guess you're right, George," I admitted. "Only I always feel guilty about avoiding museums because I don't much like them myself."

"But we liked the museum!" said Pam.

And Jane said amiably, "We like this, too!"

"Never mind, George," Harry promised. "We'll come back some day when we have plenty of time for you to dive."

"By then the rest of Apollonia will be under water, too!" said George sarcastically.

And with some truth, for the sea is still encroaching, and what was once the principal street of the ancient city is already partially engulfed, although on its landward side the ruins of three Byzantine churches have been excavated. The most impressive of these, the Eastern Church, seems to have accrued through the ages, as one wall is a remnant of a temple of Apollo, and another is built with a Hellenistic type of masonry, while its monolithic columns of marble represent the fifth century, and its mosaics are typical of the sixth century.

During their perusal of ancient sites, Pam, Jane and George, all of whom had previously visited Sabratha and Leptis Magna, as well as Cyrene, and now Apollonia, had all noted and been impressed by the prevalence and obvious superior longevity of the many places of worship in all the ruins.

The most impressive and best preserved structures, we agreed, were always sacred edifices of some sort — temples, tabernacles, pantheons, mosques, churches, et cetera, which usually represented an accrual of differing faiths throughout the changing periods of time. One formed the historical concept of a long procession of peoples down the ages, always in search of something, an Almighty, a Messiah, a Golden Calf, a fetish, a graven image, a totem, a Mumbo-Jumbo, a God, or gods. And in their eagerness to give factual expression to their search, they always built a material monument to mark their spiritual longing. Once it was built, the longing lessened, but the goal was no more nearly found.

One wonders what will survive of our cities today to mark what we are, and for what our search has been. I think we have not changed in our pursuit of the always unfulfilled goal, the search for something more than ourselves. The need to believe in something is in us so strongly that belief is a part of self-preservation.

Pam observed that after places of worship, the next most sought-after locations seemed to have been theaters, and she reminded us that the magnificent Roman theater at Sabratha was still occasionally used today. George contributed the idea that the third most popular location was reserved for the latrines and baths, as both were always sited with an eye to a good view and relaxation for the patrons. The neatly shaped, companionable rows of marble latrines at both Sabratha and Leptis Magna are some of their most photographed attractions, and tourists delight in having their pictures taken while sitting on them.

"The Romans had a goddess Cloaca," I remembered, "who was the genius of the sewers and of excrement. I'm sure there must be statues of her on all the ancient sites, if we could recognize her."

"I don't think she's in the guidebook," said Pam sadly.

Before leaving Cyrene the next day for Benghazi we were advised by Robert Goodchild to be sure to stop at Gasr Libya, where an unrivaled Christian period mosaic had recently been uncovered. Following his directions, we turned off the highway at kilometer 63, west of Cyrene, and drove north a half-mile to a small country center in the Green Mountain. Here the only building visible was an old Byzantine church, used in Italian times as a fort, and since the days of Libyan independence turned into a medical dispensary for the local people.

Near this old landmark, discovered by accident when local laborers were digging for building stone, a magnificent and almost perfect set of Christian mosaics was uncovered. A complete mosaic floor exists on its original location. It is miraculously lovely to look at, and more miraculous when one realizes that it was placed here fourteen hundred years ago, almost exactly as we see it today, by the order of

THINGS LIBYAN

Libyan wearing a Taghia

Covered with her baracan, this Libyan lady is ready for the street, with only one eye exposed. Why it is her left eye rather than her right eye, the lady does not know: her answer is tradition.

The good luck symbol of the hand of Fatima, the daughter of the Prophet, Mohamed, is widely used in gold jewelry. The design is also placed on homes and vehicles to ward off danger and evil. So also

This type of design continues indefinitely in Libyan basketry.

are the symbols of fish, crescent, star and horn

Simple symbols of sheep, goat, cock and chick are used in carpet weaving.

Classic antiquities abound.

 gazelle

A stylized camel design is used as motif in many rugs woven in the Fezzan, the desert province of Libya.

date palms

strong tea

And now oil wells flow in Libya.

the Emperor Justinian when he had the church decorated in honor
of his wife, Theodora. The central panel of the floor clearly states
that it was laid down in "the third year of an indiction by Bishop
Makarios," which makes the year A.D. 539.

The floor, as we saw it this day, was completely open to rain and
sun except for a carelessly fluttering, torn, canvas canopy overhead.
As we experienced both a downpour and sunshine while studying
the mosaic, it was freshly washed clean of its red Cyrenaican soil,
and shone with renewed clarity and delicacy under the sudden
beams of the sun. It must have been the floor of the main nave of the
church, and the mosaic consisted of fifty separate panels which depicted a great variety of living things as well as inanimate ones.
There were birds, beasts and fish, nymphs, satyrs and mermen,
males, females and probably hermaphrodites, ships, castles and temples, all done in a grandly imaginative style in gay, realistic colors. It
was the most impressive and fascinating mosaic that I have ever seen,
partly because we saw it on the very spot where it had been laid
down fourteen hundred years before, and where the Romans of that
day had stood, like us, and admired it.

Shortly after our visit, appreciation of the value of the find in all
its perfection stimulated further excavations, which uncovered two
more churchly rooms, also with mosaics. After completion of the
excavation of these rooms, the entire site was walled and roofed to
protect and preserve it. The preservation of its delicate coloring
over the past fourteen hundred years is largely due to the fact that
the mosaics had been buried most of the time, and not exposed to
either light or weathering. In the few years which elapsed while the
floors were exposed to the elements while being uncovered, more
fading took place than had taken place in the fourteen hundred years
preceding.

Harry and I were flying up to London for ten days with George,
before he went back to school in Canada. Harry loves London, and
wanted George to see the city as he had known it; not as a sight-
seeing event, but as a charmed land of endless book shops, wonderful
entertainments, and excellent food.

The day before we were to leave Tripoli, Mohamed gave a "kus

kus" party for George, inviting the Libyan boys in the neighborhood — Sayed, Sola, Mustapha, Omar and "old Mohamed" from the
Fezzan. He served kus kus made of fine-grained semolina, which his
mother had made at home, and camel stew cooked on my charcoal
brazier in the garden, and, of course, sweet tea with peanuts. I was in
bed with a high fever of unknown origin, but I could hear their
young voices laughing and chortling over the stew pot outside, using
a polyglot of languages. George had quickly fallen into the use of
"Mediterranean," the best name by which to describe the local means
of communication, which consists of a murderous combination of
broken English, Arabic, Italian and French. There was no lack of
either communication or understanding that night.

The next day we found to our horror that we had missed the five-
after-midnight BOAC plane to London the night before, on which
we had reservations. By one of those incredible slips which people
incredibly make, we had misthought 12:05 to be just after midnight
Friday, instead of just after Thursday midnight. I didn't entirely
regret it, as I had felt too ill the night before to dress. Now, after a
miserable morning of family recriminations and chest-beatings, we
were advised by BOAC that they could not give us reservations for
tonight, but that we should go to the airport and hope for cancella-
tions. This we did, and were lucky.

We arrived in London, and naturally it was raining and continued
to rain the ten days we were there. Hotel doormen, bus conductors,
taxi drivers, salespeople, everyone we met, were busy apologizing
for the weather, with what seemed to us to be an overoptimistic
presumption that it wasn't always like this in August. We were, I
think, the only people in London that summer who were pleased
with the rain, as we had arrived from Libya in a desiccated state,
after the fierce, dry summer months and the ghiblis. In every way
London was good to us, and Harry and George browsed endlessly,
buying books, while a new hairdo and clothes improved my morale,
and our evenings were spent on luxurious living we could not afford.

For us, one more goodbye in the airport marks the end of another
epoch in life with George. When we three meet again he will once
more be a different person. Always when we first meet after being
apart for some time, he seems to have changed so much that we are

strangers. Gradually we become friends again, and there comes a short period midway between meeting and the next parting when we feel easy and normal together. Then, as the time grows shorter, begins the downhill slide towards the parting. We are all three overcast by the impending distances of space and time ahead of us, and Harry becomes too thoughtful, and George too brusque and tough, while I fight sentimentality. And the end is always the same: Harry and I stand together and wave goodbye, and George goes off alone; or George stands alone, and we go off together.

Perhaps it is just as hard on children to have their parents devoted to each other as to have them at odds. To some extent parental devotion excludes the kids, while a state of marital unrest certainly includes them, unpleasant though it is to have to take sides. Still, George cannot bear to have dissention between Harry and me. If there is even a friendly (comparatively!) argument between us, George comes in on Harry's side, and says, "Ma, stop picking on Pa!" And then when Ma stops picking on Pa, George looks left out and lonely.

I think that young people suffer more keenly than adults because their lack of experience makes it impossible for them to rationalize their sorrows. Although I may be able to comfort myself with the knowledge that all things pass, a boy of seventeen has only today.

Someone said once that part of you dies each time you say goodbye . . .

It was a happy homecoming in Libya. I was pleased to be returning to a real home this time, instead of just arriving to set one up. Mohamed had cleaned house thoroughly in our absence and was delighted with himself; we had brought him a pair of gray flannel slacks and a sport shirt from London, and we were delighted with ourselves, and he with us. The marvelous Libyan autumn was rejuvenating the withered survivors of summer, and spring was in the air in October. Even the little red Vauxhall standing in the garage seemed none the worse for the ghiblis of summer, nor for George's having learned to drive it.

The next morning I was delighted to get back to my few Arab phrases when I asked Mohamed for Turkish coffee. Our coffee break gave him the chance he wanted in which to open his new campaign. He started this by saying amiably, "I like to learn to drive your car. Then I can drive for you."

"I don't need a driver. I like to drive myself."

"George drives your car."

"Yes, but George has a license, and his father had the car especially insured for George to drive."

"I like to have a license, too."

"You will have to go to driving school first to learn to drive."

"I now go to school every evening for driving."

"Well, that is very enterprising of you!"

"You let me practice on your car?"

"No, Mohamed. No one may drive my car without a license."

The next day a friend mentioned to me that he thought I had returned the week before, as he had seen my car on the road with Mohamed driving. This gave me quite a shock, but when I thought of what the car had escaped, my relief swallowed up my indignation. I had learned another thing never to do — never leave the key of the car at home on a nail when we go abroad.

Three times a week for weeks then, Mohamed left the house early to get to his driving lesson. This consisted of riding around in the back of a truck with a dozen other Libyan boys, each one hoping to get a short turn at the wheel with instruction. Although these lessons en masse were less expensive individually than a private lesson, they must have netted the instructor a huge profit per hour of teaching.

After some weeks of this, Mohamed began to take driving tests. Every week he took a test and every week he failed it. It seemed that he not only had to pass a driving test, but he had to be personally recommended by the instructor before he could get a license. I finally gave up asking Mohamed if he had passed his test because it upset him to admit he had failed, yet I felt that he must be just as well qualified as other Libyan drivers.

"Do any of the boys who take lessons with you pass the test for a license?"

"Yes, sometimes, if they are friends of the teacher."

The next time I saw my Libyan mentor, Hammet, I asked him if he knew why Mohamed couldn't get a license.

"Maybe he no give present to the teacher."

"Ah, ha. What present must he give?"

"Maybe give cigarettes. Must give something."

The next day I said to Mohamed, "Hammet thinks that you have to give a present to the instructor before he will recommend you for a license."

Mohamed looked thoughtful. "Maybe, Mother."

A week later he arrived at the house in the morning, jubilant. "Mother! I pass my license!"

"Good. Wonderful! What happened?"

"I give bottle of whiskey to my teacher. My friend from Wheelus buy whiskey for me cheap. Now I pass my test, and have my license," he said proudly.

This, I thought, explained a lot about Libyan drivers.

A few days later Mohamed arrived in a mood of deep depression, and told me that his family had arranged a marriage for him to take place very soon. With these words he put his head on his arms and burst into tears.

"Why must you marry so young, Mohamed? You have no money."

"The mother, she wants my babies. But I don't want to get married now! I want to be like George. I want to go to school, and to travel. But I never have any fun, never never! I always have to work. And now I must marry," and he sobbed aloud.

It was obvious that he looked for no "fun" from matrimony, and I expect he was right. The sad thing was that Mohamed wept for the little gaiety which should be every young person's by right.

"You haven't seen the girl you are going to marry, Mohamed?"

"Oh, no! My mother see."

"But your mother is blind."

"She know what she look like, because people tell her."

"How old is your fiancée?"

"Maybe thirteen, maybe fourteen. Is very good girl; she live in the house of the mother of Salem."

I knew that Salem's family was well connected and moderately well-to-do, as they were landowners, and that to be well connected was the most important thing in the Arab world. I thought that the girl was probably a poor relation, but if brought up in Salem's household she was sure to be a nice, capable girl. Quite possibly, she might bring a little fun and brightness into Mohamed's burdened household.

8. Nobody to Advise

HERE in Libya, for the first time in many years, Harry was taking his weekly holiday, which to begin with was Sunday, but later was suitably changed to Friday, the Moslem day of rest. As a result, we were really seeing the country, as we were on the road every free day, armed with plant presses, bread and cheese, and Thermos flasks of coffee and water. I learned more about the countryside those first two years than in all the years after.

When I congratulate Harry on actually taking his free days off, he says, "I wouldn't mind working harder here; I'd like to! My problem at present is to find *enough* to do. I wasn't sent here to go out and plant seedlings; any forest guard can do that. I came here to advise the government on forestry. But I can't find the Libyans to advise! Old Abou Babba was right about the number of experts here. There are more advisers than Arabs. He was in the office today. He wanted to know how you like it here."

"And did you tell him I'm a fully convinced Libyan, except for the yashmak?"

"I said something of the sort. He's having quite a time himself in Cyrenaica."

"Good time, or bad time?"

"Awkward. The King rather favors his Tobruk palace orchards and he manages to keep Abou Babba busy most of the time making the royal oranges grow larger, and his olive trees yield more. When Abou Babba isn't busy with the King's place, he's improving matters on the farm of the police chief, Buquwaytin, who grows a little of everything. After that, if there are a few minutes left, the Chief of the Cyrenaica Defence Force has some orchards that need expert attention. Meanwhile, the poor, ruddy plains farmers get damn little help and advice. Abou Babba himself says it's not right — but he can't refuse the King — nor the others, I guess."

"This is part of my trouble," he continues. "I was sent here to formulate a sound forest policy, and to persuade the government to enact modern legislation to implement it, but the federal government doesn't even have a forest department! There are only the two provincial ones. I can't find Libyans who know enough about forestry to be advised."

There had been some truth, I thought, in my own idea that the fewer trees there were, the more a forest adviser was needed.

"One reason," Harry went on, "I have started this collection of Libyan flora is to escape the frustration of no accomplishment in the policy line. I shall send several of each specimen we collect to Kew herbarium in England for them to verify my classification, and I shall keep several specimens here in the herbarium I'm starting for Libya. A comprehensive classified collection of Libyan flora has not been made before. This at least will be of value to the country in the future."

"Will they realize the value of a collection? Maybe they'll just sweep it out in the spring cleaning!"

"Not till I leave, anyway. And perhaps before that I can get somebody interested; Badreddin Messaudi of the provincial forest department is quite knowledgeable."

"I thought that the Italians did a lot of forest work in Libya. What's happened to that?"

"They did a great deal of excellent, very sound work here. In fact, they devised a very successful system of dune fixation. But much of their work has since been nullified, or destroyed entirely, during and after the war. Many once fine plantations here have been cut down for fuel, and goats and sheep are grazing where good plantations once flourished. It's a crime! And very shortsighted on Libya's part."

"I suppose the Libyan government has everything to learn, and all of it first."

"Land ownership is another discouraging problem. At this moment, it looks unsolvable. Until the government decides to whom the land belongs, we can't make any forest reserves, nor do any work of lasting value."

"Why can't they decide who owns the land? Why is it insolvable?"

"Because tribal ownership claims dominate all others, and these conflict with each other. Tribal claims are almost impossible to establish, or to decide. And the tribes are stronger than the federal government. If government arbitrarily establishes a reserve and plants it, along comes some old sod and says it's his tribal allotment! And no one can prove it isn't."

"Have there never been any surveys?"

"There is no accepted survey system. Tribal land boundaries are really known only between tribes. If the government surveys, then the tribes just pull up the sticks, and throw away the boundary stones!"

"We did see some cypress and juniper on Jebel Akhdar, though."

"Jebel Akhdar is a natural cypress and juniper forest area, and it *should* be a prolific stand; it was during the Italian occupation, because they prohibited all indiscriminate cutting and grazing in the natural forests. But after the war, the occupying military authorities more or less canceled the Italian prohibitions on cutting and grazing, and look what happened! The nomadic shepherds returned in force with their flocks and herds, and they have grazed everything below their knees and chopped down everything above for firewood! If they continue like this their "Green Mountain" will be a "limestone plateau!"

"Are you making any headway at all with the policy legislation to protect these areas?"

"I doubt it! I've spent countless hours and days drawing up the legislation that they need to protect their forests, but I can't find anybody seriously enough interested to push through its enactment. Basically, the Libyans are a desert people and don't feel the same as we do about forests. The shepherds and herdsmen can always shout louder than the trees! 'Better our trees die than our people!' is the politicians' motto. The trees don't vote."

"But surely it *is* better that the trees die than the people?"

"The people won't die. They didn't in Italian times; the population actually increased. The fact is that Libya is now in the last phase before final desert invasion. The Sahara is *not* being held, it's taking over more and more arable land. The ultimate future of Libya is not to produce sheep and goats; its real future is agriculture, and it always has been. Even if they should end up with oil in the Sahara, it's still an agricultural country, and its long-time future must be."

"I don't hear much talk about oil. I thought the Italians couldn't find any!"

"The Italians didn't. But if the French find oil in the Algerian Sahara, *somebody* is going to find it here. In any case, oil means money in revenues, but it doesn't supply a livelihood to the people. Agriculture does."

"Last winter when the wadi flooded, and we watched the Wadi Megenin, chocolate-brown and heavy with silt, pouring into the bay here, I didn't think there would be any land left."

"That happens every year. The best fertile layer of soil washes into the Mediterranean."

"But why?"

"Because the entire catchment area has been stripped of vegetation by grazing and cutting. Consequently, any rainfall does the land little good as it runs off into the wadis. And then whatever soil *is* left gets sanded down with every ghibli."

"Doesn't dune fixation do any good?"

"Depends on how well it's done, and where it is. If there is no windblown seed, the indigenous vegetation can't return. I want you to see the dune area where Hammet is doing fixation now. No crater on the moon could look any less habitable, or any more dreary. The wind blows constantly, either from one direction or another, as there's nothing left above the surface of the land to stop it. This is only ten miles from Tripoli, and the dunes are coming closer all the time."

Harry had not exaggerated, I thought next Sunday as I stood braced against the wind between him and Hammet, who was becoming more and more of a "son" to Harry inasmuch as he never refused any demands on his personal time to accompany us to areas of forest interest. Now I clung to Harry and Hammet as the merciless, inexorable desert wind battered us, while I looked in horror at what dear old nature — left to herself — was doing.

I said as much to Harry, who said indignantly, "Dear old nature isn't being left to herself! That's what I mean. This wasteland has been created by the total destruction by man and animal of all natural vegetation. If we can hold the dunes here, and keep men and goats off the area for ten years, nature will probably regenerate. If not — well, there you see it — a moon landscape!"

Sand, mixed with the dust of the red earth, rolled out all around me in rusty dunes as far as I could see, in the most unnatural-looking scene one could imagine. The landscape was carefully divided into six-foot squares which were outlined by closely set tufts of bristling vegetation about a foot high. The angular, mechanical design contrasted incongruously with the undulating horizon.

"Is that stuff growing?" I demanded, looking curiously at the stiff little sprigs sticking up from the sand.

"No, it isn't meant to. It's dis — so the Arabs call it; *Imperata*, really. It's just buried in the sand to stabilize it temporarily until trees can take root. All this area is going to be planted with eucalyptus seedlings, and the dis should hold the sand until the seedlings take hold. Dis fixation sometimes lasts over a year, if it's properly done. Come along, I want to show you something."

The wind battered us unceasingly, and the sand sucked at our feet as we plunged up and down across the dunes until we came in sight of the fronds of date palms — but not waving from date palm trunks, but spurting grotesquely out of the dunes themselves.

"There you are," said Harry. "Those are the village palm groves. You can't even see the cultivated land; it's buried under the dunes!"

I was content to leave the area promptly. "The desert is all very well," I said, "in the desert, but not moving up to the doorstep."

"But where is 'in the desert'? It's *any* place in Libya where you destroy vegetation — and fail to hold the soil."

On the way home I asked, "How fast will those dunes move if you don't do any fixation?"

"It is almost impossible to predict, because it depends on the winds, and on the size of the sand grains. But we do know that those dunes have moved enough in the last few years to swallow the village's cultivated land and its fringe of palm groves — I think at least fifty yards in those years."

The day we visited the esparto area on the Asaaba Plain between Garian and Jefren we met an old Italian orchard owner plugging along the gravel road shoulder behind a large gray mare. We were on the long, rolling stretch where the colossal, antiquated olive trees are, and where we thought the turnoff to the plain came. Fearing that we had missed it, we stopped the old man and asked.

It was enough, and he told us his history. Arbitrarily chosen by Mussolini twenty-five years before to be a Libyan farmer, the then young man had arrived here to become an unwilling colonizer. He had unenthusiastically planted his Tagrina land with peaches, figs, and almonds, and in the end had decided not to return to Italy. He was too old, he said, to make a new place for himself.

"Did you have any trouble with the Libyans during the war, and after independence?" Harry asked.

"No, we don't bother each other," he said. "All through the war we helped each other out when food was short. They're mostly Berbers here, and not too quarrelsome. A bit lazy, maybe. But they all know me, and we get on."

"You must have seen a lot of changes?" Harry said.

"Most of the Italians in Garian and Tagrina have left, or are farming the orchards for Libyan owners, now. I still own my own place, but as I can only sell to a Libyan, it limits the price I can get."

"This turnoff for the Asaaba Plain," Harry reminds him, "we haven't missed it?"

"No, you've a long way to go still. I can remember when the esparto was so thick on the Asaaba Plain that you couldn't see a sheep running through the grass; now you can even see an ant!"

The esparto grass situation was another of Harry's continuing headaches. This grass, or halfa as it is called here, is a tufted perennial with a branching base, which is (or has been) natural to the steppe areas of Tripolitania. Its use is for making high-grade paper, and it is especially in demand for bank notes. As far back as Turkish times, esparto was one of the principal exports from Tripolitania.

Today, the Esparto Corporation, government-owned, has a monopoly of its purchase. Thanks to shortsighted overexploitation and to injurious harvesting methods, most of the esparto stands have been destroyed, and the once natural esparto areas are becoming desert.

We finally arrived at the flat, drab plains area where the esparto was being harvested (out of season, Harry noted!) and we stood and watched the process. The grass was being plucked by Bedawi labor, who twisted handfuls of grass blades around short sticks, and then pulled in such a manner that most of the plant was uprooted. The proper way to collect it, Harry said, was to pull it blade by blade, so the root was left intact in the soil.

"Why do they let them harvest like that?" I asked. "Can't the monopoly refuse to take it when it's pulled with the roots?"

"As long as the monopoly can sell it, they'll take it any old way. A plan for esparto management control was drawn up long ago — but it has never been followed. However, the one thing that can possibly save some of the esparto grass areas is happening: the demand for esparto is decreasing. During the war, paper manufacturers found other fibres that were equally good for paper. Now the price paid for esparto by the monopoly is no longer attractive to the pickers. This will save some areas of this low-rainfall steppeland from being converted into bare, wind-eroded plains such as we are looking at now. What you see here is only what the overexploited esparto stands always become. Look!" And Harry pointed in disgust to the plain.

On our way here we had passed through one of the loveliest parts of Tripolitania, the rural countryside of Garian, where rich fruit orchards, acres of barley and wheat, fields of wild flowers, and gnarled, dignified olive trees spread out before us in extravagant array.

Now on Asaaba Plain I stood and looked — at bales of dead esparto. Even when growing, esparto is not a beautiful grass, but in desert land categories anything that is green, that grows and flowers and tufts and holds down the soil, is attractive. Now here before us, torn out, mangled, and stacked in bales is the accumulated beauty of the landscape.

Standing thirty feet high are large bundles of dried, pressed esparto ready to be trucked to the Tripoli port for export. Beyond these bales spreads the denuded land, interrupted only by scattered esparto tussocks, which are the final step before complete disappearance of the grass. Already the hungry, parched landscape is eroding into wasteland gullies and dry waterways. Already the earth's sharp, white bones jut out from her wasted body in anticipated decay.

"It's like a skeleton," said Harry. "No blood running, no heartbeat left, no sap to rise — just bone and skin and hair. A dead land, and murdered by its children!"

9. Wedding

LAST Monday Mohamed said goodbye to us before leaving for a week's festivities which included his wedding. He first embraced me warmly many times, calling me "Mother" and weeping on my shoulder, until finally I had to remind him that it was not his funeral but his wedding that he was going to. I promised to go to his house in Suk el Juma on Friday afternoon to join the celebrations, and to bring Clutha with me. Mohamed adores Clutha, Major Jack Garnett's wife, whom he often sees at our home and in the British forces book store, as she is unfailingly courteous and charming to him.

In these week-long weddings we strangers are never invited for the nuptial night. A Libyan wedding requires five to seven days of festivities and ceremonies, and it costs from one hundred fifty dollars, up to astronomical sums. Mohamed's salary is thirty-three dollars a month and his wedding is costing about four hundred fifty dollars, which he hasn't got. He is borrowing it, of course, starting with us.

When I asked him why the wedding cost so much, he itemized to me how the money is being spent: first, an extra door has been built to close off his little alcove from the rest of his mother's house; a chest of drawers has been bought for the "she" to contain her dowry things and a gift of gold jewelry has been made from Mohamed to her; a pure-silk white wedding baracan has been purchased for Mohamed; the rest of the money will go on quantities of tea, sugar, peanuts and sweet cakes for friends and relatives who must be feasted for a week.

Friday afternoon Clutha and I arrived at Suk el Juma at the agreed meeting place where I have often left Mohamed when I drove him home. Here, as Mohamed had promised, Ali, a young Arab friend, was waiting to meet us, dressed in rather bedraggled Western clothes and much less tidy and smart than our Mohamed. However, he spoke understandable English, which was the reason he was chosen to meet us, and he said he would conduct us to Mohamed's house.

I suggested that we park the car and get out and walk, as the old city streets are almost impassable for motorcars, but guide Ali insisted that we should drive on farther. With difficulty then we negotiated two very sharp right-angle turns, the second taking us through a narrow door in the city wall, and here, with an advance of barely twenty yards beyond my chosen parking spot, Ali said we should leave the car. We had now achieved a position from which it was almost impossible to turn around, and meanwhile we successfully blocked the alley.

Now guide Ali dashed ahead of us and disappeared into a house, returning in a moment with Mohamed, beautifully dressed in his new white baracan, coughing heartily, looking handsome but exhausted and dopey from sleepless festivity nights, but very cordial with his welcome and handshake, which today he followed with the traditional Moslem gesture of touching my hand to his forehead, lips and heart. He ushered us, followed by a string of curious youngsters, up a narrow lane to a doorway, and here Mohamed stopped and called out in Arabic.

An old woman whom he then introduced as his mother answered his call. The act of introducing was accomplished by our peering around a doorway at her, although she, with her blind eyes searching towards us, could not permit her face to be seen by the youngsters outside. The entrance to the house was designed so that a person standing at the doorway could not see directly inside the house. Mohamed's mother was a real old crone to look at, her face leathery in texture, covered with a mesh of fine lines, and boldly landscaped with great gullies of wrinkles which gave her the look of genuine Libyan terrain. Looking at her, I was shocked at the havoc which life had wreaked on her at an age of, possibly, fifty. Giving birth to nine children and burying eight of them had been no light task.

While I was still staggering from this sight, Mohamed gestured me to enter, and without entering himself, he pointed to us that we were to go to his room. Just then an attractive-looking, vivacious young woman, Fatima, took us in tow, and we were swallowed up among thirty or so Libyan females. Fatima introduced us all around, and soon we were engulfed in massive kissing operations. Extricated finally by Fatima, obviously a top female executive, who seemed able to control every situation, we were guided towards the bridal alcove.

The bridegroom in wedding baracan

A great deal of kissing took place that afternoon, as everybody greeted each other in this way. Knowing that kissing is distasteful to Asians, I had thought, before coming to Libya, that it might be to Arabs also, their ways being often more Eastern than Western. But I was wrong. Kissing among Libyans, and men do it amongst themselves as much as women do, is a quite different caress from our kiss of the Western world which is, in its deeper meaning, a sensual endearment. Libyan kisses are like pecks, bites and nibbles, and are made with a forceful munching of lips against other lips or cheeks, and repeated again and again, on first one side then the other, accompanied by little cries.

In due time, following Fatima to Mohamed's room, we found

Lutfeyah, the little bride, seated cross-legged on the floor, in the process of being made up by a coal-black Fezzani woman who is a professional wedding beautician. This process, we learned, would continue for several hours. Lutfeyah looked about thirteen years old, tiny and immature in her body, but with a dainty, pretty little face — or so I could imagine. Today, however, she was too much made up with rouge, lipstick, powder, henna, eye pencil and shadow for me to be sure what nature intended.

The pattern of her facial makeup followed a normal one, until it came to her lower lip and chin, and on these, neat little Vandyke beards were being drawn with eyebrow pencil, while a few dark vertical strokes like whiskers had been drawn on her cheeks. These marks signified her tribal affiliations.

Her small hands and feet were painted with intricate henna designs, her hair was carefully parted in a dozen sectors and then braided into two small shoulder-length plaits, which were being elongated by twisting into them two heavy black wool yarn braids, widely banded with silver. I later noticed that most of the women guests wore similar artificial braids tied on to their own less abundant ones.

Many times in my first months in Libya, I have thought about the lives of these veiled, secluded wives, and wondered what they would be like. I had thought they must certainly lack that Western feminine incentive for adornment, the struggle to acquire, and then to hold, the admiration of men, and especially one's own man. In the Western world the fight is fierce and competitive, and it no doubt accounts for a lot of otherwise inexplicable things we women do.

But in Libya, a woman cannot fight in the open field. It is of no use to her to have a new spring outfit to increase her charms so that her husband may see by the light in the eyes of other men that his wife is a prize. Here a light in the eyes of another man may be cause for a killing, and not necessarily of the other man, more likely of the wife. For at this time in the Libyan Moslem world, a man could look only on the faces of his mother and his wife, and no other woman, unless she was not a Libyan Moslem.

In Libya, so strictly is the rule of seclusion held up as the ideal for wives that the perfect upper-class wife seldom steps from her home after marriage. The exception to this rule comes after a year of marriage, or after the birth of a first baby, when the wife is permitted to visit the home of her parents. This narrow concept of good wifehood is symbolized by the unworn pair of shoes: in these shoes the wife was married, and in these shoes she should be buried, the shoes still shining like new. The concept of seclusion is most strictly identified with the upper class, except in possibly half a dozen cases of the wives of Western-educated Libyans who have gained a little freedom.

One may rest assured that the few sheeted female figures one sees in Tripoli hastening one-eyed through the frenzied race of motorcars, buses, bicycles, donkey carts, camels and pushcarts are *not* the wives of the charming effendi-effendis you met at the cocktail party last night — *their* wives don't go out marketing. These women on the streets may be black, white or brown, slaves, poor relations, or servants, but they will not be the "ladies" of Libyan Moslem faith.

Having thought anxiously about women's thankless lot in Libya, I was all eyes this wedding day to get a glimpse of them at their weary tasks. And nothing could have surprised me more than the hilarious atmosphere I met of gay, fierce, abandoned, primitive celebration. These, one felt, were not city-bred women from either slums or palaces, but rather Berber and Arab "bints" from the "bled," from the black tents of desert and steppe, from the troglodyte caves, and from the woven mats of the barley growers. These were women with vitality to spare, and today they were having a marvelous time.

Even my theory about women's motive for self-adornment collapsed here, when I saw the excitement and joy these women were experiencing from seeing each other's brilliant costumes, for each one had her "best dress" on, and they had dressed for each other as much as *we* dress for men. My general impression of the garments at this, my first Libyan ladies' party, was of a rainbow of color.

Ladies were draped, swathed, swaddled in many yards of metallic striped cloth, with alternating stripes of either turquoise, purple, deep blue or bright pink. Elegant gold-embroidered blouses were partially submerged under these draperies, while masses of heavy gold (apparently) jewelry rested on their bosoms. At least half of the women had babies suckling at their breasts, and all had children clinging to them. The young women were beautiful, or handsome, full of life, vitality and gaiety.

Their elders, however, looked immeasurably old like Mohamed's mother, who in actual years was not very old — perhaps not more than fifty — but looked to be a centenarian. It was as if there were no middle-aged women in this country, no what we call "well-preserved" women of mature years. Apparently they all slipped from youth directly into antiquity. However, girls of fifteen and sixteen, and up to thirty years, were ravishingly pretty in a fierce, gypsy-like way, which suited the mad spirit of enjoyment.

The majority of the girls present had dark eyes and dark hair, but a few had wide-set blue eyes and medium blonde hair, or hennaed hair. The dark girls had long, strong noses which may be described as Roman, Arab or Hebrew, as one wishes. The blonde girls had daintier faces and smaller, pointed noses, perhaps more like the original Libyan Berber stock.

There were a few very handsome Fezzani lady guests, with very black skins and pure African Negroid features. Three of these ladies were the most elegantly dressed and extravagantly jewel-laden of any present. I was told later that they were the second wives of very wealthy Arabs, effendi-effendis, as Mohamed describes such upper-class, moneyed Libyan gentlemen.

While the bride was being created in Mohamed's room, we were urged at intervals to go and take a peek at the progress. When at five-thirty she was led into the courtyard by the Fezzani beautician, her head and face were completely covered with a satin drape. It was not until traditional passes were made over her, and wedding chants sung, that she was finally unveiled to be admired by her female friends. I was somewhat staggered with the apparition, as she certainly looked more like an Oriental princess, or a figure in a Chinese drama, than a poor but warm-blooded Arabian teen-ager who was about to marry "my son Mohamed" on a monthly income of thirty-three dollars!

Lutfeyah had on silk Turkish trousers partially concealed under a number of seperate velvet tunics, each one of a different vivid hue. Her chest was hidden by gold necklaces, brooches, bangles, and gold earrings which hung from her ears onto her shoulders in loops the size of a tumbler's brim. She had wide silver anklets to band her trousers, and bracelets to hold her sleeves.

As Lutfeyah is an orphan and a dependent household helper in the home of Salem's mother, I wondered where the finery and jewelry had come from. I learned later that it was customary to borrow a certain amount of jewelry for a wedding, and that the rest of it represented a gift from Mohamed plus her own dowry, which was probably all of her lifetime's wages put into gold.

By now some wrinkled Fezzani (female, of course) entertainers were making a rhythmic, drum-like music by tapping the bottoms of dried gourds with their fingers and palms, while the guests were belly-dancing, one at a time, in the center of the ring which was formed by the guests and family. Almost everyone except Clutha and me took a turn at dancing, from little girls of two and three years up to Mohamed's mother herself, who after two rounds collapsed temporarily on the floor. The dance was always the same primitive, sensual, voluptuous belly dance, obviously aimed at the basic fulfillment of the seven days' festivities. By now everybody was ululating frenziedly, including Clutha and me.

Everyone except Clutha and me was sitting on the floor when not dancing. Although we wished to sit on the floor, we were not permitted to, and two very uncomfortable straight-backed chairs with fancy white bed pillows on them pursued us wherever we went, until we gave up and sat on them as we were intended, thus putting everyone except ourselves at ease.

It was astonishing that although no one except us spoke a word of English we all understood each other quite well, largely thanks to the spirit of warm friendship with which we were welcomed. Apparently, by making the proper greetings in Arabic when I entered, as Mohamed had taught me, and then giving the correct responses about my health in Arabic accompanied by the usual Arabic exclamations of "El hamdu li'llah!" or "Praise be to God," I had misled people into thinking I could converse in Arabic. But when the ladies, delighted that I spoke their language, started to go further in the conversation, I had to make my ignorance plain.

By seven o'clock, when Clutha and I were preparing to make a polite exit, having been there for six hours, we were literally forced to our seats again by the lady executive, who now produced two tremendous plates of kus kus, which we were invited to eat. As we had been eating and drinking all afternoon, very sweet tea, very sweet cakes, and very sweet sweets which had been tirelessly urged on us and everybody, we were completely without appetite, all the more so as no one else was being served with kus kus. Perhaps they would be later — I never figured it out — or perhaps, as is so typical of the Libyans, they were giving to their visitors much better than they could have for themselves. After we had done our best with the kus kus, there still appeared to be a good meal remaining on our plates, but we felt sure that the hordes of children hanging about would be delighted with what we left.

We kissed everybody all around, munching cheeks hungrily, babbling farewell and el hamdu li'llahs, climbing over infants and circumnavigating elders as we worked our way towards the exit. Only the bride went unkissed. She had been sitting almost motionless in her finery in the center of the room for the last two hours, both hands placed flat on her knees, her feet encased in silver wedding slippers flat on the floor in front of her. Tradition does not permit her to speak or to laugh, although her mischievous friends are all making an effort to make her do so. In her own way, she is enjoying herself, for she is the center of attention and the object of all admiration this day.

As we step outside the outer doorway we can hear the roaring good time continuing behind us. If the Libyan ladies are repressed and woebegone, as I had previously envisioned them, it certainly isn't at weddings!

Outside the house we met Mohamed again. He is living in a friend's home, as he can't return to his own home until the unveiled ladies have left. Just how and when he and his bride ever get together for the consummation of their marriage, I haven't worked out. But I think it will be some days before Mohamed feels energetic enough to do my household work again.

10. Immutable Islam

AFTER many discouraging glimpses of man ruining nature, it was very satisfying finally to arrange a trip to the fabled Sahara oasis city of Ghadames, "Pearl of the Desert," of which we had read. I don't know who first called it pearl, but no one since has failed to do so, the name so suits the view of the shining, white-walled city lying luminous on the sands as you approach.

Here, in the middle of the Sahara, on the strength of a God-given artesian water supply, that destructive creature man has redeemed himself by planting green gardens, fruiting orchards, and golden date-laden palm groves, and building to the honor of Allah a hidden city famous for millenniums through all Africa.

Three thousand years ago Ghadames was known to travelers as a desert watering place, and it is believed to be Pliny's Cydamus. It remains today a noble Moslem monument, always hospitable to desert travelers. It is even being promoted as a tourist item, I note, in Libya's tourism circulars, but I think from my own trip that it may be some time before it fulfills tourist comfort requirements. It was only after three long, hard days of Land Rover jolting over what was scarcely even a track that we arrived.

"We" were in this case Henri Le Houèrou, an FAO ecologist from Tunisia; Jan Berkelbach van der Sprenkle, an FAO agronomist; Ahmed, our Libyan driver; Harry and I; and three Land Rovers. Harry was looking for possible sites for tree plantations and Jan for cereal locations, and Henri was botanizing.

Our journey had been prolonged by a day-and-night stop at Nalut, which has no duplicate in all Libya, located as it is on the very crest of the red Jebel Nafusa, where it is more like an eagle's nest than a town. An ancient Berber troglodyte village, Nalut is positioned thus for defense against past centuries of attackers from the Phoenicians up to the Turks, for defense against change in its cold, hard Islamic sect of fanatic Abadites, and for preservation of the Berber racial stock unpolluted.

The keystone of Nalut is its old Berber fortress whose primary use was, and is still, as a storehouse of Berber valuables — in other words, the products of their tiny, sky-high lands. In a world where money has no meaning, this is the "bank" for the people of this area; here they store their crops, dates, wool, anything they may value. Each one has his own "cell," of which there are more than three hundred, guarded only by one old watchman who sleeps all the time. Yet no theft, we are told, ever occurs.

The storehouse is hewn out of the face of the solid rock cliff, as well as being built upward on top of it with limestone blocks. So high in the sky one seems up here, and so cut off from the world below, that I felt an overwhelming sense of security, tranquility, and independence from wordly limitations. The people of Nalut must be, I thought, of a different caliber, almost superhuman in their resilient toughness, compared to the plainsmen below.

We slept the night at the little "hotel" on the edge of the cliff whose door was unlocked for us by a friendly Nalut policeman. The place exuded the chill of a tomb, not having been opened for over a year. We put up cots and sleeping bags out on the veranda looking off the cliff to the distant lowlands. The Nalut sunset seen from here was unforgettable, as the orange sun sank swiftly into the red flushed land, leaving behind it a limitless orange-dyed plain with the ghosts of centuries of Berbers who have watched those desolate Stone Age stretches for the enemy to come. Today the enemy exists unrecognized in the vanishing soil and the encroaching sand.

On this flood plain Harry had hoped there might be a possibility for starting eucalyptus plantations. He now saw that without water-spreading first, it would be hopeless. And on the wind-battered limestone cliffs above, now eroded down to skeleton form, to start a plantation would require more money than was available.

We left Nalut the next morning and twisted our way through the last crags and zigzags of the red jebel, whose chief beauty here was its lurid color, which made a gaudy contrast to the tiny, land-filled pockets which the Berbers had terraced into the cliffs and planted with emerald barley and green tufted palms.

It was another rough day of progress, upward and downward as much as forward. This was my first experience of driving on washboard, which is like driving along railroad ties and is easier the faster you go — until you strike the spot where six or seven ties are missing! Harry and Henri were too busy botanizing and collecting plants to notice the ardors of the road, and Jan van der Sprenkle was probably too young to feel it, but Ahmed and I had many moments of condoling as we banged along — or came to a breakneck halt on broken washboard. Ahmed always called me Mary, for some reason I never understood, and he reckoned that he and I were the delicate ones on the trip — he because he had seven children, and I because I hadn't! Anyway, every desert trip has its surprises, and this one's, for me, was that we arrived alive.

An added interest of washboard track is that you are certain to try to escape it by getting off it, which ends in your losing the trail which is at best scarcely visible. This is exactly what Ahmed and Harry and I did, thereby leading the other two Rovers astray also, and ending up all three of us across the Tunisian border.

Fortunately, when we found ourselves traveling straight into the sun, instead of keeping it on our right hand, we realized that we had gone too far west, and must have crossed the nearby border. We hastily changed our direction, and headed the procession eastward, anxious to get back into Libya before the Tunisia border patrol should spot us. Because of persistent arms-smuggling into Algeria, the border police are very active now; I remembered Jackie Garnett's story of how he and Clutha had spent their holiday in the Tunisian police post, when they crossed the border by mistake!

By seven P.M. we were outside the famous seven-foot-tall white stone walls of Ghadames, where the crests of date palms wave above the ornamental, crenelated desert bastion.

The odd thing one notes immediately about Ghadames is that just outside the city gates lies a complete outer settlement of tents and shacks — the dwellings of the mighty Tuareg to whom the city once belonged. For although it was built as a Tuareg city, the Tuareg themselves will not live inside. They are true nomads, a veritable desert people, and they will never raise their tents, nor build a dwelling, nor take up an abode inside the walls of a city.

In slave trade days when the Tuareg manned the slave caravans, they owned numerous slaves whose work it was to build gardens and towns for their masters, who then kept their slaves and animals inside the walled enclosures, having first cut the slaves' Achilles tendons so they could not run away. Today, inside the walls, Ghadames is peopled by Berbers, Arabs, and the descendants of Tuareg black slaves.

Inside the city gate, we found the Ain el Fress (Spring of the Mare) Hotel, an attractive one-story, Middle Eastern looking structure, which, we have heard, used always to be filled with gay, holidaying families of French officers of the Fezzan French administration. Now that the Fezzan is completely Libyanized, the holidaying families (those who could pay!) exist no more.

Tonight the hotel is closed and locked. Never mind, says the policeman who accompanies us from the city gate, he will call Mohamed to come and unlock it. Mohamed, a tall Fezzani, comes, and brings with him the huge, ten-inch-long iron key, whose size is a symbol of Ghadames. As he unlocks the door, turning the key seven times to do so, he assures us without a smile that today is the first day that the hotel has been "open"! There is no food, he says, and no bedding, but we are welcome to sleep inside and fix our own food.

Harry is delighted with this answer to "Ghadames, the tourists' Paradise, the trip for everyone!" which is the latest Libyan tourism advertising, and we try to visualize a busload of tourists dumped here without a meal or beds! But anyway it couldn't happen, as no bus could make the track.

As at Nalut, a tomb-like chill and damp envelop us inside. We throw open the hotel doors and windows and take our pick among the tiny, empty bedrooms, open our sleeping bags on the beds, and ascertain that the W.C. has no water, but the hand basin has — what luck!

Now to the dark and dingy hotel kitchen, where Jan has lighted some candles and set up our little bottle gas burner, while I prepare Bolognese pasta — in other words, superior spaghetti! Ahmed helps me, and this assistance consists of adding more and more red pepper and tomato paste. By the time the food is ready, we have acquired several Ghadames policemen as guests. Henri is gregarious with Arabs, and he and Harry have been collecting the Libyan names from the policemen for the plants they have collected. This is a good opportunity for me to practice my Mediterranean, the local mixture of French, Italian, Arabic and English.

We carry the food into the hotel lobby, lighted dimly by a couple of candles, and sit about on a broken-down divan, crippled chairs, and a bedding roll and eat steaming, savory spaghetti, washed down by red wine for those who want it, Henri and I, and Libyan tea for the others. Before we finish, my eyes are almost closing, and we stumble to bed . . .

It was dank inside the hotel in the morning, and there were fat mosquitoes full of blood on the wall, and the lobby smelled of the tomato sauce and wine, but the sun shone in the courtyard, and a policeman turned up with six fresh loaves of hot Ghadames bread, and Harry soon had coffee boiling.

Ghadames is a city of two levels, with the streets of the lower level remarkably like dungeon corridors or tunnels, as they are narrow, dark passages lighted only by an occasional overhead grating or by a sudden glimpse into a courtyard. The play of light and shadow, of black on alabaster, of deep shade ripped open by a streak of blazing sun — these are the city's fascinations and add to its mystery. Just as you feel you are lost in a dungeon, you burst into a chalk-white court with an ancient seeding tree and a couple of black children pelting each other with seeds.

The entire circumference of walled Ghadames is only four miles, and the city, a maze of hidden streets with several entrances, occupies only a very small part of the area. This morning, thinking we would wander about on our own, we made a false start by going in at the nearest tunnel. We were met almost immediately by a Moslem priest, who told us that there was a mosque with a spring nearby where the women came to get water, and for this reason we must not enter here. He suggested that we return to the city gate and ask a policeman to guide us, as otherwise we might not only intrude on women, but would surely get lost.

We followed his advice, and soon another Mohamed from the police was detailed to escort us. Now we attacked the maze down another tunnel where sometimes we had to feel our way, but at other times, by rays of light from gratings above, we glimpsed various handsomely carved palm trunk doorways, though the buildings themselves were of mud. The guide assured us that at no hour would we see the women of Ghadames, except when going to the springs for water, as their whole lives were conducted on the second-level city above us, which was exclusively for women.

There are other strict segregations in this tiny, labyrinthine city, as each of the three groups of occupants, Berbers, Arabs and black Africans, occupy distinct and separate quarters, and do not mix. Even among these groups there are ironclad divisions, or castes, as follows: the descendants (1) of nobility, (2) of strangers wed to slaves, (3) of servants, and (4) of slaves.

As my eyes became accustomed to the darkness in the tomb-like streets, I began to see that every door was marked with some sign or charm, fish, horn, star, crescent, the hand of Fatima — she was the Prophet's daughter — to protect against the evil eye. Obviously, extreme followers of Islam though these people were, and firm believers in one God — Allah — still, the age-old protection of magic was not abandoned.

Wherever we found a few feet of sunlight, long mud seats were built against the wall, and here men sat huddled, lost in their baracans, austere and motionless, without occupation, ambition or diversion. Never before, I think, have I seen an entire city so buried alive. I thought back to the gay Tripolinos in sidewalk cafés watching the gay girls pass. Hamdu li'llah for changing times! Hamdu li'llah for dynamic Tripoli! More and more it seemed to me that Ghadames smelled of death. Here was immutable, static Islam untouched by the needs of life.

The corridor ended in a white-painted courtyard surrounded by dark, arched recesses lined with benches for lounging and dark, arched doors. I knew by the magnificent mulberry tree which grew in the center, looming high above the buildings and shading most of the square with green, leafy gloom, that this was the old flesh market of slave trade days. Here the human survivors of the blood-blazed African trail were bought and sold for cash.

Our guide had one more tourist item to show, the square minaret of the Djmaa el Kebir, the tall Moslem tower which dominates the skyline, and about whose base the secret city clings and hides. To look upwards at the minaret, it appears white and blinding in the sun; to enter, it is damp and deathly; but to climb to its top, it reveals the secrets of the city's roofs.

We returned to the police station and met the Ghadames city mudir, who was tall, slender, dark-skinned, with finely cut, non-Negroid features. He spoke French and seemed extremely intelligent. We also met the Tuareg mudir of the Tuareg tents, whose indigo robe draped to his bare sandaled feet, and whose indigo veil wrapped about his head and face so that only his eyes were visible through a narrow slit, for among Tuareg the man must veil, while the woman exposes her face. We also talked with the mutasarif, an Arab and a political appointee, who seemed to know nothing about anything.

When we returned to the hotel we found Clyde Adams of Mobil Oil and eight other oil men who had just landed their private plane on the airstrip outside the city gates. They had been told in Tripoli that the hotel was "open," and they were expecting to have their lunch here! We explained the situation, assured them that we had plenty of food for all, and insisted that they eat with us. We opened a few more tins, a few more bottles of wine, boiled a kettle of rice, and we all sat down. Clyde said they were out on "exploration," and as soon as we finished eating they were off again in the plane. Flying is good for exploration, but not for botany and soil-testing.

We visited the marketplace later, where lethargic merchants dozed. There was no noise, no verbose exploitation of wares; rather, they seemed to be protecting their goods from our unwelcome attempts to purchase. I finally succeeded in extracting from them two pairs of yellow-and-red woven Ghadames slippers, as I wanted a pair for George and one for our Mohamed. I also found a tiny silver Fatima's hand for good fortune, for Mohamed's soon to be born baby. Henri also wanted some slippers, but he had to order his for collecting on the day after next. We then went to the vegetable suk and bought onions, tomatoes, potatoes and sugar.

Early next morning a young policeman arrives at the hotel with more fresh bread, and a huge Ghadames key hanging around his neck. The mudir has sent him to take us to a Ghadames house and show us the interior.

Under his guidance, we stop at the first door at the opening of a tunnel. This house, he says as he inserts his ten-inch key into the rusty lock and then turns it eleven times to open the door, is the house of a rich merchant, who has many enterprises in Tripoli. Inside is a different world; the white walls are elaborately scrolled with vivid scarlet designs and three closed doors are decorated with elegant Persian panels, while numberless small cupboards set into the mud walls have doors elaborately decorated in blue, green and scarlet scrolls. The same motif, isosceles triangles (or minarets) with scrolls and flowers, is repeated many times.

The floors are covered with woven reed mats. The walls are thickly hung with innumerable hand-woven food covers, made from palm leaflets interwoven with threads of bright, colored silk and wool. These, we are told, are a part of the marriage dowry of every Ghadames woman. Each cover is about two feet in diameter and vividly ornamental, and although these are obviously used for decoration here, the same article is used all through the Fezzan to cover food. Another type of wall decoration is what appears to be brass vases in different sizes. These shining, delicately chased brasses are called narghile, and there are hundreds, perhaps thousands, of them hanging on the walls and stacked on tables. These narghile were used in times past for currency, and for this reason they are made in three exact sizes, of three precise weights, and of metal of the same alloy. The roof of the house, two stories above, with a large window for light, forms the ceiling of the room.

I think it is the gaudiest room that I have ever entered, and it shows no common touch with the outer sepulcher of Ghadames. Yet this very quality of outer austerity masking the hidden, inner flamboyance is Arabian. The decoration also is typically Arabian, as every doorway is arched and each door is deeply carved and vividly painted. A turning stairway leads up to the second level, passing on the way an elaborately decorated door which we are *not* invited to open.

The room above is a half-floor balcony, one part of which is curtained off into an alcove which the guide says is for sleeping. One wall is papered solidly with Middle Eastern colored picture postal cards and many repetitious pictures of the Prophet Mohammed telling his beads with a lion lying beside him with a smirk on its face. On the other walls there are bright Sunday-supplement pictures of Eastern and African countries, more food covers, and more narghile.

The stairs mount a half-story higher to a door which opens into the kitchen. Here are six little sinks in which to burn charcoal for cooking, and a sunken stone oven for bread. I see no provision for water or for washing.

The stairs mount a final half-story to the roof where only I, a female, may go. I step out onto the roof and go up six steps again inside a small cupola, the top of which commands a view of the white-painted housetops of Ghadames, blinding in the sun. Almost all the roofs have small, glistening domes on top which are family tombs and places of prayer, and all have serafins, or four triangular corners built high enough (three feet) to cast a shadow on the roof at any hour.

The roofs are occupied with women of every shape, size, color, and age, enjoying the morning warmth, the dry, gentle breeze and the pale blue sky. They are drying garments (so they must have water), shaking dusters, feeding chickens, cuddling babies, dozing on mats, brewing tea, shelling almonds, combing each other's hair, calling across to other roofs, laughing and gossiping: they are alive; no smell of the sepulcher here! For once the female has won.

When our policeman guide finally closes the door behind us and turns the great key eleven times, I am wondering whether the women of this house are closed in behind the unopened doors we passed. Is the rich, merchant home-owner in Tripoli making more money today? Or is this just a show house for tourists?

Later, at home in Tripoli, I found this same house described in detail, almost exactly as we saw it, in *The Magic Gate of the Sahara* by Angelo Piccioli, first published in English in 1935. More than two decades ago this same Arabian retreat was the showplace of this immutable Moslem city. Tastes have not altered; perhaps there are a few more picture postals today, a few extra Prophet Mohammeds with lions, but otherwise nothing has changed — except the human element. For the original rich merchant home owner is dead, and it is his son now whom we failed to meet, whose women we did not see, but whose house we admired.

Roof Tops of Ghadames

The population of Ghadames, so the mudir told us the next day, had fallen from fifteen thousand in the 1925 census to an estimated three thousand persons today, chiefly because there was no longer a living to be made here. Slave trade had been outlawed, caravan trade had ceased to exist, and although Ghadames still produced the finest dates in the world from the Digla palm, she could not sell them all, for dates were gradually ceasing to be the only food source of the desert, as increased Western traffic brought more imported foods. As well as Digla dates, Ghadames gardens produced barley, wheat and lucerne, to which the damage by birds and pests was great. She had grown, and could grow, among her date palms, pomegranates, figs, olives, apricots, lemons, beans, lettuce, tomatoes and watermelons — but nobody used them here.

In Ghadames, they told us, the working years were from twenty to forty, as lack of nutrition made forty a man's maximum working age. After this, the men sat on sunny benches at the end of dark tunnels and waited for death.

As we toured the Ghadames gardens the depressing facts which the mudir had just been telling us become obvious. The majority of the gardens were derelict, and had been abandoned to weeds, pests, birds and lack of water, and their owners had migrated. Today there were only four hundred people employed in agriculture.

The ancient heritage from Allah to Ghadames had been her water supply. Its best known source was the Ain el Fress natural spring, which is said to have been discovered by a soldier mounted on a mare who pawed the sand when searching for a drink. This spring still flows, but fifty per cent of its water is wasted because of seepage through its damaged walls and lack of proper maintenance. The second water supply here was from the Italian artesian well drilled in the days of Italian occupation, which is still used for irrigation. This well now produces only one-quarter of its original flow.

The third water supply was from the French artesian well, drilled in 1946, which feeds the cemented concrete irrigation canals above soil level and then flows by gravity to the land. This is the most reliable water supply. But at least fifty per cent of all these waters is lost through seepage and through lack of maintenance of the irrigation canals and the wells.

Lack of water is caused by lack of maintenance, and lack of maintenance is caused by shortage of Ghadames manpower, and shortage of manpower is partly caused by lack of water to make the gardens produce — but also by an extra factor, the desire of young men for a different way of life.

There were no tree plantation possibilities here, Harry told the Mudir before we left. Harry suggested, however, that there were good opportunities for more extensive cultivation of cereals, if a work force could be found.

But the mudir shook his head; they were gone, he said; the young men were gone — and they would not come back.

Ghadames was once a great distance from Tripoli, when the men who are now old traveled the three hundred fifty miles by camel. Now we came by Land Rover, in three days because we botanized

— we *could* have come in one day, with luck. Our friends from the oil company arrived from Tripoli in forty minutes by plane.

As we leave the "Pearl of the Desert" a few days later, I breathe a deep breath outside the city gates. I look with more understanding now at the far-spread-out black tents and mounds of earth roofed with fronds, which form the "city" of the nomad Tuareg who have camped for centuries outside the Ghadames gates.

Entrance to Ghadames

As we depart we are accompanied for almost five miles, as we drive, by a sandy acreage of thousands of Moslem tombs, all, we assume, facing towards Mecca. But so old they are, so weathered, so torn by winds and sand-eroded and sand-heaped, so indiscriminate and lacking in any separate entity, that one can only feel that here death is waiting to quench the spark that is himself in every man alive.

11. Blind Forces

I KNEW something was wrong when Mohamed didn't turn up by midday on payday. It wasn't that he never failed to come to work, but that he never failed to come on payday. I knew that something more serious than had ever before occurred must have happened in his home. My mind went immediately to little Mohamed, who at seven weeks was especially vulnerable to the by-products of the intense Libyan heat which breeds illness and death in so many local babies.

It was only May, but we were gripped in a hot spell with shade temperatures at 106 degrees, and the flies were already out in glinting hordes. Our house is screened, with the exception of the kitchen door, which has a complex French door anatomy combined with semi-attached outdoor shutters that make it impossible to screen. I now hang mosquito netting in the doorway, allowing it to lie an extra six inches on the floor, and placing bricks on this surplus. I then fight the wind and Mohamed to keep the curtains in place. I had spent the first day of the hot spell devising these curtains. Mohamed watched my labors, and then asked me if I had an extra piece of netting to spare for him to take home to cover the baby.

I was pleasantly surprised, as several weeks before I had given him a lecture on child care in hot weather, and the reasons why little Mohamed should cease to sleep, like the filler in the sandwich, between Papa and Mama on their sleeping mat, in the inside, windowless room of the old Arab house in Suk el Juma. I had suggested that I would buy a basket or crib for the baby to sleep in, and this could be covered with netting.

Mohamed had listened politely and then said, "Arab babies not the same American babies. Arab babies always sleep with mother." And here the subject ended. I knew it wasn't Mohamed, but the women at home whose ways would have to be changed, if a change was to come. Mohamed's comparative faith in my ideas would not spur him strongly enough to battle against their firm faith in traditional ideas. One couldn't blame him for his inertia, for the fact was that the women always had the last word, as they were with the infant all day. If he tried to force the issue, they would only make his life miserable at home, and still do as they wished with the baby.

So when Mohamed asked me for a piece of netting, I asked apprehensively, "Is the baby ill?"

"Yes, maybe. Maybe stomach no good. He cry all night."

"Are there many flies in your house?"

"Yes, maybe. Lutfeyah see sister of Salem yesterday. Sister of Salem gave Lutfeyah basket her baby sleep in before. Now Lutfeyah put Mohamed in basket to sleep. I like piece of cloth to cover for flies."

This was a favorable development. Lutfeyah had grown up in the household of Salem's sister and her husband, in a family which was one of the few educated families at this time in Tripoli. This family had contact with modern ideas, and Salem had been abroad for two years at school. His sister, who had six children, had introduced some modern practices in their up-bringing, and this was being passed on to Lutfeyah. Obviously, more could be done for little Mohamed through the influence of one of Lutfeyah's own kind than with suggestions from me, who had nothing in common with Lutfeyah's world except access to the ear of her very young husband.

"Mohamed, there isn't a large enough piece left from those curtains, but I'll give you money to buy a new piece. On your way home today, you must go to the store where I bought the netting, and buy a two-meter piece for Lutfeyah. It must be large enough to drape down over the sides of the basket, and tell Lutfeyah she must put weights on the corners to hold it down."

"Thank you, Mother. I do like you say."

When Mohamed left the house that afternoon I called after him on his bicycle, "Don't forget the netting to cover the baby!"

"Yes, Mother."

The next morning when I asked him if he had bought the netting,

he said he had forgotten it. As it usually takes several remindings before Mohamed achieves any objective except his own, I wasn't surprised, but told him again to be sure to buy the netting *this* afternoon.

Mirage~
The desert drowned
in blueness~

"Did the baby cry again last night?" I asked.

"Yes, he cry all night. I no can sleep."

"That won't hurt you," I said heartlessly. "But is little Mohamed
all right in the daytime? Does he only cry at night?"

"Maybe, no. He no can eat, he cry, he bring up food. Sometime he
feel very hot."

"You must take the baby to the Italian doctor in Suk el Juma this
afternoon. I am sure from what you say that he is ill. You can't wait
around when a baby is ill. Now take him this afternoon, will you,
please?"

"Yes, Mother."

"Why don't you take Lutfeyah with you?" I asked then, not for
the first time, but determined to make another onslaught on custom.
"Take her so the doctor can tell *her* what to do for Mohamed. She's
the one who takes care of him, and she's the one the doctor should
talk with."

Mohamed shook his head, smiling rather condescendingly at how little I understood the situation, and said, "No, Mother, Lutfeyah cannot go. My mother brings Mohamed with me."

Well, I thought silently, his mother had nine children and lost eight of them! One draws the obvious conclusion. "Anyway, Mohamed, be sure to take the baby to the doctor this afternoon. And don't forget the mosquito netting."

"Yes, Mother."

The next day was Thursday, also payday, and followed by Mohamed's day off, Friday, which is the Sunday of the Moslem world. When Mohamed did not arrive by ten o'clock on Thursday I assumed he was delayed, but when he did not turn up by twelve my annoyance was mixed with alarm.

At seventeen years, Mohamed carries full responsibility for support and care of an alcoholic father, a blind, ill mother, a child wife, and now an infant. In addition, he is their only contact with the outside world. He alone steps out of that shadowed doorway in Suk el Juma to see the sun, and breathe the outer air; he alone can go to market, do shopping, pay bills, arrange business matters. No matter who is sick, Mohamed must visit the doctor, bring home the medicine and, if necessary, escort the invalid — unless it is Lutfeyah, who may not leave the house.

It is too much for a boy of his age. Because he has too much responsibility in his own home, I am easy on him in ours, and he takes advantage of me, as any youngster would. And when he misses a day at work, I am never sure whether he should be scolded or pitied — and I believe Mohamed feels the same.

Today when he did not appear by one-thirty I knew that something was wrong. As I hurried to tidy the house myself before Harry arrived home, I was hoping that the telephone would ring with a message from Mohamed. The only phone in Suk el Juma is at the police station, but it may be used in an emergency.

Preparing our meal today was simple, as Mohamed was to have done my marketing. Fortunately, I had some Egyptian rice and a tin of tongue though it was just the sort of a day for a fresh green salad. While picking foreign bodies out of the rice, I regretted again that Harry won't eat Italian rice, which is glutinous compared to Asian rice, but comes in a neat carton, all cleaned and ready to cook.

Harry came, we ate, and the evening passed without word. I decided to go to Suk el Juma in the morning and find out what was the matter. I would have done so today except for the memory of times past when Mohamed had been absent without valid reason: once at a golf tournament for caddies, as he had been a caddy at Wheelus Field, once at a swimming party with friends, once at a wedding, and so on. In any case, today had been terribly hot, and the drive across the city would have been scorching in the ghibli, and I was lazy.

Next morning unusually early I heard Mohamed's step on the outside path, and the sound of the front door opening. Always when he enters the house he comes immediately to say good morning to me, and have a chat. Today when I heard the front door open I called out from the study without waiting for him to appear, "What was the trouble yesterday, Mohamed? Was the baby ill?"

There was a moment's silence. Then in flat, choked voice without coming to see me, he answered, "Baby dead." His footsteps went directly to the kitchen.

After a moment I followed, and found him by the open refrigerator putting my market food inside. I put my hand on his shoulder and said, "I am so terribly sorry, Mohamed!" Suddenly he swung around and put his arms down on the kitchen sideboard and buried his face in them. Then he gave a long, hard sob and said, "My son is dead!" I put my arms about him then, as being the only way I knew of to express my sympathy, and stood beside him as he crumpled down, frozen and silent.

I have seen Mohamed in tears many times in the past: in tears when I have shown annoyance with him, in tears when he failed the test for a driver's license, in tears when I was taken to the hospital, when we left for home leave, when he broke a piece of china (the first time only!), and when he cut his finger, and in tears when he found me once in tears. Yet, I have always found him an ebullient spirit made up of complete contradictions, wistful yet boastful, affectionate but calloused, touchy and nonchalant, ardent and dumb, quiveringly sensitive himself, but often blind to the sensitivities of others. I thought that I had seen him in every emotional state, but never before had I seen him silenced by his emotion. His sorrow today was in a different category from anything that he had experienced before.

I didn't ask him what the baby died of, or if he had taken him to the doctor. I felt that I knew the answers, and they were no comfort to either of us.

I touched his coarse black hair, well-oiled and stiff, and my eyes rested on his finely made Arab hands which always managed to be so clumsy. I thought of all the forces for good in this boy, and of the obstacles to their accomplishment; I remembered the quick, avid intelligence, accompanied by blind prejudice; I thought of the new world which he admired and the old world to which he was bound. He was the only survivor of his mother's nine children. Now his own first son had died. Were the same blind forces of ignorance to wipe out his offspring, too?

After a couple of minutes I said, "Mohamed, please make us some coffee." I spoke in Arabic, using the phrases Mohamed had taught me, a thing that always pleased him. Ten minutes later we were sitting at the coffee table with cups of strong, Turkish coffee and cigarettes, and Mohamed had wiped his tears. It isn't that such things make sorrow any lighter, but in the face of death, normal activities somehow reassure us.

The next step was to tell Sayed, Sola, Mustapha and old Mohamed from the Fezzan of his son's death. This required an hour or more, over tea in the garden. And in justice to our Giorgimpopoli American surroundings, the entire neighborhood was by now hushed in sympathy for Mohamed's loss.

It was midday when I waved goodbye to Mohamed as he wheeled off on his bicycle to return to Suk el Juma for the formalities of the burial feast. He had with him his fortnightly pay, and in addition a gift towards the burial costs of the infant whose birth had not yet been paid for, and the wedding of whose parents was still a debt.

II

Allah's Holiday

Sahara scene   fej fej

12. Allah's Holiday

WE HAD DISCUSSED the Sahara trip often enough, but something always got in the way. This time it was the approach of Ramadan, the great Moslem fast.

"But we *must* go!" says Badreddin earnestly. "We must! — in sha' Allah! Only," he adds, nodding his head emphatically, "we must be back home again before Ramadan commences!" He looks exactly now as I imagine a desert sheik might, his strong Semitic features glowing with enthusiasm in his dark, handsome face. Yet he is an extremely gentle and civilized young man, one of the best educated Libyans, and a member of the Tripolitania Forest Department.

Hammet agrees with him — about getting back before Ramadan, at least. He also nods his head energetically, saying in a shocked tone, "We couldn't travel all day in the desert without food or water!" He looks horrified at the mere thought, and hastily lights himself another cigarette from his gold lighter, thinking no doubt of the month-long daylight abstention from cigarettes.

"Could we travel on the desert at night, then?" I ask. "You can eat after dark."

"Certainly not!" says Harry shortly. "It's too cold, you couldn't see the country, and everybody gets bad tempered in Ramadan, anyway. And the oasis people will all be having their own feasts, and they won't welcome non-Moslem outsiders like you and me. Also, Badreddin and Hammet want to be at home in Tripoli to have Ramadan with their families. No, traveling in Ramadan is *out!* We can't put the trip off later than May because of the desert heat, and it's still too cold on the desert to go now."

"Ramadan comes in spring this year," says Badreddin. "If we can get away we can still have three or four weeks on the desert, and be back in Tripoli before Ramadan begins." Badreddin is almost as anxious to go as I am; Hammet is rather loath to leave his city comforts, but prepared to go "where my father goes," as he always says to Harry.

Ramadan is a shifting feast, or possibly famine, which lasts for one lunar month of twenty-nine days and thirteen hours. Its observance by strict daytime fasting includes abstinence from food, drink (including water), and smoking, from sunup to sundown, and it is one of the five pillars of Islam. To keep this ritual of abstinence is the rule for all good Moslems throughout the Arab world, although they keep it with varying degrees of strictness. It is always a period of strain, for daytime work is performed on empty stomachs, while the pursuit of pleasure goes on all night with eating and tea-drinking, card-playing, and exchange of family visits until the sun rises. Just before dawn the last meal is served, and neither food nor drink may be taken again until the sun goes down.

Libya is one of the strictest of all Islamic countries. This kingdom is orthodox Islam by government edict, by respected precept, and by personal example of its aesthetic monarch, King Idris, who is also its religious leader. Young Arabs from other Islamic countries who come here to work soon find they are keeeping Ramadan more strictly than ever before in their lives. Libyan public opinion may not be openly defied — although, as I have sometimes heard Libyans say laughingly, one Moslem alone may be quite liberal, but two together are always orthodox!

"So now we shall plan our trip for March," says Badreddin triumphantly. "Agreed?"

"Good," says Harry. "We will take the plant presses and collect specimens of flora all the way."

Hammet nods amiably, but without enthusiasm. He wouldn't be left behind for anything, but he would prefer a different goal than a Tuareg mud village on an old Sahara slave track on the southwest boundary of Libya! Now if we were going to drive to Cairo . . . !

"I've always wanted to go to the Sahara Desert!" I say to Badreddin, suddenly realizing that I always have.

"Not Sahara Desert!" says Harry. "That's redundant. Sahara *is* desert in Arabic, eh, Badreddin?"

Badreddin smilingly agrees. "And as four-fifths of our country *is* Sahara," Badreddin adds, "it is time for Hammet and me to discover it!"

Hammet gives him the Pasha glance, half amused, half annoyed, and lights himself another cigarette, the bejeweled face of his gold wristwatch gleaming brightly as he smokes. He'll be with us when the time comes, he knows — and so do we.

"So now we make plans," says Badreddin. "What Land Rovers can we take?"

"Any that still run!" says Harry.

"I shall drive the best Land Rover for my father," says Hammet firmly.

"Is No. 57 still running?" asks Badreddin anxiously, beginning to fear shortage of transport.

Badreddin is a very large young man in every way, and one who inspires confidence. At twenty-five years he is sure of himself and filled with enjoyment of life. He often wears a quizzical, amused expression on his face when he listens to us discuss Libya, and he doesn't hesitate to tell us our mistakes. He is observant and learns quickly. He never questions his Islamic faith, and is certain of the virtue of the things in which he believes, and unashamed to fight for, and speak up for, his ideals of decency and right living. He is not naïve, nor easily fooled, but he is without cynicism. He is an outstanding character, and gives me great faith in the future of Libya.

Badreddin's father was one of the very limited hierarchy of old-time Libyan teachers, at a time in Libya when education was almost a crime. That Badreddin should achieve an excellent education regardless of obstacles was, I think, inevitable from his early upbringing. He was one of four Libyans who qualified a few years ago for a two-year FAO scholarship to study at Cyprus Forestry College, where he won top scholastic honors. When he returned to Libya he joined the provincial forest department.

Badreddin and Hammet are unlike each other in character, except for hot tempers, but fortunately they never get angry at the same things. Hammet's dominating personality which reminds people that he is still a Pasha is seldom in abeyance, but when he talks in a manner that Badreddin calls "big nose," Badreddin laughs at him and calls him "effendi-effendi," a sort of superlative of gentleman, and they both laugh. Their characters almost complement each other; perhaps for this reason they remain firm friends.

Both so sure of themselves, and both so different — yet both types are necessary here: one sophisticated and worldly, who hurries to meet new ways; the other steeped in the Islamic past which he carries with him into the future.

Hammet has now been working with Harry for a year, and although he has had no professional training he is proving very helpful. He knows all the people of importance, and between his wife and himself he is related to most of them, a deciding factor in the Arab world. As the government failed to designate any local counterpart for Harry to work with, Harry is trying to transfer to Hammet some knowledge of administrative training, and enough interest in the forestry program to keep it alive when he leaves. Hammet now speaks English well enough to express himself.

When I talk with Hammet and Badreddin and Suleiman and Salem, and others like them, I find it almost impossible to believe that Libyan education was practically nonexistent until 1951, the year of Libyan independence. These young men have had one advantage above the majority of Libyans; they represent a very small privileged class, which means that they are of the limited few who have not had to support themselves from infancy.

Hammet, Badreddin, Harry and I were the early nucleus of the desert trip, which soon included Gerry Van Hoorn, an attractive young Dutch expert in hides and skins, the most eligible bachelor in the FAO Mission — and the most efficient at remaining so. He was thoughtful, he was kind, he was just what women like; it was impossible not to love him, and impossible, it seemed, to get beyond that. Accompanying Gerry in his Land Rover will be Assad, his young Libyan assistant and an excellent driver.

March comes; we are six now, with two Land Rovers "still running," as Harry says. It is inadvisable for one vehicle to travel alone in the desert. Three of us are Europeans and foreigners to Libya, and three are Libyan Moslems, but we are all equally strange to the Sahara, the Libyans being sightseers there as much as we. Only they speak the language.

Before we leave Tripoli, four more people with two more machines arrange to come with us, for desert trips are catching. Later, part way to our objective in the desert, the party dwindles back to the original six.

I had read enough about past desert explorations to know that our insignificant little trip would represent nothing in the line of an accomplishment. With go-anywhere trucks, the desert is becoming a tourist item — although it still swallows some, and others turn back. The nomad on his camel is no longer surprised by blue jeans, he may even be using a pair for his underwear, and the little Arab urchin in the oasis may be dressed in a US gift flour sack. The days when Rosita Forbes had to disguise her sex to travel to Kufra by camel are vanishing. Freya Stark, the intrepid Arabian chronicler, is no longer a woman alone in an Arab world. T. E. Lawrence would turn pale at the liberties taken with his overwhelmingly masculine kingdom. These simple facts one cannot alter.

The only thing that is important about this trip is that no one — not we, nor the Libyans, nor anyone else — can possibly know and understand Libya by sitting in a sidewalk café in Tripoli, or Benghazi — or even in the gilded desert capital city of Sebha. The important thing about this trip is — that we went.

Our traveling preparations were varied. I packed food for Harry, Gerry and me, on the basis of a non-Moslem diet, which included smoked sausage, salami, pork and beans, coffee and whiskey, tinned corned beef and stew; I packed another diet for the Moslems with sardines, tuna, cheese, spaghetti, salmon, tinned cake, pudding, tea, and lots of sugar. We hoped to get oasis bread as we traveled.

Additions to the menu turned up on the day of departure, with Assad bringing a huge bag of greens and a bag of special bread, while Hammet and Badreddin had eggs, tomatoes, beans, onions, oranges, potatoes, green peas, and more sugar — not all of which items travel well in the bottom of a Land Rover!

For washing and cooking, I brought along a disreputable old galvanized bucket, two ancient cooking pots, one medium-size and the other very large, in which to cook spaghetti, and a large metal colander to drain spaghetti. This colander immediately became Harry's relentless enemy because it had two obtruding handles and never fitted anyplace. Harry threw it away several times, only to have it retrieved by the following Rover and surreptitiously returned to me. Finally, one handle came off, the body bent into an ellipse and then it fitted nicely into the bucket, and was acclaimed a success.

We also took along the FAO plastic traveling equipment which was beautiful but suitable only for picnics, we discovered. We all had bedding rolls and camp cots, either our own or borrowed. We also had with us numerous large containers full of water, which we hoped to be able to refill at wells as we went along. And perhaps the most vital to ensure our return, we carried a full load of spare parts for the Land Rovers.

As the distance you could travel in a vehicle in the desert was largely determined by the amount of gasoline you could carry to bring you home again (these were the days before oil company gasoline dumps), we had an extra gas tank installed and were carrying two hundred liters. We knew we would be able to refill our tanks at Sebha, the Fezzan capital, and possibly again further south, and we hoped to reach the southern Libyan border. We started out with Hammet driving one Land Rover, with Harry and me in the front seat and luggage jammed tightly in back, and Gerry driving his Land Rover with Badreddin and Assad.

For centuries in the past, Tripoli has been the principal Mediterranean marketplace for black slaves, as a result of its location at the northern seaboard tip of slave trade caravan routes which have crossed Africa south to north and southeast to north from the countries of Nigeria and Sudan. We were planning to follow in reverse one of these old caravan routes, going from Tripoli east to el Buerat, where the sands of the Sirtic Desert meet the sea, and then south through the Sirtic Desert, passing through Hun and Sokna, old caravan stops, then through Sebha, the capital of the Fezzan, and southwest to Ghat on the Libyan-Algerian border. This caravan route continues south through Air in French West Africa to Kano in Nigeria, but Ghat was as far as we expected to go, as the business of our expedition was primarily Libyan flora, not African caravan routes.

Ghat we knew by our reading as one of the oldest caravan stops in existence, built centuries ago, probably by the slaves of the Tuareg, who are themselves the original caravan people who transported chained African slaves in stumbling, starving thousands over the cruel sands and lived on the profits. The most romantic and bloodcurdling stories of the Sahara are those told about these white-blooded, Aryan desert people, the Tuareg. Fantastic tales of glory and foolhardiness bathe them in a mist of romance, through which the tall, veiled men parade with fantastic majesty, so that today when you look at a Tuareg, the cloak of the past hangs almost as clearly on his shoulders as does the long, draped indigo cotton garment which sweeps the desert floor. Although Ghat is known as a Tuareg town, its history suggests that in reality most of its inhabitants are the descendants of black slaves who have adopted Tuareg custom, for the Tuareg himself rarely lives in a town; he merely works out from it on his self-appointed job of "protecting" the central Sahara.

We left Tripoli late in the afternoon, as we planned to travel one hundred forty miles east along the coast over a good, Italian-built road to Misurata, where we would sleep in a little Italian hotel. We would get off to an early start the following morning for the first desert stretch. At Misurata we joined the other two Land Rovers and their four occupants: Peter, an English FAO agronomist; Elham Talaat, an Egyptian FAO assistant agronomist; and Aminta and Carlo, driver-mechanics, both Italian.

The following morning we left at eight, as everybody had different ideas about what was an early start, Harry's being six and Hammet's being nine. So far, we had traveled east along the Tunisian highway, which parallels the coast. Now, we continued sixty miles further in this direction to el Buerat on the edge of the Sirtic Desert. Here we stopped again at the little signboard arrow pointing across an open sandy plain with the simple words scratched on it — TO THE SAHARA. There is always something audacious in the sight of this little handmade shingle standing boldly beside the best highway in the country and confidently directing traffic to take off across an open stretch of desert, and knowing its directions will be followed.

We follow the arrow, and now the road consists only of occasional stone cairns piled up to suggest the desirable direction, and this marked path becomes worse than the plain, and develops into a "corduroy" track, progress along which is comparable to driving on the sleepers of a railroad track. Corduroy, if consistent, is best driven fast, and three Land Rovers diagnosed this piece as being fifty-mile corduroy and set off at this speed, their drivers shouting advice to us as they passed.

Stung to action, we tried fifty and found it better; instead of banging up and down we vibrated violently. We were just congratulating ourselves in chattering syllables when we struck a three-foot-wide sand pit. There was a noise like passing the sound barrier, and perhaps we did! Anyway, the luggage shot up in the air, and the pots, pans, colander, blankets, pillows and Hammet's suitcase shot forward on top of us, and we came to a halt.

But no necks are broken, and the wheels still turn, so we continue. Each time, just as we work up to a good speed and relax we strike another sand pit. My neck seems to me to be snapping perilously, but I remind myself that I have read that the human body can stand as much as a mechanized vehicle can. Fortunately, I do not know at the moment that we have already cracked the Land Rover's steering arm!

Meanwhile, I see between sand pits that we are passing scattered bits of scenery, historic Roman monuments, crenelated Turkish ramparts, great seas of dusty gravel, occasional lakes of pale lilac Matthiola, and long drifts of sand. There is a ghibli rising and the air is full of dust. Although we call ghiblis sandstorms, they carry dust more than sand, according to Ralph Bagnold, who, in *The Physics of Blown Sand and Desert Dunes*, says that sand seldom rises above six feet and is too heavy to stay long in suspension without great velocity.

Now, with the dry visible yellow wind on my face, with the desiccated sand plain stretching before me, with vegetation in chalky outlines, I am convinced at last of the reality of the Sahara. Three-foot-high rivers of wind-blown sand are flowing about the car. After miles of swimming upstream through a wind-born landscape, we come to Bu Ngem, where an abandoned Italian fort perches strategically on top of a sandy hill.

It seems a good idea to take refuge from the ghibli inside the fort while we eat lunch. We find the mud-walled fortification occupied by laborers, who tell us they are working on the road — probably digging those sand pits! Anyway, they are very courteous and sweep up one corner for us to use, for which we give them fifteen cents. Then Hammet starts to boil water for tea, and we get out the food.

Meanwhile, I am looking for a distant, secluded corner. I find a place in full blast of the ghibli, but out of sight of man, and have just unzipped my slacks when a small Arab boy hustles around the corner, dragging behind him a baby gazelle. He jumps into a sales talk on how much I need that baby gazelle, and please give him some money for it. But I wasn't in the mood at that moment for gazelles, nor small boys!

I return to our corner of the fort, and we eat a fly-menaced lunch of sardines and bread, with a choice of coffee or tea. While I am now beginning to revel in the drama of the ghibli, in the opening up before us of the Sahara and the escape from Tripoli life, I see that our Libyan friends are distressed by the fly-covered sardines, the sand-sprinkled bread, and the intense heat. As we are all still strange to each other as travel companions, conversation continues on a high and impersonal level.

We are under way again by three. We lose the ghibli as we approach the shadow of the tall cliffs of the Jebel Uaddan, but the road continues to be corduroy, and often we leave it to bowl along the gravel plain in false security, until at top speed we strike a dry wadi bed, which almost breaks our necks; then we return to the corduroy and vibrate on it until the plain seems preferable, and so on. I was to learn later that this strip of corduroy before reaching Hun was not the worst in the run, but no other stretch ever bothered me so much again. It was a day devoted entirely to shaking up the liver and loosening the womb, and when both were still with me by nightfall, I called the day a success.

About six-thirty we see a dark strip on the horizon which turns into a fringe of dusty palm trees. We lose this glimpse of the oasis temporarily to twist through a series of outlying sand dunes until we find signs saying, STAY ON THE ROAD. THIS AREA IS HEAVILY MINED! But where *is* the road? Presumably we are on it, as we aren't being blown up. The Sirtic Desert was a battlefield in World War II, and Hun itself was intermittently used by both sides as a military airstrip. Even today a boy guarding his sheep, a woman fetching water, a man looking for firewood may be blown up.

Suddenly we emerge from the dunes, almost in the shade of the dusty date palms, and find ourselves about to enter a bright, white, clean looking little village, which is Hun. Already I can feel the dust less heavy on me, my throat less parched, and the struggles of the day retreating.

We find the government rest house, unload our food and liquid gas stoves on the veranda, and take the bedding rolls inside. Four of us set up our camp cots in one room, and six in the other. The party consists of ten persons and four vehicles, an unwieldy group, as no one (except me) acknowledges a leader. This is too many vehicles and persons for speedy travel.

Now that we have stopped for the night, the drivers devote themselves to the vehicles, much as a good rider devotes himself to his horse, while the passengers breathe down their necks giving unwanted advice. We have had two blow-outs and Carlo is helping Hammet patch the tires, preliminary to putting inner tubes in. Aminta goes over every possible nut and bolt in his Land Rover, tightening it. I don't see how any vehicle can stand such shaking. It is eight o'clock, and the last daylight is fading before the men leave the vehicles.

It would be gratifying to say that meanwhile I had cooked a fine spaghetti dinner for all of us, but the fact is that I could not get that damn fancy gas stove to burn, and no one paid attention to my shouts for help, so I gave up (rather easily, perhaps) and sat down and drank gin which made me, at least, feel amiable. Meanwhile the rest were tired and cross and picking on each other, except for Gerry who is never out of sorts, and Carlo who is a cheerful, handsome Italian boy filled with tireless energy.

In the end, Carlo boldly took over the stove and operated on it with a reckless hand and apparent success, for suddenly blue flames shot veranda-high. In no time at all my caldron of water was bubbling and ready to cook the spaghetti, and I temporarily relinquished to Carlo and Aminta my ambition for cooking. They prepared a marvelous pasta meal in best Italian tradition. Meanwhile, I locate the lime juice for our Moslem travelers, and the whiskey for those who favor it, while Hammet builds a fire of twigs to boil the tiny blue teakettle. Very shortly the morale of all is greatly improved.

It was here that Assad's liver was discovered. We were stuffed with hot food and staggering tired, and we went happily to our closely stacked cots which were arranged side by side in two tiny rooms. The Libyans, in deference to me I think, had all gone together with Elham Talaat in one room. This was a temporary segregation which soon wore off. Gerry, Peter, Harry and I were in the other room. Between the two rooms was a small bathroom with modern fixtures and no water, and the usual W.C. without any W. Harry and I visited the outer darkness and the great outdoors.

I have just fallen tiredly apart in my sleeping bag and am nearly asleep, when I hear the unmistakable sound of somebody trying to vomit. All about me my room companions are sizzling soundly in sleep. I pull my sleeping bag completely over my head, but there is no escape. Somebody touches me on the shoulder in the dark — Badreddin.

He whispers loudly in my ear, "Have you anything that is good for nausea? Assad is sick."

"He had better just be sick, and get rid of it," I suggest.

"He already vomits many times. Now he is very cold. I think we should do something."

I pull myself together, and wriggle out of the sleeping bag, thankful that I have gone to bed with my trousers on. I stumble to my suitcase, and fumble in the dark till I find the old faithful hot water bottle, brought with me to lessen shock in case of an accident. I know that Harry has morphine injections, painkillers, sleeping pills, dysentery remedies, a variety of emergency drugs, but nothing as simple as soda bicarb.

Badreddin rebuilds the tea fire outside to get hot water for the bottle, while I go in and talk to Assad. He certainly looks ill, and is chilled. I feel his diaphragm carefully, with the thought of possible appendix trouble, but find that the tender spot is on the opposite side, under his ribs.

"Do you have any trouble with your liver, Assad?" I ask.

"Yes, the doctor always gives me medicine for it. Today my head aches very bad all day, and everything goes around and around. Always at home I must eat just vegetables, and special bread which my wife makes." I remember his huge bag of greens and bread, then.

"I think the jolting of the car has upset your liver. Here is Badreddin with the hot water bottle now, and we'll get you an extra blanket. You'll feel better when you are warm."

I ask Badreddin to bring in the big army blanket from our Rover, and soon I tuck Assad in with the hot bottle and blanket. "You'll be better tomorrow, I'm sure," I promise Assad, who doesn't think so at all. Nevertheless, he thanks me politely for trying to help him — and promptly gets sick again. All the others sleep noisily on.

I stumble back to my cot in a trance, and fall asleep instantly; through my dreams all night I hear somebody vomiting. Obviously, weak livers should stay at home.

Harry and Gerry and Peter and I are up at six the next morning, and make coffee while the others are still asleep. I describe Assad's liver to Gerry, who says "Mamma mia!" I suggest to Gerry that if "everything goes around and around!" for Assad today, Gerry had better drive the car. Gerry says "Mamma mia!" again, and agrees.

We look again at the others inside, and they are still asleep, Assad looking very yellow. By persistent nagging, Harry gets them moving by nine-thirty, everybody tired and edgy. The first three days out are the worst, I know from experience.

Packing up the provisions, I observe that the whiskey is practically gone and the lime juice almost untouched, and the entire week's supply of liquid gas has been consumed by Carlo's magnificent cooking of the first meal.

Assad retires to the Land Rover where he sits drooping and sad, with his bag of greens untouched. Gerry takes the wheel. Peter takes the wheel. Aminta takes the wheel. Hammet takes the wheel. Mamma mia! We're off!

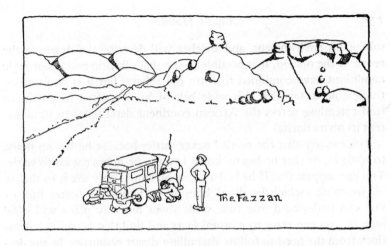
The Fezzan

13. The Fezzan

THERE are only two facts about the Fezzan that people never try to dispute: it is the southern province of the United Kingdom of Libya, and it is desert. Except for these two things, the area may be correctly described in apparently contradictory terms, according to the temperament of the narrator.

Desert oases are regarded by some people as miraculous phenomena and have been made into the themes of beloved fables. One of these is the story of the sophisticated mare who was both steed and friend of a Moslem soldier of fortune traveling across the Fezzan. Failing to find a well where they expected it to be, both horse and rider grew thirsty, and the mare became so distressed at seeing her master suffer that she pawed furiously on the desert sand. Suddenly, from the spot where she pawed, a spring gushed up to become the perpetual, always-flowing Ain el Fress at Ghadames, or Spring of the Mare — which has recently almost ceased to flow! Other people may explain desert oases more scientifically by means of geology and hydrology, but to me this makes them seem only slightly less miraculous.

One person may describe the desert nomad as the inevitable result of his environment, and another will describe the desert as the result of the nomad. It is possible to say that climatic and geographic conditions have combined to form the Sahara; but it is also uncontradictable to say that this wide belt of barren, often mountainous land extending across the African continent determines to some extent its own climate.

You can say that the nomad never settles because he has no home to settle in, or that he has no home because he doesn't wish to settle. You can suggest that if he had a house he would only use it to shelter his livestock (which he does) because he knows no better life; or you can understand that four walls about him any place will stifle him; or you can refer to pastoral facts and find that he shifts habitations from the need to follow dwindling desert resources. In the desert the narrow path between sufficiency and starvation, between survival and extinction, is often indistinguishable except by the result. Here, reality is a mirage and truth is nebulous. Here the sandstorm is a dust storm; the highest temperature in the world is registered at Azazia near Tripoli, yet Tripoli has a Mediterranean climate; and the inhabitants of North Africa are not Africans but Arabs and European Berbers!

Our first stop is the government experiment date farm just outside Hun. This is run by government under management of the FAO date expert, Jef Dowson, who spends much of his time here. He has done wonders with the date palm cultivation in this area, and is enthusiastic in plans for the future. Jef himself looks more like an Egyptian famine than any of the Arabs who are working with him; desert life is harder on Europeans than on those who are born to it, perhaps because they work harder. Jef speaks excellent Arabic. He loves date culture passionately — perfectly adjusted to the desert, I guess!

A few miles from Hun we come to Sokna, also famous in slave trade history. Sokna exists where it does because of the wells in the oasis, which for centuries have brought caravans here to call. The village is completely enclosed by a high, white limestone wall, finished on top in a distinctive crenelated design all around the wall.

The same design had been repeated in the Ghadames walls, also on the slave route.

We stop at a well just outside the village to watch while water is drawn up by man and camel power exactly as it has been done for centuries. The camel, with the water container, which hangs inside the well attached to him at the end of a long rope which passes over a pulley above the reservoir, stands close to the surface opening apparently supervising, while the container is submerged and filled by a series of expert, man-made jerks. Then at a signal from the man the camel, with a supercilious look, ambles away from the well, thus drawing the container to the top.

There is a magnificent *Acacia nilotica* growing beside the well, and in its shade I sit down to sketch. This is the first *Acacia nilotica* I have noticed since leaving the Sirtic Desert. Upon inquiry, we learn there are a number growing in Sokna, planted here by the local people for the *Acacia*'s economic value; the pods are used in tanning hides, and have for centuries been used for trade and barter. Gerry as a tanning expert is interested in this.

Peter has led in everything so far, setting speeds, calling halts, telling people to hurry, slowing them down, saying let's eat or let's not eat, contributing the last word on everything; after all, he is an Expert. The problem is that he is accompanied by Experts Talaat, Van Hoorn, and Keith, who have their own Expert ideas on matters. How fortunate that I know nothing.

After leaving Sokna, those who think they know desert travel best take the lead. This means that Peter and Aminta in their Rovers are in front, breasted by Hammet who can't bear to be second, breasted by Gerry who thinks there must be an emergency someplace! Neck and neck, the chariots race over a sand and gravel plain where the marked path is corduroy and the unmarked one is gutted by dry wadis, until Harry suggests to Hammet to drop back in second place.

"But my father," says Hammet, unwillingly slowing, "you are the leader! You should be first."

"Damn it all, I want to see the country!" says Harry. "Slow down."

But there's a fever in group speed, and soon we are seeing the whites of Experts' eyes again, though rather bloodshot, and coughing in each other's dust. Behind us is the beige, gold and bisque of sand dune country with its friendly fringes of oasis palms backed dimly by the shape of Jebel Uaddan. Before us opens a very different landscape shadowed by long, forbidding dark humps of mountains which change to purple and black as we approach and look as if molten lava had been poured over them, as indeed it probably has been in ages past. For this is the forerunner of Jebel Soda, the Black Mountain, a volcanic massif once entirely lava-covered, now weathering slowly down to plains.

The track on which we travel is now stripped in distinct and varying colors according to the different geological strata we are crossing. I could never have imagined anything like it! Here is the pale, shiny lime green of gypsum, here a yellow strip of sandstone, now the rusty red of iron, now the chalk white of lime, the black and purple of basalt, and sometimes a sand drift of salmon pink blown up from the Red Desert. Fantastic and incredible, and a page of pastel colored stripes in my notebook must be a reminder of this.

As we go southward, the coal-black humps become angular and geometrical in shape, rising up sheer and straight from the plain, examples of hard strata which have survived erosion. Lesser brown humps lie amongst them like giant ant hills which have had buckets of coal tossed over them.

We have been warned to watch for *Maerua crassifolia* in Wadi Tengesir, a dry wadi which descends from Jebel Soda and runs north into the flood plain approaching Sokna. *Maerua* is almost the only tree which still survives in the Jebel Soda region, probably because it does not burn well enough to be cut and carried away for firewood. All the other trees such as *Acacia tortilis* and its variety *raddiana* have been destroyed, from Hun to Sebha, for firewood, just during this century.

Badreddin, in the leading Rover, spots the first *Maerua*, a tree about twenty feet high with smooth, white bark and dark green foliage which grows in a dense, full crown and makes a beautiful display against the bare, black mountains.

Now large, lustrous black boulders lie all around us, weathered from the lava mass and still weathering into black rocks, black stones, black gravel, and ultimately black sand. The track is marked by single boulders pried out of chocolate sandstone and standing upright like a parade of penguins, with one black side, one brown. Under their guidance we are being swallowed into a world of dark shapes.

We stop at Wishka, on the divide, which Hammet says is the last place we will find water until we reach Sebha. There is an artesian well here and we water the motors, fill our bottles, and take long, cool drinks. The water is clear and sweet, quite different from the brackish water in the oases below. We are about 2500 feet, the approximate level of Jebel Soda plateau. Yesterday sand, sky and air were all one medium; today blackness and brilliance alternate. Up here, filled with cool fresh air and sweet cold water, we are truly gripped by the holiday spirit, and Hammet and Badreddin are "fooling about" like teen-agers, a circumstance I could never imagine taking place in Tripoli! Only Assad remains melancholy, more a matter of liver than mental dejection.

One distorted, wind-bent, sand-bitten tree stands alone on the steely sunstruck plateau before us. For as far as we can see in any direction there is no other vertical object visible except this one desiccated tree, and it is the only sign of almost-green for several hours.

The midday sun is blinding, but the wind is cool and fresh up here where the weathering rock dust is too heavy to be lifted in the current. The basalt tableland, sheeted over with glittering gravel, gives off a blackish sheen except where the clear blue waters of mirages swell and ripple over it in soundless, shifting floods. We park the Land Rovers, and as we start towards the tree on foot, the shimmering, pale blue, mirage lakes seem to break before us and pour away, then close in silently again behind. In all this fantasmic, unreal scene, the mirages alone seem real.

Arrived at the tree, Harry says in respectful tones, "This must be the tree the Tuareg talk about. The *Maerua crassifolia* is the only tree beside the *Acacia raddiana* that will grow on top of this plateau."

"How did it get here?" demands Badreddin. "By windblown seeds?"

"Who knows how this one came?" says cautious Harry. "It's rare, but it's native."

"Perhaps the seed was spilled from a caravan in the old slave trade days," I suggest hopefully.

"Why should it be?" says Harry.

"Why shouldn't it be? They spilled plenty of human seed along the way!"

"How old is it?" asks Hammet.

"I can't say," says Harry, who never makes a guess.

Anyway, it is a tree, although compared to the *Maeruae* we found in Wadi Tengesir, with their rich bottle-green crowns, it is a sapless, fleshless, bloodless, almost colorless relic, a victim of hunger and thirst — but still it lives! Now the investigation begins, the measuring as well as marveling, and everyone has something intelligent to say about it, except me. I can think of only one thing that fits this tree, and I can't say it. As a forester's wife, I was soon weaned from my early pleasure in "Trees" by Joyce Kilmer, the bane of foresters who like to consider themselves as being solely responsible for tree production. But today there *is* only one suitable phrase to quote about this tree!

The men photograph it, circle scientifically around it, search for seeds on and near it, scrutinize the trunk, branches, leaves and bark, which is white as a bone. At last we turn away, and the blue ripples of mirages retreat before us, then close in again behind, leaving the thirsty specter growing in a lake. Someone looks back and says, "And it's really only a miserable, scruffy little thing!"

And this is the real truth of the desert. A miserable, scruffy little thing may be a miraculous sight in a long day's travel, a thing of pure beauty, a proof of fertility, a sign of God, and a promise to man. Yet undeniably it may still be only a miserable, scruffy little thing. In the desert, of all places, beauty is in the eye of the beholder.

There is no permanent human settlement any place in the Jebel Soda. The massif sometimes receives up to an inch of rainfall in years when there is none at all on the desert floor. In such a year nomad herdsmen drive their livestock up to graze. What they graze on I can't imagine, as we haven't seen a glint of green, except the *Maerua* which was scarcely green, nor a spear of grass in six hours of travel.

What agony this stretch of the journey must have been for the slaves driven over it in barefoot herds in caravan days! Yoked neck to neck, naked men, women carrying babies, crying, sickly children, with their black skins gray with dust and broken with sores, stumbled on bleeding feet over the sharp rocks, lurching and almost falling, held upright only by the wooden yoke which tied them to their neighbors. Each night the ill and the dead were cut loose from their places between those who had survived, and left behind in the wilderness to perish. Today, mounds of human bones and camel skeletons are still found along all these routes, and not all of these are centuries old, for "the trade" lasted well into the twentieth century. Slave traders used to estimate to lose eighty per cent of every human cargo and still make a good profit!

It is a long way to come from the inferno of those days to the carefree wonder of sailing through mirages in a Land Rover. My former concept of a mirage as a neat little pastel picture, possibly upside down, projected into the middle of a sandy, yellow desert is all wrong. Instead, I am projected into the mirage, which itself dominates the landscape, absorbs it and drowns it, and me with it, to such an extent that it seems that *I* may be imaginary, or an optical illusion, but the mirages are real. Sometimes as we drive, the road is only a slim peninsula surrounded by sea, and sometimes it narrows to a thin strip of blue tape which unrolls as we go, and rolls up after us. And thus lost in light waves and tricked by sight I am momentarily existing in a painless medium, when suddenly the leading Land Rover comes to an abrupt stop. We breast it, and shout, "What's the matter?"

Peter gives the answer with sweet reasonableness, "Matter is it's three o'clock. Let's eat!"

The idea pleases everyone, and we park the cars. I walk some distance from the vehicles, and turn back to make a sketch of four little Land Rovers looking ridiculous and insignificant on a large black plain. A vindication of the feeding instinct comes when Harry sees in the distance in a wadi bed a few sparse tips of green, which on investigation prove to be an *Acacia tortilis* accompanied by a few miserable *Cruciferae*, all very tired and wan, but vegetation.

After bread and tinned tuna, we continue across the steely surface, now pursued by a new set of mirages with yellow sand dunes floating in them like custard on pudding. We know by the maps that sand is not within view from here, and the mirage dunes must be promises of what is still beyond our sight. After another hour of travel the dunes begin to solidify, while the mirage waters withdraw to the horizon with the lessening intensity of the four o'clock sun. Soon the sharp outline of the gravel plateau softens to an undulating one caused by the stealthy appearance on our right of a long line of symmetrical, saffron-colored dunes. These creep up as we travel, until they predominate over the blackness of gravel, and suddenly all about us there lies the beige of sand.

There are high dunes and low ones, sand drifts and sand shadows, and smooth, rippling yellow sand is coated thickly over all the landscape, with one exception. This is a hard, brown sandstone peak looming ahead of us, which in weathering seems to have taken the shape of a sharp featured face; this is known as Garibaldi's Head. We have crossed the border now into the Fezzan.

We stop here to photograph, Hammet and Badreddin with mad enthusiasm photographing us all against Garibaldi's Head, and getting us to photograph them against every available landscape oddity. I nag Harry into taking a couple of snaps with me in them (it *is* the Sahara!), but he would much prefer a tree. Peter, who has stopped with us, approaches his photographing precisely, meticulously and without sentiment, as a thing that should be done with the minimum amount of enjoyment.

The color about us is marvelous, the sky still Madonna blue, the sand golden against chocolate hills.

"Oh, isn't it beautiful!" I say to Peter.

He answers me rebukingly, "Our ideas of beauty differ!"

I realize then that the color green is missing, and Peter has the English love of a green countryside, and a pastoral one. "But I love the emptiness of it, the barrenness — it's uncluttered," I say.

"But you wouldn't want to live here?" Hammet asks, with horror.

"In the desert? I'd like to try it, anyway. Would you?"

Both Hammet and Badreddin shudder, "No, no, in sha'Allah! No, no!"

Harry finds three naked spears of grass, *Aristida plumosa*, nearby, and then we leave, but not before deciding to change the name of Garibaldi's Head to Pasha's Head in Hammet's honor, as he is probably the first one to visit it.

Pasha's Head rises from the foot of the pass which we now descend to reach an undulating valley floor, crisscrossed in the distance by small, choppy blue waves which prove to be hills. These are the sand hills and dune masses of Ramla Zelaf, turned a glorious cornflower blue in the lessening light. After the austerity of Jebel Soda the scene before us has a pleasant pastoral quality, in which the rippling sands look like ripe wheat fields, and the blue hills might easily be abloom with lupin.

However, the way proves far from pastoral, and for two hours we crisscross sand and stony desert, with the road frequently blocked by long golden dunes of migratory habits around which we must drive, or try to. We have just passed Peter, who is really our best driver, stuck in a dune, when as we slow for the turn our car settles softly down into the sand. For a moment Hammet churns up the sand in a last four-wheel effort to get out, then he switches off the motor and we all jump down.

Shall we try it again, with a lightened load and two of us pushing? Or try the second step first (as each failure digs the car in deeper), and scour the surroundings for dried vegetation to place in front of the wheels to give them traction? The third step of untying the long sand tracks we try to avoid because of the time needed to attach them securely again to the vehicle.

At this moment Gerry and Assad whizz past, waving. They apparently see our trouble, find a hard spot ahead to stop their car, and return on foot to help. Now, with all of us pushing, the car pulls free — just as Peter's car passes, once more in the lead! It's a game, with the drivers, and no one can afford to feel superior — although each one does. It seems unavoidable, when you look at a car stuck in the sand, not to feel that *you* could have sped it safely on. Except for myself, and I marvel that we are not stuck all the time.

Just before seven o'clock we near new Sebha, the provincial capital of Fezzan. Unlike those of genuine oasis villages, the approach to Sebha is not heralded by sight of a welcome strip of dusty palms which to the traveler mean water, for modern Sebha does not owe its existence to the vital fact of water, nor to any vital fact. It is a synthetic town built to the dream specifications of a provincial capital, and it houses imported government personnel, plus experts, foreigners, and weekend visitors who usually come by air.

The one interesting architectual feature of Sebha is visible immediately: the old Italian fort on a nearby hill, called Forte Regina Elena by the Italians, which fell to the French forces in World War II and became Fort Leclerc. Under the French postwar administration of this area, Fort Leclerc was occupied by the Foreign Legion troops, principally of German nationality. When by agreement with Libya the French evacuated the Fezzan in 1956, they removed all pipes, plumbing fixtures, and fittings from Fort Leclerc before turning it over to the Libyan military forces, who now occupy it. This fact is uppermost in my mind as I look up at its looming mass and try to visualize the problem of carrying water in buckets up that hill.

Except for this local military background, Sebha looks like any suburban real estate subdivision project whose promoter has suddenly run out of funds. Its three or four streets, intersecting each other at right angles, are unpaved and deep with dust and sand, but lined by ornamental light posts — without lights. With thousands of kilometers of Sahara space about them, these little white box houses stand close together, side by side, and stare into each other's windows. All have water "laid on," but there is no water this year.

We have heard in Tripoli of the attractive new Sebha Hotel, with a bath attached to each room, and we have wired from Tripoli for reservations. This is now our goal, and a line of parked cars indicate it. Here a small, neat, white stone lodging place, blinding in the sun's last beams, proves to conceal a pleasant interior courtyard which overflows with men in blue jeans and cowboy hats, sack suits, tweed jackets, khaki trousers, all arguing with Haji Mersah, the Levantine proprietor, about having room reservations. Harry joins the argument, and I have just decided that I must relinquish the idea of a bed and bath tonight, when Harry comes back and says we're in.

We go to a nice clean room with a comfortable-looking double bed and an adjoining bath, but no water in the pipes. Meanwhile, Hammet, Badreddin and Assad have found a place for themselves at the police barracks, and Gerry and the others have managed to farm themselves out with Sebha contacts.

Now our Levantine proprietor sends in several buckets of water with which we sponge off the top film of sand. My hairline and scalp are still salmon-colored and, though I brush vigorously, my dark hair stays gingery and stiff. I scoop sand out of my ears, scrape it out of my nails, put on a clean but sandy shirt, as red dust has penetrated my valise, and hurry to the hotel bar, where our entire party has met, for iced drinks and a hot meal. Very soon I am forced to admit that the synthesis of Sebha out of sand and cash is serving to make me very comfortable!

The next morning the men devote to overhauling the Land Rovers, and we find that ours and another one have broken steering rods which must be replaced with new ones from the load of spare parts with which we travel. So far, our car has had four punctures, and three new inner tubes are completely demolished. It is quoted that after every eight thousand desert miles all the spare parts of a desert truck need replacement, but we seem to be reaching this goal too fast with Sebha only eight hundred miles from Tripoli.

14. Marianne

As I HAVE no mechanical advice to give, I am free this morning to go with Marianne Lapper to visit the Fezzani families of some of her students. Marianne is a UNESCO education expert who teaches adult education in old Sebha, called Sebha Gedid, the original Sebha oasis. To go from the capital city of Sebha to old Sebha requires only five minutes travel, but it is five centuries removed in time. Old Sebha is as obviously impoverished as the Sebha capital is pretentious and improvident.

Marianne Lapper, a slender, blonde, blue-eyed young German woman of keen intelligence and great sensitivity, is completely dedicated to her work. She and I met first by chance in the British military hospital in Tripoli, where she was under treatment for dysentery and I for an infected kidney. We found ourselves so sympathetic in outlook, that I think we both enjoyed our stays in the hospital. Marianne is a talented Orientalist and linguist, and speaks Libyan Arabic fluently. She is also "Dr." Lapper, but everyone in the Fezzan calls her Marianne, including the local policemen. They do it in such a respectful yet affectionate manner that "Marianne" spoken thus becomes a veritable honorific, and one soon forgets both "Lapper" and "Dr."

We park the car in blinding sunshine, just outside the old mud city wall, and pass through a narrow doorway to enter the city. Inside it is dark and cool, for the street is really a covered passage-way with the upper floors of dwellings meeting together above the street. We follow this alley in dusk, and I trip in several ruts as the sloping path climbs, turns two corners, and stops before a closed door. We knock; voices answer from above, and Marianne replies in Arabic, and then we open the door and enter.

In contrast with the dark passage outside, the interior of the house seems bursting with hot, white sunlight which pours down on us from the open sky two stories above. This is the first southern oasis house I have entered, and knowing that they are built without windows in order that no man may see the women inside, I was not prepared for the flood of brightness.

Steps lead to a second story above us and then continue upward to the roof. The house is built of mud blocks, with construction beams of palm trunks, the only available desert wood. There is no furniture of any sort, only a woven reed mat rolled up against the wall, and several homemade pottery cooking pots standing near on the earth floor.

Three women are waiting to greet us; in a house of this simplicity personalities dominate surroundings, and these women are like flames of desert life.

Two of them are middle-aged; one has an oval face with aquiline features and blue eyes, and the other has a broad, round face with brilliant, black shoe-button eyes. The old lady, their mother, remains seated on the smooth earth floor. Her face is heavily lined with both sorrow and laughter, and her eyes sparkle with wicked humor, and malice, too, I think. They all have tan skins, but are certainly not Negroid, although the word Fezzani usually introduces a person of black African blood. As in most Libyan homes and all oasis ones, several generations of a family live together.

They greet me with the Moslem welcome, a handshake followed by a kiss on the back of one's own hand. They welcome Marianne, however, as a sister, as one of themselves, as one who enters their house by right of mutual trust and deep affection. In fact, they express a feeling for her which, if I had not seen it, I would not have imagined could ever exist between Libyan women and any foreigner. I was deeply impressed by the honesty, strength and simplicity of this relationship. I had heard from Marianne, when we were in the hospital together, of some of the difficulties of her first year in the Fezzan, and it seemed to me that in the relationship I saw today her reward was being won.

The woman who looked youngest unrolled the woven mat for us to sit on, and from then on there was never a silent moment. My

Arabic is still limited to polite exchanges and queries about health, but I knew enough to realize that the conversation was about me, and I knew exactly what they were asking. In gay, animated voices full of vitality and curiosity, and accompanied by forceful nods of their heads, they were asking for my vital statistics: How old is she? Is she married? Has she children? How many children? Fortunately, fate had provided me with acceptable facts, and Marianne was able to make the correct answers for me; and my two children, one male and one female, half the world away, were strongly approved of, even if not numerous enough.

The old lady, however, said to Marianne about me, "My, my, my, she must be terribly brave to go away and leave them! *I* could not ever leave *my* children!" This is a true comment on Arab family life. That in their own time my children had left me as truly as I had left them was something she could not have understood, either.

Meanwhile, I was greatly enjoying the flow of conversation around me, and marveling at the fact that Marianne's pronunciations, more especially her intonations and rhythm of speech, were identical with those of the women with whom she spoke. I was reminded anew that Arabic as spoken by women is decidedly more melodious than that of men.

Our friends offer us a choice of either tea or goat's milk, and we choose goat's milk. While we are drinking this the conversation is interpreted for me by Marianne as concerning the health of those present, and of our various families. Meanwhile four children arrive; one, a girl of twelve, Fatima, with a charming, bright face and blue eyes, brings in a basket of wheat grains from which she is cleaning chaff.

Another girl, a few years younger, with a pinched, sad face, comes dragging herself along the floor by use of her arms alone, her helpless legs dragging behind her. Marianne tells me later that she has been crippled from birth with an inherited disease, probably syphilis. The girl's small face fills with joy at sight of Marianne, and she hurls herself on her in an ecstasy of affection, clings to her tightly, and finally settles at her feet with an arm resting on Marianne's lap and her eyes focused adoringly on Marianne's face.

A third girl, with a darker skin and rather frizzy hair, but a happy, round face, comes in carrying the most treasured prize of this collection of children — a boy of eighteen months, who is happily king of the castle. He is a husky, cheerful infant and probably handsome, if one could see his features clearly, but his sugared, sticky lips (he sucked a sweet), his runny nose, his whole immobile shiny face is studded with large, shimmering iridescent-winged flies. The flies don't fly at all; they just cling, sticking to his lips as if to flypaper. Marianne makes motions at the flies, and sometimes they flutter slightly, then settle back and cling. Although the child's lips are iridescent under the shine of fly wings, he seems quite undisturbed by them.

Marianne asks the eldest girl, Fatima, to show me the baby's sleeping basket which she has made. Fatima does so with pride, demonstrating to me that Marianne taught her to make it by weaving the leaflets of palm leaves together for this new purpose. Now the little king, called Mohamed, of course, as he is the first-born boy, sleeps alone instead of between Mama and Papa.

Before we leave, Marianne asks permission to take me to the rooftop from which we can survey all the other rooftops of Sebha Gedid. This is banned territory for men, as all household roofs are strictly for women only — the rooftop is woman's only freedom.

After taking proper goodbye formalities, we leave the household, I very much impressed by the apparent brightness and gaiety of these women who live their lives behind closed doors, in a life that to me would be unbearable. As we close the door after us, Marianne calls my attention to the fact that it is made from split sections of the trunk of a palm tree which have been joined together to make a very attractive door.

We visit several other friends of Marianne's and find one who is very ill with a liver complaint, and is, as we visit, receiving a massage from a friend for her malady. Marianne tells me that this patient went first to local Arab doctors and made no improvement, then to a French doctor, still without apparent benefit, then she returned to a local Arab doctor again. He has just finished giving her a course of treatment which consists of burning her flesh with a white-hot iron, as a result of which her ribs and back are covered with long scars. This treatment, the patient tells Marianne, is giving her some relief! It occurs to none of them that her illness may be beyond cure.

As it is midday now, we start back along the covered passageway, walking slowly and talking.

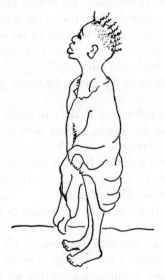

"Is there much illness in old Sebha?" I ask, my eyes still filled with the sight of those long, raw, red scars caused by cautery.

"Well, what you saw today was probably the result of a lifetime of bad diet. Certainly, undernourishment and trachoma are the greatest problem. Although of course social diseases have further-reaching effects through the children — like little Lila today! No one can possibly estimate how widespread these diseases are, except to say that there is an overwhelming amount, more than any report would dare to say. As to trachoma, among the fifty girls that I have at school, forty-nine of them had trachoma. All have been treated through the school, and most have been cured."

"About what age do the local girls marry?"

"Any time after eleven years of age — and from then on they are usually perpetually pregnant. Some of them have never menstruated: they were married, and presumably became pregnant just before they would have had a first period."

"Can't somebody try to teach them family planning, or birth control?"

"Agnes dear! You are talking centuries and centuries ahead of us here! In any case, the women don't wish to escape pregnancy, because as long as a woman continues to get pregnant her husband has less excuse to take another wife. Also, children are very much wanted here and receive a great deal of affection — even if they can't be fed properly! But a tremendous number of children die before they are four years old. That, I suppose, holds down the population."

"What do the children eat?"

"Dates. Especially the black Fezzani. The lucky ones may have goat's milk, but many of the oasis children, after stopping with mother's milk, eat nothing but dates up to the time they are nine or ten years old. To them, food *is* dates."

"I remember a little Fezzani boy," I recall then, "who came up from the desert to live with some friends of ours in Tripoli. He actually refused to eat at all for days, until they finally got him some Fezzani dates. He wouldn't touch the sticky Tripoli things they sell in packets. He had to have his sugary, caramelized, sun-dried Fezzani date! They're wonderful for flavor — I never tasted anything like them; but I hate the sand in them. But I guess a Fezzani doesn't notice sand! The modern Tripoli youngsters won't eat dates at all now; think it's too provincial, probably!"

"The Fezzan people could never exist without date palms," says Marianne. "Nothing is wasted; even the stone is ground up and fed to livestock. All these local mud houses here are roofed with date palm fronds plastered with mud. Sayed Umar Sha'aban, the father of one of my pupils, set out the other day on a journey of several weeks to guide a camel party across the Rebiana Sand Sea to Kufra. I was at the house visiting his wife the day after he left, and I asked her what he took to eat. She said his pockets were stuffed with Fezzani dates, and he had a sack of them tied at his waist, and he had a little packet of tea, and a full water bag, and that is all that he took! Think of crossing one of the worst stretches of the Sahara like that!"

"I don't mean," Marianne continued, "that all the oasis people use nothing but dates. Some of the farmers grow barley, wheat, millet, onions and tomatoes. Many of them make bazin from barley flour; they knead it into dough and eat it uncooked, and it's nourishing. Some even make wheat flour into pasta, like spaghetti — but those things are eaten sometimes, dates are always used."

"What about their sheep and camels?"

"Sheep here are *never* slaughtered for food! They're only used for wool. Camel — well, most people can't afford *any* meat of any sort. Sometimes a very old camel may get slaughtered, if he's too old to plow, and too weak to carry! People don't use money here, they don't have it! A family income averages about twenty dollars a year."

We pass through the gate in the old city wall now and step outside, into the sunshine, into a different world. The shadowed one we have left was welcoming and friendly, but not, I knew, a world for *me*, only for the women of a Moslem world. That world has its own strength and power which reside in its very exclusion, its walls and closed doors, its secret thoughts and unexplored minds, its faith in old ways and in the following of ancient rites. Here the old order and its followers now survive spiritually with self-respect. Tear down the walls, open the doors, draw in the sunlight, destroy old rites and bring reason to bear on old faiths — and what would be left to them here? Where and how does Fezzan life offer them any living substitute, or alternative?

Speaking my thoughts aloud, I ask Marianne, "But could these people survive in a different life? A leap out of darkness into full sunlight is as dangerous as from sun to darkness."

And Marianne answers, "They are already successful in part in handling their incredibly difficult and dreadful desert environment. Their primitive ways meet their primitive needs. They depend only on desert resources. I do not wish to change them; I only hope to teach them to use more completely their own resources. Sebha Gedid is centuries old, and in future centuries it will still be here. But *new* Sebha? Well, stop paying people to live there, stop importing their food and goods for them, and new Sebha will vanish like dew on the sand!"

"And are these women content to follow the old ways?" I ask.

"Of course! They know nothing else. They accept the old tradition of complete seclusion unquestioningly, and the home is the woman's only world. She *is* the home; its problems and burdens are hers."

"What about bringing water to the house? I know that's a woman's job always."

"Oh, every household can produce some poor relation, or somebody sufficiently déclassé to go to the well and bring water!"

Before we separate for lunch Marianne promises to take me with her this evening to visit her education classes in Sebha Gedid. Classes for women must always be held at night so that the pupils may go there under cover of dark without danger of any man seeing more of them than a shadowed shape.

It is a moonless night, but the brilliance of the stars in the indigo sky makes shadows on the desert as Marianne and I walk to the old town. Behind us lies the artificial yellow shine of new Sebha's tawdry houses, and the nocturnal noise of its ceaseless radios.

Arriving at the old city wall, we pass through the narrow gateway, unlighted of course, and lose the starlight completely as we feel our way along the covered alleyway. As before, I stumble in two ruts, trip on a rock, and fall up the sloping ground while Marianne, who knows every rut by heart, tries to guide me.

"It's terribly dark!" I comment needlessly.

"Of course," she agrees. "If it were not so dark, the women could not leave their houses to come to class! On bright moonlight nights we do not have a class."

Around another corner, we stop at a doorway and Marianne feels for the keyhole. Finding it, she opens the door into a room lit dimly by a streak of light which shines down a stairway from the floor above, from where I hear young voices chattering in Arabic.

"They are already here," Marianne explains, "because my best pupil comes early, and starts the class for me. She assists me now in teaching, and I come a little late on purpose so that the girls will learn to carry on their work without me, and to be responsible to themselves."

As we start up the narrow stairway, vigorous young voices are already calling down to Marianne, and before we top the stairs she is conversing gaily with her still unseen pupils. I am again astonished and delighted by the identity of her Arabic with theirs, by her concord with them, by the harmony of response and answer between herself and the girls. This is what speaking a language really is, not learning its words alone, but understanding its heart. There cannot be many Western women who will ever converse in this manner with Libyan women, who themselves add to the language difficulty by their custom of seclusion.

I find, above, a small room with ten rough tables and benches which are occupied by twenty-five young women whose ages, Marianne tells me, range from twelve years to thirty. After thirty, they are usually grandmothers, and considered too old to learn! There is only one babe in arms, a fact that is unusual; frequently there are six or seven infants whose mothers must bring them in order to attend themselves. Now Marianne is engulfed by her pupils, who obviously consider her one of themselves. That she has extra knowledge in some matters, however, they accept, and tonight her ability at knitting, which is the current class lesson, is badly needed, for they have reached the heel of the sock. The wool they are using is homespun from their own sheep.

Meanwhile, I am sitting in front of the class where I can look at them and they at me, a matter of mutual satisfaction, as I stare and they stare, and we are all content. Some of them come close and run fingers up and down my nylon stockings which they call my "skin," and feel the fabric of my clothes, and investigate my nylon slip, and underthings. In turn, I touch their hands, their hair, look closely at the tattoos on some faces, and feel the fabric of the woven, dark wool "melhafas," the voluminous draped garment each one wears, which takes the place of the white Tripoli baracan. Here, tonight, these robes are thrown back from their owners' heads and faces; but outside the schoolroom door the melhafa will be draped completely over their heads to hide the face, except for the left eye.

I have exhausted my little list of Arabic greetings, and the girls are asking me questions, the Arabic of which I do not follow but the content of which I know by heart. How old am I? Married? . . . And so on.

As in the morning, Marianne makes the answers for me as she knits sock heels. Again, my married and maternal statistics are warmly approved of while the class gets on with its knitting, but nobody stops talking for even a moment, and barbed interchanges draw constant laughter. The beginners are still practicing their stitches on mufflers, but the advanced ones are now inextricably entangled in socks. The problem looks quite unsolvable to me, and I would give up wearing socks sooner than knit them, but the girls are undismayed and knitting madly, except when they are unknitting madly.

It is the gayest classroom I have ever been in, not in physical surroundings but in the invincible quality of high spirits and exhilaration of its occupants, the "little women," as Marianne always calls them. There is no imposed foreign standard of behavior here; rather, the girls are behaving by their own best standards of politeness and courtesy, which include giving hospitality to me and paying loving attention to Marianne's instructions. But this is not done silently with downcast eyes, in an atmosphere of well-regulated gloom such as might exist in a Western schoolroom, but which they themselves would hate. Instead, there is a sparkling round of merriment, spiced with touches of malice, such as they themselves like, and they compliment Marianne and me by believing we will like it. This is good breeding of its own individual brand, and as such I find it infinitely superior to seeing Libyans imitate foreign gestures of politeness, the reasons for which they will never know.

One thing I ask myself, but decide the answer is easy: why is school such fun, and the occasion for high spirits? Of course, it is obvious that for young people who live completely secluded in their homes, any meeting with other young people is going to be a wonderful time. Weddings and burials are the only excuse outside this school which can bring females together here.

During an hour in which I listen to the lilt and rhythm of a guttural language spoken fluidly and watch bright young faces of every shade of skin from tender bisque to ebony, all with eyes and minds focused on their teacher, I also reach some conclusions about Marianne.

I know that she has been living in Sebha over a year, remaining here throughout the cruel summer when temperatures go over 120 degrees Fahrenheit in the outside shade, and remain above 100 degrees all through the nights, even inside the mud and stone houses which are built for coolness. I know that she has been the only European woman here throughout the summer, and what this means in learning to live alone only Marianne can tell. She has existed with empty boxes for shelves and packing cases for furniture, with dysentery and boils to deplete her strength; yet none of these things has defeated her.

But one thing almost did, she told me: during the first year of classes, she came home each night from her work, mentally prostrated and almost hysterical from the strain of following in her (then) Algerian Arabic the Libyan Fezzanese dialogues of her pupils, and then answering back in kind the subtle, witty, puckish repartee which is true female Fezzanese and must be answered back in kind, or you have acknowledged defeat. Tonight, I see proof that Marianne is undefeated.

In that first year she must have learned as much as her pupils did, and it is one of Marianne's gifts that she herself can learn. Another gift is lack of smugness; she does not feel that she comes here to civilize. What need is there for that, she asks me, when these girls are truly civilized by their own standards? And she loves them, and it is perhaps the supreme gift to be able to love. So many people only love the reflection of themselves in others; but Marianne loves others.

She has plans drawn up for a teachers' training school in Sebha to which in time one girl from each lonely little Fezzan oasis will come to study and then return to her home oasis to teach. Marianne says that the Governor of Fezzan Province has been very encouraging to her. It is a revolutionary idea here to try to enlarge a woman's world in any way. The great part of the Libyan Arab world of men opposes it, if only by mute immovability. Against this, I wonder what one pale blonde German girl can do?

I was later to discover not so much what Marianne could do, but what the men of the small desert world could do to her, a brave young woman who did so much for their women, and whom their women so truly loved. And possibly the very meanness of their masculine reactions to her magnanimity was commensurate with the character of the brutal desert struggle which had bred them — tough, lusting, and merciless.

15. The Oasis People

To UNDERSTAND the people of the oases one must first visualize the vastness of the desert area in which an oasis stands and the utter isolation of each tiny group of date palms, vegetation, dwelling places, hidden women and plodding men, each oasis usually having less than a hundred persons. These spots are like pinpoints on a clean sheet of paper with nothing connecting them to each other, or to anything else. Yet no one point is located by accident; each one is placed exactly where, by necessity, it must be; exactly where, and only where, water may be obtained by digging for it.

For the treasure of the Fezzan is a buried treasure: it is not gold, nor salt for which gold was once traded in equal measure; nor is it the notorious, million-dollar African slave trade of days gone by; nor will it even be oil, in the long run of future years. Wealth of the desert lies here in the huge, buried layer of water-permeable rock forming a geological basin which underlies the entire circular structural basin of the Fezzan. Under the wind-beaten, desiccated desert of today, this deep, porous layer of sandstone and conglomerate rock has been accumulating water during thousands of years, and while man was busily destroying his resources above soil, nature was busily storing up treasure for him below in this priceless water reservoir. Ground water is the secret of every grass blade, barley grain, and date palm which grows in the Fezzan.

Here is a land almost without rain, without even a cloud. In some years, precipitation is completely nonexistent; in others there is only a trace. The average yearly rainfall was estimated to be, throughout a period of the last eight years at Ghat in the southern Fezzan, a half-inch; and it is the opinion of a French meteorologist who has just completed a study of this area that rainfall is steadily growing less.

With half an inch of rain falling on a parched surface, there can be no runoff or catchment. There exists here only this many-centuried safe deposit of ground water to make existence possible for man, animal, or plant.

Fezzan oases are located along four narrow areas where the water table comes close to the land surface. In such an area, wells of varying depths, which tap the porous underlayer, will bring water to the earth's surface. Sometimes water is also found in natural-flowing springs. In such an area, very shallow wells of only three or four feet in a dry wadi bottom will often flow freely because they draw water from the wadi floor alluvium which itself draws water from the underlying sandstone layer. This explains why a wadi may suddenly appear across a desolate gravel plain, looking as green as a green pencil stripe drawn on white paper. Yet if you stop and search you will find no visible dampness, not even a drop of water nor a drink, but vegetation will find it.

Because of its buried water table, there is much talk nowadays about the Sahara's "having water" — but this phrase is a misleading one for people who think of water as I once did, in terms of bathtubs full. One day I watched ten Tuareg women — the Tuareg woman is unveiled and free — at the well at Bir Um el Ufrar on the Red Plateau fill their goatskin bags with water to carry on their backs to their tents five miles away. Bir Um el Ufrar well is pumped just once a week by camel power and once a week each woman comes and fills her gerba, which holds about five gallons of water. Then she carries it home as the week's supply for her family of three to six people. This means that less than a quart of water a day is used by each person for all purposes, for cooking, drinking and, if one can imagine it, washing and bathing. This is the water consumption of a group of people who live *near* a well, and who are an example of *fortunate* Sahara people with water! It is not surprising that the real nomad who never settles any place does not touch water to his person; instead he "washes" with sand.

Actually, not bathing is less difficult to reconcile oneself to in the desert than other things which accompany water shortage. Next to being thirsty, I think that washing dishes in desert sand is the most objectionable result of no water — I can get the dishes clean, but *I* end up covered with an edible layer of sardine tails, tuna oil, salami skins and savory sauce, ground in with sand and an odor which Harry calls "Nuit de Targi," instead of the old favorite Nuit de Noël.

There may be only twenty or fifty people living in an oasis, or a hundred, or several hundred, but each oasis is surrounded by an uninhabitable area which makes it as isolated as an island. Its date palms and inhabitants are constantly enveloped in one of two arduous climates. During part of the year the dwellers swelter and bake in a blinding sun, and are swept by the merciless ghibli, which crosses the Sahara like a yellow tidal wave, sometimes drowning whole villages in seas of sand, and destroying vegetation, camels, and men with all their mortal relics. The ghibli leaves behind it, in poor exchange, new mountains of bone-white sand, fresh pink scallops of shifting dunes, knife-edged crescent-shaped ones, and black granulous plains. During the rest of the year temperatures drop during the night to freezing, veering winds turn cold and damp, the sun is bright but comfortless, and no rain descends.

Physically, the desert people just barely survive, but spiritually they are strong because they are steeped in their own cultural tradition which has developed from the urgent needs of their lonely lives. Desert necessity is their essence. Until their needs change, their way of life cannot do so. For any outside force to try to alter their ways without changing their desert exigencies would be as destructive as to take fins from a fish and replace them with feet, and then throw him back in the sea.

Between the oasis people and our Libyan companions, Hammet, Badreddin, and Assad, there is a great gap, yet all are Libyans and Moslems. Between the Tripoli young men and ourselves now there seems to be no gap, yet we are Europeans and Christians, and they Arabs and Moslems. I even suspect that Harry and I could settle to an oasis environment more easily than Hammet, who has a wide streak of playboy in him, for Turks are true Europeans, and we are only Anglo-Saxons!

Having been off on my own with Marianne for several days observing local fauna, I have neglected Sebha flora, which is easy to do, as it is almost nonexistent. We occasionally see *Panicum turgidum*, a desert-colored grass which looks like a bundle of straw. Good for fixation, because anything is. Another miserable specimen is *Calligonum comosum*, a distorted shrub with scraggy, jointed branches dry and brittle. Of course, there is *Cynomorium*, which sticks erectly up out of the sand in phallic shape in an eight-inch column of bruised, reddish flesh. Zeb el Turk, the Libyans said! Parasitic, too. In all the nearby oases there are the date palms, and *Acacia tortilis* and its variety, *raddiana*.

The most spectacular thing on the sands is the *Citrullus colocynthis*, the Apple of Sodom. This is a gourd of a bright pumpkin color when fresh, which in time fades out to white. It exists on a scrawny little colorless vine on the ground, but the gourd is visible from a long distance. It grows from hen-egg size to ostrich-egg size, and is very light and easily wind-blown. The other day I pursued one for some distance over the sand in the unrealistic hope that it might be a prehistoric ostrich egg. It wasn't, but it might have been. Although there are no ostriches here now, there were in the Stone Age days and even in Italian times, and ostriches abound in rock paintings. Things like eggs can travel on moving sand crests by being jostled along from one grain of sand to the next, a process which sounds to me something like a dry version of osmosis. By this process the egg arrives in strange places just as indubitably and mysteriously as the sap rises in the plants.

On the track between Sebha and Murzuk there exist huge cross sections of fossilized trees which put to shame any trees living in this area today. These are relics of the Pleistocene times, when the climate of the Sahara was probably comparable to that of Europe today.

It is just outside of Sebha that I have my solitary experience of being a heroine. I expect I shall never let any of my fellow travelers forget it.

There are some fine Stone Age rock drawings some kilometers from Sebha, and these Marianne and I went to see early one morning with a young Sebha policeman, presumably to escort us, but really because he wanted to drive the Land Rover. Of course there was no road or trail, but Marianne knew the way. Although the sand was soft in places, the policeman and I shared the driving and had no difficulty in arriving at the slightly mountainous location where the paintings are. I was extremely enthusiastic, as these were the first I had seen on site, although compared to those of Lhoti's book on the Tassili N'Ajjer the Sebha ones were unspectacular and lacking in variety. Still, anything that one sees oneself on the site is more exciting than a great wonder which one reads about.

Marianne and I decided that Harry and Gerry must come to see the pictures in the afternoon, as we were leaving Sebha the next day. Consequently we started out just after an early lunch, with Harry and me in one Land Rover, and Marianne and Gerry in the other. As our Land Rover had been loaded for the next day's start, it was very heavy, and we soon found that the sand, which in the early morning with the night chill on it had offered a crusty surface and good resistance to our wheels, was now mushy and soft. Gerry and Marianne in their unloaded Land Rover, with Gerry a more skilled sand driver, were sailing along, while Harry and I bogged down twice and had to dig out, and once used sand tracks.

As it looked as if our loaded vehicle couldn't make it, I suggested that Harry shift into the other Rover and go with Marianne and Gerry to see the drawings and leave me behind in our Rover to sketch. This was agreed.

"We'll be back in two hours at most," Marianne estimated, "as we are only three-quarters of an hour from the gara now."

"Be sure to wait right here," Harry warned me. "Don't try to get smart and drive off any place on your own, as you'll surely bog down, or get lost. And your Rover has the sand tracks."

"Yes, dear. I know you wouldn't like to lose the sand tracks!"

They skimmed off at a terrific rate, which is the only way to keep going on sand, and almost immediately they were lost to sight beyond the long dune on my right. Even their sound vanished like magic, blocked by the sand dune stretches.

"Suppose *they* get lost!" I thought, feeling suddenly very alone. "Or, if the wind rises and covers their tracks from here, how will they find *me* again? And if they don't come in two hours, what do I do?"

Well, it had been my idea. I got out my pencils and paper to

Jebel Jinn

sketch, and found nothing to draw but one lone dune and another lone dune, and another. Anyway, there was *too* much time for sketching; I had gotten used now to being hurried every moment as I sketched, to get back in the car and not delay the others. Finally I gave up and wrote in my diary. Then I went for little walks in all directions, always keeping the cartop in sight.

When I stood on top of the dune I could see off in every direction, and there was nothing to see but more dunes. I saw by my watch that it was four o'clock, and the others had been away two and a half hours. I sat in the car and waited another half-hour, meanwhile thinking carefully about what Harry had said — "Don't drive on your own, or you'll bog down, or get lost!" But *I* had the sand tracks, and if they had bogged down, they would need the tracks.

Three hours now. Something twitched in my fingertips, and the next moment the Rover was moving. "Dear God," I thought, "It isn't getting killed that I'd mind — but just don't let me get stuck!"

I had my plan in mind. I headed in the direction the others had disappeared in, only I mounted the dune and remained on top. I intended to stay on the crest of the dune where the sand was always hardest, and travel its length. Meanwhile I was praying for another longitudinal dune running in the same direction which would join mine, so I could mount it with a running start from my present dune. Still I saw nothing of the other Rover.

I traveled about half an hour, gaining confidence with every minute, as I skimmed the crest of the well-organized dunes which obligingly laid themselves end to end, almost overlapping. "It's easier than it looks," I thought. And at that moment I saw I was coming to the end of my dune range. "I'll not go down," I determined. "There's sure to be soft sand at the dune base, and I haven't the guts to risk getting stuck. While I'm on top, I can always turn around and go back."

But could I turn around on the narrow crest? Well, I couldn't back up all the way! Before I tried the turn, I stopped the car and decided to progress on foot to the extreme end of the dune for a final look around for the others. I did this, and unbelievably, scarcely crediting my own eyes, wondering if it was a mirage, I looked far down the soft end-slope of the dune and saw way below me three very small, very busy, sand-digging figures, and a Land Rover bogged in sand up to its springs!

One seldom experiences such a moment! There was I, unstuck, unlost, mobile, and bringing the rescuing sand tracks! Admittedly, it was also nice to meet up with one's companions again!

I gave them a shout. They looked up. They were shocked. They couldn't believe it. Not Agnes! We told her to wait! Then with one mind, they all started crazily waving me back, and shouting, "Stay on top! Stay on top! Don't come down here!"

I thought myself that it was time for them to stop giving me *their* advice. *I* was the one who was mobile.

So we unlashed the sand tracks again, we dug them out this time, and the Rover got going. I went back to my darling, adorable, reliable vehicle and prayed that by God's good grace there would be just space enough for me to turn it around on the crest.

There was. Thus the day ended in my only triumph of the trip.

We left Sebha at eight this morning, and I think we were all glad to go. New Sebha is too synthetic to attract devotion. One cannot be loyal to a lightless lamp post, a dry bathtub, a W.C. without W., a village without villagers, and a soulless city filled with transient inhabitants who count the days till they can leave.

Peter and the three in his two Land Rovers leave for Brak, an oasis north of Sebha, from where they will return to Tripoli. Now we are down to the original six persons and two cars, headed south for Ghat. It is a glorious morning with a brisk, cool breeze, and clean, dry air — one of those days which I didn't know existed when I was describing the arduous climates of the oases!

Only a few kilometers from Sebha we strike a strip of fej fej, large-grained sand which does not pack solid and is the most treacherous trap for sand-driving beginners. We dive deep into this and stick, and everyone starts giving advice. Invariably, those who were *not* driving feel that they could have avoided getting stuck, but it takes a brave and foolhardy man to say so. This isn't a bad bog-down, as the sand is not above the wheel hubs. We lighten the car, dig out the wheels, put some *Caligonum* branches under and behind them and, using reverse four-wheel drive, struggle onto solid sand without using the sand tracks. We are just going well again when we have a blowout, and stop to put the spare on the front and the good front tire on the back.

Under way again, we travel parallel with a chain of black mountains, often pyramid-shaped, which are part of the Hamadet Murzuk, or Rocky Desert, a prehistoric conglomerate mixture of sandstone and clay which is weathering to a bedrock plateau. This rocky buttress curves southwest and outlines the huge series of Sahara sand dunes known as the Erg of Murzuk. Long sand shadows of hibiscus red sand creep in from our right, and sometimes there are patches of vegetation with a straw-like *Panicum*, *Acacia tortilis*, and *Maerua*. Black stone cairns mark the track, which is absolutely straight except for rise and fall, and widely varied as to color, with crosswise stripes again.

We cross a plain of vivid sunset sand against a background of gently rippling hills (which I cannot find on the map), and here the desert suddenly blossoms, or so it seems. The dunes are dahlia red, the sand floor ripples like a field of golden mustard, and the hills bloom violet as if with iris, while black pyramids race beside us. I never dreamed that deserts held such miracles of color, such sunset hues, and such subtleties of mood. Meanwhile Harry gloats at the sight of unexpected strips of vegetation and a few small trees in dry wadi beds. Sometimes now we can see salmon-pink sand hills which have been brought by the Hamra wind all the way from Hamada el Hamra, the Red Desert.

Now dark, jagged shapes and pyramids surround us, the advance guard of the black mountains on our left, and tough old survivors of the battle of time against conglomerate rock. Hewn from the Nubian layer, the antique giants may once have known the footfalls of dinosaurs and wingbeats of flying snakes. Faced by such Mesozoic forces, my sense of egoism oozes from my mortal self into the ancient landscape, and I feel I should apologize for thinking that I matter. "My life!" one says. Yet here a lifetime has no meaning, desire has no significance, intention has no value and deeds have no worth. No wonder that the Moslem, faced by this landscape, gives his submissive answer with submissive shrug, "In sha'Allah" — "If God wills."

But we are not Moslems, as Harry reminds me, and we didn't grow up in the desert surrounded by Nubian sandstone. It is our fate to squirm through life twisting and straining as if things really mattered, trying to do this and to avoid that, to attract some and to repulse others, to persuade fate or resist it, always in revolt against what in the end we know we must accept. And at heart we like it this way. I think this element of revolt is the basic difference between the philosophy of East and that of West.

Yet already we know Moslems in Tripoli who are withholding the submissive shrug and the quickly spoken "If God wills!" and are fighting for their fate. They are contaminated, I suppose, by the West. If the Nubian sandstone is right, contamination does not matter, only conglomeration counts!

With the old black battle-axes still hounding our left flank, we came to a long, green strip of oases on our right, backed by the Ubari sand hills. This strip of fertility extends for more than a hundred miles from el Abiad, the oasis we are just passing through on the way to Ubari, our day's goal. In addition to having a water table close to the surface, these oases have the advantage of being located in a valley between the Hamadet Murzuk and Erg (sand hills) of Ubari, and consequently they benefit from both elevated areas, as the moisture from them sinks to the lowest level.

Gone for all time is my picture of an oasis as a little circle of trees.

In this small settlement we see it as an isolated strip of trees, date palms, water, wells, gardens and people. *Acacia tortilis,* despite the fact that it is always being cut back for charcoal, follows this strip in an almost unbroken belt.

A handful of sparse living centers string along this fertile strip, all with date palms and barley fields, which are the most beautiful, vivid, shiny green of anything one sees in the desert. Hedges of thatched palm fronds surround planted areas to break the wind. Structures for wells are also made from palm logs, and house doors are always built from split sections. It is no wonder that the date palm is lovingly referred to by the oasis farmer as "my father's aunt"! The big sex scene in oasis life is the mating of two date palms — even though it is done by artificial insemination!

We stop at the small village of Twish to photograph, as this is the first place where we have seen the Sudanese-style circular beehive huts. These are made entirely of palm fronds plastered together with mud, as are also the circular corrals and livestock shelters.

"Look, Mother, look! They are all black!" exclaims Badreddin, amused and fascinated by the sight of a place completely dominated by black Africa and showing little of Arabia. Hammet regards the whole scene distantly with the supercilious air of one who feels no connection with what he sees. The fact that he is now wearing a vari-colored Fezzani skullcap purchased in the Sebha suk makes his air of superiority slightly inconsistent.

Twish is such a tiny place that it is seen in one sweeping glance; or so it seems until I walk parallel to it and find a typical, mud-walled Arabic village cuddled down beside it. The only people to be seen any place are black, and no one seems interested in us, although others may be hiding inside the dwellings and watching.

Harry is photographing extensively here, as the minute village outlined against the Jebel Messak Settafet is dramatically over-whelmed by the tall mountains above and behind it.

Under way again, and traveling a little further south we find vil-lages which have nothing but beehive huts. A mud-and-thatch wall extends from the hut in a larger circle to form an animal corral into which the house door opens, and of which the house wall is part. Stopping to eat our invariable midday sardines marinated in sand is

Twish

a psychological struggle among the six of us. Badreddin, Gerry and Assad in one car are always hungry by one o'clock and looking for a place to stop. Hammet and I are hungry also, but Harry, the party's elder statesman, with whom we travel, could go on forever without food.

Every hour or so our cars are accustomed to draw together to see that all is well, and to ensure that no car is out of sight of the other too long. The lunch battle begins when somebody (not Harry) looks at his watch and says, "Isn't it time to eat?"

"What! You chaps hungry again?" Harry says.

No answer from the embarrassed others, but the Elder Statesman's wife says plaintively, "Well, I feel stronger after I eat."

"Very well then, chaps. We'll just go on until we find a nice little picnic place with a spot of shade, and stop there." We know then that we are doomed, for no such spot exists.

For the first few days our car led, theoretically searching for a picnic place, until three or four P.M., when exhaustion set in. Then I suggested to Gerry that about lunchtime he should grab the lead forcibly, outdistance us a bit (hoping that Hammet would not take up the challenge to race!), then stop his car at any possible place and get the water bottles and a few lunch items unloaded before we could arrive.

This usually works quite well. Today, Harry is ranging the

nearby desert floor bent double and looking for vegetation, while the rest of us open tins of sardines and tuna and unwrap the large Edam cheese and Hammet boils tea on an infant fire made from charcoal and twigs. We have invested in a sack of charcoal, which proves more reliable than bottles of liquid gas.

Harry brings in a few chosen sand-colored items which he places carefully in sacks, and will press tonight for the collection which is going to Kew Gardens. Now we eat. It is unbelievable how good it tastes, even the sand!

We arrive at Ubari by six o'clock, report to the police and ask permission to use the rest house overnight. The Tuareg police lieutenant in charge has done police duty in Tripoli, and proves to be an old friend of Hammet and Badreddin. He makes us welcome and sends an old man over to clean up the rest house, which stands across the square from the police station. Here we find two rooms for sleeping, unload our cots and then prepare food on the veranda.

I always prepare the food at night, as I do little of the driving during the day. Sand driving is exhausting physically because of the wheel drag, which is a strain on the hands and wrists. We are all tired out by the time we stop, and the first thing I do is locate the gin bottle and take a drink, while the men are putting up the cots and unrolling the sleeping bags. Badreddin fixes a fire for me, charcoal and twigs tonight, sometimes the GI stove when we have no twigs, and we put on a kettle for tea, and a caldron of water to boil.

Our mainstay, night after night, is either spaghetti or macaroni, as these are the two things that all of us can and will eat, and I'm too tired to make separate menus. It takes the water at least an hour to boil in the huge, deep stew pot which I brought from home for the pasta. Meanwhile, I mix a hot sauce of tomato paste, hot peppers, red pepper sauce, and Tabasco which I add to thinly sliced onions fried in olive oil, then simmer gently, add more oil and simmer again. This sauce goes with the spaghetti, plus grated Parmesan cheese, and that's dinner. We have tins of fruit, stew and soup with us, but the Moslems eat nothing with tinned meat in it, unless they know it has been killed with the ritual of the Koran. Tinned fruit is nice as a delicacy, but a trip like this doesn't need delicacies to tempt the appetite.

Badreddin has asked the police officer at Ubari to have tea with us, and by now he and another Tuareg friend are sipping their tea and listening avidly to news of the outer world. We find courtesy every place and hospitality freely offered, even from impoverished conditions.

To have Libyans traveling with us is itself an introduction, but not only because of language. These Tuareg, who consider themselves the caretakers of the south Sahara, have their own language, Temaheq, quite another language from Arabic, although many of them speak Arabic, too. Badreddin says that the Tuareg speak only Temaheq amongst themselves, but as a matter of courtesy they speak Arabic with Arabs. A nice point!

Assad, now that his liver has established friendly relations with him and his greens have been consumed or abandoned, proves a great social asset. He has a studious nature and an inquiring mind which questions everything, including the distance of each day's run, the components of tinned margarine, the past participles of English verbs, and the grammatical construction of sentences. When at home, he studies English in the British Council class, and his conversation is the most nearly correct of the Libyans. Badreddin's vocabulary, however, is the most colorful, as he refuses to let lack of grammatical knowledge or vocabulary stop him from expressing himself, and he makes up words to suit. One of his nicest is "charmingfulest."

For me, these tea-drinking, general powwows which we have each night sitting on the floor in the dusk with only a flickering candle or the light of the campfire, these are the parts of the trip I shall never forget. It is not only the exchange of ideas, but the companionship with people whom I like and admire and in whom I am interested. So different from European social life in Tripoli, where one is constantly saying things that mean nothing to people who mean little.

I think there comes a time, if you live away from your own country in a strange one, when you either intensify your feelings of strangeness into antipathy or begin to identify yourself unconsciously with the new country. For me, Libyan identification begins with this Sahara trip.

16. The Road to Ghat

NEXT morning we say goodbye to the police and leave for Uweinat, also called Serdeles. Every place in Libya has at least two names, an Italian one and an Arabic one, and here on the desert there is often a Tuareg one, too. At Uweinat we hope to be able to fill the gas tanks again. With luck, we *may* arrive at Ghat tonight, though this is one of our longest runs in mileage, over a hundred miles. The track, they say, is very bad, and travel very slow.

That a hundred miles is a long, hard day's run seems ridiculous in terms of highway travel. However, on this trip I think we traveled as far vertically as we did horizontally, and we halted constantly to examine scraps of vegetation. And as the trip was primarily to study the country, with the thought of finding possible areas for fixation, for regeneration, for plantations and for cereal uses, we frequently did just that — stopped and studied the country.

The only thing that desert travel has in common with my earlier Borneo jungle trips on foot is that sometimes they are both remarkably slow. I know that ten miles a day in heavy jungle is more than most jungle travelers can do. Ten miles in dune country or sand sea may be quite impossible.

On our vehicles we carried metal sand tracks about six feet long, lashed across the front of the vehicles. It is quite possible in areas of soft sand or of the large-grained fej fej to be forced to make your labored advance entirely over sand tracks. This means you place the tracks under your two front wheels and, assisted by pushing from the rear, you drive the car onto the tracks and just beyond, then drag them forward and place them in front of your wheels again. With luck and energy you may be able to move the tracks twice in five minutes, making about a twenty-five-foot advance every five minutes, or three hundred feet per hour — which is less than a mile in an exhausting ten-hour day — assuming you don't drop dead before! We didn't have to do quite this on our trip, but I mention these facts to show that a hundred miles in a day is not lazy going.

We were also acquiring car weaknesses to struggle with. I cannot conceive of any concentration of machinery capable of completely withstanding the jolting of such travel. Screws unscrewed and bolts fell out, despite persistent attention, while unyielding metal parts snapped and overly resilient ones became elastic. Tires were a constant anxiety. We had started with two extra new wheels complete with tires, plus three extra inner tubes. After Sebha, I stopped counting punctures (they gave me a chance to sketch!), but the men seemed to be patching tires at every stop and shifting them from front to rear, or rear to front, according to individual theories. We would never have set out from Tripoli with such tires as they have now become! Yet now we look at them with growing pride at the end of each day's travel — for rolling still! We are developing strong loyalties to our vehicles.

Much of the time I make notes in my notebook, kept open on my knee as we travel. Although the writing is almost undecipherable, I find this better than waiting until we stop at night, when I am too tired. From Ubari on I make numerous rough sketches, both traveling and when the car stops for a moment, to chronicle a scene which to me is strange, and fascinating. The contrast from darkness to brilliance in the semi-desert landscape is almost unbelievable, and we have found that sand stretches require the same technique to photograph as snow. One cannot even believe the exposure meter, the glare is so blinding. As well as light and shade and color range, there is great contrast between the spheroid, malleable look of sand masses and the sharp, ragged outlines of weathering rock. The desert is a place of extremes — in heat, light, color, asceticism and voluptuousness.

Just out of Ubari we pass a solitary flat-topped hill rising alone from the plain. Such a hill is called gara in Arabic, a word I hear constantly now because the gara is typical of this area. After Ubari, the oasis belt disappears, and we become more conscious of the mountain mass of Amsak Settafet which is south of us. We are traveling on a coffee-colored plain or steppe strewn with large black boulders which look like lava, but are ancient, weathered sandstone. Hammet is having trouble with the Rover, and we stop frequently. It is something to do with the petrol feed. Our hopes for reaching Ghat tonight begin to diminish, as this is one of our longest runs in mileage and the track is the worse and our travel is slowest.

By midday we cross the northern end of the Erg of Tatta, a yellow dune mass which curls and spreads itself like a sleeping, golden cat. We stop again, and Hammet and Assad once more screw and unscrew all available nuts and taps in the Rover. My only contribution is to keep silent, but I'm the only one who does. Finally Assad removes the petrol feed, cleans it and returns it, and full of hope, we start off again — only to find that now the petrol is leaking more copiously into the sand. Loss of petrol is the last thing we can afford; we stop again and renew investigations. The leak is lessened slightly, and we decide that the best thing to do is proceed to Uweinat and hope we can get mechanical attention there. Esso Oil Company is prospecting in this vicinity, and oil companies have good mechanics and are famous for their generous assistance.

Now the track climbs through geometrical, caramel-colored layers of rock, and a landscape completely sterile. Harry says that this steppe area is believed in the past to have had considerable numbers of *Acacia tortilis* and *Zizyphus lotus*, all of which have now almost entirely disappeared, thanks to the nomad's destructive habit of cutting all vegetation for fuel and charcoal. Later we cross several trucks headed north and loaded with *Acacia*. When we ask them where they are going, they tell us they are going to Misurata with a load of firewood contracted for by Misurata contractors. Apparently even these few remaining trees are not benefiting the needy local people, but are being sold to an area which is entirely well off.

Our interest in scenery is waning as the way to Uweinat stretches on and on. Maps here are seldom accurate and distances are never definite, and consequently no one of us knows how far from Uweinat we are, but we *do* know that our gas is going. When at the end of a long up-grade we come on a couple of palm-thatched houses, sure sign that an oasis is near, we feel much brighter. Then we see some shining wheat fields and date palms, and the next second we are driving between mud-walled houses and gardens and arrive suddenly in the center of a tiny town in the shade of a truly magnificent *Acacia albida* tree of whose historic past we have read.

This *Acacia* has been written about by travelers for more than a century, and probably venerated during all its lifetime, because it is a marabut, or shrine, and marks the burial place of a holy man. The practical application of this sanctity means that the tree may not be cut nor harmed in any way, which is probably the only reason that it has survived. Even its seed may not be picked, but can only be collected from the ground. It stands about sixty feet high, with an enormous trunk, surrounded by many small trunks which have grown up from the suckers. It is in flower now, and delicate, pale yellow *Acacia* blooms cover the tree.

The feeling of peace and sanctuary this shady, holy, ancient tree gives to the little African village is enhanced by the sight of several old men sitting gossiping in its cool, dark shadow. At the same time our own hopes are raised by the sight of an oil company truck parked with its cab in the shade. At this moment, a tall, thin, angular figure dressed in long, full Fezzani trousers, with bare feet struck into Tuareg sandals and bearded face partly hidden under a ten-gallon Stetson, comes ambling up to Harry, looks at him and says, in an American drawl, "Hi, didn't I meet you at the Underwater Club in Tripoli? I'm Pete Howard."

Harry looks again at the exotic figure, now half-Tuareg and half-Texan in costume, and says, "Yes, we did meet there, but you can't blame us for not recognizing you today! Are you stationed out here?"

Pete laughs, quite happy at the idea that he looks very different from a Tripoli oil clubman. "Yes, I'm here in charge of the exploratory camp for Esso. Our camp is just around the corner. What are you folks doing here?"

"On the way to Ghat," says Harry. "But one of our cars has a gas leak that we can't find. We'll not get far at the rate we are losing fuel."

"I have a top mechanic here," says Pete. "Let him look and see what he can do. We're equipped for any type of shop work out here for our own vehicles."

Harry accepts the offer gratefully, and a few minutes later the German mechanic, one of Rommel's corps once, Pete says, has located the trouble and says a welding job is needed. Pete tells him to go ahead and do the work, while he takes us out to visit his camp. Pete loads Harry and me and Hammet into his own Rover, which has no top and is stripped of all extra weight to give it extra mobility. The other car is to follow us.

Pete's camp, described by him as "just around the corner," turns out to be something rather different. We turn at right angles to the track we were on and take off across country, leaving Uweinat behind, traveling as the crow flies and in midair, it seems, such velocity the stripped car has. We turn a dozen "corners" of dunes and crawl up and down sand pyramids like flies, Pete riding the car like a horseman. At the top of the steepest sand slope we come to a small, high plateau where camp has been established, camp being a dozen tents with Pete's tent set slightly apart. Pete unloads us here, and then as the other car has not arrived he turns back again to see why.

It turns out that the heavily loaded Rover has balked at the final slope. Leaving the car where it is to await our return, Gerry, Badreddin and Assad get in Pete's car and return with him to the camp, where Pete has suggested that we eat. Welcome news to all of us, as it is three o'clock and we are starving.

Our host has eaten long ago, but his cook promptly produces some hot, thick, black bean soup which clings most comfortably to our insides. Well fed now and able to take an interest in things, I ask Pete, "Do you like working way out here?"

"Yes. I am completely happy here."

"You don't get lonely?"

"No. Anyway, we get oil company visitors by air — too many! And Mamie flew out the other day, but she hates this place! Wouldn't stay a night for any price!"

Mamie is Pete's charming wife, much better known to us than Pete. Mamie is a very attractive young woman, the soul of gaiety and friendliness, with a lovely singing voice — but no hermit's wife!

"Do you find many artifacts here?" Harry asks.

"Plenty! It's an archeological gold mine — as well as an oil mine."
Pete shows us some arrowheads, and a Stone Age adz. "It's not just
the geology and archeology that are interesting in this area, it's the
people. There are some marvelous old Tuareg characters about. I've
got one old boy who's teaching me Temaheq."

Pete's attitude here in the desert is far from being that of an oil
man in exile. In fact, the geologists of the oil exploration period
whom I have met have considered themselves in exile when tied to a
city desk.

After lunch, he returns us to the shade of the *Acacia albida* where
the Land Rover is awaiting us in good condition again, thanks to oil
company mechanics, but empty of gas. Then begins a dicker with
Pete about gasoline, of which he also is short. He agrees to give us
what he can spare, which we hope will get us to Ghat, and commis-
sions us to collect there on his behalf the gasoline which he has previously loaned to a police Land Rover in Ghat — *if* the police at
Ghat *have* any gas! That gas, assuming the police have any, should
get us back to Uweinat, by which time, five days from now, Pete
hopes to have more gas himself, and promises us enough to take us
back to Ubari. And thus begging, trading, doing anything except
buying it with money, whose value vanishes completely out here, we
get gas for Ghat.

We wave goodbye to Pete and pull out of Uweinat, noticing a
number of *Acacia tortilis* trees on the outskirts, but no more *A. albida*, as the marabut's shrine in Uweinat is the only *A. albida* in all
Libya. It is now four o'clock, and we have close to one hundred
miles still between us and Ghat, and Pete has said that the road ahead
is worse than that behind us. I don't notice any difference, myself, as
bad is bad. All travel here is a competition between man and machine
to see which will break up first. So far, we have outlasted the machine, which is fortunate, as we have no spare parts for ourselves.

We cross an arm of the Monti Acacus at 4000 feet, and turn due
south and follow the Wadi Tanezoft, a dry valley which lies between the Acacus Mountains now on our left and the Tassili N'Ajjer
mountain range. The latter is located mostly in Algeria, just across

the border which we are now paralleling. These mountain masses have peaks between 5000 feet and 6000 feet, and although a mile is no height in mountains, these bare, stark, rocky masses without trees, shrubs, grass or clouds to hide in look higher than they are.

Jebel Jinn

In this region of the Tassili N'Ajjer massif in Algeria the oldest caveman art in the world exists, discovered here a few years ago in Tassili caves by French explorers. Some of the rock frescoes date back to 8000 B.C. The story these pictures tell is one of the most amazing things in the whole Sahara. The lives they depict and the activities they portray, combined with the beauty and delicacy of their style and the sophisticated technique and expert perspective of their execution, provide one with a new concept of the phrases "Stone Age" and "caveman." One hundred fifty tracings on paper and exact color reproductions have recently been made of these works of art, and placed on exhibit in the Museum of Man in Paris for the world to see. By these, it seems that we are due for a revolution in our ideas of Stone Age man.

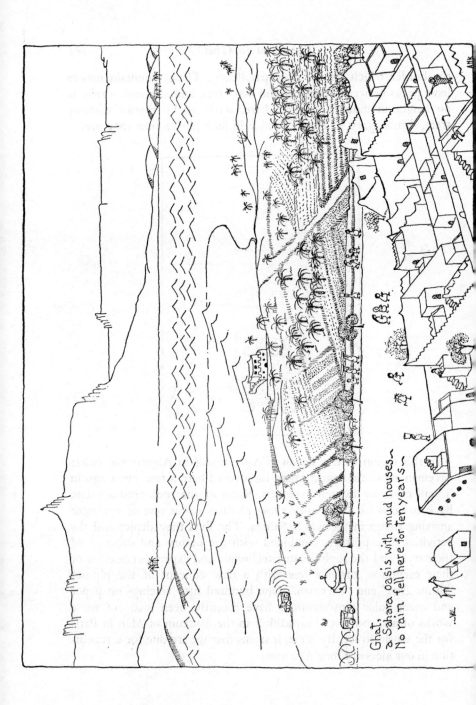

Ghat,
a Sahara oasis with mud houses~
No rain fell here for ten years~

In my notebook for this pre-Ghat area I have drawn a sharp-edged outline of dark geometrical shapes, quite unmountain-like, but part of the Hoggar massif. At the bottom is scrawled, "We are rushing madly towards this!" On the next page I have a collection of small, round black mushrooms afloat in a bowl of brown gravy, with the note that "These mushrooms are mountains." Then as the sun goes down behind the distant massif, I have noted, "Little brown ant hills (several hundred meters high!) pop up in front of us, quickly turning purple in the lowering sun, except for a shimmer of white calcium on top like drifting snow."

With the sun now lost behind the mountains the shadowed landscape grows increasingly ghoulish. It is quite fitting that at this moment we should arrive at the foot of the Jebel Jinn, a craggy, tortured pinnacled mountain which, according to legend, is inhabited by powerful and unpleasant supernatural jinn. Looking at this landscape at sunset, black and ragged against a burning sky, I feel quite willing to leave it undisputed with the jinn.

Rapidly the scene about us turns dark violet then black, and soon there is nothing to tell us where the road is except when we get off it and suddenly strike a wadi bed — and my neck snaps. It is eight o'clock when we suddenly realize that we are traveling smoothly on a real road. Then all in a moment, with no warning of lights ahead, no glow even in the sky, the road twists abruptly — and we are in Ghat. By the starlight we can see white walls running beside the road, and dark shadowed palms, and then proceeding slowly around another twist we arrive at the police station. Here we exchange greetings and ask directions, and then with a policeman walking amiably beside us carrying his oil lamp to show the way we are led to the rest house.

17. The Tuareg

HERE we are immediately with friends, for in Ghat, a Tuareg oasis, both men and women are free to come and go as they wish — almost too free for our good repose. All night in the rest house courtyard where we are trying to sleep we are visited by interested onlookers and spectators who have come to see the new arrivals. All night, dozing pleasantly, all of us travelers lying together under the great *Zizyphus spina christi* tree with its white bark shining and its canopy spread over us, I hear cheerful Fezzani voices making us at home with, "Lebas, lebas, lebas, Hammet! Lebas, Badreddin! Lebas, friends!"

We are up early the next morning and head for the marketplace, of which every village has one. Here in a small square partially enclosed by low, mud-brick shops we find eggs, tomatoes, bananas, peppers, woven baskets, food covers, gaudy, glittering colorful glass beads, woven bead belts and long necklaces in vivid blues, reds, yellows and greens combined in geometric patterns, and silver anklets and bracelets, and sheathed arm daggers attached to bracelets. Both the inhabitants of the marketplace and everything edible in it are heavily plastered with sparkling, iridescent-winged flies, of best and largest breeds.

As Ghat is a Tuareg oasis, or at least one which exists under the Tuareg tradition, the work is all done by either serfs or women, as the men never work. The women are all unveiled. The market ladies are certainly tough-looking babes; it was one of them, it seems, who was trying all night to get into Hammet's bed! She couldn't have been much to our elegant friend's taste. Still, it is pleasant to meet with friendly smiles, and natural curiosity without antagonism. It is good to escape from the too great contrasts between Moslem women and Western ones, which I find in Tripoli — a contrast which makes the Western woman seem bold and shameless and the Libyan Arab woman slightly ridiculous. Here in Ghat there is a relaxed atmosphere and the girls neither run and hide nor look embarrassed. And if they behave a bit boldly, this is accepted in their own tradition, and they are only doing what comes naturally. In fact, illicit love affairs amongst the unmarried women are not a disgrace, as the Tuareg women have a completely individual code of behavior and morals.

Now in the morning, in the glittering white sunlight, the market women sit cross-legged with their food items spread on round trays on the earth floor, and balancing their less breakable wares on their heads. They are dressed in dark, draped robes of black or indigo blue cotton with bright-colored head scarfs and baracans floating about their heads. They look decidedly grubby and smell very strong, and I can easily visualize them as washing with the desert sands! Nevertheless, Ghat has a wonderful artesian well and good water supply, and later on I found crowds of women at the public watering place, washing their clothes and themselves with great gusto. Perhaps it was I who smelled strong this morning!

The most objectionable inhabitant of Ghat is the fly. In a desert oasis one never sees a lone fly; instead one sees a fleshy aura of them surrounding every particle of food and every person. They are furious and frenzied, seldom seem to be airborne, and never travel alone. They mass in solid formations and cluster in large beady bunches like berries. They settle on the sticky mouths of children like blackberry jam, swarm on the watering eyes of infants, and turn small black baby faces iridescent with their shimmering gray wings.

For above all they love babies, and every infant carries a buzzing halo about his head. They stroll on his eyelids, flutter in his lashes, crawl in and out of his nostrils, cluster in the drip from his nose and cling to his baby lips. They never desert him; stark naked with all his orifices exposed, he is perfect fly-bait, and they go with him wherever he goes, his blackness a-shimmer with wings.

The Tuareg aristocrat has three outstanding physical characteristics: he is tall and white-skinned (if you can see his skin!) and has straight hair. As most people of Ghat are dark-skinned with kinky hair, they are probably not true Tuareg, but the offspring of slaves still working in the farmlands for the benefit of the aristocrats. The Tuareg themselves scorn all forms of work. They are, by tradition, warriors only!

Tuareg males are brought up on the saying, "Shame enters the family that tills the land!" and the men literally have never worked the land. The women do all the business and handle all the cash. They are also free to love where they wish, although I didn't see much to tempt a man in the market today.

In days past when the Sahara was a battle place for semi-nomad, wandering desert tribes, each one battling for survival, the Tuareg was the supreme warrior and was happiest when he was engaged in a bloody brawl. With the coming of comparative peace in the Sahara, once severely enforced by the French Legionnaires with the help of the Chaamba camel legions and now generally accepted, the warrior Tuareg has literally fought himself out of his old, once-respected job and place in desert life, and today the Tuareg men seem to have no valid reason for being. They sit about all day on the desert floor outside the city walls, covered from head to foot in indigo blue drapes, their faces completely veiled in dark blue folds of the litham, with the narrowest slit for their piercing black eyes which are all too frequently dimmed by trachoma.

They never remove their blue garments, and their bodies themselves are permanently dark blue from the effect of perspiration on the indigo dye. They do not remove their veils for sleeping, or even when eating, for by the Tuareg code of etiquette the mouth should never be seen, and to eat visibly is considered an ace of indecency. Consequently, they shove their food up under the veil, and suck it down. Reason suggests that these decadent, grubby, unsanitary men are pratically worthless in the world of today, but one still cannot escape a gasp of admiration at the sight of a tall, very straight, blue-robed Tuareg sitting like a ramrod on his racing camel.

These former warriors of the desert have always been a challenge to Sahara explorers, who are inclined to see them in a cloud of romance, perhaps because their lives embody overcivilized man's subconscious yearnings. In more than one way, Tuareg history justifies respect, for they not only fought their way up and down the African continent, but have in past years been responsible for trans-Saharan transport by camel convoy from Kano, in Central Africa, north to the Mediterranean Sea.

"Lebas, Hammel, lebas!" Ghat

Yet here also, in their second capacity as desert convoy leaders, one sees them balked by the twentieth-century changes which send trucks with huge-surfaced wheels, like sand-paddle-wheel steamers, and go-anywhere desert vehicles, which surpass the camel himself for sand travel. Today, the old slave trail from Kano north through Agades, through Ghat and through Ghadames to Tripoli may be followed by wheeled vehicles which take less than half the number of days that a camel caravan requires. Admittedly, no vehicle can travel alone, nor travel without a full stomach of gasoline and a complete assortment of spare parts, which in my mind should include a wooden leg and a liver replacement.

The Sahara is bathed in historical bloodshed whose truth is more lurid than fiction; its explorers have to be tough, hard, and brave — at the same time, they sometimes have a softer side.

In July 1825, Major Gordon Laing, a determined, courageous, conceited but lovable English Saharan explorer, was in Tripoli making preparations for an extensive desert trip to Timbuktu. He fell in love with Emma, the daughter of Hanmer Warrington, the British Consul there, and Emma fell madly in love with him. The Consul describes his daughter's attachment as being "wild, enthusiastic and romantic," and says that "every remonstrance was unavailing!" The two were determined to be married before Laing left for his trip.

The ceremony was performed in Tripoli by the British consul, no other means being available. But Warrington had doubts as to the legality of his performing the ceremony for his own daughter, and would not permit Emma to stay with her husband as his wife. As he himself said, "They were never one second from under my observation!" Consequently, Laing left for the Sahara with his love unfulfilled.

Near Wadi Ahennet in the Hoggar, Laing was attacked by Hoggar Tuareg and left for dead, with ten saber cuts on his head, others on his body, a bullet in his hip, both legs injured, both hands mangled, and one almost severed from his arm. Incredibly enough, he didn't die. He was nursed for three months by Arab friends, and recovered enough to cover four hundred miles of the worst desert in the world on his way south to Timbuktu. The city he rediscovered in the name of the British, though it had already been discovered by a Florentine, Benedetto Dei, by the Portuguese and by the French. Laing alone, however, left a journal of his trip.

He stayed two months in Timbuktu, and then left for a journey home. A few days distant from Timbuktu, and less than a year after he had been nearly murdered by the Tuareg, he was attacked by an Arab tribe and killed. He died from numerous spear thrusts, after which his head was cut off. Although a variety of Arab shieks and Timbuktu personnel were accused of complicity in the murder, there was no real proof of anything except that he was dead. And in the sun-warmed port of Tripoli, young Emma Warrington Laing became a widow without having been a wife.

The great human tragedy of desert explorers is not the lonely death in the sandstorm, or even death of thirst, but the unnumbered deaths of those who have utterly trusted the desert people, who have loved and idealized them, have believed they understood them, who have felt secure in their hands, perhaps because they have wished to feel secure, and who have in the end lost their lives at the hands of those whose ways, traditions and urgencies they have so much admired — but whom they failed in the crucial test to understand. Perhaps our bodies can travel more swiftly than our customs can change. Harry always likes to say about me, whom he believes to have a too trusting and romantic disposition, "They'll cry whilst they cut your throat!"

Charles de Foucauld was another romantic wanderer who loved the desert to death. De Foucauld, a member of an old, aristocratic French family and himself a marquis, first traveled in North Africa in Morocco in 1883. Here he became a Trappist monk in retreat at Beni Abbes. In 1904 he joined a desert patrol with the Frenchman Laperrine, famous for his Sahara air explorations. They traveled through the Hoggar, the tremendous and terrifying red desert massif which sprawls along the Tropic of Capricorn, and is peopled by the fiercest and most war-like of the Tuareg groups, the same who had chopped up Gordon Laing.

Here Father de Foucauld settled again in the very heart of the rust red rock surrounded by Sahara, and here he built his hermitage at Tamanrasset, which is today known as Fort Laperrine. Father de Foucauld had no ostentatious missionary zeal; his only aim was to lead, by a selfless example, some of the desert people whom he loved to what he saw as The Truth. Whether or not he succeeded in this, it is certain that through his scholarly study of the people he produced a dictionary of the Hoggar Tuareg dialect, called Temaheq, the only book of its kind and one which is in use today.

In 1916 a series of ferocious raids took place on all the French Sahara outposts. These were executed by the Tuareg of Ghat and the Fezzan, and probably instigated by the warring European powers who were at this time deeply involved in the western desert in Egypt, Cyrenaica, Tripolitania and Algeria. Most of the Tuareg raiders were armed with European arms which had come to them through the Senussiya who were promoting and exploiting the spirit of Islamic revival.

In December 1916 in a raid on Father de Foucauld's Hoggar hermitage Father de Foucauld himself was murdered by the raiders. Although the hermitage was in reality well armed, Father de Foucauld, rather than take arms against the attackers, met them unresistingly and fell a martyr to his own ideals. One is glad to say that the assassins were not De Foucauld's own Tuareg of the Hoggar but those of the Fezzan and Ghat groups, which existed in a state of perpetual warfare with the French desert outposts. For this reason De Foucauld's murder cannot justly be regarded as an act of treachery committed by those whom he had served and loved, but rather as one more example of the outcome of desert worship: those who love the Sahara will choose to die in it sooner than to survive away from it.

The old slave trails from Kano to the Mediterranean are marked by little heaps of bones, both human and animal, of slaves and camels who dropped by the track to die while the Tuareg caravan continued on its way, herding the miserable files of barefoot human beings across the shimmering, scorching landscape. In later days, the Sahara was marked again with other crosses with the mute statement, MORT POUR LA FRANCE. And today it is being marked once more, this time with MORT POUR LE PÉTROLE.

The Tuareg history is one of great warriors and careless murderers, of men who dealt out death recklessly, with no more serious thought than that with which we drown superfluous kittens. Yet today the master warrior sits veiled and silent in the sun while flies crawl unnoticed and unmolested over his unblinking eyelids.

Midday finds me standing alone in the old fort on the hilltop which overlooks Ghat. The fort was built by the Italians during their occupation of Libya, captured by the French in the Second World War, and finally turned over to Libya in 1956, the year in which the French theoretically gave up their administration of the Fezzan.

This is a perfect place from which to inspect the village, as most of the mud-walled houses are without roofs, or at least with only a small part of the housing area covered, and I can look down into the houses and spy on Fezzani family activities. The walls have delicate picot edgings, with triangular pyramids at the corners to give shade. I presume that the disregard of roofs is due to several facts, one being the almost complete lack of rain in Ghat, where there has been no rain, at the time of this visit, for ten years.* Add to this the facts that the women do not live in purdah but conduct their lives and loves openly and that men are in any case hidden behind their veils, even in their own homes, and there seems little need for roofing.

This fort is a wonderful place to meditate, but I really came up here to sketch the scene below. The massif around which we skirted last night, appearing then to be a black monster, today lies bare and angular and white in the sun's blaze. Between the monster and the oasis, and in all other directions around me, the desert glares in sculptured golden wavelets. Here at my feet, as if dropped by parachute from paradise, lies the most lovely oasis of all, feathered with the dainty green of palms, *Tamarix*, *Acacia* and Christ thorn and spread over with the pleasant verdure of gardens growing with Egyptian beans, peanuts, pumpkins, tomatoes and plots of shining barley.

The road by which we entered last night is now outlined in the bright green of cultivated gardens, as it comes sweeping in from the stark barrenness of the gravel valley which lies between the two great mountain masses of Monti Acacus and Tassili N'Ajjer. From utter vegetative desolation, one suddenly arrives in the center of the lush oasis.

This miracle of greenness exists because ground water is abundant here and found close to the surface. An artesian well in Ghat, originally dug to supply the Italian fort, flows constantly, and ditches carry its water to all the gardens. The lavish ground-water supply may in part be due to Ghat's location at the low point between two mountain masses, where humidity is bound to collect. It is also due to the fact that in the past a layer of water-bearing sandstone was raised by monoclinal flexure close to this area's land surface, and that this layer is still under sufficient artesian pressure to cause water to flow in dug wells or drilled ones.

Now to my ears comes faintly the most precious of all desert sounds, the rustle of running water, as below me the artesian waters move gently through the narrow ditches, spilling from level to level, with a legally regulated amount for each garden, as the blessed liquid

* A few years later, half the mud houses of Ghat were to be liquefied in an unprecedented "cloudburst," in this "cloudless" district!

finds and feeds the thirsty land. In this pleasant scene sounds the secret of oasis survival.

I climb down the hill and return to the village just in time for lunch at the rest house, or is it the police station? — the two are often combined — where we slept last night.

Harry and Gerry, Badreddin and Hammet have just come from a long discussion with the mudir of Ghat, and the amenokal, the chief of the local Tuareg, about the future of Ghat. The sad fact is that Ghat has no future; her Negro slaves who work the land are dying off, and her young men are leaving because there is no longer a living to be made.

Her prosperity in times past has been derived from the caravan trade which traveled north and south from Kano through Ghat to Tripoli and back to Kano, carrying slaves, gold, ivory, ostrich feathers and leather work and returning with salt and silks. Now the caravan routes have decayed, from the abolition of slave trade and the competition of the Mediterranean sea routes. For in the past it was not the Tuareg nor the Arab, but the Negro slave who cultivated the oases and beat back the Sahara.

My companions are also discussing the fact that a small girl has been offered for sale to Hammet to take back with him to Tripoli!*

I observe with pleasure that Badreddin is preparing a couple of chickens for a fresh stew to be eaten with our spaghetti. I am especially grateful to see that Badreddin is plucking the chickens himself, a job which I hate.

After a tremendous meal to satisfy our rapacious appetites we all settle down in the shaded courtyard to snooze. But the biting flies do not permit this and we are wide awake when the informal afternoon reception begins, as various persons of importance arrive to pay their respects — or possibly for us to pay our respects to them. I am usually in a state of confusion as to who is honoring whom, as Arab salutations are so copious and customs of hospitality so lavish that all

---

* The fact that such a suggestion is regularly made to travelers in the desert is a cause of great embarrassment to the Libyan government, which does not countenance the traffic in human beings any more than does any other respectable government. However, it is not always possible to see that the law is respected in every isolated oasis of the Sahara. The law is the responsibility of the state, but its observance is the responsibility of the people.

persons present seem to be honored. As we are six and our visitors are also six and there is no place to sit except our cots, we all settle down in close propinquity on them, while Hammet prepares tea.

Gerry's cot has two people on it already, and when the seventh visitor later arrives, a tall, wide, robust policeman who settles down on Gerry's cot, the cot, with a loud splintering noise, collapses on the pavement. Tremendous roars of joy from everyone greet this disaster, and from then on the success of the party is assured. Just why I laughed so hard when this happened and still laugh when I remember the scene, I am not certain, but I suspect that it is because I have now acquired the Eastern habit of laughing at all disasters which do not happen to me. Perhaps hilarity is based on a sensation of relief at one's own escape, more than rejoicing at the bad luck of others. Anyway, the collapse of the cot completely and immediately assured the true success of the party, and from this event onward, with the cot flattened out like a skeleton on the floor, risqué stories were told (being purified and partially interpreted for me by Hammet) with uproarious success.

The locals all had personal memories of the desert, which we listened to with awe, while our party had hair-raising stories of city life which grew in size and excitement as the evening waxed. By nine o'clock we were all dear old friends and there was no sign of our guests' departure, and I was growing hungry again. Our food supplies could not be stretched to entertaining seven lusty policemen, and I was trying to resign myself to a night of tea and anecdotes when I saw Badreddin moving off to where he had stacked the cooking pots, which he now began to scour in a suggestive way. Then Hammet started to move restlessly about, and Harry disappeared in a corner to fuss with his plant presses, first asking for assistance from Gerry and me. In time, seeing their audience disappearing, our visitors began to wander away, not forgetting many expressions of thanks for tea and promises to see us all in the morning. Very swiftly then, Badreddin and I once more put spaghetti on to cook, this time without any stew.

We all sleep in the courtyard each night to escape, if possible, from the smell of the waterless W.C. which has been accumulating its burden since the last slave train came through! It is awkward being in the center of town, and having to dash to its outskirts morning and evening. I should prefer to camp outside the town on the desert, but the hospitable police insist that we stay here — and use the modern conveniences! Anyway, this courtyard, for me, is unforgettable; the *Zizyphus* tree is a spectral white mother in the starlight above us as we lie in our cots each night.

This is our last night here; we are in bed, but no one seems sleepy. Badreddin is talking with Harry.

"Did you know that the people of Ghat are the most individualistic in all Libya?" Badreddin asks.

"I thought you were all that way!"

Badreddin laughs. "Yes, perhaps. But these people never think alike about anything, the policeman says. That is the reason that Ghat is divided into two quarters, the 'Yes' quarter, and the 'No' one."

"Is that big policeman himself from Ghat?"

"No, Ghadames. He's a real Tuareg."

"The ancestors of these people in Ghat were certainly black," Harry says.

"I think the original people of Ghat were the Atara; they're black. Only the Tuareg doesn't describe the Negro as black, he calls him blue; and he says that the Hausa is black, the Arabs are white, and the Tuareg are red!"

"What about the Jebel Jinn," Harry asks. "Do the evil spirits ever come down here to Ghat?"

"Oh, yes. But there are holy men in Ghat who can throw out the evil spirits of the jinn!" says Badreddin, laughing.

"Maybe we take one holy man back to Tripoli with us!" suggests Hammet.

"Instead of that little girl!" somebody says.

"Is it still true that the Tuareg won't work?" I ask. "That he thinks it is a disgrace?"

"Oh, yes, my mother. He must save all his strength for love! He is an 'Expert' for love!"

Much laughter.

"Very nice life!" says Hammet.

The next day we are looking back at Ghat in the early morning light, slightly nostalgic but not actually discontent to be on the road again, our hearts filled with mixed pictures of this Sahara oasis. In our memories we can feel the blazing sun and the welcome coolness of shade, and see the jewel-green foliage and the glowing color of sun-drenched skins, the white teeth of laughter in dark faces, the wrinkled visages of "old crones" of thirty years, the round, dusky smoothness of young wives of twelve, the immobility of babies' eyes outlined by metallic-winged flies. We can smell the reek of rotting vegetation and the stink of dirty drains, and hear the silence of the star-strung sky by night, and the splash of falling water.

Hammet did not buy the little girl. But as a parting gesture, just as we were all packed into the Land Rovers, one of the old market ladies came up and tried to sell *me* a slave! All principles of human freedom aside, the last thing I want to be responsible for is introducing any more primitives to twentieth-century civilization.

18. The Sahara Is Desert

"THERE have always been odd characters who love the desert. I am one. Hammet hates it; Badreddin takes it in stride; Assad is preoccupied, whether by sand or by sea, with his liver; Gerry is happy any place; Peter prefers his caravan in England to a Rover in the Sahara; and Harry seldom admits to perfect contentment. But I know that not one of us would have missed this trip."

I wrote these philosophical words sitting in the Land Rover at Uweinat waiting for Harry to find Pete Howard, who we hoped had gas for us. The friendly Ghat police, having had their own gas supplies renewed by police transport, had at Pete's suggestion supplied us with the gas that they owed Pete, and this had brought us back here to Uweinat. Now we were hoping that Peter had received his new supplies by lorry and that he could give us enough for our return journey to Sebha, where gas would again be a commodity to be bought with money. Then we could return the gas to Pete from Sebha (a gas drum can usually hitchhike a lorry ride) or repay his company in Tripoli.

Harry doesn't find Pete, who has flown to Tripoli, but has left word with his mechanic to replenish our gas tanks when we come, hamdu li'llah! It is interesting to think of the number of fortunate coincidences on which this kind of trip must depend. If one allowed for every emergency, the Land Rovers could never roll. Nevertheless, it's a wonderful feeling to know that your gas tanks are full.

Filled now with sanguine expectations for reaching Ubari in good time, we turned our backs on Uweinat in the early afternoon, securely set on the road home. Though the basic mileage would be the same, we anticipated making the return trip to Tripoli in less time than the voyage out, chiefly because we had now explored the flora and landscape thoroughly. And there was Ramadan to keep in mind.

Hammet was driving, and we were alternately slithering swiftly over untracked sand, with the soft, whispering sound and lack of vibration which is so exhilarating, or jolting our kidneys and guts on a horrible corduroy track. I was wedged in the middle between Hammet and Harry, trying to brace myself against the bumps and keep my head from hitting the roof. Harry, however, was relaxing and going limply with the motion in an apparently successful manner.

Odd characters who love the desert.

"Don't brace yourself," he advised me. "Just let yourself flop. It's much easier on you."

So I relaxed and flopped and vibrated in a teeth-chattering state.

"Get her up to seventy, Hammet," Harry suggested. "She'll go smoother on this washboard if you go faster."

Hammet got her up and we shivered instead of vibrating, and it was certainly better.

"Yyyyou were rrrrrrright, Hhhhhhhhhharry," I nattered. "Rrrr-rrrelaxxxxing is bbbbbbest!"

Bang, bang, smash, bump, and God knows what! Suddenly I hit the roof with my head, then hit the seat with my tail bone, felt an excruciating pain mid-spine, and collapsed under the load of the rear seat luggage which shot forward on top of me as the car plunged to a shattering stop in a sand pit. We had come on one of the great soft sand gaps, probably a collapsed foggara,* in the hard corduroy surface of the track, and it had stopped us dead. There was no good reason why we hadn't turned over. No one spoke for a minute; we were too surprised at being alive.

Then I tried to straighten up and felt again an excruciating pain in the middle of my back, and screamed. Hammet looked horrified and asked if I was hurt, and Harry said I'd be better in a minute, we were lucky to be alive!

"Take the bloody suitcases off my head," I begged. "I've broken something, and I can't straighten up!"

Just then Gerry's car hauled up to us and he jumped out, and ran over, looking anxious. "Everyone O.K.?"

By now Harry and Hammet were repiling the luggage in the rear of the car and roping it in again. I tried once more to straighten up, and screamed again. Gerry's expressive face distorted with sympathy, and he put his arms around me and lifted me bodily into an easier position. "You must have strained your back!"

"I think I've broken one of those things in my spine — a disc, or something. It feels exactly as if two of them had got pushed together."

Naturally, nobody believed me, but in any case the show must go on in the desert with dusk coming and the campsite not reached. Before we started up once more Hammet insisted on putting his nice white embroidered pillow (all the rest of us had dirty ones by now) under me, and I sat on it on the outside seat, and hung like death to the door to take the weight off my seat, but the next three hours were hell.

"Drive carefully, Hammet," I begged.

* Subterranean water passage.

"Yes, Mother, I am." Bang, crash, bumpety bump, for no one can drive carefully, gingerly or gently on desert tracks at sundown.

"Can't you go slower, Hammet? If you hit another sand gap I'll be dead!"

"Yes, Mother, I am." But fifty miles is the speed for washboard, and fifty we go.

"Is your back better now, Agnes?" asked Harry.

"No, it's horrible. If I could only sit on my stomach instead of my bottom for a while! I'm afraid I'll stiffen up tonight, and not be able to get to my feet tomorrow."

"It's sure to be better tomorrow!"

"I don't think so. I can feel the things crunch! There's just one thing I want to think about now — that's the whiskey I'm going to drink when we get to Ubari!"

Finally we got there, to the dear little rest house across from the dear little police station, with the same dear little policemen, all of whom came over to tea with us once again. It was like home, it seemed. Maybe I'd live!

Meanwhile Harry and Gerry got me out of the car and onto my feet, and I found I could stand better than I could sit, which cheered me. By now, the idea of being a charge on my companions' patience worried me as much as the pain. Still, I had nursed Assad, I reminded myself, when he had a bilious attack, and held his head when he vomited and given him my hot water bottle when we thought he had appendicitis . . . Hot water bottle! An inspiration!

An hour later I was sitting on the hot water bottle and holding a hot whiskey toddy in my hands, and although it sounds like treatment by counter-irritation, my back felt better.

I regret to say that in the long run whiskey did not mend my disc, and Harry had to haul me to my feet next morning, and every morning for the last seven days of the trip. If I could have gone to a doctor when the pain was most acute, I would have gone. But the Sahara doesn't specialize in expert medical services, and by the time I got back to Tripoli, which is no medical paradise either, the pain was lessening. I managed to persuade myself that time would heal me — and it did, although medical examination some time later showed that I had had a fractured disc.

Of course discs differ, also treatments. If you have red, white and blue discs and belong to the American aid group or the Embassy or the Air Force, you are flown to Germany or the States for expert treatment. If you have a nationally unattached disc and belong to the United Nations, you push your disc back into place and fix it with a thumb tack, or ask your husband to put in a washer.

Having come from the extreme southwestern boundary of Libya at Ghat, we are laboriously but happily retracing our steps in a northeastern direction.

A return trip always has both its sorrows and consolations. I admit to enjoying the privilege of regular baths, hair shampoos and manicures, and these loom pleasantly ahead as we travel towards Tripoli; now there is the additional incentive for arrival of not having to bounce up and down on my sore disc. There may be letters waiting for us from Jean and George — doubtful, but always to be hoped for! I already look forward to seeing Mohamed, and hearing his new problems and suggesting possible solutions. I want to see if the little Damascus climbing rose is blooming now, and if the tiny new cactus in the pot is going to flower with a petal like a drop of blood, and if the grass is taking hold at last, despite the sand and worms . . .

Yet I dread being caught up again in the endless round of conventional actions which make up my daily life in Tripoli, but which count for nothing out here under the Sahara stars. I dislike discoursing in polite banalities — yet cannot conceive of a cocktail party at which one shouts the verities above the tinkle of iced drinks, into the unlistening, unhearing ears. I look forward to a swim from the rocks at the Underwater Club, and a mixed drink at the bar — not half as strong as the ones we drink unmixed in the Sahara — but served at the Club with smart girls nearby. But smart girls of whom I can only stand a limited amount! Perhaps it is the duality of my life in Libya which makes me enjoy it so much, for it is both basic and gay.

Now I have a bond with the Sahara. Before leaving Tripoli I was reading ethnographic notes by a French historian of the Libyan desert, who wrote of the joy of the desert men in singing their nomadic songs of the seasons, especially of the harvest season, and of the winds of the Sahara. The historian translated some of these singing poems from Arabic into French, and I, translating with my stumbling French, wrote them out for myself in English. They were simple, primal, imaginative, and steeped in the essence of the abject dependence of the nomad on the moods of the Sahara. Who, except a follower of Islam, could accept destruction after destruction as sent by Allah and make a song of it; suffer loss after loss, drought, famine and sand flood and sing again; celebrate every success of crops, increase of flocks, birth of a child, or vista of beauty as sent to him by Allah and sing again of Allah's will be done? Job, perhaps. As I read those songs in Tripoli, they seemed far away from me in time, as well as in space.

But now I have a bond with the Sahara, and I more clearly hear the voice of the nomad when he sings. When he hymns the brutal force of the Sahara winds, I feel a bond. When he tells his children that the wind of the ghibli leaves nothing living behind it on plain or dune, "not even the fetus in the mother's womb," I recognize his cry. When he tells his children that the wind from the north draws up from the earth the shrubs for his flocks to feed on, and makes women fertile and men virile, while the child in the womb grows strong, I hear his song.

Now, from Ubari we pass through African-inhabited Twish, and then along an oasis strip where a string of tiny places is noted on the map only as "potable water." We are working our way up towards Sebha now, and before we approach it we sight what I remember so well — the vivid pink dunes brought south by the winds of the Hamada el Hamra, the Red Desert, as it weathers its stony red plains. These gaudy dunes have drifted against the jagged black shapes of the distant monsters of Jebel Soda, Black Mountain.

For a couple of days then the suffocation of Sebha grips us. Marianne has flown to Tripoli, but the men of our party are here to discuss their findings from Ghat and Ubari with the Fezzan ministers and directors. The story is always the same; the oases are dying from loss of young male life. If matters are to be mended, not only must plantations and other projects be begun, but manpower must be inveigled back and young men must be shown a better oasis living.

Can this be done? The oasis mudirs have shaken their heads at us all along the line; the young men won't come back! And if they do not come? Well, a little more time and the oases die.

From Sebha we got to Wishka, the divide, where we drink joyfully once again some fresh, cold, nonsaline water. We cross through the wicked Jebel Soda, covered as if with scattered fragments of jet and cut steel of celestial origin, the most vicious-looking stretch of the trip, all glittering, angulated black. We come to Hun and buy some dates to take home, but we do not sleep here. Instead we hurry on to have the last night of the trip where we spent the first night . . .

All the way back we had counted the days to Ramadan, and in the final dark nights out we had searched the blackness of the sky for the possible appearance of a new moon. It was useless for Harry to remind us that it was all written down in black and white in the almanac: we didn't have an almanac, and anyway, no good Moslem likes to challenge the control of Allah by predicting even an unalterable date.

Now, just after dark, back again in Misurata and only a few hours away from Tripoli, we realize that the trip has worked out as we had planned it, and we will be home for the beginning of Ramadan. Already Hammet, Badreddin and Assad have ascertained from the Imam of the Misurata Mosque that the new moon of the ninth Moslem lunar month was seen tonight in Zliten, that the guns have boomed with sunset, and that tomorrow with sunrise all Moslems will begin their daylight fast.

But Ramadan is a time of feasting as well as fasting, a time of celebration as much as prayer. It is a time when there is a drawing together in all the Moslem world amongst all Moslems, with a resultant exclusion of all nonbelievers. For this reason, there is amongst us tonight a feeling of nostalgia and a tinge of melancholy, for we all realize that our fraternity will soon be split.

We are sitting quietly in the small, hideous little hotel parlor waiting for supper to be ready; I am thinking sadly that this is our last night, yet at the same time I am thinking fondly of the wonderful, long, hot bath I will have when I get home. Harry, Gerry and I are drinking whiskey, while Hammet, Badreddin and Assad are drinking small glasses of sweet Arab tea.

Suddenly into this tranquil scene comes rushing a thin-faced, tense-looking little European in a bush jacket. He greets Harry as a long lost friend, and Harry returns the greeting with equal enthusiasm. I immediately understand that the little man must be engaged in Harry's profession or an allied one, perhaps botany, or ecology, agronomy or agriculture, if not actually in forestry, for Harry's enthusiasm is usually more scientific than social.

The newcomer proves to be Mr. W. W. Rajkowski, a Pole by birth, who fought with the free Polish forces in the desert and after the war became a British subject. He is in Libya now to study tribal land laws, he tells us, for which work he is being financed by an infinitesimal geographical research bursary from Durham University. A doctor of science whose hobby is botany, his chief pleasure in life is making small pastel sketches of the wild flowers which he collects on his travels. Diffidently, he shows us his notebook filled with many delicate, lovingly drawn flowers, fragile desert specimens which have survived in brave defiance of the brutal climate. As he shows us his dainty specimens, Mr. Rajkowski's eyes gloat adoringly over this small, painfully come-by storehouse of beauty.

But it isn't the sketches which delight my Libyan companions, but the fact that Mr. Rajkowski speaks to them in Arabic of such excellent, precise and fluent quality as to make them exclaim with joy, and praise him enthusiastically as a true Arabist. Glowing with pleasure at their praise, Mr. Rajkowski soon confides to us his sanguine plan to travel to Kufra, the famous desert oasis in the southeast Libyan Sahara, traveling exclusively by camel, accompanied only by a Bedawi guide. He expects to collect botanical specimens on the way, and to live in Bedawi fashion with desert frugality. He assures us that his experiences in the desert fighting forces have fitted him for a trip of this kind.

Our Libyan friends now look fully as alarmed as Harry and I do at hearing his plan. Their lives as city Arabs are as far removed from those of the desert nomad as Harry's life and mine. But Mr. Rajkowski is obviously delighted with his camel plan! He says that he has no money to supply himself with a desert vehicle, but even if he had, he still prefers camel travel, which by its very slowness is the best way to study both vegetation and living beings, human and otherwise.

This is true, we all agree, but the question arises now whether there is still time in Libya to continue at a camel's pace. Where retrogression already has momentum, should one attempt to halt it by whatever means possible? Or should one ignore it, and seeking still the perfect answer instead of the practical one, continue slowly by camelback?

Mr. Rajkowski, at least, is completely satisfied with his plan for a camel-pace expedition, and throughout dinner, which he eats with us, he is the center of conversation in both Arabic and English. He glows and sparkles in both languages, and his ordinary, not physically very attractive little face, is redeemed by intelligence, interest and animation. Here is a man whose very essence is loneliness, and most of whose days are undoubtedly passed in solitude; yet tonight he has found companionship.

This story has a sequel. Months later we were again all traveling together in the Fezzan desert. Listening one night to a nomad guide's story of desert tragedies, we learned that a body had been found on the tremendous desert stretch known as the Rebiana Sand Sea, which is notorious as the cruelest obstacle on the route between Sebha and Kufra. At the time of finding the body it was not easy to recognize, although after investigation it was identified by a book of flower sketches which lay beside it.

Some time before this discovery, a Bedawi who had been traveling with Mr. Rajkowski as guide had arrived at Kufra and reported that his companion had died of thirst in the Harugh massif. Just that — just died of thirst.

There may have been foul play, but there probably was not. What a Saharan Bedawi, desert born and bred, could survive might easily be the death of a fair-skinned, northern European. One lifetime does not adapt a body to desert conditions; it requires generations. The little Pole might easily have become too weak from thirst to travel long before the Bedawi would collapse. Bodily endurance won.

To those who know the desert the story the Bedawi told is neither strange nor mysterious, but a familiar tale told once again of the outsider who challenges desert stretches. Thus, to the end, Mr. Rajkowski was a lonely little man.

A death of this sort is one which anyone with imagination who travels the Sahara will have experienced in his fancy more than once.* We love to hear tales of the miraculous, desert-bound wells, the wonderful spring-fed oases, the life-giving water holes that every true desert nomad, rat, camel or human being can find. But we travelers do not encourage the stories of the years when the miraculous wells go dry, when the once green oases lie seared and arid and unfed by the springs, and when the water holes are only dry, caked clay bordered by bleaching bones. Yet these are the normal years. For the fact is that these amazing sources of drinkable water found in great stretches of desert desiccation seem miraculous, and that is exactly what they are — and miracles don't take place every season.

And now the trip is ended. We had all gone out to see the Libyan desert, Libyans and foreigners together, all equally sightseers there, with a common Sahara goal. But more than the desert, we had found in its desolate stretches something memorable that we hadn't bargained on — a period of complete, perfect and unblemished companionship regardless of religion, nationality or race. This was true for Harry and me, and I know that it was the kind of relationship which had to exist for all of us, or it could not exist for any of us. In the desert, we had quickly come to accept and take for granted this miraculous companionship.

But here tonight in the semi-civilization of a small village hotel on the edge of Tripoli, with Ramadan about to divide our group in halves again, we become acutely conscious of the precarious and precious quality of this fragile relationship. Now suddenly we fear that this may slip from us. Now sadly we see that life may never be like this again.

Next day outside our Giorgimpopoli villa, in the glare of the sun and the cool of the sea, our Mohamed welcomes us home with cries of horror at our sand-coated condition, and secret envy of our trip. There is a great stack of mail inside, he says; already the world closes

---

* *Time*, June 25, 1965, gives the report of five German travelers who died of thirst and exposure on the way to Sina in the Libyan-Egyptian border desert.

in. Gerry and Assad say salam 'alekum and addio, and head for home. Hammet is fidgeting to get home for a bath; Harry is anxious to go inside and press his plants. Only Badreddin and I are melancholic, unwilling to end the trip.

"In Arabic," Badreddin recalls, "Sahara *is* desert. Shall we go again, you think, my father? In sha'Allah?"

In sha'Allah! If God wills! In sha'Allah!" Harry says.

Who can say more?

19. Marianne's Little Women

Only he who understands is sad.

Arab Proverb

I HAVE been putting off writing the end of this story, waiting for time to dull my indignation. Time doesn't.

Our Giorgimpopoli telephone rang one glorious, breathless, African evening. To hear the phone, which so seldom worked, ringing magnificently gave me a shock; an even greater one was to hear the clear, sweet voice of Marianne, speaking in Tripoli instead of in the desert.

"I'm in the Grand Hotel, Agnes dear, and I want very much to see you. I've just flown up from the Fezzan. There's something that worries me, and I must talk to you."

"Marianne! It is wonderful to hear from you! I'll come right in, and bring you back home for dinner with us!"

Twenty minutes later Harry and I picked her up in the lobby of the hotel. I thought she was looking rather too pale and thin, but ghibli season in the Fezzan is no health builder. Still, she was full of enthusiasm, as we drove home, and she described her success with the plans for the new training school to be built in Sebha, the first school of its sort ever built in the Libyan desert.

"And just think!" Marianne said triumphantly. "The husband of one of my old night school pupils has given us the land free, an outright gift forever, on which we are going to build the Sayyida Fatima School! It's to be named after the Queen, you know. Just think what that gift means! This man's own wife was our pupil, and he likes the result so much that he gives us the land!"

"Well, so he should, Marianne, after what I saw of your work down there! But your training school is considerably more ambitious than your night classes, isn't it? You say that you want one girl from each important oasis to study at the school. And after that, what does she do?"

"Oh, dear Agnes, this is the real point. She goes back to her own oasis and starts a little center there to teach the girls of her own village what she has learned. This is so important. Each one of our Sayyida Fatima pupils is to become a focal point of her own."

"But *can* each one? Not every girl can teach others, and enthuse others."

"I think that these girls will be able to because our school goal is so simple. That is the best part of it. We do not try to supplant Arab traditions and customs with Western ones. We do not wish to introduce machinery for work that hands can do. Our only aim is to teach these young desert women to use more fully the natural desert resources around them. They have always been dependent upon these resources, and they may well remain so forever. We only try to show them every possibility in these resources, and perhaps to give them a fresh outlook on them. These desert women are so wonderful, so courageous, so proud, so resourceful, that I know they can do it.

"Our school will be built as a Fezzani house is built, of stones and mud. Our kitchen will have a Fezzan fireplace, exactly the same as the girls have in their homes. We shall help them to learn to produce better meals in the same surroundings as their own. Do you know what they eat at home now? Bazin and dates and sometimes a little wheat pasta! *Any* improvement in this diet will help them. Any changes which the girls see in our school kitchen will be such as the girls can make for themselves in their own homes. In our school we shall accept all the desert limitations, but we intend also to realize its best possibilities."

"Marianne, if I hadn't gone into those Sebha Gedid homes with you myself, I could never have appreciated how completely without possessions these people are!"

"Yes, these girls come to us from houses which are unfurnished except for mats which they weave from reeds and a few pieces of homemade cooking pottery and basketry. Our girls will come from the poorest level of Libyan life, and that is the level to which they must return. Any improvement they can make for themselves must be costless, but it will be priceless to them."

Marianne's little women.

"Has LPDSA* definitely promised the money?"

"Yes, it is definite. And now I must travel to all the oases to select my pupils, and then persuade their fathers and mothers that they should come to Sebha to our school. This is going to be my most difficult job. We wish to take only twelve girls to start out with, but it is a two-year course, and they must come for the full two years. This means that there will be no wives, for no husband would permit his wife to stay away from home for such a long time. However, a divorced wife can come. There are divorcées there as young as fourteen and fifteen years. If a girl has children, she may bring them. We really need at least one baby in the school for the pupils to practice on when they study infant care."

"Exactly what will you teach them?"

Marianne swiftly reeled off a curriculum of reading and writing in Arabic, sewing, knitting, washing, cleaning, cooking, hygiene, sick nursing, spinning, weaving, basketry, pottery, embroidery, baby

* LPDSA — The Libyan Public Development and Stabilization Agency funds came at this time from British and other foreign aid monies to Libya.

care, preparation of raw wool for use, and good behavior and etiquette in the best Libyan tradition.

"Who will pay the running expenses of the school?" I asked.

"The Libyan government is going to pay. But the annual expense account is ridiculously low, only about fifteen hundred dollars per annum. We kept it to the bare minimum in order to be sure the school can continue even after foreign aid stops."

"Marianne, I think it is marvelous! I am truly thrilled. It will be a dream come true, and *your* dream. I don't think that *anybody* — UNESCO, in the United Nations, or in Libya — will ever know how much they owe to you, except perhaps your 'little women.' "

"And I love my little women! What I want more than anything in the world now is to see Sayyida Fatima School functioning."

"You will. The worst is over, surely. You have the land, the plans are made, and the cash is promised. What can possibly interfere?"

"Well, people might," said Marianne uneasily. "The Fezzan Council could. A certain man could."

"What *do* you mean? Who is after you? A Libyan?"

Then Marianne named to us a powerful Arab sheik in the Province of Fezzan.

"He followed me up here to Tripoli by air today, and he's checked in at the Grand, too. Ever since we got in he's been trying to make a date with me for tonight. 'To go over our school plans again,' he says. You know he's on the Council. But I know what he wants. I've already told him not to come to my little house in Sebha. Even to let him inside my house could ruin me. He always pretends he wants to talk about the school, but I know his reputation, and everybody else does, too. I simply can't have any scandal or gossip; it would ruin the school. Fathers would never let their daughters come if there was talk about me. That's one reason I came to Tripoli this weekend, to try to get away from him for a few days. He's the head of the board that has to do with the school, and he has been very helpful. Now he thinks that I owe him special thanks! If I am nice to him, it will ruin me, and if I'm not, he has it in his power to ruin the school. I'm frightened, and I'm furious — and I don't know what to do."

"Don't you think he'll drop it when he finds it's useless?"

"I'm afraid not. He's too used to getting his own way. If he doesn't get it, he'll retaliate. And I want that school so much!"

"But surely he wouldn't try to stop the school? It's for the benefit of his own people!"

"Oh, Agnes dear, you don't understand these people! The school is for the *women*, and the women don't really count for anything with most of the desert men. Or rather, they count for only *one* thing! Oh, I don't really think he'd try to stop the school — but if he gets angry with me I know he'll do something to hurt me, and the best way is through the school. I suppose he might even get me thrown out of Libya — or my contract might not be renewed."

I looked at Marianne aghast: I knew it was entirely possible that he might do just that.

"When does your contract end?"

"This year. But I have promised LPDSA to stay on for at least another two years, in order to get the school going. I had to guarantee to stay in Libya before they would promise to provide the money. They were afraid of getting stuck with a big investment in the school plant, and nobody down there in Sebha to carry on the program."

"Surely then, LPDSA, or UNESCO, will back you up, even if al Sherif should make trouble."

"Nobody backs up anybody in this ratrace," Harry interrupted dispassionately. "It's our business to be liked."

"But Marianne's liked too much!" I suggested.

"Harry's right," Marianne agreed. "We're all here at the request of the Libyan government, and we stay only at their pleasure. They can call me 'persona non grata' tomorrow, if they wish, and give no reason — and I'd have to leave."

"And the *dis*pleasure of al Sherif is a better reason than they usually have," Harry said pessimistically.

"They'll never get another woman to do what you are doing for the Fezzan women," I said indignantly.

"Well, I love them," Marianne answered quietly. "They are marvelous, gay, intrepid women. And most of the men are all right, too. At least, they are neutral. But nobody dares to lift a finger against al Sherif!"

"The Fezzan is no place for women," said Harry.

"And when I think," Marianne said sadly, "how all these many months in the Fezzan I have carefully avoided having any social contact with any of the men in the French community, the doctors, the military officers, the technical aid men, just so that there could be no possible gossip about me, and no prejudice felt against me for having any connection with the French community! I never even played tennis with a man!"

After we had finished dinner, Harry and I went over with Marianne the now completed school plans. I marveled at the fact that, backed by UNESCO, she could have supplied the entire initiative for the idea of this teachers' training center which would be unique in the Libyan desert, and probably in the entire Sahara. She had first formed the concept of the school when, in her Sebha night classes, she had observed the quick, intelligent response of the desert women to every opportunity to make their lives more fruitful. Now the dream was a plan fully worked out on paper, backed up by hard cash, with annual maintenance promised.

The school seemed to us to be perfect. The entire establishment was conceived to be just the small amount better than the girls would have at home so that they could see the possibilities of installing the same improvements in their own homes later. The high-walled school compound was designed for privacy, with sleeping and living quarters lighted only by tiny, high windows, while the schoolroom had windows opening on an inner courtyard only, to give light without the possibility of being overlooked by any men. The kitchen had the typical open Fezzan fireplace for cooking, and a kitchen garden was to be planted in the courtyard.

When we drove Marianne back to the hotel about midnight, she asked us to come up and wait in her room for a while to see that all was well. As we came through the lobby, the desk clerk gave her a note saying that the effendi from the Fezzan had telephoned, and would call her again later. We had just settled ourselves in the bedroom when the phone rang. It was, of course, al Sherif.

"No, we can't go over the plans again tonight," we heard Marianne say firmly. "I have friends here with me now — Mr. and Mrs. Keith. No, after they go home it will be too late. It is already after midnight. I am very tired and I shall go to bed shortly. Please do not call me again, as I shall be asleep."

Marianne turned from the phone with a gesture of frustration.

"I think you should come home with us and sleep at our house," I said. "There's a perfectly good couch in the living room."

Marianne looked at me despairingly. "But suppose I stay with you tonight? There's still tomorrow — and the day after — and all the days after that down in Sebha!"

There was nothing to be said. We all had the unhappy knowledge that the last word could not be hers.

That summer Harry and I went home on three months' leave to Victoria, British Columbia, Canada. Like everyone who goes on home leave, the moment we had said goodbye and were airborne we left our Libyan problems behind. We had a good holiday in what seemed a completely separate world where people were all equally busy with their own problems, and not at all interested in Libyan ones.

Shortly before we were due to return to Libya, we found ourselves losing all interest in the holiday life, storing away our heavy clothes and putting summer apparel in our suitcases again, being commiserated with on leaving God's country and secretly rejoicing, but most of all wondering what had been happening in Libya in our absence. By the time we touched down at Idris Airport, Tripoli, with Hammet, Badreddin and Suleiman welcoming us and Gismondi smiling hello, we were avid for Libyan problems again.

One of my first interests was Marianne and the Sayyida Fatima School, at whose inception I felt I had been present. Almost immediately I heard from Marianne by letter. The school now existed in material form, and was almost ready for occupation. She had been busy all summer (temperatures 120 degrees in the shade, and no shade) going by Land Rover to the oases to select her pupils and persuade their parents. She thought she had a promising group. Two teaching assistants were expected to arrive soon from Egypt. Nevertheless, she had many worries at present. She only "hoped" that all would go well! Knowing Marianne's normal tremendous enthusiasm, I felt sure that all was *not* going well.

Some days later I received a distracted letter from her saying that she was flying up to Tripoli to discuss with UNESCO and LPDSA serious personal problems.

"I hope it's not that man again!" I said anxiously to Harry.

"I hope not. He's the local Bluebeard, but he's also the mainspring of the Fezzan!"

As soon as Marianne met us, she told us what we had feared. The Fezzan Council had briefly informed UNESCO that they no longer wished to retain Marianne on the program. The school was built; the pupils were selected; the curriculum was arranged, and a couple of young Egyptian ladies would now take over its conduct and instruction.

"Can the Egyptian girls do it, Marianne?"

"They can, if they will! The worst thing about the Egyptian teachers is that they feel so superior to our little desert girls. You might think they had no desert and no Bedawi in Egypt and that they were all college grads! The Cairo girls who have just come to Sayyida Fatima are chiefly interested in keeping their fingernails painted and their lipstick on."

"I know it's a dreadful disappointment to you, Marianne," Harry said, "but you are really better off out of the Fezzan, and out of this country. It is no place for a young woman alone."

"I have never believed that before," said Marianne. "I would never give in to what 'people' said. I always felt sure that if one behaved carefully so there could be no misunderstanding one's conduct, the men would respect it."

"Are you sure that al Sherif is behind this?"

"Do you doubt it? He *is* the Fezzan government. The ridiculous part is that if I said 'Yes' to him, the school was ruined; when I said 'No,' I'm ruined!"

"What does your organization say? Will they fight for you?"

"Fight for me! They just say, 'You see? We told you the desert province wasn't a suitable place for a young European woman!' Or else they take an even more annoying attitude that I'm just being hysterical. That young unmarried women often get these fancies that they are being pursued! Oh, they are quite kind, and very superior about it. I suppose that they will give me some stupid assignment in some non-Arabic country where I can't use my dear Arabic language — but where I'll be safe from pursuit! And I'll live in comparative luxury, and hate it. I love the Fezzan; I love my girls there. Perhaps I should say 'Yes' to al Sherif!"

"Do your girls know there is any trouble?"

"Of course. Everybody knows everything about everyone down there, whether it's true or false. The sands never cease whispering."

"Have the girls been turned against you?"

"Not yet, but they will be. In their world, the man must be right. The dreadful thing is that everything I have done for the girls and for the school has been done with all my heart, because I love them. But they'll probably end up thinking that I was just a sham and a show-off, and maybe no good, to boot!"

Desert breed

"Well, they'll never get another girl like you down there."

"They don't want one like me," she said sadly.

And this is the way it happened that Marianne left the desert she loved. A few years later were to find her employed in an excellent German embassy post, housed in a charming embassy apartment, in a beautiful and exotic capital city in the French-speaking part of the Arab world. There she is Arabic adviser to the embassy, but she speaks no Arabic to Arabs, as Arabs there speak only French. Marianne is indeed "living in luxury," compared to the Fezzan — but she would trade it all to be back with her little women of the Libyan desert.

20. Move to Benghazi

THE CRISIS was here! We were moving to Benghazi to live, and Mohamed must remain behind. For how could Mohamed, the only male of his family, its only contact with the outer world, whose young wife was now pregnant with their second child, how could he leave his crippled household and go five hundred miles away to live with us in the new capital city of Benghazi? The answer left us all depressed, but it was obvious. Now every day Mohamed's face was long with tragedy, he was fighting tears, and his entire conversation was, What shall I do when you go?

"You'll have no difficulty getting a good job, I'm sure, Mohamed," I said. I knew that he wouldn't, with the magnificent testimonial I had inscribed for him, though my recommendation rather overestimated his practical gifts for homemaking and laundering and his industry. But these matters, I felt, were more than made up for by his good character and intelligence, which would burst upon his new employer as a happy surprise.

"I don't want to be a houseboy," said Mohamed somberly, "I want to live with you and go to school like George."

"I know, and I wish that you could. But who would take care of your family? Now please don't cry, Mohamed. We *must* go to Benghazi, and you *must* stay here."

"Will you try to get me a job in FAO Mission here?"

I knew that a number of members of the FAO Mission who were attached to the Tripolitania provincial government, and not the federal government as Harry was, would be remaining in Tripoli to work in this province. That night I suggested to Harry that he should try to get Mohamed an office orderly job; but Harry has ethics about such things, and he said that Mohamed must get the job on his own merits.

"Yes, of course," I said, "but I think if you or I just write a little note, it will give a personal touch, and his merits will be more obvious and get more consideration. So I'll write. Is that all right?"

"I suppose so."

Being short on ethics myself, and knowing that Arab states function on nepotism, I wrote another really excellent letter for Mohamed telling of his ability with the English language which he was now learning to write, his quick intelligence, his aptitude for learning and his business acumen and ambition, and mentioning that he also had a driving license. This letter was addressed to a friend in FAO, to be presented after we had left Tripoli.

The change in capital cities was something which we had always known might happen. The constitution of Libya, in an attempt to guarantee justice to everybody, and possibly to harvest votes from all fields, specifies the existence of two capital cities — Tripoli in the Province of Tripolitania, and Benghazi in Cyrenaica Province. For the last two years the seat of federal government has been in Tripoli, where the majority of voters reside; now the time had come to shift the boom benefits of a capital city to Benghazi.

The fact was ignored that Tripoli already had efficient, Italian-built buildings to house its government departments and administration, and a rapidly growing number of housing units for families of government employees, bilateral agencies, consulates and embassies and, last and least considered, UN personnel and families. Whereas Benghazi, never much more than a Bedawi village, unredeemed by any lengthy Italian occupation (against which the Cyrenaicans never ceased fighting) and partially destroyed by Second World War bombing, had at this time neither administrative accommodation nor private housing.

However, both the King and the constitution were determined that the government should move and, as was frequently pointed out, it might be possible to change the constitution, but not the will of the King. For His Majesty King Idris, modern statesman and efficient politician, benevolent ruler compared to some, was still an Oriental potentate.

The King had been fortunate in his former prime minister, Ben Halim, a beautiful little Arabian Nights man with beautiful little wives and an inspired political brain which, though he himself was a Cyrenaican, never let him forget that the majority of voters lived in Tripolitania.

The new prime minister, Abd al-Majid Kubar, a Tripolino, had come to office in the reflected glory of his father, who had been murdered by the Italians as a resister and become thereby a martyred patriot. Kubar himself had been Speaker of the House under Ben Halim, and was a wide-awake and practiced politician, necessary attributes in a federal government whose actions were constantly being conditioned, if not nullified, by the overly dominating provincial governments.*

The Benghazi move was extremely unpopular. I came in contact with no one, either Libyan or stranger, who was pleased with the idea. Most Libyan ministers had by now wangled themselves good houses in Tripoli, and lesser Libyan government servants were housed at ridiculously low rents, with three and four generations of the same family living under one roof. It was financially impossible for such families to upkeep separate households, and the wage earner foresaw having to leave his wife and family in Tripoli if he retained his job with the government in Benghazi. Many of them would give up their jobs sooner than go.

As for the foreigners, most of us had established ourselves out of town in what Harry called the American ghetto of Giorgimpopoli, which had developed specifically to meet the foreign demand for out-of-town housing with running water, sanitation, and a little garden space, and whose continuation as a suburb depended on the occupants' ability to pay a comparatively high rent, a qualification which still limited the district to foreigners. A few years later, with the arrival of oil prosperity and increased government pay and rents paid by government for its employees, Libyans moved in waves to

---

* The first ten years of Libyan independence were a prolonged battle between federal and provincial ambitions and authority until, in 1963, the separate autonomous provincial governments as such were abolished by the King and an act of parliament.

Giorgimpopoli, therefore putting the lie to the idea that they could not appreciate more spacious living.

Suddenly, at thought of moving to Benghazi, we in Giorgimpopoli who had in the past complained about lack of garbage service, no paved roads, no city water supply, electricity failures, telephone breakages and no mail deliveries began to count our mercies, mourn their impending loss and hymn our undying love for the dear old ghetto of Giorgimpopoli. All we could do was to hope that the present government would fall, and Ben Halim return to power with an eye on the Tripoli voters again!

Crenelated wall—Sokna

Meanwhile there was a rumor in the air of a scheme which seemed then like a ridiculous dream: a third new capital city was to be built at el Beida in the Green Mountain of Cyrenaica. Beida, at this time, was only a whistle-stop in the eyes of a passing foreigner, the home of a famous Islamic tomb to a Moslem, and to no one a real city. But never mind, el Beida was to be built, stone on stone, into a great

Moslem Arabic capital city at the cost of hundreds of thousands of pounds of what? Of foreign aid money! A dream! we said.*

During that last summer in Tripoli George flew out again to spend his vacation with us. So that he should meet other young people, for Tripoli was a favorite holiday spot for American and British young-sters whose parents were employed here, we planned a swimming and lunch party for him at the Underwater Club, girls now in-cluded. The day the party was to take place, somebody tossed a bomb into the garden of the American ambassador, for what reason I forget; one reason is as good as another to an enthusiastic bomb tosser. After this, at the ambassador's request, all social gatherings for young people were canceled.

It was then that George and Don, who was also eighteen, and holi-daying here from England, became friends. They clicked instantly, perhaps because they both had English fathers and non-English mothers, a combination which encouraged nonconformism in both.

George and Mohamed had quickly resumed their companionable and affectionate relationship this summer. But after the bomb inci-dent it became temporarily inadvisable for young Westerners to go to public places where young Libyans gathered, and Libyans were not welcomed in Western clubs. It was not for fear of another bomb, but fear of the quick tempers of young people which might end in serious trouble, that our boys were told to stay at home.

Mohamed, whose heart was filled with good intentions and affec-tion for almost everybody and especially for "brother George," could not visualize any such problem occurring. Harry and I hesi-tated to give reality to a nebulous threat by telling George not to go about on the street or the beach with Mohamed. So we were not sorry when Don and George dreamed up a plan to travel together on the cheap in Europe until Don had to return to England to school. George was then to meet us in Benghazi, where we hoped by that time to have a house, and to stay with us for a year while he com-pleted his final high school term by correspondence course.

This European travel plan was a great blow to Mohamed, who longed to go, too. I felt almost personally culpable that our son had

* But a dream which came true in 1964.

several kinds of freedom, one of which was supplied to him by our cash, while Mohamed had none. It was useless to talk of equality in a world of inexhaustible disparities.

The government was by now officially in Benghazi. In Tripoli, the federal government had been said to exist in a state of organized disorder; in Benghazi it existed in disorganized disorder. If anyone asked for a file, he was given three glasses of tea and a kind word; if he asked for a minister he was told to go to Tripoli; if he went to Tripoli he found the minister was in Italy for his health. Many of the ministers developed ulcers, and the ulcers needed Roman air.

Meanwhile those of us not gifted with ulcers had to move to Benghazi, as the job of the United Nations and FAO was to advise the Libyan government, and this action required mutual propinquity, whether or not the government took the advice.

The rush for housing was on. For three months we had been negotiating from Tripoli for a Benghazi house. The houses didn't yet exist, but financially gifted Arab landlords, from the moment when they laid the first clean, white limestone block on the house site, were renting their nonexistent houses for high rentals of two hundred to three hundred dollars per month to strangers who fought with each other to sign the lease. By the time we agreed to pay a rental which we thought too high, somebody else had paid a higher rental and started to move in. Finally we managed to nail down a house, and by moving quickly and stealthily we got into the premises as the walls rose about us.

Our house was in a new suburban district which had been grazed clean by goats and later used as a garbage dump, and now was being transformed overnight by far-seeing Libyans into a foreign suburb. Garden City, Fuihat, the area was named. It was on a vast, limestone-eroded, red dust plain which lifted five feet in the air with every wind. No one ever forgets the red earth of Cyrenaica, which turns all the washing red!

At last we had to say goodbye to Mohamed. At one period in my association with the Libyan boy I had begun to wonder if all Mohamed wanted from us was a soft job with steady pay. Well, he did — who wouldn't? — but that wasn't *all*. As our days in Tripoli grew shorter, I saw something else which greatly surprised me. Mohamed, living close-packed in his rabbit warren of relatives, was still painfully alone, and lonely.

He had no one except myself to talk to about the things which now interested him most: about the Western countries, their behavior and culture, good or bad, which fascinated him and with which he was just now coming in contact in Libya because of the influx of Westerners. Mohamed had an avid desire to know, a tremendous capacity to learn, and a great urge to discuss. More and more, as our departure neared, I saw what a lonely child he was, head of a family though he might be. I realized also that the day for young Libyans to follow unquestioningly traditional edict had passed: they were bound by it still, but not with unquestioning acceptance.

On our last day in Tripoli we had asked Mohamed to wait in the house for the landlord and give him the key. As we walked out of the house for the last time, he stood at the door. He did not say goodbye. He followed us to the high iron gate and put his head down on his arms and leaned against it with his face hidden. I touched his head as we passed. Harry went out and got in the Land Rover, and I got in the old red Vauxhall which I was to drive to Benghazi, and we started off. I looked back, but Mohamed's face was still hidden, as he stood there, alone. Of all my memories of Mohamed, this is the one that remains.

III

Poor Relatives of Allah

21. The Dump Develops

WE HAD called it a dump, and hated to come, but our year in Benghazi proved to be one of the happiest of our lives. Here on the edge of the Libyan Sahara we lived a small, cozy life in the little Bedawi tribal village, which dabbled its Arabic feet in Mare Nostrum while its backside was smitten by saffron winds. The shift of capital turned out to be a first-class real estate promotion deal, and tides of foreign prosperity poured in on the sandy, red air.

The fact was that the place grew on you. Its dilapidation, its fierceness, its sadness, its guts, its tattooed Bedawi dames with their high, orange-calf boots and gaudy striped baracans, its tattered, untamed, gentle-spoken men, its enclosed, secretive suk, its incandescent salt plains shimmering in the sun, its closer contact with friends and its increased simplicity in living, all took hold of your heart as no big city could. If the government was in a state of confusion in Benghazi, so were the various aid agencies whose job it was to accompany the government wherever it went and pour advice into its deaf ear. The confusion was now so all-encompassing that even the Western eager beavers began to follow the government's lead and settle for tea and cakes, instead of psychotic frustration.

Shortly after our move to Benghazi, Jan van der Ploeg, the Chief of the FAO Mission, a diplomatic position as liaison between the FAO Experts and the Libyan government, went on sick leave to Holland, leaving Harry to act as Mission Chief in his place. Harry continued to be the advisor on forestry, but was also responsible for assisting each of seventeen Experts to implement his own program. In simple words, Harry had to persuade the government to assist rather than to impede the Expert in carrying out the work that the government had asked FAO to send an Expert to do! This sounds contradictory, and it was.

Harry had always said in the past that he preferred to deal with forests rather than people. Now when he told me that his time would be taken up by dealing with people more than with his own profession, I said, "But you haven't the patience, have you?"

"Why not?" he said indignantly.

He proved to be right; in fact, he astounded me. He developed wonderful patience and persistence in all his dealings, and, in spite of his pointed wisecracks, he had tremendous sympathy with all kinds of human beings. He was constantly bringing home the story of some unique person who required some unique form of assistance — which he invariably received. Harry had a broad experience in everything to do with agriculture as well as forestry, and this was fortunate, as the FAO Libyan Experts had to do with agriculture and agricultural products, animal production, marketing of products, agricultural cooperatives, forest research, veterinary work, animal health, tannery instruction, horticulture, farm mechanization, agronomy, rural institutions, soil survey, water utilization, and fisheries. In addition Harry was acquiring a border-to-border knowledge of Libya that few Libyans had.

The name Benghazi will mean most to those who remember, or who fought with or against, Rommel's African campaigns. Benghazi — decimated by retreating armies, bombed by advancing ones, torn to pieces by its protectors, thrown to the dogs and retrieved again by its friends — Benghazi somehow, but God knows how, survived its delivery.

By the end of 1942, a British military administration was established in Libya. After the war, regular British forces with their families were stationed in Benghazi. Every available room or apartment was suddenly rented, and a few new ones were tossed up; British military money flowed into the shops, and the little starved village began to eat again and to smile. The pink-skinned soldiers with their blonde wives and babies became part of the village scene.

Two years after Libya had become an independent kingdom, Great Britain signed a treaty with her which specified an annual payment to Libya by Britain of eleven million dollars for the right to maintain military bases here. Now the British military uniform, tattered portions of which already clothed most of the impoverished Cyrenaicans, became an accepted and not unwelcome sight in the country.

But a crisis came with the Suez trouble in 1956, when the use of British forces from Libya against Egypt seemed probable. Libya, however, refused her consent for the embarkation from Libya of any British military forces for an attack on an Arab neighbor. Britain acceded to Libya's refusal, and it became obvious then that Libya could have little further value to Britain as a base for an attacking force. At the same time, atomic weapons and guided missiles had lessened the strategic value of all Western bases in Libya. The following summer Britain withdrew most of her forces from Benghazi, and by the summer of 1958, when we arrived there, she had completed their withdrawal, except for a token group.

The yellow rows of battered, dismantled barracks-like flats stood empty and miserable, and the Libyan ex-servants of officers, trained to say "cheerio," had no one to say "cheerio" to and no one to pay them the monthly thirty dollars on which entire families subsisted. The shopkeepers had closed out their little stocks of imported British shirt buttons, nylon stockings, wool socks, Bromo, elastic, oil stoves, and tinned biscuits, and put up their shutters and drowsed outside in the sun. Onto this moribund scene burst the capital.

Out in our graceless, gardenless suburb of Garden City it only matters that we have a house, when it seemed for a while that we would have to put up a tent! Although history claims that trees grew here in Roman times, trees and Romans have long since gone, leaving as sole survivors of the arid land, goats, sheep and Bedawi. The three have combined to destroy, consume, and burn every branch, twig and leaf of possible vegetation.

Here once the breeze blew sweet and clean through hardy native pine trees, whose searching roots bound earth and stone, whose quivering needles reached for rain. But now, when the south wind whistles day and night, it comes to us heavy with the sands of limestone decomposition and the ochre dust of the dying earth. Yet this is not Libyan desert; this is only deserted Libya, not four miles from the sea! Today, this is the scene outside our garden wall, which fortunately stands five feet high.

Inside the "garden" there is great activity. George, who is to be with us for this year in Benghazi, has just returned from Europe in time to help.

"Hi, Pa, how deep do you want these holes?"

"At least two feet, or the trees won't take hold."

"But Pa, this is solid rock!"

"That's right! Pure limestone. You'll have to dig as far as you can, then fill the holes with water and let it stand overnight. Then dig further next day."

"How many trees did you say?"

"Badreddin sent us three hundred seedlings by truck from the nursery."

George and Harry stand silent and swearing in the sun, as they contemplate the idea of three hundred holes to dig.

"Guess ours will be the only house in Garden City with a garden!" said George.

"Digger Jones has a garden, with flowers right now," I suggest. "But we'll have a forest twenty years from now!"

"If the goats don't get in!"

Standing on our veranda and looking beyond the gray stone garden wall, I see a winding, would-be road and a few stone houses like ours scattered about without reference to the road, and at odd angles, standing partially shrouded in the local yellow wind which almost always blows.

Camels with heavy, creaking loads pass hourly, carefully cushioning their steps with the sway of their torsos, placing their great padded feet with faultless rhythm on both sand and rock. Disregarding the road, they pass just outside our gate, their haughty heads undulating smoothly above the wall. Their utilitarian, inelegant desert-adapted bodies and their disregard for the discomfort of the terrain well merit their supercilious expressions.

Camels are admirable, but donkeys I love. Unlike camels, they follow the road, dancing along on their high, twittering feet, their movements a ripple of high-heeled shocks, and the air about them quivers with their haste as they bounce their loads of ancient Libyans homeward. If I ever have a pet in this land it will not be the famous African Seluki hound which Harry talks of, nor the sad little gazelles which we regularly refuse to incarcerate, but some little gray donkey who has collapsed under his huge load in front of my house. Then I shall go out and pick him up and carry him into our garden where he will live forever after on a diet of Quaker Oats — while I languish in a cell for stealing!

Bevies of Bedawi women cross my vision at intervals, swirling up the road in full sail before the dry wind as they hurry back to their torn black tents. They are well swaddled in vivid baracans of flame and yellow stripes, indigo and gold stripes, which wrap around their legs above the edges of their high-topped crimson or chrome-yellow kid shoes, which must be the original of all high-topped shoes and are especially made for them in Benghazi suk. Sometimes the heavy baracans blow back from the women's faces, or are thrown defiantly back to reveal coffee-colored skin, wild, flashing eyes, and clean-cut features whose delicacy is confused and lost under heavy indigo tribal tattoos. Meanwhile, sheep in all numbers wander about, and if our gate and door stood open they would be in our kitchen; less gentlemanly goats actually assault the gate with evident intention of gnawing their way inside.

The Libyan landlord who constructed our stone villa is building its duplicate next door. He is using the same combination of sand instead of concrete, the same vintage of secondhand fixtures, of salvaged plumbing and corroded pipes, and he is working under the same delusion that he is building a new house. He is employing the same impoverished-looking workmen who are still dressed in rags and seem to exist solely on tea and Arab bread. Yet presumably they must be amongst the fortunate few here, for they have jobs, and jobs mean pay.

Or so I assumed, until Ali made us his confidants. Ali is one of the workmen, or possibly the foreman, as he talks more than he works. He has three languages to do it in — Arabic, Italian and English; English, as he was in British military service in the desert.

As soon as we started to move in, he made acquaintance over the garden fence with Maddelena, usually called Lena, the young Italian woman who had surprised me by agreeing to leave Tripoli and move to Benghazi. Here she lives with us, creating housekeeping bliss in a disordered household, and making us all so dependent on her that I am already plotting to see if there is any possibility of taking her to Canada later. As Lena is not very pro-Arab, I was surprised to find her responding politely to his friendly overtures. Soon I understood why: he speaks gracious Italian, and he carries with him an air of happy self-confidence and well-being (God only knows why!) and the assurance that Allah is always on his side. His psyche is the exact opposite of the other local workmen, who look lugubrious and downtrodden, no doubt with good reason. Ali has an erect, slender figure with a happy, swaggering walk, and a piquant, vivacious face which expresses good cheer no matter how black the circumstances.

Speaking over the wall the other day, Ali told Lena and me, with the brightest of smiles and gayest of laughs, that neither he nor any of the workmen had been paid for four months.

"Why don't you all quit work, then?" I asked. "There is a great deal of building here now, and you could get other jobs with a different boss."

"Yes, but other Libyan boss no pay, either."

"But why don't they pay? When they rent these houses to us, we have to pay!"

"Maybe by-and-by Libyans get money. But he no have money when build the house."

"But I hear that our landlord is a rich man. His family is an important family. His brother is in the Majlis.* "

"Yes, very important man, very rich man, but no money! Plenty of land, plenty of wives, plenty of friends, but no money!" says Ali. "He get rent from your house now?"

"Three months paid in advance, and we pay each month, too!"

* Parliament.

"Maybe he pay us some money soon," says Ali philosophically.

"What do you live on?"

"I no cost too much. I sleep here in new house for watchman. I drink tea and eat bread."

This chat gives me a new slant on wealth and poverty in Cyrenaica, amongst both landlords and workmen.

Meanwhile this vast red plain with its filthy red dust, its tough, unconquered people with their ragged dignity and their tattered black tents, its chalky white houses for its pallid foreign friends, is already taking a grip on me.

Pucci

22. She Did It to Annoy!

THE HORN of the FAO car sounded as Harry drew up in front of our gate.

"Hurry up, Signora, the car is here!" called Lena.

"Hurry up, Ma! Pa's waiting!" shouted George.

Pa has a reputation for not liking to wait. Now he was headed for the Benina Airport to catch a plane for Tripoli, and he was stopping at our house just long enough to pick up his luggage and me. Beep! beep! went the car horn again.

George rushed the suitcase out, and I grabbed the briefcase, coat, hat, and bundles from the bed and dashed through the hall to the living room, headed for the front door. All our floors are polished Italian ceramic tile, and on my second turn I skidded with extreme momentum on my favorite small bougainvillea-colored Benghazi rug. The rug and my feet continued in a forward direction, while my body went leftward. With my arms still filled with bundles, I lit full force on the floor on my left elbow and hip bone, and there is nothing to equal polished Italian tile for a graceful crash landing.

Fortunately, I was wearing a light kidskin jacket, or my forearm might have flown right off and been lost forever when I landed, as the only thing that seemed to hold the lower arm to the upper part was my jacket sleeve. The extreme limpness of the broken member startled me, but the hip hurt worse.

By now the crash had been heard through all of Garden City, and Lena, George and Harry came running. As they looked at me on the floor, it is hard to say what emotion was uppermost on their faces — surprise, distress or annoyance. To slip on a rug is an inglorious accident, and worse when it happens at an inconvenient time. I found myself apologizing for the delay, even while I begged them not to touch me till the pain lessened. Just then the driver beeped the horn again.

"I've broken my elbow," I said calmly, a quality which is not mine by nature but which I cultivate for crises, the calmness measuring the crisis.

"Nonsense!" said Harry. "You couldn't break your arm with such a little fall!" Harry thinks that if he denies a misfortune which he doesn't want me to have it may disappear.

"I don't know why not!" I said indignantly from the floor. "Other people break bones when they fall. Look!" With my good right hand I picked up my left hand and arm, and it was obviously not well connected with the rest of me. Now George and Harry were lifting me cautiously to my feet, while my hip screamed out. The car beeped again.

"I've got to catch that plane," said Harry. "You ride out with me to the airport — there are some matters I want to discuss — and you'll feel better for the air. Then if you still think you have broken your arm, get the driver to take you to the government hospital for an X ray. Ask for the German doctor who came to the house to take care of Jan. Dr. Klug, I think his name was. Come on now, or I'll miss the plane."

They got me into the motorcar, Lena looking horrified, George uncertain, and Harry and I resigned. Half an hour later we drew into the airport just in time, and Harry's last words to me were, "Now take care of yourself, dear. It's probably just a sprain, but perhaps you'd better let the doctor see it."

I said nothing, and expect to be rewarded in heaven for it.

When we left the airport I asked Mohamed, the driver, to stop at the house and pick up George to go to the hospital with me, as by this time I did not feel equal to delivering the baby myself. The government hospital is a large, rambling, Italian-built group of buildings which branch out from a center courtyard, with endless nooks where doctors can get misplaced. We couldn't find Dr. Klug, but George found a kind Italian Sister, who came out to the car and clucked her tongue solicitously over me, and hurried away to return with Dr. Guerera, a young Italian surgeon who had studied at the Mayo Clinic and later proved to have profited by it.

By now my hip was almost immobile, and I began to fear that I had broken it, too. My elbow was X-rayed, and proved to be broken in two places; my hip was also X-rayed, and it was not broken, but dislocated. I was so relieved at this that I felt quite philosophical about my elbow.

I had assumed that my arm would be put in a cast immediately, and that I would more or less walk out. But when they cut my jacket off, an extravagant action which broke Sister's heart, my arm had more than doubled its girth by hemorrhage, and the doctor said it could not be set at present. By now we had arrived in the anteroom of the operating room, a cozy place filled with patients of all kinds, including two little girls with nim nim, as the Arabs call measles. A polite elderly Arab gave me his seat, a small, tall, slippery stool off which I almost fell when Sister gave me an injection to lessen the pain. At this stage, all the other patients gathered around me to watch what was happening and to cluck their tongues at the revelation of my swollen, congested arm. Meanwhile, the door to the operating room stood half open, and we could see a policeman lying on the operating table — to have a bullet removed, someone said. We knew it was a policeman from his big, shiny boots on the floor by the table. Asepsis seemed to have no place here.

Dr. Guerera and Sister told me that I would have to stay in bed with the arm completely immobilized until it could be set in five or six days' time. They agreed, however, that I "wouldn't be comfortable" in the hospital, what with bedbugs, tea being brewed in the corridors, and Arab radios tootling! I assured them that I could be taken care of at home, where I had an excellent Italian woman living with me, if the doctor would attend me there. This he agreed to do. With my arm well swaddled and resting on a board, and George to help me, I limped out, feeling that I had gotten into enough trouble for one day.

I have always been accident-prone; at least, a great many things have happened to me. But ever since I read that accident-prone people are that way because they subconsciously want accidents to happen to them, I have felt guilty if anything happened to me. Yet I am quite certain that I did not slip on my favorite rug in order to annoy!

A not unpleasant few days followed at home in bed. My arm was a revolting, gangrenous-looking, blue-green object, but Dr. Guerera, who came every day, assured me that it was "very nice." My hip hurt much more than my arm, but I was so thankful that I had not broken it that I was almost pleased with the situation. There was life in the old bones yet! Lena took good care of me and learned to comb and dress my long hair, which I always wore up, which she insisted was her most difficult task.

George provided our diversion, with his circus of field mice. The collection started with three mice brought to him in a little box by our Arab driver, a gift much treasured by George, although we had plenty of our own mice, outdoors and in. George built his pets a miniature playground with ferris wheel, ladders, and athletic apparatus, and fed them, and put them under a cotton curtain to sleep at night. But every morning regularly the box was empty and the kitchen was full! Daily, they were recaptured and placed in their zoo, a real test of loyalty for Lena, who hated mice in any location.

My UN friends came to see me, and everybody said how lucky I was not to have broken my hip, and how their friends had fallen on polished tiles, too! Nobody suggested I was stupid to break my elbow, and I began to reconsider about being accident-prone, and decided to blame it all on the tiles.

After six days away, Harry was due to return home about midnight on Friday. We had telegraphed to him of my condition, knowing that if I weren't at the plane to meet him he would assume that I had been hacked to pieces by hostile natives.

Meanwhile my six-by-six-foot bed had become the scene of all our activities. As we awaited Harry's arrival, George was sprawled across the foot of the bed, and Lena was sitting on the side. We heard the FAO car arrive and minutes later Harry hurried in carrying a cardboard box and a bouquet of stupendous, deep pink carnations, which had been flown from Italy to Tripoli and thence to Benghazi, where not a flower bloomed. Here they represented the height of luxury. But the magnificence of the carnations was almost forgotten when Harry opened the cardboard box and out tumbled the most beautiful little Maltese puppy I have ever seen.

Undisturbed by the confusion of his arrival, he tottered over the mountainous sheets to me, and curled up amiably in the palm of my good hand. There was no hesitation amongst us; in that instant each one knew that this was fated to be the dog of his life! The dog knew, too, and graciously permitted us to adore him.

"This is the pup Barbara promised to George. He's just a month old. Not bad, is he?" said Harry.

"Not bad! ! ! ! ! This darling dog! ! ! ! !"

"He was no trouble at all on the plane. We gave him an aspirin first and then popped him in the box, and he went to sleep. Slept all the way. Natural-born traveler!"

"Didn't the airline people say anything?"

"Why should they? Didn't know I had a dog," said Harry complacently. "He's a Maltese working dog, they say."

"What's his work?" I asked curiously.

"He guards the sheep."

"Let's get him some sheep!" George suggested.

Our new darling looked like a small silky ball of fluff in three colors — white, rose-beige and gray, and shining out of his long, silky hair were a black, wet nose and glowing black eyes, while two silky, sooty ears hung gracefully down. I was glad he was so small and hoped he stayed small; our last dog, Kam, had outgrown us.

Kam was a boxer whom we had brought home from the Philippines, who ate expensively and grew to great proportions. He jumped out of upstairs windows, frightened postmen, tipped over garbage bins, pushed over babies, and ultimately annoyed Harry by remaining a puppy in his outlook, regardless of size and advancing years. When we returned to the Philippines and left George in school at Shawnigan Lake, Kam stayed in our Victoria home with a housekeeper. When this poor lady dropped dead of heart failure, Kam was sent into a kennel, as we were to be in the Islands for a year longer. Finally, sooner than keep Kam confined indefinitely, and pay out a fortune, we gave him to friends who had a summer home in the Vancouver Island woods and who wanted a watch dog.

Remembering that Kam's size had worked against him, I was pleased that this one was small, for there is something incomparably endearing about small things. Having been a tall thing all my life, I know this. People may love us, but they seldom long to protect us. Tonight the idea came to me that at this moment we all three of us probably loved this helpless little creature on my bed as much as we loved each other.

"Nice little fellow," says Lena, who is just learning English. "Bellisimo Pucci Fellini-Fellini!" combining the name of her favorite songster with her favorite Italian picture director.

"Little Coeur de Poulet!" says George admiringly, as the pup attacks George's finger which is tickling him. "He can sleep with me."

Lena looks dubious. "There's more space in my bed because I'm small," she suggests, longingly.

"He can sleep right here between Harry and me, like a Libyan baby," I say generously.

"No dogs between you and me," says Harry firmly.

Thus Pucci's life with us began. To say he never gave any trouble would not be true, but he was worth it, and he soon became the best-loved dog in the world. He was wooed by both Lena and George, but Lena won, perhaps because she and Pucci were both Mediterraneans. They certainly spoke the same language, and they enjoyed a mutual empathy.

As Pucci grows older, this empathy becomes more marked. When Lena gets out of bed on the wrong side, Pucci, who sleeps with her, follows her to breakfast with a scowl, his eyes rolling till the whites show, his lips drawn back from his sharp teeth. The whole day long the two are heard growling and snapping at each other, though neither knows why. The next day there is honey on their tongues, for no reason.

The day after Pucci's arrival I returned to the hospital to have my arm set. I feared that this would be a terrible ordeal, as I have always understood that having a limb set is excruciating, and I didn't imagine that the hospital had many modern ideas about sparing the patient's nerves.

Once again the operating room was seething with patients, and I was sitting on a small upright stool braced for horrors, while the kindly Italian Sister gave me a hypodermic injection. An elderly Arab hospital orderly sat behind me and held me firmly back against his chest, making pleasant little sympathetic noises as the doctor worked, while another Arab orderly held my shoulder tightly with my arm extended to the surgeon. While I waited for the agony, Dr. Guerera worked gently with his hands and fingers, massaging and pressing and feeling the bones into place. It was all done so skillfully, and so without brute force, that I could scarcely believe it was finished when they started to wind on the plaster-soaked bandages. When my flabby, useless arm was finally firmly encased in plaster, I had a wonderful feeling of security. I started to count off the days for the three weeks to end and the cast to be removed.

It had by now ceased to be a question of George's keeping mice and become one of the mice's refusing to leave. The kitchen was tiny, and overflowed with refrigerator, stove, sink, closets, pots and pans and foodstuffs, and the mice had much more fun here than in George's box. We couldn't put either poison or traps out because of Pucci. What sealed the mice's fate was a cold spell which brought all their friends in from outside, and all night we could hear them browsing and carousing.

The next morning Harry and George entered the kitchen with a .22 air rifle and closed the door behind them, warning Lena and me to stay away. I called after them that the corpses must be disposed of, whether of the mice or their own. The blasting began. I saw, mentally, ricocheting bullets which took their toll of Harry and George, or at the very best left holes in my refrigerator. The blasting continued, soon amidst laughter. Pucci, Lena and I had our noses at the door. Then silence. "Are you all right?" I called.

"Sure, Ma! Just a minute, we're going out to bury the bodies!"

It was the end of mice in the house, and I think it was the only shooting Harry and George did in Benghazi.

The time had come for me to have the cast removed. George drove to the door of the hospital operating room, and while waiting for the doctor to arrive we sat in the car and watched the game of life. There always seems to be an air of calloused lightheartedness amongst the lesser personnel in hospitals all over the world, a feckless, frivolous air which is especially apparent to the patient who sits in pain awaiting the doctor.

Today there were two very wide, old Fezzani ladies, possibly jani-tresses, who were carrying on perpetual titillating games with the various Libyan orderlies. The ladies' costumes were gay but not se-ductive, although eighteen inches of bright azure underwear was showing between the bottoms of their henna and blue striped bara-cans and the tops of their tall, yellow calfskin boots. However, bara-cans, being voluminous, bulgy and bunchy, and nontransparent, are not erotic costumes. The shining black Fezzani faces were unveiled and constantly lit by the view of white teeth and wrinkled smiles, which were possibly less gay than simple-minded.

A dozen young men of assorted ages, dressed in soiled medical coats, ran back and forth across the scene, not, as I at first believed, in haste to reach the patients, but in playful pursuit of each other. The veranda and entrance corridor, which were overflowing with patients and blue with the haze of tobacco smoke, made an ideal jungle for stalking and chasing. Unlike most hospitals, the patients also seemed to enjoy the game, and sometimes stuck out a playful foot for somebody to stumble over.

All the patients were Arabs or Fezzani, and mostly, of course, men, although in this nomad community the women sometimes come. Most of the patients had at least one eye which looked dis-eased or closed or wandering, in addition to their other obvious ail-ments such as ulcers, carbuncles, infected wounds, and fly-clustered sores. Several red-rashed children with the always popular nim nim were sniffling and twisting and wiping their fingers on their papas and their papas' friends. A baby in its father's arms was believed to be dying, I was told. I thought it might well die of suffocation, as its head and face were completely covered in a dingy woolen blanket and the day was already hot. None of the people present appeared to be operating cases, but all had gathered at the operating room, as this was where the doctor would come first.

While waiting here this morning, I realized for the first time that in all of my now numerous visits to the government hospital, I had never seen another European patient. The Seventh Day Adventist, American-staffed hospital must get them all except me.

When Dr. Guerera arrived he looked tired and pale, but he smiled pleasantly and had a kind word for each of the patients. This was a man whom I really admired. He was the only surgeon in this hospital, which serviced the entire Libyan population of Benghazi. He was on duty every day, and on call for emergency surgery or childbirth every night, and was paid the equivalent of two hundred eighty dollars a month. No "colonial oppressor," he!

I had no idea as to how a plaster of Paris cast would be removed, but Dr. Guerera told me with some pride that with the modern electric saw which the hospital had it was a simple operation. I had assumed that the doctor would do it, but as I sat confidently down between the two attendants, the doctor merely stood by. Today, the elderly one, against whose chest I had leaned when my arm was set, was in possession of the saw, which looked very large and sharp.

He positioned the saw lengthwise on my cast, turned on the electricity, and pressed firmly down. The noise and the vibration were nerve-shattering. I stood it for several minutes, while the saw cut deep into the cast. Then suddenly I felt heat and dampness all along my arm, and knew that it was blood running inside the cast. He had cut too deep!

"You're cutting my arm!" I said, trying to say it quietly, not wanting to hurt the man's feelings but not wanting to sit quietly and have my arm cut off.

The Arab smiled gently, "Oh, no, Signora. That is just the heat of the saw you feel."

"But I can feel the blood running! You're cutting too deep, I know!"

"Oh, no, Signora, you must imagine it," with another gentle smile, while the saw bears down.

Now Dr. Guerera leans down to say in my ear reassuringly, "Ahmed is our very best assistant. He has been attached to the hospital for twenty-two years. It is his job to remove all the casts, and he has never cut anyone yet."

I realized then that the doctor was telling me that Ahmed would have been slighted if the doctor had removed my cast instead of Ahmed. Well, I didn't want to hurt Ahmed's feelings, but I hated to lose an arm! Perhaps the stump would heal quickly! Fortunately, at this moment the saw stopped, the cast began to spread open under Ahmed's trained fingers, and I watched for the blood to stream out. . . .

"You see, Signora," Ahmed said kindly. "The cast is off, and the arm will soon be perfect."

I looked at it in surprise. It was an arm of fish-belly color, but quite, quite without blood.

Dr. Guerera smiled and said, "You see, Signora Keith, that Ahmed has very skilled hands."

I could gladly have embraced Ahmed. "I think he's wonderful!"

Six months later, when we were in Canada on leave, my elbow was examined and X-rayed again, and I was told that the setting and healing were perfect. I decided that I had met two miracles in the Benghazi hospital — Dr. Guerera and Ahmed.

23. Strange Christmas

THE STREAM of somber khaki flows steadily along under the green, red and black pennants of Sciara Tousson Maidan, the main street of Benghazi. Here on the shores of the Mediterranean, on the fringe of Africa and the edge of the Sahara, December twenty-fourth is not the day before Christmas, but Libyan Independence Day, the seventh* in Libya's history.

At nine in the morning the day is benign, with a pale azure sky and a sun which dazzles without giving warmth. A sharp wind sweeps northward from the desert and steppes but fails to chill the rejoicing crowds.

To describe the Libyans as they appear this day, I must first say that on all other days Benghazi is probably the worst dressed place in the world. Here, even more than in Tripoli, khaki-colored rags prevail, left over from military occupations. All garments are thoroughly patched, and some outfits are nothing but patches. Ordinarily, children race about in the chill desert wind in assorted rags, piled layer on layer without benefit of sewing. An air of well-being and good cheer is the last quality to associate with a Benghazi crowd.

Today, all is changed. Even the ugly, yellow mud-covered buildings, usually lethargic and secretive, are charged with vigor and life of their own, under their floating Libyan banners. People pour through the streets with laughter and gay salutations to smiling friends. Motor traffic flows patiently around small islands of large Libyans who stand in the middle of the road shaking hands enthusi-

* 1958.

astically and, regardless of traffic, pursuing to their legitimate end
the extravagant Arabic greetings which rank courtesy above safety.

Almost all the men are wearing the true Libyan dress, their voluminous baracans draped across their shoulders in heavy, yellowed
folds of natural wool. Like the Roman toga, this garment enhances
the wearer's dignity. The long sleeves of the kaftans, or inner coats,
show at the wearer's wrists, and are vividly ornamented with braid,
and the bright blue, green or purple, baggy-seated Arab trousers are
visible below the baracan, gripping the ankle and outlined in braid.
And almost everyone is wearing shoes!

This great national day is a family day such as the American
Fourth of July. Every child within walking or riding distance, arriving by donkey, camel or bus, is here on the city streets to see the
parade. Think what it means to children who have grown up watching foreign armies march through their streets and begging alien
troops for bread and pennies, to see today their own army, well
trained, well dressed and proud, proclaiming this country as theirs!

The children are dressed as never before in their lives, for they
have been born into postwar misery and country-wide poverty: but
today they are in neat, new, gay-colored dresses or suits. For the
little girls, cut velvet is the favorite fabric in shades of turquoise,
tomato red and cerise; metallic cloth is next in favor; while less elegant rayon and cotton fabrics compensate by being multi-flowered
and multi-colored.

Little boys, too, are self-consciously proud of their loose, three-quarter-length tunics, or jellabia, which are frequently of bright saffron yellow, the schoolboys' color. The children all trail through the streets hand in hand, attached to each other in long chains like paper doll cutouts, one end anchored to the largest child and the other end anchored to Papa. But never, of course, to Mama, who must remain at home, unseeing and unseen, preparing the kus kus, the feast day dish of semolina mixed with vegetables and stewed meat.

Standing here in the close-pressed crowd and watching the long military parade, I am impressed by two things. First, that I can stand here engulfed in a crowd of Libyans, Arabs, Middle Easterners, I, a foreigner among them, a woman and a Westerner, and be not only safe but welcome. They even politely urge me forward towards the front of the crowd, better to see the parade! Where else will I ever be treated like this? One may be safe, one hopes to be welcome, but where else will I ever be pushed forward to see a parade? My second thought is astonishment that a country of only one and a half million people can present a military parade which takes an hour and a quarter to pass.

"They walk as if their feet hurt!" Harry, beside me, says as the infantry pass.

"Probably they do hurt: they use sandals or go barefoot most of the time. Those army boots must kill them!"

"Except for flat feet," Harry admits, "they really do look fine!"

"But what I notice most of all is that they all look so proud of their uniforms and of themselves."

"Well, so they should be! I think this military display proves to every young Libyan that now he *has* a nation!"

Perhaps no soul can fail to stir at a military parade. The heartbreaking thought that the finest and fittest young men of a nation are being trained to die for it will always both torment and excite us.

"Here come a lot of soldiers on horseback now! Who are these? They have the same beautiful gray horses we used to see the Arabs riding at Zavia!"

"This must be part of the Cyrenaica Defence Force, special guard of the King. They act as mounted police, but they are really military." They pass with a clatter of hoofs.

Next come the mechanized units, making horrible noises in the effort to go slowly, and keeping the horses in front of them on edge and prancing. The young men of these units, with nothing to do but sit and look severe and occasionally swivel a gun, are self-conscious and hot in their tin hats, but nobody twitters or grins.

"Well, I never saw so many different shades of skin in all my life!" I say. "There is everything from white to tan to brown to black! And some with blue eyes, too. Berbers, I guess. But they are all so serious."

Now a wave of excitement sweeps through the crowd, broken by the clucking of tongues in admiration. "Here comes the prize!" Harry says. "The Cyrenaica Defence Force Camel Corps!"

"Walahi! Walahi! Walahi!" sweeps over the crowd, in admiration. "Aiyah! Aiyah! Aiyah! Tck-tck tck-tck tck-tck! Walahi! Walahi!" as the tall, swaying camels, mounted by khaki-clad soldiers with turbans draped desert-style and carrying rifles, move almost soundlessly down through the center of town. After the rattle, bang, clatter of horses and jeeps, the solemn camels with their high, mounted riders and their unhurried pace seem to move in a desert vision.

"Walahi!" I say excitedly. "That's one thing we'll never see in a parade at home! Thanks be to Allah that we got here before the camels were mechanized!"

"There is no doubt in Benghazi but that the Camel Corps is the favorite," says Harry. "But if this parade were in Tripoli, they'd shout their heads off for the mechanized units!"

"It really is a wonderful parade. I don't see how they managed such a good display."

"They've had British military advisers for years now!"

"Yes, I know. But what impresses me is the individual seriousness of everyone in the show today."

"You know what strikes me more than anything?" asks Harry. "No women!"

"I know. Depressing!"

"Here they are trying to make a nation out of a desert, and an army out of a camel corps, and they lock up their women!"

"Do you remember what Mrs. Anabtawi told me? That clever girl who came from Nablus, the very strict Moslem town in Jordan? I asked her how she had managed to get free from her family and go to the university and then marry the man she chose for herself. She said that as soon as her family realized that she had as good an earning capacity as her brothers, they were willing for her to get out and work, as long as she gave them part. Being a woman was no longer a disadvantage, if she could bring in money! She said that the key to unlock the door to the women's quarters was a woman's capacity to earn."

So far Mama has found no place in the great undertaking of this Libyan nation. The stunted harem life of the Arab women of the cities is crippling the country more than any other factor. Human energy is priceless, yet local woman-power remains untouched in order to perpetuate an outlived social tradition.

A woman's first obligation is to her home, her husband and her children. Most women agree to this. The question in Libya is: how can a Libyan Arab* woman fulfill this duty in the circumstances of her life here?

She may not go to market to buy the food.

The only Libyan women in the marketplace in Benghazi are the cheerful black Fezzani dames who squat outside selling fresh eggs to Europeans and shelled peanuts to Libyans to steep in their sugary tea. With polished charcoal faces shining and wide smiles, with kinky hair tied up in magenta or purple headcloths, ankle-sized earrings dangling on their shoulders, and huge, gilded necklaces lying like slave chains across their bosoms, still — they are free.

"Good morning, missus! Big, large, nice eggs, missus?" Their greeting follows me as I enter the market and join the invading foreign housewives from America, England, Italy, Germany, and Jordan. I push through the market square making the rounds before buying, pinching fruits and prodding vegetables, all of which come by truck from Tripoli, a sunny, two-day run over an uneven road. I

* Tuareg women are a special category — also the Fezzani Negro women.

study in confusion whole carcasses of lamb and famine-beef, which defy a butcher's chart, and ask the fish man for anything but tuna, which fish he sells under every name, and talk with the poultry man whose chickens still cackle and flop. Jostling beside me, a few Negro servants from wealthy Libyan households bargain in Arabic, the only females in Benghazi who mix with the white market invaders. Market shopping is done by Libyan husbands, before or after work.

In Tripoli, a virtuous woman may not leave her home to go alone to the doctor for her own ills. Sometimes her husband goes on her behalf, relating her symptoms to the doctor, who is not permitted to see his patient. If the woman goes, her husband must take her in a closed vehicle, taxi carriage or car, with her body, head and face covered with the indispensable white baracan. Does the doctor see under the baracan? Oddly enough, he does. The woman is quite willing to be examined — only the husband suffers embarrassment.

More trying still, a woman may not on her own initiative take her ailing child to the doctor, but must wait for her husband to return from his work at night, and do so. . . .

Ahmed is to be circumcised. He is the first-born child in a good Libyan home, of educated, intelligent, handsome, healthy parents. Samira, his mother, teaches at a girls' school nearby, to which she, covered by her baracan, is delivered daily by Majid, her husband, who also escorts her home in the afternoon. Majid enjoys a professional government appointment.

Ahmed is a husky, healthy child of six months. As Majid is a modern, Western-educated young man, he is going to take Ahmed to the government hospital to the doctor for the operation, rather than to the barber, or a Moslem neighbor, as a less enlightened father would do. Samira would like to go with little Ahmed to the hospital to be near him, but she knows that she may not go to a place where men may see her.

The Egyptian doctor gives Ahmed an anesthetic and performs the minor operation. He returns the semi-conscious baby to Majid's arms, with these instructions: "Take him home quickly while he still sleeps. You must keep him in his bed and completely quiet for at least four hours, as there is danger of hemorrhage. He will become restless when the anesthetic lessens, and he will be uncomfortable, but you must keep him from moving about, even if you have to hold him down. After four hours, there is little danger of hemorrhage."

Majid returns the baby to his mother, who looks at the little creature sadly as she sees blood on his clothes.

"Never mind, Samira. It is all over now, and by tomorrow he will be fine. I shall wait here four hours as the doctor told me, to keep him quiet and to see that there is no hemorrhage," reassures Majid.

The two sit beside the cot where Ahmed, strong and vigorous at six months, and now decidedly uncomfortable, is trying to thrash about. Together, they keep him moderately quiet until the four-hour period elapses. Now, having fulfilled the doctor's instructions, exactly on the last minute of the fourth hour Majid hurries from the house to his government office. Samira leaves Ahmed in the care of the little eight-year-old Fatima, the "poor relation" which every Libyan household has, and goes to the kitchen to fix some broth for him. Soon she hears Ahmed crying loudly, but Fatima, who adores the infant, is singing to him, and Samira wants to finish the broth.

Five minutes later Fatima screams out in fright, and Samira goes running to the cot to find Ahmed covered in blood from a hemorrhage. Terrified, Samira tries to think what to do. She is by no means ignorant, and she knows the child must be taken to a doctor to stop the hemorrhage or he will die. She has no telephone with which to call Majid, or any outside help. She knows that *she* must not take the baby in her arms and dash out for a taxi or a carriage and take him to the hospital herself. Cursed by the outworn tradition of her country, her child is dying now before her eyes.

Frantic and half-crazed, she screams out to Fatima to run as fast as possible to the house of Majid's brother, five streets away, and if he happens to be at home — in sha'Allah! — to beg him to come immediately to take the bleeding infant to the hospital. Fatima shoots out of the house like a frightened mouse, and runs all the way, thanking Allah as she goes that she is still free to run!

Samira bundles Ahmed up ready to go and stands just inside the door, holding him and sobbing and praying for the brother of Majid to be at home, and to come — to come — to come — in the name of Allah! Bismi-llahi! Bismi-llahi!

Her prayers are answered. Majid's elder brother, with a carriage in tow and Fatima beside him still gasping for breath, arrives at the door. Samira thrusts Ahmed into his arms, and begs him to go, to hurry! The blood-soaked garments tell what the trouble is.

Now Samira and Fatima wait alone in the house without news of the child. Samira has never in her life before suffered like this, not even when the baby was born. She is frenzied, hysterical, almost crazed, walking about the house, peering out of the curtains, wondering what is happening to her son. She prays, and she cries, and she prays again, but she cannot say, "If God wills" — "In sha'Allah" — to anything except Ahmed's recovery.

It is two hours before Majid comes. His brother has called him from his office to the hospital. Ahmed's life has been saved by a blood transfusion, and he is asleep in the hospital. El hamdu li'llah, el hamdu li'llah.

Majid knew that Samira had suffered terribly. Yet at no time, I think, did Majid question the rightness of the custom which forbade her to rush from the house to the hospital with her child who was nearing death. If Samira questioned the custom at the time, she accepted it again later — for after all, her child *was* saved, by the will of Allah, the Compassionate. And without Allah's will, what could Samira do?

A woman may not escort her children to school, and does not have any contact with their teachers. She has no knowledge of the widened world which it is the aim of education to introduce to her children. There is one teacher training school for females in Libya, run by an Egyptian headmistress, where there is an opportunity once a year for mothers and teachers to meet in a women-only soirée. This is attended by a few mothers, who represent the most "advanced" wives of government ministers.

Child experts claim that education must begin at home. It seems hopeless to attempt to battle ignorance, superstition, lack of hygiene, habitual undernourishment and endemic disease with school training for children who must return each night to the Middle Ages of their homes, to mothers who live in a medieval world.

Such are the conditions of a woman's life in the Libyan cities.

These conditions cannot be blamed on following the Koran, for this is the century in which other Moslem countries are sponsoring a normal way of life and comparative freedom for their women. Kemal Ataturk lit a chain fire when he ordered the women of Turkey to abandon their veils and harems — and enforced the order. I can imagine the distress which exposure probably caused many traditionally reared older women, after a lifetime spent in hiding. Exposure to them was probably as bad as nudity. But Ataturk was a realist, and he recognized the power potential of women and the need of his country to use it.

In the light of Turkish Ataturk's twentieth-century enlightenment in his attitude to women, it is surprising to know that the veil and seclusion were first imposed on Libyan women during the time of Turkish rule and Turkish Pashas. Seclusion is not a part of Islam. The object of the imposition was to preserve morality in Libyan homes and to protect women against the invaders' unwanted attentions. But rules of conduct which may have been appropriate to conditions several hundred years ago can have little application to the life of modern Libya. This is a nation which I have found to be nonviolent and civilized in every way — except its attitude to its own women.

It is a noticeable fact that when you travel outside the cities here, amongst the Cyrenaica Bedawi, amongst the desert nomads, and with the Jebel Berbers of Tripolitania, the code of the harem has little weight and less observance. Wild, gypsy-like figures pop out from every shrub and give back stare for stare. Sometimes the startled female figures make token gestures towards hiding their faces in their blazing, henna-colored baracans, but more often they scrutinize you as frankly as you do them.

In Libyan country life, women of necessity take an important place. They share with their men at least two essential duties, that of helping to sow and reap the crops and that of guarding the flocks. In addition, the women alone are responsible for a third equally urgent task, that of supplying the family living quarters with water, carried by hand and brought on foot, frequently from isolated wells many kilometers distant. At such wells, water may be drawn up by donkey or camel power only one day a week. Whether to their tents or mud huts or thatched beehive dwellings, the job of carrying water is exclusively a woman's duty. Thus in the daily routine of rural life, the Libyan woman is a vital force.

In city life she has no comparable vital position. She is not allowed to fulfill her own capacity as a human being, much less her potential to contribute to family prosperity and welfare. Her home responsibilities are limited; she has no civic duties; and she has not yet been discovered as an economic asset.

And yet in these few years before the facts of physical womanhood betray them into hiding, it is the little girl children who bring to the Benghazi streets their only beauty. These small girls sparkle with energy and life; they plunge like fiery colts, tossing their dark, ringleted hair, while their brilliant eyes snap as they stare boldly, defiantly, or just curiously into the eyes of a stranger like myself. Their lips may seem set in a sullen, downward bow, until as suddenly and silently as a streak of sunlight through an opening door their faces break into friendliness with a lovely smile. In such a moment, one sees what the men have hidden away for themselves behind high walls and closed doors, in hidden interior courtyards. This is the same golden smile which I have seen to my delight and astonishment in meeting with the wives of our friends in their secluded homes.

Among the Libyan townswomen whom I know well, only two wives, Insaf and Badria, have both cared and dared to break their purdah. These two have much in common: both of them achieved their new status through the desire of their husbands that they should do so, both girls within the first year of their marriage; both married educated young men who had selected their wives with this intention.

Both marriages were arranged, with an understanding by the parents also that the wife should share in the pleasures and duties of wifehood and family life, and that she should be unveiled when possible, and not live in seclusion. I say "when possible" because a woman *recognized* to be a Libyan might still be stoned on the Tripoli streets by ignorant young men, if she went unveiled.

Kadija of Libyan broadcasting fame, who conducts women's programs over the air and is the first Libyan woman ever to speak on the radio, is an exception. She always goes unveiled and is respected everywhere, but as a public figure more than as a wife, although she has been married.

Both the wives I speak of came from prosperous homes, both had educational advantages, and both had fathers with advanced ideas. In these girls' homes it was the ambition of the fathers that their daughters should step beyond the shadow of seclusion. Both became teachers, and Badria is a headmistress.

It is both impossible and undesirable for Libyan women to break from seclusion without the full approval of their husbands, and also of their parents. It would be almost impossible for the average Libyan woman, with her ignorance of life outside her own home, to visualize a break with tradition, much less plan and work for it. Her husband, who already knows the outer world, must envisage it for her. She may be too shy to emerge easily. Brought up as she has been, closed away from all males from the age of twelve until she marries, she is bound to suffer emotionally when, with her face exposed, she faces a room filled with both sexes.

Even if it were possible for a Libyan woman to plot her own freedom, she could neither obtain it nor keep it against the wishes of her male relatives. It is quite possible that she would be done away with, quietly and quickly, at the desire of her husband, brother, or father, if she violated tradition in any way that could be interpreted as "shaming" them — and the act would be considered justified. There might be a slight stir amongst the police, a few gestures towards justice, but in the long run the affair would soon be forgotten.

For women of the Western world, used as we are to freedom of thought and movement, the Libyan woman's life would be unbearable, a prison. But the fact is that for the Libyan woman herself, life is not unbearable; it is not a prison; it is not even unthinkably constrained — it is just, well, just normal life as she and all her friends and family know it. And she is gay within the circle of her home.

And if she herself is moderately contented, why should anyone agitate for things to be different? Why should anyone urge her to be discontented? Why do I feel that my two young friends who have emerged from seclusion have done something desirable? Why don't

I feel that they might have been better off in the old tradition, as men's playthings, or fecundity figures, or symbols of sex, if they were content to be so?

The full answer to this question is not simple, but the practical aspect of it is. Libya in 1958 is a poor nation except for oil, which is still a gamble. To exploit her oil resources to the full, she must have people with knowledge and techniques. She must have intelligent spenders, not ignorant wasters. She must utilize to full capacity what is in the end any nation's greatest natural resource, its human energy and human power. Today, with her women in seclusion, fifty per cent of Libya's potential power is untouched.

Libya is understaffed for every type of employment, and especially so for work which requires training rather than muscle, and skill more than strength. The average income of a Libyan wage earner is infinitesimal, and so also are the salaries of her best-trained personnel. Young men holding responsible positions in government service receive little more than do domestic servants in foreign households. Any increased family capacity to earn is vital.

Inside the home, knowledge of hygiene and child care are primary needs. Knowledge of diet and how to prepare foods is vital. Outside the home, women are crucially needed for nursing, teaching, social services, typing, secretarial jobs, telephone exchange work and work in factories and canneries. For Libya to prosper as a nation, her women must start to live to the full extent of their energies, both inside and outside the home.

Libya has neither geographic nor racial unity. Her three provinces are glued together by mutual dislikes more than by common love. Here is an Arab nation, with her Arab spiritual attachments in the Middle East and her material assistance coming from the West. If she turns full East, she starves; if she turns full West, she will be attacked from the East as a traitor. Today, she faces slightly West with an open hand extended, but the eyes in the back of her head are on Cairo, and her heart beats for Nasser, who is the hero of the Middle East and Arab Africa.

Yet even in this difficult position, the words that Libya speaks are measured ones, when the words of those about her are violent; her voice is calm, when those around her shout; her actions are restrained when sister nations stab and kill, and the Libyan smile is friendly when others scowl.

Much of this is directly attributable to the influence of her king, Sayyid Muhamad Al Sanusi Idris, already in his seventies, a man of God even before he is a monarch. His benign influence and moral dominance is incalculable. It is constantly said that while King Idris lives, there will be no violence. But the corollary is also voiced: what will happen when he dies?

The other day I went to visit Insaf, a young, educated Libyan woman, the wife of a friend. As I arrived, she was about to leave her apartment to walk to the girls' school where she teaches, but with true Libyan hospitality she insisted on returning with me to the apartment so that I might see little Ali Nasser again, and enjoy the miracle of his handsome, healthy growth. Ali, who is now six weeks old, rests in the care of his Bedawi grandmother, who lives with Insaf and her husband, while Insaf is teaching.

It is grandmother who opens the door to us, dressed in her Bedawi garb with long, baggy Arab trousers plainly visible below the copious draperies of her handsome red and orange striped houli. Her skin is olive, and blue tribal tattoos mark her face, but her eyes are bright and warm. She and I can only exchange limited polite greetings in Arabic, but graciousness, hospitality and warmth of welcome emanate from her like the odor of spices.

We find Ali Nasser asleep on the foot of his parents' bed, cocooned in white baby blankets, his pink and white face framed in an embroidered Viyella bonnet and his tiny hands emerging like crumpled blossoms from the sleeves of his hand-sewn Viyella jacket.

Mother, grandmother and I all hover admiringly over Ali, although there can scarcely be three women less alike than we three — a young and beautiful modern Libyan mother, an elderly Bedawi grandmother, and a middle-aged American visitor. Yet we behave much the same as we worship at Ali's little feet. Suddenly Ali, as if conscious in his sleep of his admiring audience, obligingly gives a big, beautiful smile. His mother swiftly presses her two tapering hands together and whispers in English, "My son smiles for me!"

Meanwhile, grandmother whispers loving Arabic words to Ali, and obviously accepts the smile for herself.

Here in this room everything is spotless. Through all the little apartment which I know well, with its treasured belongings of new-lyweds, its oddly assorted and lovingly cared for wedding presents, everything is shining and polished. Here is the white, flowered-china English teapot, and there is the tiny, blue enamel one for Bedawi tea; here is a cotton flower-printed tablecloth, and there are the round, reed-woven Libyan food mats; here are faded chintz pillows on the divan, and there is a woven sheep's wool rug spread beside them. There is a bowl with a few artificial flowers, because there are no flowers in Benghazi, and there is a locally woven baracan beside them.

Here, in this house where a newborn Libyan infant flourishes, the hiatus of centuries and of countries has been spanned. Here one is conscious of no painful gap between the desert Bedawi grandmother and the little new citizen of the modern kingdom of Libya. Here under this roof the great span from Stone Age custom to modern infant training seems to have been covered in the gestation of one womb.

Insaf and I leave the apartment together, and, dressed much alike in wool skirts, jerseys and tweed coats, walk towards her school, gossiping. The wind from the desert is strong and cool about us, the sky is midday pale above us as we walk and talk together — two women most fortunately free to know and feel and see all things about them.

24. A Pinch of Magic Powder

A YOUNG Arab and a Bedawi girl of perhaps eleven years arrived at the front gate this afternoon, and asked Lena to call the "Mama." When I went out to see what they wanted, they said that they had come to ask me to go with them to the nearby nomad settlement to see the girl's father who was ill. The young man, who looked familiar, quickly identified himself as Ramadan, the son of the sick woman whom I had been asked to doctor some weeks before, in the same Bedawi slum. This woman had been coughing up blood when I saw her, and I had taken her to the government hospital.

"How is your mother now? Is she still in hospital?" I asked the boy.

"No, Signora, she did not like to stay. She cannot have her strong tea when she wishes at the hospital. You know that our strong shay is very strengthening. Also, the doctor becomes cross with her for spitting, and in any case there is no one to nurse her in hospital."

"Who nurses her at home?"

"My grandmother takes care of her. Now my grandmother is burning my mother's back in cross directions, and this is curing her cough."

At this point I wondered why Ramadan had brought the girl, Halima, he called her, to ask for my help, as I was not yet prepared to practice cautery on the backs of my invalids. Yet even as I wondered, I knew that my answer was written in their anxious young faces. They were hoping, and looking, without yet believing, for help of some sort from any direction. There just might be a pinch of magic powder in my pocket!

Harry had just arrived home, and I asked him rather apolegetically to go with me to see the man. "I don't know just how I got into this medical practice," I said guiltily. "I'm not anxious to imitate Florence Nightingale!"

"I know how it began," said Lena accusingly. "It started when you bandaged the wounds of the workmen next door when they had accidents. Now they'll always come!"

"And *that* started when Ali's friend chopped his foot, and came here for help, and *you* called me to go and fix him!" I defended myself.

"Anyway, Ma *had* to bandage him," contributed George. "He was bleeding all over our rugs!"

Although neither George nor Lena would at first take an active part in my involuntary local aid program, they were always to be found breathing down my neck and giving advice, as I washed strange wounds in the bathtub. Before the victim left, George would have donated a cigarette, and Lena a cup of coffee, which probably did as much as my treatment. At this time, we were the only local source of running water, and undoubtedly, washing the wounds clean did more for them than anything else.

Now Harry looks at me with a noncommittal look and says, "Come on before it's dark."

As we left the house with Ramadan and Halima in tow, Lena sniffed disapprovingly; she would have sniffed more disapprovingly if we hadn't gone. The car was parked in front of the gate, and surrounded by kids from the settlement who were on their way home from school, where the afternoon session lasts until four-thirty. Their sixth senses had discovered Ramadan and Halima in our house, and they were determined to get in the car with us and have a drive home. I think eight managed to get a foothold, and, studded inside and out with little heads, we started across country following Halima's directions. We left the road and bounced over the lime-stone plain, successfully avoiding potholes and caves and arriving in a few minutes at a cluster of lean-tos built from scraps of corrugated iron from cannibalized barracks roofs.

A wall, or zariba, of tight-stacked dead brush formed a little courtyard, and inside this were a neatly groomed cow, two goats, several lean dogs, and innumerable youngsters. We entered the single room of the lean-to and met a middle-aged woman, two youngish men and seven children. Lying on a woven mat in the corner was a painfully emaciated old man. I say old; he looked old, but he was probably about forty. This was the patient. Everybody including the sick man greeted us with extreme politeness, using both Arabic and Italian salutations.

Seeing how ill the little man looked, and how miserable his surroundings, I felt quite ill myself to think that they had nothing better to appeal to than me. Yet if I didn't try to help them, they would have no help. No doctor would come out to these cases here, for the doctors were all too overworked in the hospital. The old man couldn't get to hospital as the buses didn't come out here. There wasn't a bicycle in the settlement, and if there had been, a sick old man couldn't have ridden it across the city to the hospital. And a taxi — well, who ever heard of a nomad calling a taxi!

The man seemed to be suffering a great deal, and when I asked him to show me where his pain was, he placed his hand on his right side low down and almost in the groin. He also had pain in his back. I felt the areas gently with my hands, wondering about the possibility of appendicitis, or a urinary trouble. When I touched the valley in his groin, he groaned. Harry examined him also, and we agreed there was nothing we could do on our own responsibility, the man must go to hospital for a doctor's care. To my surprise, everybody present agreed willingly, especially when we said we would take him to the hospital in our car.

All in the shack quickly surrounded the little man to dress him, a process which consisted simply of crowding his poor bones into an old British Army overcoat which hung on the wall, and which was, I imagine, the family overcoat. Then the entire family moved in under the patient, like ants under a large particle of food, and swept him out to the car. We told Halima to come with us, as she spoke some English.

We arrived at the hospital in a few minutes, and while Harry parked the car we deposited the patient at the emergency ward.

Here the Egyptian doctor examined him superficially, on the stretcher, and said he thought he had renal colic.

"Bring him back tomorrow," he said, "and we will X-ray him for kidney stones."

"I can't take him home and bring him back again," I said. "He is too ill! He groans all the way coming and going, and his family can do nothing for him. Please keep him in the hospital, and try to treat him."

"Is better you take him home. Our beds are full."

"I can't take him, he's too ill. Can't you give him a mat and blanket on the floor, and give him medicine here? He has no bed at home, anyway."

While we argued, Halima, who has a charming, bright, intelligent face, was busy examining me, the doctor, the orderly, the room and everything about her, with keen interest. Finally the doctor agreed to keep the old man for examination for three days. She got the gist of the conversation immediately and quickly asked me if I would bring her to see Papa tomorrow — a suggestion which I ignored, but to which I will undoubtedly accede.

The doctor brusquely told the patient to go down the hall to the admittance office. As he was quite incapable of doing so on his own, Halima and I got him off the stretcher and into his ancient overcoat again, and the three of us tottered down the hall to the office. Here the old boy fell into a chair and sat submissively, looking like an old soldier's ghost, while the orderly quizzed him for odd bits of information, which the old man did not have, to put on his entry card. Here we left him.

Halima was now filled with trust, while I was beginning to wonder if I had done the old boy a kindness to bring him.

"But what else can we do?" I said to Harry. "We couldn't leave him in that hovel without any medical help — but at least he had friends there. Here in the hospital they just don't care!"

"Fact is, that we can't do anything," Harry said. "But we don't like to admit it!"

The dusk had fallen, and Halima was bouncing about in the back seat as we threaded our way across the cratered plain at some risk in the dark. "Anyway, Halima is enjoying it," I thought. We arrived at the little brush stockade, and the car was instantly surrounded by a crowd of waiting children into whose midst Halima descended, but not forgetting her manners.

"Goodbye, Signora, Signor. Thank you, Signora. Halima go with you see Papa tomorrow?"

"Maybe, Halima."

Halima

The next morning by seven o'clock Halima was calling for "Mama" at the gate in front of the house. Was Mama ready to go to the hospital? Lena told her that it wasn't time to go yet, to come back in an hour. Two minutes later I looked out of my bedroom window and saw her wispy, tatttered, wind-blown figure parading along the top of our garden wall until she arrived close to my window. She waved at me then, and shouted from the wall, "We go now for my papa!"

"No," I called back. "We go see Papa at ten o'clock. Too early now to see visitors."

"No, no," shrilled Halima, madly waving a green paper slip at me. "Papa home now. Papa ready now to go hospital for picture."

"Holy cow!" I thought in amazement and wonder. "Papa's got

more energy than I have!" I hurried outside and took a look at Halima's green slip. Sure enough, it was a hospital admittance slip for an X ray.

"Hurry, now," said Halima. "Papa go hospital for picture."

"How did Papa come home?" I asked with respect.

By now Ali, who was listening over the fence, involved himself in a dramatic dialogue in Arabic with Halima, as a result of which he said to me, "Her papa walk home last night because hospital no give him place to stay. Now her papa more sick today. Halima say you take him back to hospital for make picture, please."

I was absolutely wordless before the mental picture of the old soldier's ghost tottering painfully back alone across the cratered plain in the dark. I was far from wordless in what I hoped to say to the hospital.

"All right," I said calmly. "I'll take him back now. But he *must* stay at hospital because he is very ill, and I can't take him back and forth every day. He *must* stay."

Halima nodded her full and convinced agreement and jumped off the wall inside the garden and trotted towards the kitchen, where two minutes later I heard Lena giving her coffee. I myself was torn between tears and laughter.

I got out the car, and Halima and I drove back to the shanty for Papa. I had stopped trying to guess what to expect, whether Papa would emerge on the wings of an angel, or riding a bicycle, or be drawing his last breath. I waited outside this time, while all the neighbors rushed in to prepare Papa. After five minutes of confusion Halima came out to me and said, pounding her little fists together to emphasize, "Papa no can get out! Papa too sick. You come."

I went inside and saw that Papa was semi-conscious and delirious, groaning with every movement, and apparently completely helpless. Beside him stood two tiny little old men, looking equally helpless.

"We *must* get him to the hospital," I said, determined that Papa was not to die here without my making a last effort. Between them the two tiny old men, less fragile than they looked, carried, pushed and pulled Papa into my car, the tinier one getting in first, and then holding the invalid in his arms. A pair of worn-out shoes was carefully handed in after him, and the family overcoat was placed gently over him. Then, Halima riding in front with me, we started off again.

At the hospital I drove directly to the admitting gate to find the Egyptian doctor who had promised me last night to take Papa in. There was no one in the office except a few odd patients, who told me that doctors and assistants were all at the outpatients' office this morning.

I next drove to the X ray office, whose location I knew from the time when my broken elbow was X-rayed. I parked the car immediately in front of the office, leaving Halima, Papa and the tiny ones in the car, and I went in. The office was jammed with patients, but no radiologist was there. I went next door to the operating theater, and I found the Italian Sister who had given me a hypo when they set my arm. She thought I might be having trouble with my arm, and when I told her it had mended perfectly, she said I was very fortunate. I assured her that it was all due to the marvelous bone-setting of little Italian Dr. Guerera.

"Today I have brought in a very ill Libyan," I said, "who is to be X-rayed, and then must be admitted to hospital as a patient."

She shook her head sadly, and said, "We have no vacant bed in the hospital."

"Well, please come and see him, anyway. Perhaps you can fix some place for him."

She came out with me to the car. My little Bedawi flock sat in depressed silence, except for Papa's groans. Seeing that my patient was really ill and unable to walk, Sister said that she would try to get the operating room stretcher as soon as it was vacant.

Half an hour later a patient was wheeled out of the operating room on a stretcher, and a few minutes later, the patient having been snatched off it, the orderly wheeled it over to us. He and Sister got Papa on to it, and Sister went with him into the X ray room. She promised that after the doctor had seen the patient's X rays she would try to find Dr. Guerera to talk with me about the patient.

Halima and I waited an hour, and then Salem, the tinier Bedawi, who had gone with Papa to the X ray room, came back and asked me to go in and see the radiologist. I went in and found a young Englishwoman, who said, "You can take the old man home now. The pictures are finished."

"It is impossible for him to go home," I said. "He must remain in the hospital."

She said, "That is not my business. Please see Dr. Sgair, the Director, who admits all patients. The orderly will take you to him."

Outside the X ray room I met Dr. Klug, an efficient German physician whom I had first met when he came to our house to treat our friend, Jan. Like all the Germans one meets, he had been anti-Nazi and anti-Hitler, he told us. Surprised to see me today, he also asked, "Well, what are *you* doing here? I heard that you broke your elbow. Is that what's troubling you today?"

"My elbow is perfect now, thanks to your wonderful Dr. Guerera. No, there is nothing wrong with me. I have come about a Libyan . . ." And I explained again as briefly as I could.

The doctor smiled rather cynically, I thought, and said dryly, "Very kind of you, I'm sure. You seem to be a good neighbor," in what seemed to be a sarcastic tone. I could see him swiftly cataloguing me as one of those naïve American do-gooders who are, if possible, more trouble than the Ugly Americans. Anyway, his tone touched me off.

"No, I am not a good neighbor, and I am not trying to be, and I don't ask anyone to think so!" I said testily. "This is a case of negative values. Here is a sick old man, poor and helpless, and his child asks me to help him. I have the ability to assist him. I am not a benefactor for doing so, but I'd be a bloody brute not to! This man is ill and he needs care. You'll have to take him into the hospital. I refuse to kill him by dragging him back to his hovel again!"

"Then we must go and see Dr. Sgair," said Dr. Klug quietly, beginning to credit me with more sense than he had done. "The surgical ward is already overflowing. But perhaps we can get him into the medical ward, if need be. First, we must see what the diagnosis is."

With the orderly trundling Papa on his stretcher, Salem trotting beside, and Halima holding my skirt, we crossed the court to the main building, picked our way through the ragged patients, and approached the inner sanctum of Dr. Sgair. In answer to my knock, a large, rather belligerent-looking man appeared. I breathlessly unloaded my case on him, and he retreated hastily before me, saying, "Better see Dr. Sgair," and beckoning me after him. Just then Dr. Klug appeared, and together we entered the inner office and approached a gray-haired, gray-faced, tired-looking man with one clear eye and the other one blue-veiled and almost sightless — Dr. Sgair. Dr. Klug introduced me to him as a valued friend, and at his invitation I sat down and once more told my story.

Dr. Sgair listened without comment, and probably without understanding my English. Dr. Klug, however, spoke up quickly, and said, "I know we sound calloused to you, but as we do not have beds for all, we must select whom we take. Also, we cannot take patients whom we cannot help, who are incurable and will just fill the wards until they die. They must give place to those whom we can help."

"I am sure this man is really ill," I answered. "I am not a doctor, and I am unable to help him except to bring him to you. This is the only place in the world this sick old Libyan has to come for help, the only place he is entitled to be taken care of. Perhaps in the long run I am doing him no good by trying to help him. But am I entitled, or are you, to throw this man's life away?"

Dr. Klug hastily said, "Of course, as a doctor it is always my duty to try to save life. But we have many who come here and pretend to be sick, because either they are tired or they just want to escape from work. One man has come in here five times complaining of extreme pain from renal colic. Five minutes after he is admitted, he is brewing tea in the corridor and walking up and down, smoking."

"I know that you have a lot to put up with here, Doctor. And I know that you do a wonderful job without good working facilities, as witness the way Dr. Guerera cared for my elbow. But I am sure that my little Bedawi is *not* faking."

"I shall examine him myself, and see his X rays, and if necessary we will admit him in the medical ward somehow. You had better come to my office and wait while I examine him."

I shook hands with Dr. Sgair, who had not said a word and seemed relieved to have escaped from making any decision. We left his office and, followed again by Papa on the stretcher, pushed by the orderly and trailed by Salem and Halima, we crossed the courtyard to another building and went upstairs. Here I lost the stretcher, and

entered Dr. Klug's office. He introduced the attractive young German woman at the desk as his wife, and I sat down. After estimating
each other silently for a moment as females, suddenly we both
smiled and relaxed.

"Have you been here long?" I asked her.

"Several years — much *too* long!" she said with a sigh.

"You don't like it here?"

"How can I like it? We have no peace, ever! My husband works
at the hospital all day, and when he comes home at night the people
follow him to the house at all hours and ask for his help. They will
not take no for an answer. They wait and they wait outside, and in
the end they insist on getting inside in some way or other to see him.
He cannot work day and night both! He also is human. I must try to
stand always between the people and my husband. Because of this, I
have come to dislike the people. I cannot be always sorry for them,
because they annoy me too much! They climb over my wall, they
come in my door, they wait beside my motorcar! Sick, sick, sick
people all over the place! I think this also make *me* sick!"

I could visualize perfectly the perpetual stage of seige of the doctor and his wife by just recalling Halima's determined arrival over
the top of my own wall. Sick, sick people all over the place! And
what could one do about it, unless one could give them ten times the
hospitalization, a hundred times the number of doctors and nurses,
and complete, country-wide courses of home hygiene and infant
care?

The doctor returned in a few minutes, and said that he had seen
the X rays and examined the patient. "We shall admit him to the
hospital to stay for the present," he said.

"Well, thank you very much, Doctor. What did you determine is
the matter with him?"

"Our X rays and diagnosis suggest that the patient has tuberculo-
sis, pneumonia and kidney stones."

I said goodbye to the doctor and his wife, very grateful indeed
that he hadn't handed the patient back to me to be taken home to
die, as one on whom they could not waste a bed! On my way down-
stairs the tinier Bedawi passed me, hurrying upward carrying Papa's
shoes and his overcoat, which I feared he would not need very soon.

Halima was waiting for me in the car, and when Salem returned we drove back across the limestone plain to the brush-fenced enclosure they called home. We made a quiet arrival, as most of the children were away at school, the goats were out chewing on Garden City gardens, and the cow was manuring them. Salem and Halima thanked me very politely for taking Papa to the hospital, and before I had time to leave, Halima said, "Halima go see Papa tomorrow?"

I had been expecting this, and I said, "Bad bukra," or "Day after tomorrow," thinking that each day we missed was something gained.

25. Instead of Dirty Rags

THEIR wounds are always tied up with dirty rags. I think it is the dirty rags which so unfailingly involve me; I must get rid of that dirty rag! And then, once having exposed the wound, I might as well wash and bandage it. After all, I have running water, and the nomads around me do not; I have clean bandages where they have soiled rags. But don't think that I see myself as a Samaritan; more exactly, I am a person with a strong desire to tidy things up — rags, wounds, people, or houses.

Now the scene from our windows, seen through the red dust, has been gradually changing. In front and to the left of us, three houses have sprung up, and over the middle one flies the Soviet emblem. This house is the Soviet embassy, and the walls here have been heightened above those of its neighbors, its iron gates have been made impervious, and before it paces the police guard.

Up and down he paces, until the change of guard comes, when, after a chat, he sometimes drifts in our direction for a cup of coffee (one should always be friends with the police!), and after that, down the road to the little Arab shop for bread. This shop has been thrown together from the inevitable ex-war rusty pieces of sheet metal. The shopkeeper, a fierce-looking man with amiable ways, is always surrounded by a group of gossiping Arabs, smoking and spitting and talking politics.

The little shop was here to service the nomads on this plain long before Garden City was dreamed of, much less built. It is prospering now, as workmen and Arab boys come here for Arab bread, which must be fresh daily, for tomato paste, chili peppers and salt, and maybe, sometimes, a small tin of sardines. The shopkeeper even makes "sandwiches" now for his clients by cutting a whole loaf of bread lengthwise, then sprinkling it with salt and tomato paste. We Keiths also come here for the crusty, tasty, nourishing Arab bread, which is made from full wheat flour.

The other day the embassy policeman drifted by with an eye wide open in hope of coffee, just when Lena, George and I were having espressos on the sunny veranda. Along with exchanging Arabic greetings — How are you? Very good, thanks to Allah! Very well, thanks be to Allah! And how are *you*? Very good indeed, thanks be to Allah! Very well, and Allah be thanked! — we asked him to come in and drink coffee with us. He gladly accepted, and while he was drinking his cup of strong, sweet, fragrant coffee I saw that his thumb was tied up in the real, original dirty rag, a thumb towards which I felt an immediate irresistible urge to tidy. The policeman gladly permitted, and then went his way to the shop for bread. From this involuntary action of mine, I trace the spreading news of my irresistible urge to replace rags with bandages.

As usual, this morning the gate bell was not rung, but a dark Arab face pressed against the ironwork peering earnestly in, while a voice called, gently but urgently, "Signora! Signora!" I heard, but was anxious not to, as I was writing.

Lena hurried out, and I heard her chattering in the sun in Italian. Soon footsteps entered the house, one pair shuffling along in Arab slippers. Lena came to me in the study, and said apologetically, "It is the Arab shopkeeper. He has cut his hand. He asked me if the Signora Doctoressa is at home!" and she had to giggle at my new title.

I laughed too, having only myself to blame. But I said, "Damn! I've just got started writing! Is he badly hurt? Could you bandage it this time?"

"Oh, no, Signora!" She looked at me in horror. "There's a lot of blood! And he wants the lady doctor!" She giggles again.

I went out to the little man, who had his left hand wound up in the usual, but twice as much of it and already soaked with blood. When he unwrapped it I had a shock. He had split his thumb lengthwise, starting at the tip and down through the nail to the first knuckle. He said that he had been holding a loaf of bread in his hand and cutting lengthwise down it with a blow of his heavy knife, which had slipped and continued into his thumb.

I knew the wound should be stitched, and I said I would drive him immediately to the hospital.

"I cannot go to hospital, Signora. I have my shop to care for. You please bandage my hand," he said determinedly.

"I don't think I can. This needs stitches," I said.

"Signora, if I go to hospital today, the doctor tells me come tomorrow, and day after tomorrow, and I cannot go. There is no bus, I have no bicycle, and I have my shop to keep. Please bandage my hand, Signora. I can come to you every day."

"Better try, Ma," urges George, appearing from the study always glad of any excuse to stop studying. "Better try. We can do it!"

"Yes, Signora," Lena agrees. "He will not go to the hospital, I know. Is better for you fix it than leave it like this."

With my cohorts behind me, I escorted Mustapha to the bathroom, where I held his hand under running water for a time, then soaked it in Dettol solution. Then I held the two pieces of finger tightly together, and placed around them a thin piece of gauze bandage greased with penicillin ointment to prevent sticking. Then I wound adhesive tape tightly around the finger to keep the pieces of flesh close together. I put the hand in a splint to stop him from using it, and told him he must keep it upright to lessen bleeding. He agreed with everything gladly, promising not to use the hand more than necessary. I told him to return the next day as I wished to watch for signs of infection. He thanked me earnestly and with dignity, and left.

"Will it be O.K., Ma?" George wanted to know.

This was exactly what I wanted to know. "I hope so. It needs to be stitched, of course, but I think the tape may hold it tightly enough so that the flesh will heal together anyway, especially if he doesn't use it. If it doesn't get infected, I think it will be all right. Anyway, it's better than a dirty rag."

Mustapha came every day, and no sign of infection appeared. On the fifth day I cut open the bandage and found the finger was quite clean, but the two pieces of flesh were not firmly held together. I put the tape directly on the finger this time, and held the pieces more tightly together. A few days later my examination showed that the flesh was now growing together.

By now he was using his hand considerably, and when he returned a week later the bandage was very soiled, and the wound showed infection. Now we started a series of hot saltwater fomentations, and I sent him home daily with his hand tied up with wet salt bandages inside a plastic bag to keep them damp. A week of this subdued the infection and we returned to dry bandages. Soon I was able to leave this off, too. The finger was not beautiful, but it was completely useful again.

Meanwhile, Lena, George and I had all become attached to Mustapha. He had marvelous independence of spirit and complete lack of servility, and in a way we all four enjoyed his calls. He was always cheerful, polite and grateful, and he often brought up a few fresh eggs or oranges when he came. He always asked after "the Signor's" health, and thanked Allah earnestly for the good health of all of us and of himself. The day I took off the final bandage and told him he need not return, I marveled at how a man from such a different world, and with such a completely different personality, could have fitted so pleasantly into our life.

The three-day feast of Id el-Fitr has a tremendous religious significance in the Moslem world. It not only marks the close of Ramadan, but these are the special days on which Moslems give alms or food to the poor, give presents to friends, heal any feuds, if possible, and acknowledge, with some gift, all debts of gratitude.

This was our first Ramadan in Benghazi, and I was rather missing the visits of our dear friends, Hammet and Badreddin, and the honey cakes and feast cakes which they used to bring us along with the spirit of Ramadan. As the second day of the Id began, I thought sadly that there was no one here to bring us the real spirit of the feast. But . . .

The first to come was little Fedal, whose ankle had been cut by scrap iron when he was working on the house next door. Ali had recently told me that Fedal had a new job now, driving the Coca-Cola truck. Fedal arrived at eight A.M. at the front door with a gift case of Coca-Cola for us! This was accompanied by many thanks and hamdu li'llahs to us for taking care of his ankle.

Soon came Halima with withered carnations and a few of the plain's tiny wild things. The carnations, I knew, had been recovered from somebody's scrap heap, but they looked good to Halima, and she felt sure that they would to me. Poor Papa had died, I already knew, but Halima looked quite cheerful this morning, her rags no more ragged, her wisps no more flimsy, and today her hair was nicely combed. She remembered her hospital rides with pleasure, and said, "Halima say thank you to Mama!"

Then came the very poor boy whost infected foot Lena had treated, much against her own qualms and fears, when we had been away on leave. He brought her six fresh eggs. Lena came rushing in to me with a disturbed, yet delighted, expression, and said, "Saad brings me these eggs, which I am very unhappy to take because he has so many children. But I must take them, or I offend him!"

"I think he is happy to give them, Lena. A Libyan never likes to receive without returning."

Then came gay little Ali, who is always on a pig's back for good spirits. He brought a dozen eggs and a load of gossip, and we all had espressos together.

Last to arrive was Mustapha of the chopped thumb. He had closed his shop for the day, and he was neatly dressed in blue Arab trousers, with two braid-trimmed vests of different lengths, and a pair of store shoes, still very rare among Benghazi Arabs. Mustapha brought a box of Cadbury's (imported from England) assorted chocolates in a fancy box tied up with ribbons! Another coffee was served.

It is an odd thing to recall that I have frequently heard foreigners in Libya express the opinion that Libyans do not show gratitude. Now at the close of this feast day I had to say, as I had said in my childhood about Christmas, that it was the best Id el-Fitr I had ever had.

My Mohamed had never failed to give something to a beggar. Hammet always did the same, brushing the beggar away from me and saying, "Malesh!" — Never mind — but always giving himself. Badreddin, too, would stop me from giving (Libyans are proud), but gave himself without fail. Suleiman, treating me to coffee at the sidewalk café, motions the beggar away from me but brings out a coin to give.

I have never seen a Libyan fail to give a coin to a beggar who asked. As a Moslem, he knows that he himself is blessed by giving alms to the needy, and the waiting beggar thus gives him the opportunity to be blessed. The Libyan gives a small coin, and the beggar thanks him.

But the beggar's sense of comparative money values is well developed. If I give the same small coin to him, he follows me down the street cursing me in Arabic for my impecuniousness.

It is in the nature of the beggar's business that he should dress the part, and perhaps it is necessary for him to be dirty, as he probably comes from a Bidonville where there is no water. Often a beggar is blind, and accompanied by a small child who leads him up to you, palm out, and waits. Sometimes small children carrying babies are on the street begging. One knows the baby is a prop — but perhaps this brings a double blessing for the giver.

When I first arrived in Tripoli I was regularly followed by a disagreeable-looking old man wrapped in a filthy baracan, his feet swaddled in rags and his head wound up in them, and the sum total exuding a musky smell. As he walked along just behind me, he would beg in a whining tone, interspersing his pleas for cash with blessings of Allah upon my head if I gave him some. I started by giving him a couple of piastres (five cents) each time, to get rid of him — but it worked in the opposite way. Soon he never ceased to follow me until I gave him something.

At this time there was a certain amount of purse-snatching in the city, and one of my chief objections to giving to street beggars was that, with my arms full of parcels, I was forced to open my purse and fish around in it for cash, leaving my purse exposed to snatching.

Finally one day I could no longer put up with the dirty shadow just over my shoulder muttering whines and incantations, and I turned on him and said, "La! La! No! No!" and went into a shop. But he was waiting when I came out and followed me for several streets, but without giving me Allah's blessing. I hoped this was the end.

But no, he knew my habitats too well, and he still followed me daily while I did my shopping. His approach was polite while he still had hopes, but it soon changed to imprecations. His persistence was admirable, and long after he had given up hope of cash he would wait outside shops for me in order to curse me. It didn't work, for now I was tough.

Then we moved to Benghazi. I had learned my lesson: I would never give to a street beggar. But here I found no beggars! There were poor people, yes — but no professional poverty.

Then one day, whom should I see waiting on the corner of the main thoroughfare, but my dirty old friend! He greeted me like a long lost relative, and started to follow me again. Giving up my errands for the day, I dashed away from the modern city center and hurried towards the suk. I dodged in the city end of its long covered concourse, and never stopped until I came out at the other end. I had lost him; I must have known the Benghazi suk better than he did.

I avoided going to the city for a few days, but when I returned I did not see him. I never saw him again. He had come to the wrong place; Benghazi does not approve of beggars. Where all are poor, no man may beg.

26. Nomad Heritage

NOT ALL of our friends in the nearby black tents and scrap metal shanties were ill and suffering or asking help. In general these Bedawi were an independent, self-respecting, hard-working group, who asked and expected nothing more than survival. Most of them lived as semi-nomads, spending the entire dry season on the Fuihat plain, so Halima told me.

One clear, crisp afternoon about three I heard a familiar shrill, horase voice intoning persistently outside my window, "Mama! Mama! Lady! Signora!"

It was Halima making her usual top-of-the-wall arrival, from which vantage point she could look into my study, and also my bedroom, and decide if it was a favorable time to speak. If I was alone in the study it was; if I was in the bedroom dressing, best return to the front gate and ring! Timidity never caused her to hesitate; it was just a matter of deciding which approach was most diplomatic.

Today I called out to her, "Halima, please get off the wall! Go back to the gate and ring the bell!"

"Yes, Mama, I go," dancing on the wall. "Mama, today I bring friends to visit!"

"Through the gate, please, Halima," but I glanced quickly down the wall, half expecting to see several other youngsters dancing on it.

"Yes, Mama," and she smiled delightedly, a wild, sweet smile, and skipped down the wall, trampling Harry's climbing vine, stamping on the infant clematis, and knocking down a flowerpot.

I went to the gate, and there were three bright faces with piercing eyes pressed against the grating, confidently waiting for the invitation to enter. As introduced to me the girl, Kadija, was about eleven, Halima's age, and the boy, Fuad, was a year or so younger. They had true desert good manners, and each one snatched my hand fiercely, touched it to his breast, forehead, and mouth, still holding it in his own hand, in salutation.

As they entered the house they looked all about them, not rudely but with honest curiosity. They immediately noticed my Libyan-made ceramic tiles with Fatima's hand emblazoned, as these stand above the fireplace. Kadija and Fuad made a quick Arabic commentary between them, while Halima, with a nod at the other two, said complacently, "No speak English. *Me* speak English. Fatima's hand good!"

While we waited for refreshments to arrive, they all sat on the edge of their chairs, a fact which I appreciated in the hope that they might leave fewer fleas behind. Soon Lena brought Kitty-Kolas, peanuts, caramels, and Turkish coffee, meanwhile receiving her own share of polite salutations. Although there was little conversation, a well-developed air of satisfaction soon engulfed us.

"Do Kadija and Fuad go to school?" I asked Halima.

"No much. Fuad help the Papa make barley."

"And Kadija?"

"Kadija help Mama with babies. Three babies. Too much babies!"

"They have house? Or black tent?"

"Very good house. You come see?"

I hadn't planned on a social afternoon, but if I was going to have one anyway, I thought I might as well see more of the nomad way of life. And the kids would enjoy the ride home.

"I come, Halima. First we finish eat."

With considerable dignity, the three managed to eat everything in sight, but slowly, daintily, to show their enjoyment, and quite without gluttony. Exchange of food and drinks is necessary Arabic hospitality, but it must be done graciously and unhurriedly, and not just for food value — or so it must appear!

As we were about to leave, Halima, who with typical Arabic good manners had saved the real reason for her visit to the last, asked me very casually if I had any extra pieces of that "stuff," and she pointed to the mosquito netting which hung in my back door. Our house was screened, but there is always one door which the landlord leaves screenless, apparently assuming that the flies will gallantly avoid that door. I always hang mosquito netting in the unscreened door. Halima had evidently noticed this "stuff" on a former visit.

"Yes, I have a piece," I said. "You want?"

Typically, Halima now deprecated any real desire for same, and said, with a shrug, "You no like to give Halima, malesh! You like give to Halima — O.K. I take!"

I found I had a two-yard length and rolled it up for her. I was longing to know what she would use it for, but felt I shouldn't ask. I showed her the weights I had sewn in the bottom of my own curtain, and said, "You can put stones. Stones good." Halima nodded knowingly, but volunteered nothing.

This time we drove a bit beyond Halima's group of shanties, to a house with mud walls which stood slightly apart. Apparently, last-minute additions had been made to mark the growth of family or livestock, and these consisted of long palm branches leaning up against the mud walls in lean-to fashion. The roof was scrap metal. Standing outside the house were two ex-army jerry cans which were undoubtedly used as water storage tanks. None of the Arab dwellings here had running water, but a limited water supply was available at a well about half a mile distant. As usual, there were goats and sheep wandering about, and a camel tethered near, which marked this family as a moderately affluent one.

I knew that inside the little house there would be no lights, no water, no heating, no cooking arrangements, and probably no clock. There was sure to be, however, a little blue enamel tea kettle and small tea glasses; and I could already hear a battery radio blaring forth in Arabic!

By now a woman has wandered out of the house with a tiny, swaddled baby in her arms and a naked two-year-old boy trotting beside her.

"This Mama of Kadija," says Halima. "Her name Amina."

Amina is wearing a henna and indigo striped baracan, and she has not bothered to throw it over her dark, swarthy face, where blue tattoos on forehead, nose tip and chin proclaim her tribal alliance. Like most Bedawi women, she wears silver bracelets and anklets. Her age is imponderable; but as her eldest child is eleven or twelve years, I think she must be at least twenty-four years old, and not more than twenty-eight. Yet she could be sixty by her wrinkles and angles. There is no youthful softness or roundness left in her face; perhaps there never was any, for there is little even now in Kadija's. But there exists in both these female faces something to admire — a spirit of unsubdued fierceness and endurance, which is breathtaking.

Amina greets me in Arabic with the phrases which every foreigner here learns first, and which to me are now filled with warmth and sentiment. Kefhalek? Kuwais. Bahi. Kefhalkum? Kuwais bahi. El hamdu li'llah! El hamdu li'llah! How are you? Are you good? I hope you are well. I am well. I am very good. Make yourself welcome, Praise to God. How are you? I am very good, Praise to God. El hamdu li'llah! El hamdu li'llah! Hand-kissing, hand-kissing, hand-kissing!

Bedawi
wife.

Just as we finish our courtesies, out of the house pops a middle-aged, well-built, dark-skinned man, barefoot and wearing baggy Arab trousers of dark blue cotton, topped by an ancient khaki battle jacket. He shakes me firmly by the hand, and says in good English idiom, "How d'you do?" The khaki battle jacket gives me a clue.

"This Papa. Name Abdullah. He speaks English good," says Halima.

"I fight war in desert with English soldier," says Abdullah proudly. "You come in my house, please? Take shay, please?"

An invitation to drink tea is as much a command as a request, and necessary to good relations. One never enters a Libyan abode, no matter how humble, without being offered something to drink, which in courtesy one should accept. Although the concentrated, sweet, black tea, in which the tea leaves have been left to stew in boiling water and sugar is piled high, is not very palatable to a Westerner, it is the main source of energy and stimulation to the Libyan, as it is his chief source of sugar.

The tea ritual is also a spiritual luxury, without which the materially poor Libyan would be truly impoverished, and I accept the invitation with appreciation, and enter the single-room mud house. The door and window openings are partially closed by handwoven hangings of goat's hair, and there is no furniture except the small "tea table," which stands only ten inches high, homemade from pieces of tinned tuna crate, as markings show. On the earth floor there are handwoven reed mats which serve as beds at night, for a nomad must naturally limit his belongings, the chief of which must be his tent, to what can be placed on his camel's back. Apparently a necessity, however, is the small battery radio, which is now bleating out Radio Cairo.

While I sit on a mat and look curiously about, and estimate the number of fleas I will take home, Amina has made a charcoal fire on the floor, and her teakettle is stewing. Kadija jiggles and kisses the baby, Halima mothers the two-year-old, and the four-year-old, another boy, comes sauntering over to me to feel my silk skirt with sticky hands. I wonder why there isn't a six-year-old, and an eight-year-old? Perhaps they have died.

Now Abdullah is happy to practice his English. "You English, lady?"

"No, American. But my husband is from Canada."

"Canada? Where is that country?"

"Canada is near the United States." The US, I have found, is the only country that North America means in Africa. "You have farm here in Fuihat, Abdullah?"

"Yes, lady, two miles away. I grow barley, also fûl* and tomatoes. I have date palms near."

"You do not need to buy much?"

"I buy only tea and sugar."

"Kadija and Fuad go to school?"

"La! Fuad must help me farm, and watch the goats and sheep. My sons are my wealth, hamdu li'llah! My baby boys are too small, but they will grow, in sha'Allah! A man must keep his sons for work."

"Kadija can go to school?"

"Kadija must help Mama to weave, carry water, and care for babies. Very soon is time for Kadija to marry, never mind school! Sons are more good for her than school!"

Abdullah speaks what for him is the truth. In the past, Libyans have always of necessity been farmers and shepherds, and every man's wealth was in his sons, who were his unpaid laborers.

Today, the fashion for schooling is spreading, and doors are opening into a new kind of world. Sons are becoming discontent to labor in their fathers' fields and to wander the desert shepherding their fathers' flocks. Sons are developing ambitions of their own which are marked chiefly by the determination *not* to be as their fathers were before them.

If Fuad were sent to school to study, an occupation to which an untrained boy does not settle easily, I can imagine that his ambition would soon be to escape from both schooling and farming and learn to drive something mechanized. The more that the modern world invades Libya, the more that paradise, to Libyans, seems to lie in mechanized wheels and coils. The farmer wants a tractor for his half-acre, the camel driver wants a truck, the donkey merchant wants a Land Rover, the bicycle rider wants a Volkswagen, and Hasan al-Rida, the Crown Prince, only travels by airplane! Machines offer the quickest escape from environment.

"At what season do you leave this house for the desert?" I ask,

* Popular Egyptian bean.

knowing that semi-nomads must have two homes and exploit two habitats in order to exist, so impoverished are their local surroundings.

"After the rains, when desert pastures begin to turn green, then we take sheep and goats south to the desert pasture of my tribe. Always in all times past, my tribe has a pasture south. There also is a wadi bed which I plow and plant with barley."

"And your house in the desert?"

"My house is my tent."

The black goat and camel's hair tent will go on his camel's back, anl Amina and Kadija and Fuad and the lesser ones, including a new one every year or so, accompanied by the sheep and goats, will walk for many miles southward to the immemorial pasturage of Abdullah's tribe, which no other tribe can ever challenge without a fight, and where the black tent is home.

There will still be no plumbing, and now no water, except what Amina and Kadija will carry once a week in goatskin water bags from a well some miles away, and this will be used only for drinking. The washing will be done by rubbing soiled surfaces, including the skin, with sand. Once again, the children will have no school, for on the desert there will be even more work for them to do.

"What do you eat on the desert, Abdullah?"

"We eat bazin, and dates, Signora. Sometimes we have tomatoes and oil with bazin. We are not rich like the Tripoli Libyans, but we do not starve."

Bazin is made from barley flour, which Amina will grind from barley grain. She mixes the flour with water to form a paste which she may bake in coals, or drop like a dumpling into boiling water, or she may just mix it and give it to her family to eat as a cereal. Bazin is a desert necessity; to have peppers, tomato paste or oil to flavor it makes it a luxury. The dates will be sun-dried until they are almost crystallized: the sweetest dates in the world and the most luscious — and full of sand from the desert winds.

"When will you return, Abdullah?"

"Ah, Signora, we wait in our tent until summer, when the barley is ready to cut. We do not leave without our harvest."

And as he waits for the barley to ripen, Abdullah must hope that the desert pasturage holds out, and that the wells don't go dry, so that his flocks will survive till the barley is reaped, *if* the year is good and there is some rain. Then Abdullah, with his barley harvest, with his family and flocks, will live to return to the mud-walled house where we sit now, and another year in his life will have passed without gain — but without loss, hamdu li'llah!

And will Kadija wish to be as her mother is? Married at twelve with a child every year, and the life of a shepherd, field harvester, pack animal, water carrier, and drudge before her?

It is not easy for a woman to escape.

Malesh! Never mind what Kadija wishes, for her life is already written for her by Allah, and as Kadija well knows, there is no God but Allah, and Mohammed is his Prophet.

27. Diversions

Keeping up with the nomads of the red plain was only one side of Benghazi; the other was the small, cozy life we carried on inside our white stone walls.

We were a family again for this year — with George alternating between schoolboy and man, with temperamental, dark-haired, pixie-faced Maddelena glowing one day and glowering the next, with Pucci already developing a Mediterranean temperament, with me talking execrable Italian and loving it, with Harry always too busy, yet working devotedly in "spare time" on his Libyan flora — while I held my breath not to disturb the magic of the year. It was a time to make memories.

There was the day when George and I tried to drive across the salt flat which turned out to be a mud swamp. Half sunk in mud, we were discovered by some nomads who, in exchange for what small change we had and a few cigarettes, lifted the car out bodily and put it on the causeway. We wondered afterward if perhaps they lived behind the bushes waiting for cars to get stuck! As George and I had the reputation of getting into trouble when off on our own, we made mad haste to hurry home and clean the car before Harry came home. Then we told him about it — after he could see that all had ended well!

We all three drove about a great deal, with the good excuse of collecting Libyan flora and always accompanied by plant presses and plastic bags for specimens. Our friends had to collect, too, never escaping without instructions as to how to care for the specimens. It never occurred to Harry just to take a drive for fun. Fortunately, the new seacoast, the Green Mountain, the Barce Plain, even Cyrene with its lion-strangling nump, all offered flora opportunities.

I studied considerably at home with George on his high school courses, which presented old subjects under new names. He was taking high school correspondence courses in preparation for the college exams which he planned to take during our leave in Canada. Mathematics was still beyond me, but geography was a fascinating subject now that I could trace my own travels on the map, and George, at eighteen, had already left a trail through Asia, Europe and Africa. History, I found, had many redeeming features, especially if it were taught showing its direct relationship to the present.

I was also doing a great deal of Libyan reading, which I had not found time to do in Tripoli. In London, Harry had discovered a beautiful calf-bound first edition (1827) of *Northern Coast of Africa*, by the Beechey brothers, filled with fantastic, delicate steel engravings made from H. Beechey's own drawings and delicious stories about Benghazi. Here I found a fable by Kazwini, translated from the Arabic, which expressed perfectly an historical truth. . . .

Many years ago a traveler passed through a large and well-populated city and asked one of its citizens at what date it was founded, and what was its history. Oh, sir, came the answer, this is an ancient and eternal city, and it has always been in existence!

Five hundred years later, the ageless traveler passed again, and the city had vanished, leaving nothing but open country. He asked a countryman to tell him how the city had been destroyed. Oh, sir, he answered, there was never a city here! It has always been country such as you see.

Five hundred years later the traveler passed where the stretch of country had been, and it was covered by the sea. He asked a fisherman he met to tell him when the country had been inundated. Oh, sir, it has always been thus — a great sea!

Five hundred years later the timeless traveler passed again. The sea had dried up and there was land. He asked the first person that he met what had happened to the sea that had been there before. The peasant gave him a surprised reply — Oh, sir, it has always been dry land, as you see!

Five hundred years later the tireless, timeless, ageless traveler, footsore and limping and determined that this was his last time around, passed by again, and here he found a large, well-populated city. He asked a citizen to tell him when it was founded, and something of its history. Oh, sir, this is the ancient and eternal city, and it has always been here!

After that, the traveler stayed at home, and wrote books about ants, whom he decided were easier to understand! . . .

To each person his own episode in history seems set apart, unique, and without reason. To the traveler in time who seeks a connecting thread, the episodes have always one thing in common, the comment of the unwitting observer — Oh, sir, it was always so!

It was in Benghazi that the nature of Harry's work changed. He had been appointed to Libya as a forestry adviser, one of a number of FAO experts grouped together for administrative and policy purposes, into what was called the FAO Libya Mission.

The Chief of FAO Mission, as he was called locally, or the FAO Country Representative in Libya, held a diplomatic position as liaison between all the FAO experts and the Libyan government. The Chief was responsible for an FAO program in the country which satisfied both the desires of the government and the needs of the country as diagnosed by the experts.

When Jan van der Ploeg, the Chief of Mission, was taken critically ill in Benghazi and medical diagnosis showed that he must remain permanently in Holland, Harry was appointed Chief of Mission in his place. This job required considerable general knowledge both of the experts' programs and of Libyan needs, but even more it demanded sympathy, patience and tact in dealing with both sides.

Although sea bathing is one of the diversions of European Benghazi life, it has never produced the fanatic water fans that the Tripoli coastline has. The sea off Benghazi, perhaps because of sand and dust in the air, seldom has the cobalt clarity in its depths, or the blinding jade transparency in its shallows, of the sea off Tripolitania, which in my mind is the most beautiful seacoast in the world.

Although Tripoli also suffers many ghiblis which sweep northward from the Sahara, the city's outlying Italian-planted fringe of eucalyptus and almond trees, apricot and olive orchards, cultivated acres of peanuts and beans, and the sand dunes recently stabilized by fixation to some degree protect the city from the worst fury of the scorching, sand-laden wind. Not entirely, for I have seen Tripoli lost in a bilious cloud for days at a time when the dusty air met the ocean humidity and hung there. I have been in Malta and watched a Saharan ghibli arrive there and remain for three days, having traveled intact with yellow dust across the Mediterranean to the rocky island's shores.

Benghazi is a separate case. The little city has been dropped on the edge of the sea and is fringed by salt flats and the limestone plain and is almost without vegetation and trees. Any wind across this plain produces its own local dust storm. When flying over Benghazi, I have seen the village clear and clean below us, but the plain is enveloped in a cloud of dust so thick that the airport is hidden and the plane cannot land.

When I was driving home from Benghazi to our house one day the sand poured down my wind screen like red rain. By midday, in the house, we turned on all the electric lights in order to see. The windows, of course, were closed, but now we closed the wooden shutters. In spite of this, everything, including the interiors of the bureau drawers, was painted red with dust.

When I looked out the window, it was like looking into a glowing, peach-colored curtain draped against the glass. The atmosphere inside was thick with dust, and had an oppressive, impenetrable texture. I thought of our Bedawi neighbors on the plain.

Pucci didn't like it at all and hid under the wardrobe; Lena didn't like it either, but couldn't get under the wardrobe! The electricity was off now, and we lit the Coleman kerosene lamp. It seemed to be growing more difficult to breathe, possibly because of changing barometric pressure.

By five in the afternoon the wind was down and the dust was settling, but the air was still heavy with it. We washed the dining table and three chairs and a few plates, and ate the stew with sand gritting in our teeth.

It was useless to attempt much cleaning yet, as the dust was still in suspension. George's bedroom was the worst, being on the windward side of the house, and it was so sandy that we swept it out. I should say we shoveled it out, as by actual measure we filled half a bucket with sand from his floor.

It was difficult to read by the kerosene lamp which smelled bad anyway, and difficult to breathe with the dust settling on us: we all took sleeping pills and went to bed.

But malesh the dusty days, for Benghazi still has its secret paradise. Cross the wide plain with eyes averted, struggle up the zigzag, shrub-lined road to a half-mile elevation, and you are in a dark green, aromatic-scented, wind-swept area of juniper, pine and arbutus trees. This is the Green Mountain, Jebel Akhdar, pride of the province.

Here growing wild in spring are many flowers, chalky white narcissus, small mauve gladiolus, bright blue iris, pale lavender cyclamen, fields of flaming poppies, and asphodel the color of a hazy summer sky. Higher on the Barce Plain are long stretches of wheat and barley, wide-spreading olive orchards, smaller groves of figs and oranges, and stretches of old, rich wine grapevines, the result of Italian cultivation. Here nature has been kind, and even goats and nomadism have not succeeded in completely destroying the proof. This plain was a producer of wheat for the Romans, the Phoenicians, the Carthaginians, the Greeks and, in the twentieth century, the Italians. And it can become again a fertile paradise for the Libyans, if they will make it so.

Up here today Benghazi visitors love to picnic on a high-protein cheese sandwich and salami diet, while they comment caustically on abandoned Italian farms let run to ruin, on animals stabled in the houses while their nomad masters live in tents, on gardens now overgrown with fûl, on orchards uncultivated, and on wells no longer clean — meanwhile themselves drinking local wine from local grapes in the shade of ancient olive trees. Nearby, a little nomad boy in rags stands close and stares, with three smaller replicas beside him, all fly-dotted, dirty-fisted, and semi-fed. Their bones stick out, and their bellies protrude.

"Baksheesh! Baksheesh!"

"We mustn't give them baksheesh," someone says smugly.

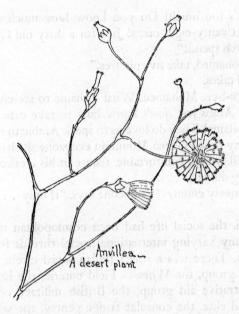

Anvillea
A desert plant

"Yes, yes, it's bad for them! It spoils them, accustoms them to beg, encourages a bad habit," they all say sanctimoniously on full stomachs.

"Fêlus! Fêlus!" *

"Oh, dear. Well, let's give them our crusts of bread, instead!"

"Oh, good idea! Here, Mohamed! They're always called Mohamed, you know! You divide with the others, Mohamed."

Mohamed snatches, and doesn't divide.

"Cigarette? Cigarette?"

"Why, the idea of children like that smoking! No wonder they're stunted. Don't give him any."

"He only wants them to sell!"

Mohamed picks up and pockets a half-smoked stub. Now Mohamed produces a worn, flattened circle of something which might be a slug, or might be a coin. "Greek coin? You buy?"

"Is it real? How much does he want?"

"Ten piastres."

* Money.

"Oh, that's too much! Do you know how much that is in *real* money? It's twenty-eight cents! Just for a dirty old Greek coin that I couldn't even spend!"

"Here, Mohamed, take five piastres."

Mohamed takes.

"Well, bye-bye, Mohamed. What a shame to see children so neglected! The Arabs just *don't* know how to take care of their kids! Bye-bye, Bisilama! They do love us to speak Arabic to them!"

On the way down Green Mountain everyone sits back half asleep, well fed, well wined, comfortable, secure in his rectitude, and going home to a big dinner.

"What a lovely country!" someone says. "If only . . . !"

In Tripoli, the social life had been cosmopolitan to an extreme, with too many varying international social threads for any one to predominate. There was a smart Italian social circle, an American bilateral aid group, the Wheelus Field coterie, the British financial and administrative aid group, the British military contingent, the ambassadorial elite, the consular fringe gentry, the semi-diplomatic "also presents," and the United Nations and its agencies, who seldom met. You could shop in Tripoli, for instance, without running into your friends; you couldn't shop in Benghazi without meeting most of them. The place was too small for acquaintances to escape each other.

My closest friends in Tripoli had been among the Libyans, although in general there was no social mixing between Libyan and foreign groups, except at ministerial level. Nobody had casual Libyan friends who just dropped in uninvited, I think, except ourselves. We had been fortunate in meeting, through Harry's professional interests, a number of young, intelligent, educated Libyans such as Hammet, Badreddin, Salem, Ali, Suleiman, and Assad, who had no exalted government status. Lack of status meant they could speak honestly with us. Such young people supply the lifeblood of any nation. These young Libyans were all that I missed of Tripoli.

Libya is a difficult country to feel that one knows or understands. Libya wants it this way. First, Moslem society does not welcome infidel intrusion. Second, foreign contacts are usually either with the ministers, who politically speaking may not talk, or with domestic servants or starving nomads, who cannot talk. And lastly, Libyan women are not available for conversation.

As age is greatly respected here, I as an older woman am able to have certain privileged contacts with both men and women. Nevertheless, I often find myself wishing to ask questions but hesitating to invade Libyan privacy; yet Libyan friends do not hesitate to ask me questions.

An Arab female is referred to by her given name only and uses a surname only for purposes of identification. After marriage, she is not referred to by her husband's name as Mrs. So-and-so, except to identify her to European friends. My name, as spoken by an Arab friend, is Agnes, rather than Mrs. Keith. Now, to some friends I have become Mother Agnes, a designation of dignity which I value.

A few days ago our Tripoli friend Mabruk, of the Agriculture Department, arrived in Benghazi on his way to Egypt to take up his year's scholarship in the Egyptian University. He is staying with us for three days. Yesterday, while we were drinking morning coffee together, he volunteered some very frank thoughts to me apropos of his own personal life and recent marriage. His candor surprised me.

"We have a great problem in my family," he began. "My father has made a great mistake!"

Without an idea what he was hinting at, I said, "Please tell me what the trouble is."

"My father, who is more than seventy years old, several years ago took a second wife who is very young. This is a great mistake by our standards."

I looked at him with surprise. "But I thought that no stigma attached to having more than one wife. Your Koranic law allows it, doesn't it?"

Mabruk, a devout Moslem, answered earnestly, "We believe that a second wife should be taken only for serious reasons. If she is ill over a period of years, or unable to function as a wife over a lengthy period, or is sterile, a new wife may be taken by mutual agreement. My father has none of these reasons. He had ten children by my mother. He just wants a new woman!"

I could think of no comment to make, and after a short silence

Mabruk continued, "Our country, Libya, is living in ancient history! In ancient times men took extra wives because many men were killed in warfare, and there were too many women, and they had to be taken care of. There was a reason, then. Today, we modern Libyans do not approve of it."

"Well, I don't see how you can afford more than one wife today," I suggested.

"We can't. And it always makes trouble at home. Everything must be done equally for both wives in both homes, and for both sets of children. The children are always jealous because they are brought up by their mothers to consider the children of the other household as their rivals."

"Is it so that the husband must divide his conjugal favors equally?"

"Exactly. The poor husband has no security at home. He must try to live in *two* homes and share his affections equally, and he ends up with no home, and the true affections of no one. Or else in the end he divorces one wife and settles for one household, but he still has the other children to support."

"Then, so far as I can see," I said, "your women feel and behave very much as we do in our monogamous society. A Libyan woman loves and clings to her man and suffers when he leaves her to share his love with another woman. Psychologically, it doesn't work happily in your society, either, then?"

"Exactly. In the old days, it may have worked because nobody questioned plurality; today it doesn't work. And as you see, nobody in Libya can afford more than one wife. I myself had to wait some years to get married and to afford children."

"Where does your father live now?"

"He left the house of my mother and took a house for his young wife, and my mother does not wish him to come back. We all suffer by my father's mistake."

"How do you mean, Mabruk?"

"You know I have five brothers and four sisters. Several years ago, after my father told us he would take a new wife, we all talked together about what we could say or do to stop him. We decided that we could not stop him, no matter what we did. So it was better to say nothing. If we spoke the truth to him then, what we said or did would never be forgotten by him. And still we knew that it would not affect his plan to marry, so better we keep quiet."

"What happened when your mother found all this out?" I asked.

"When my mother finds out, she becomes very ill, she almost goes crazy. Many Moslem women do really go crazy when the husband takes another wife, or they become very ill for ever after; frequently they kill themselves!"

He paused, perhaps wondering if he was saying too much. He was indeed giving me a different picture from the prevalent myth of the happy harem household, where love and babies are communally shared, while the husband is beloved by all.

"Is your mother recovering from her suffering?"

"For a while my mother became to us, her children, like one of *our* children. We took great thought for her, and showed her a great deal of affection; we treated her as a "special case" — like the American lady whom you and I were discussing yesterday who is unhappy because of *her* husband. So all my mother's children comforted her, and now she is gradually becoming normal again."

As Mabruk talked, I was impressed by the honesty of his attitude. It has always seemed to me to be slightly ridiculous and against nature for us in the Western culture to keep up the pretense of "friendly" divorces. And it has seemed equally unbelievable to me that in Moslem law a husband can be successfully shared.

"Then perhaps, Mabruk, the worst is over now, if your mother is reconciled?"

"The worst is not over," said Mabruk firmly, "because my father married a young girl, and already he has three children by her! In a few years my father must, by law of nature, die, and then he leaves the wife and children, who become the responsibility of myself and my brothers!"

"Good heavens! And you have been waiting for years to afford to marry and have your own children!"

"Exactly. As my father was determined to marry again," Mabruk speaks in a tone of unconcealed irritation, "he should at least have married an *old* woman who would not give him more children!"

Mabruk was obviously overlooking one important fact in life — that old men do not care to marry old women!

"It is not just the money to take care of these children — and that will certainly be very difficult indeed! It is also that we must try to see that the children grow up in a good environment and in the right way. If they were the children of a brother, and he died, then I would be proud and happy to take care of them and bring them up. But the children of my father! No, he has made a great mistake."

I knew that Mabruk, carefully and traditionally brought up, would never have voiced a criticism against his father if it had not been well deserved.

"What about your own marriage, Mabruk? Are you happy and contented, as you hoped to be?"

"Well, I am not really married yet, because although the betrothal was made two months ago, my wife is not yet living with me. In fact, I have not even seen her face since she was thirteen years. She is my cousin, you know. But we have decided that we will not live together until we can get our own apartment in which to live. We do not intend to live with my family."

"Will you find a place in the medina, near where your family home is?"

"No, indeed. That was my uncle's house you visited with me; I have never lived in the old city. I do not like it; it is dark and closed-in there, and I always feel cooped up and depressed. No, I have asked Hammet to look about and find me a modern apartment like his own."

"Have you seen Badreddin since he returned from Oxford? He is to be married soon, I hear."

"Yes, he is home, and he has told me much of his year at Oxford. He says that the first four months he was there he found it almost unbearable. The bad climate, the different ways of life, and the food were almost past enduring. But he forced himself to eat, and he just ate to live, and slept from exhaustion, and worked all the rest of the time. But by the end of the year, he said he had grown to like it, he felt at home, and he could even eat "fish and chips!""

"How does he feel about Libya now that he is back again?"

"Now our way of life here does not seem as satisfactory to him as it seemed when he looked back at it from England!"

"What about Libyan food? Is he glad to return to it?"

"He felt better on the food he ate in England, and he thinks that much of the illness here comes from poor diet and strong tea. He has made up his mind to live in the modern way, and although, of course, his coming marriage is an arranged one and he has not seen the bride since she was a child, he hopes that in time she will unveil and go about with him."

"I have already invited him to bring her here after their wedding and stay in our house, as we will be away in Canada on leave."

"The idea is good, as here in Benghazi his wife is a stranger, and she can unveil while she is here. It is easier to unveil here than in Tripoli."

"Will your wife unveil?"

"I wish her to do so in time, when people have learned not to criticize. It is too difficult still in Tripoli. But my daughters shall *never* cover their faces."

28. We Are the World

As Chief of Mission and Country Representative, Harry carried the responsibility of forming FAO programs for the future in Libya. Here in Benghazi the experts and families of FAO and the United Nations agencies all drew together. In the limited small town environment we found each other; we also found the core and heart of the United Nations Mission, the resident representative Harold Caustin and his wife, Kathleen. They are English, and I don't wish to embarrass them by compliments, but I do intend to say that they did more for the United Nations spirit by their own personal examples than any other persons I have ever known.

Harold's job was to represent the United Nations and its experts with the Libyan government. He had the intellectual capacity, the judgment and the sensitivity which one expects to find in a man in his position, but he had in addition a tremendous belief in what he was doing and in the United Nations. One might think that this was only natural in a man working for this organization — but it wasn't. It seemed almost a local habit to disparage the job you were doing while accepting a good salary for doing it.

The technical knowledge of United Nations experts was unchallenged, but their conviction of accomplishing anything in Libya was sometimes weak. This was understandable, as the Libyans themselves provided difficulties: they were not yet well enough trained to work along with technical experts in any line. On the other hand, Libyans had to start some time! When the government had failed to provide Harry with a Libyan to train, he had taken on Hammet. Hammet would never be a forestry expert — but he could do a little of everything else!

Kathleen was the perfect wife for Harold's job, and very good for the Mission and everyone in it. Fearless of responsibility, she never shied away from giving her time, her strength, or her cash to those who needed help. As she always told me, she did it because she liked to, and I am sure that she did. When I sympathized with her once about her frequent and lavish entertainments for the UN personnel and visitors, most of which I knew the Caustins paid for themselves, Kathleen's answer was, "Oh, but we love to entertain! I should do it anyway, whether or not we need to."

She was gifted with a gay spirit, a loving heart, a gracious personality, a tremendous ability to like people, and a pair of rose-colored glasses. The only times I have ever been annoyed with Kathleen were when her convictions of what was good for the UN Mission caused her to put on her pink spectacles and, after a cautious look, to declare with complete conviction and a serious face that the dirty gray ghost in the cupboard was really a lovely pink sprite! And quite possibly some dirty ghosts did turn into pink sprites for the sake of Kathleen. No pink sprite I, but she sometimes shamed me into more charitable actions, if not views.

Here in Benghazi I found the real reward of being attached to an international organization; your obvious social contacts and the people with whom you are thrown are by nature international. You need not seek outside your own group for variety, diversion, or a good laugh, as it is all there in abundance. We are the world: we are its problems, and in us lie its solutions, or lack of same.

In the Mission of the United Nations and its agencies, there were about one hundred persons, and they came from the following countries: Burma, New Zealand, Jordan, Turkey, Syria, Ireland, Lebanon, Egypt (now UAR), India, the Federal Republic of Germany, Poland, the United Kingdom, Canada, the United States of America, Italy, Yugoslavia, Netherlands, Australia, Iraq, Belgium, Pakistan, Sudan, France and Denmark. Many had their wives and families with them.

We foreigners have a habit of regarding the country we enter with an eye as to how it can be best used to please us. As most Anglo-Saxons like picnics, they promptly seek picnic sites. Picnics are not a

Libyan habit, as a Libyan infers that one naturally prefers to eat one's food without sand.

Not long ago there was a favorite picnic site on a delightful, clean, white, sandy beach at Juliana, not five minutes' drive from Benghazi. Harry, George and I went once or twice when we first arrived here, but not being dedicated picnickers we did not think of going again for several months. Then, when I suggested to Kathleen that she and Mary come with us to this same clean, sandy spot, she looked at me in surprise, and said, "Sorry, my dear. We can't go there, you know. It's covered with broken glass now!"

"Broken glass! On the beach? In the water? What has happened?" I asked, without a clue.

Kathleen, the most charitable soul in the world, and no gossip, didn't want to voice the plain facts, but finally she told me that the beach had been ruined for bathing by a group of sophisticated Libyans who met there to imbibe the alcoholic aspect of Western culture. Now broken beer, wine and whiskey bottles made the sand unsittable and the sea impossible to enter.

It is unlawful in Cyrenaica to serve an alcoholic drink in a public place to any Libyan, and this law is enforced, but it is obvious that a number of Libyans are capably serving themselves. One of our least desirable and most dangerous Western habits has been one of the first to be transmitted to our Libyan friends. Already, more than one brilliant Libyan career has been ruined by alcoholism, which seems to take its strongest hold among the most intelligent people. Fortunately, those who use alcohol to any extent here are very limited in number and make up only a fractional proportion of the Libyan population. Most Libyans can't afford alcohol, don't approve of it, and don't like it.

There has always been legby, a Libyan farmer's drink, made in the country by collecting the sap from the central stalk of the date palm. Legby is drunk both unfermented and fermented, in villages where date palms abound, and it is intoxicating in its fermented state. Although the date palm may be tapped more than once in its life for the drink, it will not supply dates after having been tapped, a fact which effectively limits the farmer's yen for legby, as his date palms are his joy.

One of the pleasantest excursions in the world is to start out under a blue sky and a blazing African sun with a good companion, a bathing suit, a Thermos of cold drink, a map which is sure to be old and incorrect, and a vague desire to find the Garden of Hesperides, or Rommel's Pool, a pothole where Rommel bathed, or a good place to shoot quail, or the hole where the River Lethe disappeared, or just a few tiny specimens of desert vegetation.

Girl of The red plains.

No book ever touches on Benghazi, which was known in Greek times as Eusperites, without mentioning the Garden of the Hesperides and the river Lethe, and no two books precisely agree where the garden is. Pliny, two thousand years ago, was the first to locate the garden near what was to become modern Benghazi, on the red limestone plain which today is crossed by the road to the Benina Airport.

The Benghazi plain is pitted with large caves, potholes, and subterranean passages which are not visible until you stumble into them. Some of these have been formed by the process of subsurface undermining erosion, followed by collapse of the surface limestone, while others are merely the remnants of rock quarries. Some are full of marshy water, mosquitoes and snakes, but others have cultivated gardens blooming in the bottom where topsoil has washed down.

These have an eerie, unnatural quality, as one is more accustomed to seeing gardens growing up a hillside than down into the interior of the earth. To come upon one of these jagged-rimmed holes in the unlovely limestone and look unsuspectingly down on the shining tops of green trees, plots of golden corn, patches of bright jade fûl, glowing scarlet tomatoes, caper clusters among the rocks, and maybe a glossy little black donkey grazing makes one look about to see where the trolls are hiding. Although the Garden of Hesperides has not been described precisely like this, as Scylax makes mention of "acres of thick planted fruit trees," I personally prefer a garden of the trolls.

The Benghazi version of the River Lethe is an underground lake in a limestone cave which is located on what used to be Royal Palace ground. This lake exists in utter darkness. It is an eerie thing to see, or rather to feel, as one usually finds it by stepping into it, after having descended the steps into a black cave which is illuminated by an electric light fixture which doesn't work. But the lake is undoubtedly there, and it extends further than one can see when flashing a strong torch along it.

No visible stream feeds it, and Libyan legend claims that its waters come directly from the river Nile through subterranean passages. A more modern suggestion is that it may be fed from a porous substratum leading from a deep desert reservoir. The lake has been tested and found to give a continuous yield of water which is too saline for human use but useful for agriculture. Probably the trolls are using it in their gardens.

Meanwhile, "my son Mohamed" was far from forgotten. We had received two letters from him, written painstakingly, with his scrap of pencil gripped as in a vise, I felt sure, and his tongue on his lip and his nose almost touching the paper, but the letters were almost illegible. The combination of his idea of our printed alphabet, which he had not fully conquered, and his own phonetic spelling produced a hieroglyphic message which had to be known to be understood. But in any case I pretty well knew what his letters were saying, as I had news of him through Libyan sources.

His second son had now been born, el hamdu li'llah! He did not get a job with FAO, as there was nothing open at the moment. He was working as houseboy with an American friend of mine whom he liked very much. She was very kind to him, but he didn't like houseboy work. He missed us and wished we would return. How was Brother George? Would I please write him another letter to somebody else in FAO, and get him a job?

His next letter a few months later I interpreted as saying that his new son was doing very well, and my American friend for whom he worked was showing Lutfeyah, his wife, how to take care of the baby in the modern way, and this son would surely live, el hamdu li'llah! Would I please write again to FAO about giving him a job?

As I was convinced that the only way Libya would get ahead, and Libyans would learn how to function in trained jobs, was to start training Libyans themselves in these jobs, and as I was convinced that my Mohamed was one of the most promising of Libyans to train, I had no compunction in writing a letter. This time a job was found for Mohamed in the FAO Tripoli Mission.

Very shortly then, through the personal interest of a young Swiss expert in the use of small tools — a phrase which always sent Harry, who admired Mohamed's ambition and his cheerful willingness to attempt anything, into roars of laughter — Mohamed was given slightly more responsible work as Peter's assistant.

When on a visit to us in Benghazi, Hammet brought me direct word of Mohamed's improved status, of the baby's continuing progress, and Mohamed's affectionate messages to us all, I felt happier than I had ever felt about Mohamed. Perhaps, in sha'Allah, he really might escape from the ever-pursuing shadow of obstacles too great.

29. We Pack Our Tents Again

ONE OF the greatest pleasures of the semi-nomad life which Harry and I have lived for thirty married years is that just as we feel that we are settling we migrate, either for home leave or back to the job. It adds great zest to life, and perhaps the Libyan nomads find this, too. Although too poor to take holidays and to travel, they can at least change their living environment. I doubt if a nomad is ever cured of nomadism.

Now having settled cozily into the Benghazi scene, having put up our tents and planted our crops, and not yet having reaped them, the time had come for our home leave. Harry, George and I were flying to London, then going by Italian liner from Southampton to Quebec. Here we planned to buy a secondhand car and drive across Canada through the Rocky Mountains to Victoria on the Pacific coast, stopping in Seattle first to see our married daughter, Jean, and her husband, Harold, and their four children.

Before leaving Benghazi, we ordered an Austin Gypsy Go-Anywhere vehicle for three months' delivery, so that I could accompany Harry on his long-planned trip to Kufra oasis when we returned. The Gypsy is similar to the Land Rover, a heavy service machine with special sand tires, and said to be less heavy to steer. Ours was to have an extra gasoline tank for desert travel. Then we said goodbye to Lena and Pucci, who were keeping the house on the red Fuihat plain open for our return, George saying goodbye rather sadly as it seemed probable that he might not be in Libya again. In saying goodbye myself, I was delighted to know that I would return, for the country and people had embedded themselves in my heart.

On our return to Benghazi three months later, to our two Mediterraneans, Lena and Pucci, and our white stone house with its cool, shuttered interior hidden away from the blazing African sun, with its garden of three hundred saplings now rooted and growing, its clematis and Damascus rose now climbing, its high walls beyond which the camels and donkeys pass, and its friends of the plain who hail us now, we found news by hearsay awaiting us before we had opened our suitcases.

The Libyan government and all assisting agencies, embassies and consulates were urgently required to move back to Tripoli immediately. Such moves were always immediate, urgent and most urgent to get them accomplished at all, as moving the capital was popular with no one except the King. It was certainly an expensive policy for a poor nation to pursue, as the cost of moving the government was considerable, and to this was added the cost of moving the United Nations agencies and families, which was also paid by the government.

Our first step was to fly immediately to Tripoli to look once more for a house. Here, prices had doubled as soon as landlords heard that the government was returning. I had had ambitions to find a house in Garden City, but I soon gave this up, and again settled for a villa in Giorgimpopoli on the wrong side of the tracks.

Meanwhile, the Gypsy Go-Anywhere car had arrived. But Kufra oasis, once less than a thousand miles southward, was rapidly vanishing from our sight. Instead of being on the way to the historical oasis as we had hoped, a few weeks later found us on the road to Tripoli with two cars to drive across the desert now, instead of one.

There was something sadly familiar about our departure from Benghazi because I had my usual mishap the night before. We had packed ourselves out of our house and were trying to find a hotel room for the night. Benghazi now (1959) was full to bursting with oil explorers, searchers, testers, diggers, drillers, riggers, planners, buyers and sellers, and there was no empty hotel room available. Finally, we found a small, unlighted two-room apartment down a dark alley where Lena, Pucci, Harry and I could sleep for the night.

Gratefully, we tossed our jam-packed suitcases inside in the dark, and turned around to go out again and find some food. The alley was unlighted and black, and there was a two-inch step down from our door, and I need go no further with my story. My ankle swelled up instantly out of all proportion to the two inches which had betrayed it. Lena was all commiseration and apprehension, Pucci covered me with kisses, and Harry, who was feeling tired (women don't feel tired!), just looked long-suffering. He was undoubtedly wondering why he had married me, and so was I.

That night proved unforgettable, not for the sprain but for its treatment. Harry had in his suitcase a bottle of Sloan's Liniment (for horses, we discovered next day), which I decided to try. I rubbed my ankle well, and went to bed. Fifteen minutes later I was up and trying to wash off the liniment, and the rest of the night I spent sitting in or on the bathtub soaking my foot in cold water in an effort to get rid of the unbearable burning. No horse should be treated like this!

During the long hours of the night, spent on the cold edge of the bath alone with my conscience, while Harry snored happily in one room and Lena breathed deeply in the next, I wondered what the day would bring. We were two people with two cars, and I knew that nothing but death would stop me from driving one car to Tripoli. But the thought of death was tempting. I tried to think which foot I always used for the gas, but I can never remember how to drive a car except when I am sitting in it.

The dawn broke, I welcomed it, and we dressed for our early start. I couldn't get a shoe on, but I hadn't expected to. Harry looked at my foot and said, "Well, fortunately it's not the foot for the gas!" We packed the cars, and forgathered with Ricardo, who was driving the FAO Land Rover. We took off for Tripoli.

It was the first day of December. There had been no rain the previous winter and, as yet, none this year. We had heard plainsmen and desert Arabs grumble about the drought, the dried up wells, the burned out pasturage, and the dying crops. We had heard this, we knew this, our minds accepted it, and we regretted it — but it was easy to feel that it went with a desert land. This was what they had to expect in a land with three-fourths desert. Now, if it had happened in the United States!

Today, the marvelous blue sky, the golden sands, the glimpses of turquoise sea, all the beauty of the fierce and awesome desert were still the same, but now they had become the background for dead and dying flocks. From Adjedabia on, about eighty miles from Benghazi, ghosts took us by the hand and led us through a haunted landscape. Sadder than the skeletons and dead bodies were the sheep and goats lying beside the road, who just lifted their heads mutely to look, too weak to get up, when our cars went by.

We wanted to stop. Lena begged to get out and do something, but there was nothing to do. It was wholesale death — by the will of Allah. Perhaps there would be rain *this* year. In sha'Allah! In sha' Allah!

We made Sirte in good time, el hamdu li'llah! By not shifting gears I found I could drive without much pain, and as much of the Sirte road is straight, I just put my good foot on the gas and kept it there. By this excellent method we arrived early, il hamdu li'llah! Although tempted (but not by me!) to drive through to Tripoli now, Harry said we would stop at Sirte for the night. Hamdu li'llah twice! Death lost its sting!

While we were eating spaghetti in the restaurant that night the little mongrel bitch that belonged to the Italian proprietor came over and tried to make friends with Pucci. I discouraged the association because of fleas, but Lena, who takes a dog's view of life, said no harm could come through a little fun. But Pucci, who was still recovering from anti-rabies injections in Benghazi, didn't feel like fun, and soon the rejected female retired.

The following afternoon we arrived in Tripoli, a beautiful, gracious, sophisticated city to people who had just crossed the Sirtic desert. We checked in at the Racing Camel Hotel as we had done four years ago on our first arrival in Libya. The rooms were still tiny, there was a urinal this time instead of a toilet, the birds still made nests in the courtyard bougainvillea, and the morning coffee still smelled of beer from the bar — but now the hotel was filled and overflowing with petroleum experts. The odor of oil was stronger than the smell of whiskey, Texas voices were louder than the call to prayer at the nearby mosque, and money was in the air, if not yet in the pocket.

The next day Pucci was taken ill, vomiting and refusing to eat. Lena and I took him to Blue Cross, the government veterinary hospital, where for the first time we met Abdullah, the big, gentle, soft-eyed Libyan assistant, who is not a doctor and cannot prescribe drugs but does all the handling of animals.

The young Sicilian veterinary in charge stood several paces away from Pucci, to whom Abdullah was talking soothingly, and asked us to describe the patient's symptoms. Dr. Baretto then diagnosed distemper — possibly, I thought, contracted from the friendly little bitch at Sirte. The doctor prescribed an injection, which fortunately had just arrived in Tripoli and which he said must be repeated daily for a week. Standing fastidiously far removed from his patient, while Abdullah readied the hypodermic needle, the blue-eyed doctor began a tentative flirtation with Lena. While Lena and I held Pucci, Abdullah gave him the injection, and then massaged and quieted him. By this time the doctor had secured a date with Lena for the future.

Picking up our shivering little Pucci, Lena and I left, promising to return tomorrow for another injection. The doctor walked us to the car, but without a word for the patient. If he had known Lena better, he would have wooed his way to her via Pucci.

Nomad tents

IV

Friends from Allah

30. Mohamed's Babies

IT ONLY needed a few hours for our former Libyan friends of Giorgimpopoli area to spread the news of our arrival.

Here were Sayed and Sola, both still employed in the neighborhood, now with an Air Force captain at Wheelus Field. Sola's bad eye now looks very bad, and the hospital doctor has told him there is danger that it will infect the other eye, too. His captain is trying to arrange for an operation at Wheelus Field to remove the diseased eye. Sayed is full of his usual complaints, and as always looks downhearted. He is not yet seventeen years old, has been married two years, but has no children. He is about to be divorced, and a second wife is already chosen for him. He says that Mustapha, the eldest brother, a very handsome young man, has just taken a second wife. Sayed promises to send word to our Mohamed ben Mukhtar that we are here.

Old Mohamed from the Fezzan calls also. Our communications with him are all in sha' Allahs and hamdu li'llahs, as he has no teeth, is quite deaf, and in any case is inarticulate. But his glowing, smiling black face speaks the same message always — courage, endurance, patience, resignation and kindness. He brings me a small bouquet of flowers, picked almost stemless from the nearby neighbor's garden, no doubt, where he is watchman. He never advances beyond watchman, and I think he has no ambition to. He gets a small cash sum, a place to sleep (all Libyan watchmen sleep!) a few throw-outs of food and discarded clothes. He lives mostly on tea and the Fezzan sugar-choked dates which he brings back with him from his annual visit to his wife in the Fezzan. For the four and a half years I have known him he has always lived in the old khaki military overcoat, which is supplemented now by secondhand blue jeans. Old Mohamed is one, at least, who should enter Paradise without question!

Today he keeps repeating, "Mohamed," meaning, I am sure, *my* Mohamed, and indicating small children. I know that on the next feast day old Mohamed will be back again with a fist full of tightly gripped flowers for me, and some Fezzan dates for Harry.

On our first Friday here, as Friday is the Moslem Sunday and a government holiday, our "son" Mohamed arrives to make an official call, bringing a bouquet of market flowers. To give fresh flowers is not a Libyan habit, as Libyans prefer waxed plastic flowers in vivid, unfadeable colors, but they see that we Westerners value fresh flowers, and they wish to honor us in our own way. This day Mohamed has the flowers in one hand, and little Ahmed, his twenty-month-old son, is gathered up in the other arm. Ahmed, a well cared for, bright-eyed child, is dressed in brand new, American style little boys' clothing.

I had wondered how Mohamed would feel when he saw Lena filling his place in the house; I was glad that he had other work with FAO which I felt sure he preferred. However, there was to be no problem. He greeted me as "mother" and embraced me, and tried to urge Ahmed into my arms. Naturally, Ahmed backed violently away with nasty noises, until Lena swiftly produced sweets, soft drinks and coffee. When Lena had disappeared, and we settled down, Mohamed said, "How you like the girl?"

"I like her very much. This is girl's work in the house. How do you like your new work?"

"Not bad. I don't mind." A Libyan is seldom enthusiastic, about work, anyway. "My boss is very good man."

"Your boss is Mr. Weismann?"

"Yes. Very good man. I like."

"What do you do beside drive the Land Rovers?"

"I also help in office. I *assist* Mr. Weismann," said Mohamed with considerable pride.

"Good. I am so pleased. How is Lutfeyah?"

"Lutfeyah good."

"And the new baby? What is his name?"

"Umar. Your friend Mrs. Harvell very good for Lutfeyah when

the new baby come. Mrs. Harvell come my house show Lutfeyah everything for baby. Show for bath, and for dress, and give very good powder for skin."

This I could very well believe, knowing my friend's kind heart and efficient ways. "What did your mother say when Mrs. Harvell came?" I asked, knowing that the old lady's antediluvian practices had been Mohamed's great problem with his first-born son, who had died.

Lutfeyah, Mohamed's wife

"Maybe she no like, but malesh! I like my sons grow strong and big like all American boys."

I didn't disillusion Mohamed about the hundred per cent health of American children, who, in Libya anyway, were undoubtedly bigger and huskier than Libyan children. Our slum children don't travel abroad to advertise the fact that we also have the underprivileged.

It was pleasant to sit chatting once more with Mohamed over coffee, watching again with amusement his little finger daintily extended beyond his coffee cup, seeing him take one little biscuit, one little sweet, and denying more than one to Ahmed also, for the sake of good manners. It seemed odd, though, to sit like this without Mohamed maneuvering to ask me for some favor.

"Where is George now?"

"George is in London studying — I hope!"

"He come here again?"

"Yes, for Christmas."

"Good. I come see him."

"Yes, of course, Mohamed."

But I was glad to see that Mohamed's former intense concentration on George and George's way of life, George's occupations and pastimes, had largely passed. Mohamed had become a satisfied husband, the father of two sons, and employed in a man's work. It was the only life he could achieve, and the life that Allah had written for him. As I had felt in the past when listening to Mohamed and George daydream, a time comes when dreams must be reconciled with reality.

"You come to my house one day to see Lutfeyah? You bring the girl, too?" with a nod towards the kitchen.

"Aiwa! Yes."

"I go now, Mother. Next time I bring Umar with me, also."

"You can't carry two kids on a bus!"

"My friend will bring me on his motorcycle, so I bring babies."

I wrap up the remaining biscuits and sweets for Mohamed to take home, along with a pack of cigarettes, and a small cash gift for baby Umar. I expect Mohamed will drop in on Sayed and old Mohamed before catching the bus. I feel proud of my Mohamed; he looks so clean and neat, and is so self-respecting, and he has grown up a lot.

George came from London a few days later for the Christmas holidays. Don wasn't coming down from England this time, but for once, George seemed perfectly happy to stay at home and sleep and eat and drink, play his favorite records, and read. It was a wonderful interval for Harry and me, as we became acquainted with him again, this time with a more mature George, who had become an avaricious reader of good books.

He and Mohamed spent an evening together, going first to the

Arabic cinema, and then sitting and talking for hours over coffee at a sidewalk café.

"Mohamed is very smart, he's modern!" George tells me the next day. "He says I can see his wife next time I come. It's O.K. because I'm not a Moselm, and I don't live here."

"Mohamed likes his job, doesn't he?"

"Yes, and he says he's going out to the desert on a trip soon. He's never been out of Tripolitania, you know, and he's crazy to see the desert."

"Yes, I know that he's wanted to go to the desert ever since Pa and I went down to Ghat with Hammet and Badreddin. Did Mohamed ask you about London, and what you do there?"

"Yes, he's interested in everything. I was telling him about the men in Hyde Park who stand up on a soapbox and tell everybody what's wrong with the government, and nobody tries to stop them. You couldn't do that here, Mohamed says."

"No, you couldn't, but Libya is entirely different. This country has only been independent a few years, and the great wonder is that the country has held together! She can't afford any disgruntled perfectionists, or disappointed politicians. She's fighting for her life as a nation."

"British government is built on the right to grouse, Pa says," George quotes. "It makes Britons feel better to complain! Anyway, I've heard people complaining in Hyde Park about the government, but they never have a very good plan for making things better."

Fascinated by Hyde Park, by the anarchistic speeches, by the protest marches, by London bookshops, by Cockney guts, by an Anglo-Burmese friend, Bill, by London nightlife, George was having the time of his life, even though he said that as a Canadian he was made to feel a complete outsider. But the lessons he learned in London were mostly not out of school books!

We next saw Mohamed during the feast of Id el-Fitr, which ends Ramadan. He arrived with his friend Ali on Ali's motorcycle, with Ali at the control, Mohamed on the pillion seat with Ahmed astride in front of him, and little Umar, ten months old, held in Mohamed's arms, along with my bouquet. I remembered having met friend Ali at Mohamed's wedding, at which occasion Ali looked very seedy. Today he is dressed in the classic young Libyan male costume of blue jeans, red and yellow tails-out sport shirt, and new store shoes. He says he has a job with an oil company, and obviously he has good contacts with Wheelus Field.

Mohamed is at his happiest exhibiting his tidy, prosperous friend who owns a motorcycle, showing off his two beautiful beady-eyed little boys who have *no* impetigo, and presenting me with flowers. In his Libyan way, he represents the successful man. While Lena prepares soft drinks and coffee, I ask Ali to go for Sayed, who lives in a nearby garage, and bring him back to have coffee with us, for this is an occasion,

Sayed arrives promptly, taking the opportunity to bring with him a letter in English, which he wants me to read to him. Seeing the letter is addressed to the surgeon at the municipal hospital reminds me of Sola, and I ask, "What about Sola? Is he going to have his bad eye taken out?"

"The Wheelus Field doctor no can do because Sola is a Libyan," says Sayed.

This does not surprise me as I know that both the American Air Force hospital and the British military hospital have strict rules against accepting Libyan patients. The hospitals not only have little control over foreign patients, but usually cannot communicate with them, and if anything goes wrong with the patient it can cause a serious problem. Consequently, Libyan patients are now admitted at Wheelus Field only by the specific request of the American ambassador. This rule was made after a Libyan baby had been left at the hospital for treatment at the father's request, and the rest of the family then complained to the police that the child had been kidnapped by Wheelus Field.

The letter which Sayed wishes me to read is from the Air Force captain for whom Sayed works, and it is addressed to the surgeon at the municipal hospital. I feel some compunction at reading a letter addressed thus, but Sayed insists the letter is about Sola, and that he must know the contents, so I read it. The letter asks the municipal hospital surgeon to give the best possible care to Sola's case, which has been diagnosed at Wheelus as needing to have the eye removed.

The writer guarantees the payment of hospitalization for Sola and any extra fees after the operation.

"Well, Sayed," I say, "this letter is wonderful! Your captain must be a very kind man, and a generous one. He says he will pay for Sola to stay in hospital after the operation. You tell Sola he must be sure to take this letter to the hospital doctor."

Sayed looks at me, still suspicious. "Is O.K. that letter?"

"Yes, Sayed. Of course. Your captain is a very good man."

"O.K., then. Sola can take letter."

"Didn't you know what was in the letter?"

"Yes, captain he say same like you say. But I no can read letter. I think maybe captain say bad things for Sola. So I ask you. You say letter good, so Sola take."

This was typical of Sayed, who always expects the worst. I wondered who else had read the letter.

"I wish George can be here," says Mohamed, looking happily around him, filled with satisfaction at having done the correct thing. "Next time George comes home I bring my sons to see George."

"When do you go to the desert, Mohamed? Soon?"

"Maybe in a few weeks, now Ramadan is finished. I like very much to go. When you and Mr. Keith go with Hammet and Badreddin, you never take me!" he reminds me reproachfully.

It was true we never had. First, because we had to leave someone to sleep in the house in our absence, but also because I visualized that very young Mohamed as being an added responsibility for me. In those days, he was always stumbling, tripping, losing, breaking; suffering with stomachache or sore feet, headache, or cut fingers. I had felt certain I would end up taking care of him, and I could only just take care of myself on a desert trip.

"Well, you are going this time, Mohamed. Please come and tell me all about it when you get home."

"I will, Mother. And I'll bring you a present, too."

I always keep a few toys on hand for visiting children, and some of these I put in a bag for Ahmed and Umar, along with sweets and biscuits and, for Papa, cigarettes. We fit them all in, men, babies and bundles, onto the motorcycle again, an Ali starts off raising a storm of Giorgimpopoli dust. Mohamed twists around to wave goodbye, his sons glued to him. He is a picture of the successful Libyan paying a feast-day call on a foreign friend, accompanied by his children in brand new clothes, and traveling by motorized transport. Praise be to Allah!

31. Bread Pirates

BACK in Tripoli again, my first visit is to Bread Street at eleven one morning for fresh Libyan bread just out of the oven. How good it smells! The narrow lane outside the suk is crowded with donkey carts, old gray mares staggering under loads, camels rocking and rolling along to slaughter, bicycle side-carts sideswiping pedestrians, and bicycles proceeding sanctimoniously on the wrong side of the road. There is no space to park a car.

I drive the street length slowly, breathing in the fragrant bread smell, thinking how friendly everyone looks and how nice it is to feel at home here. The stands on this street are all piled high with bread, but the first stand I pass seems to have the largest, most perfectly browned loaves, so I maneuver the car around slowly and return. Turning is a perilous job, as traffic never stops for an obstacle but dodges it, and a Libyan cyclist usually fixes his goal when he leaves his doorstep and doesn't detour. I drive back at a walking pace until I come to the favorite bread stand. I call from the car window and ask the man to give me two of his loaves of the largest size. He hands them to me and says, "Six piastres!"

"Six piastres?" I say. "No, four piastres. That is the price!"

"Six!" he shouts.

But I know that the price of bread is government controlled. Bread is the basic diet of city Libyans, many of whom eat nothing more all day than a loaf of bread with a pinch of salt and a dip of tomato sauce. Many imported foodstuffs here are now double the price that they were a few years ago, but bread stays the same. It is the only luxury of Tripoli life which today sells cheaply, and it is the best bread in the world for the lowest price.

Made from full wheat flour, molded in round loaves, beautifully browned in large charcoal-burning ovens, baked fresh twice a day, at dawn and mid-morning, it is the working man's staple — and mine.

The loaves are three sizes, the smallest one for one piastre, the equivalent of three cents, the largest for two piastres, and the mid-size for mid-price. The catch in buying bread is that there is no exact standard by which the customer can measure the loaf, and no strict dividing line between the three sizes. The Libyan buyer can never be fooled, but the bread man always hopes to fool the foreigner, except for the Italian housewife, who is a foolproof shopper. A Libyan customer picks over every loaf on the table in his search for the largest, pinches them all to avoid an air bubble, and then pays the minimum price for the size.

Libyan bread is not popular with Americans for several reasons; one, because it is well handled, not to mention well dusted. For who in Libya has failed to see the overloaded bread cart wheeling down the road and accidentally discharging some of its loaves on the street? Somebody shouts at the bread man, who stops and runs back, picks up and dusts off the bread, and restacks it, and hurries on. But malesh! The bread is good. Or so I think.

Americans are accustomed at home to large white loaves of very light texture and quite without taste, and the golden Libyan bread does not taste good to them. The Italian bakeries produce something they call Italian bread, which sells widely to Americans because it is produced under more hygienic conditions. But this bread is an insult to Italian bread as made by Italians in Italy.

In Benghazi we were deprived of Tripoli bread, as the Benghazine bakes himself a long cardboard loaf of cardboard texture and flavor, while the Bedawi bakes his own flat, unrisen discs of bread. For foreign consumption, several Greek bakeries turn out flavorless imitations of British bread.

Now, as I argue with the man about the price of my bread, I feel sure it is four piastres for two large loaves, not six piastres.

"Six piastres!" shouts the bread man again, "or you give me back bread!"

As I do not have four piastres in change, I must give him a ten-piastre note, which gives him the final word, and he only returns four piastres.

Two piastres, six cents, is not a big incentive to fight, and I tell myself that perhaps the control price of Tripoli bread was raised during our stay in Benghazi. Anyway, the bread is too good to leave behind.

That evening I ask Hammet, who has come to see if he can assist us in settling, if the price of bread is up. Hammet's family, like many of the best families, make their own bread and pay a small sum to have it baked at the nearest baker's oven. Hammet assures me that the control price of bread has not been changed.

The next day I return to Bread Street, which is so flooded with livestock traffic that I park my car outside and enter on foot. This time I have exact change of four piastres. I go to the same man, select two large loaves, and hand him four piastres. He says, "No, six piastres," with his hand still extended.

I say, "Four piastres," and start to turn away.

He pushes the four piastres back in my hand, and grabs at his bread, repeating, "Six piastres! Six piastres!" determined to have his bread if he doesn't get six piastres. A crowd is gathering and gawking, and I am telling myself that even if he is cheating me, it is very good bread, the largest and brownest on the street, and two nice loaves of bread are probably worth two extra piastres. So I give him two more piastres, and retreat with the bread.

For a week, then, I daily pay the man six piastres for his bread, consoling myself that it doesn't matter much if I *am* being cheated — the bread is good.

One evening when we are dining out with friends, a discussion of bread arises. For lack of anything better to say, I tell about the man who always collects two extra piastres from me. My story is met with groans of disgust and a collected opinion poll which shows that no one else there would accept such treatment, and I must be weak-minded to do so! As I am beginning to think so myself, I decide to make a test the next day.

The following morning I take Lena to town with me. Italians usually get market goods for a lower price than Americans or British, chiefly because the Italian housewife raises hell if she doesn't, and the Libyan shopkeeper is still in awe of her.

I park the car before we enter the street, and I ask Lena to go to the first stand and buy bread while I wait in the car. She goes, handles the loaves carefully on the stand, chooses two large ones, pays for them, and returns to me sputtering with indignation. "Signora! This man is mischievous! Wicked! I find two large loaves; I ask if these are the biggest. He says, 'Yes, two piastres each!' Signora, he is wicked! He is cheating you *too* much!"

I thought so, too, although as an American I am accustomed to being cheated. Lena and I drove slowly down the street past the bread man, stopped the car where he could see that we were together, and said "Buon giorno," and drove on. He looked decidedly confused.

The next day I return alone to Bread Street, leave the car, walk to the bread man and choose two large loaves. I slap down four piastres and hurry off before he can do anything. I thought that I had won.

The following day I proceed as before, laying down only four piastres, but the man is too quick for me. He grabs at the bread in my hands, shouting in real anger, "Six piastres!"

"No!" I shout indignantly. "Four piastres! You sell to my Italian friend for four piastres. Why you ask me for six? I only pay you four piastres!"

"Six piastres!" he shouts, gripping the bread, and trying to force the four piastres back in my hand. A crowd gathers, mouths hanging open, pressing in around us.

"Four piastres!"

"Six piastres!" and the bread is being mangled between us.

The crowd presses closer, breathing hotly on us, not yet angry but slightly hostile, vitally interested, and too close for comfort. I am isolated on Bread Street, not only because I am a foreigner, but because I am out of my class. Had an educated Libyan been present, I think he would have stood up for my rights, or had there been a policeman, he would have made the man sell the bread. But there were only Bread Street men, to whom I am an alien both by race and by class.

It seems undignified to continue struggling in a dirty alley over two loaves of bread and two piastres. I drop the bread, pick up my piastres and leave. It is the first time during my years in Libya that I have been angry with a Libyan.

I didn't go back for several days because the incident annoyed me, and hurt my feelings. As Harry said, "Bread Street is no longer your spiritual home!"

Best friends—
Lena and Pucci...

I went back once again and bought bread from the stand next to the unpleasant man. He pretended not to see me. The loaves were inferior, but I paid the correct price. There was no further incident. But Bread Street had changed; they had made me an alien. In that swiftly gathering crowd of faces slowly growing hostile I had seen a hint of what might happen if my car were run into by some bright lad riding his bicycle backwards on the wrong side of the street and the lad were injured.

Now, Harry's driver picks up the bread at a little shop he passes daily. We pay the proper price. The bread isn't fresh. I'd rather have the better bread for two piastres more. But I can't do it. It's not the piastres, it's the inference of the bread man's action. "Only two piastres each to the Italians who ground our noses in the dirt for years! But three piastres to the Americans who send us gift wheat!"

Now that we are back in Tripoli again we see much more of Hammet; Harry sees him daily in the office, and we hear about him on every side. Hammet is very determined on his own way, which is not always in accordance with either best Libyan usage, or Western. He is equally determined to have the approval of those he cares for, and to do the things he knows they do *not* care for. This disaccord between actions and ethics requires some nimble-witted explanations to which he is quite equal. The irrisistible fact is that he makes himself believe his own explanations, even while he is making them. He is a compelling person whom one must like without judging, I guess.

Usually Hammet makes his explanations to me, destined to be conveyed indirectly to Harry, by which time they don't seem as reasonable as they did to me. I tell Hammet, "It is better for you to tell this to 'your father' yourself."

And Hammet says, "He is too busy to listen!"

I know very well the "too busy" ploy, designed to protect Harry from just such explanations!

Both Harry and I worry about him, ineffectually of course. When you like a person so much you do wish that he would permit you to approve of him. Of all the young men whom we have met in Libya, he is the one who I am sure will succeed materially — but never be happy. He is after two worlds, and wants both unconditionally, and doesn't expect to pay for either.

As far as women go, as soon as he has conquered one, he ceases to find her desirable. What a vista! In this matter of wives, women and divorces in the Moslem world, it is not my business to judge. But I do know that Moslem women have hearts exactly like the rest of us, and I don't like to see my friends' wives hurt.

Yet what can I personally say about a person who is consistently thoughtful of me, kind to me, who never fails to arrive at our home on Libyan feast days with an appropriate delicacy or gift to include us in the celebration, who honors me with his confidences, and who tries unconditionally to assist Harry? — and whose current wife I love! One thing I know — it is fortunate that I am too old to attract him as a female.

Harry always says, "Hammet has never failed to accomplish successfully anything I ask him to do. I rely on him."

So, unreliable though he is, Harry, at least, can rely on him. There is no mystery to equal that of a human being!

32. Harem Party

I SAT hastily down beside Elsa Taher, the taffy-haired, American-born wife of Ali Taher, a brainy young Libyan, at one time a minister of state, who had taken his university degree in the United States. Elsa, who married him there six years ago and is now the mother of four children, seems to remain quite untouched, perhaps deliberately so, by Libyan ways and Arab contacts. Today, in this very volatile Arab atmosphere of an extremely gay Libyan harem party, she makes no effort to respond in kind to the voluble Arabic salutations of her friends. In fact, she pays less attention to them than I do. She might be a tourist passing through, looking with alien eyes on antics which don't concern her.

"A very nice party," I suggest.

She looks languidly around and says, "I never enjoy these female things. All this chatter. And the food is so horribly sweet! You can't keep your figure on that stuff."

"The Libyan ladies aren't trying to keep their figures."

"Some of them are! You should hear them talk about their 're-gimes!' Only six sugar goodies instead of eight! Saha is on a regime, she says, but you can't tell the difference before and after. It's like when they have babies. Gosh, look at that dress!"

Saha Beshir, our hostess, is one of the few Libyan women today in Western dress, and it is certainly the wrong one, a bouffant black taffeta floral print with huge turquoise roses, probably purchased in London when her husband was in the Libyan embassy. The dress does nothing to suggest that her pregnancy has ended and that this party is to celebrate the happy birth of the eighth little Beshir, a son.

But Saha has an irrepressible capacity to enjoy life, warm, easy manners, a pale, transparent skin, eyes that are glowing, and strong, glossy, hennaed hair — *and* she has given birth to five sons.

"She always looks happy, anyway."

"Yeah? She wants to go back to London, though. Hates being cooped up here. She adored shopping at Swan and Edgar — bargains in nylons, and all that. The three older boys are at school in England, and they have almost forgotten their Arabic. Hate coming back to Tripoli for holidays! Say they don't know what to do!" Elsa stops and looks about her disinterestedly, and says, "Saha's a scream, though. Did you ever hear her tell about how Sadik got a house for them in London? At first, she and the seven kids all trailed around with him, when he was trying to rent a place. Every time a landlady saw all those kids she said, No! So Sadik told Saha, You must all stay in the hotel, and don't you dare to come out again until I get a house! So he went off alone, and got a house, and Saha and the kids moved in at night."

The party has grown to large proportions, and the sunny veranda which surrounds the luxurious duplex is filled with varicolored café tables laid with cutlery, and at least a hundred women are seated already. As our hostess is the wife of a prominent Libyan, everything is being done in lavish style.

Most of the guests are Libyan, and they have all arrived swathed in their huge white baracans, which have been quickly flung aside to reveal some very elegant Libyan costumes. These are built around the drapings of an inside baracan, woven of cloth-of-silver threaded with turquoise, purple, or cerise and worn pouched out across the stomach so that everybody looks permanently pregnant. This is the most extravagantly gowned Libyan group that I have ever seen, and it is certainly a sign of the increasing Libyan prosperity. The well-to-do Libyan woman always has one handsome outfit to use for feast days or parties, but today there are Libyans here whom I see frequently enough to recognize that their outfits are new for the occasion.

Our hostess, Saha, assisted by her three sisters, her two pretty little daughters, and a variety of family dependents, has seated her guests so that they can all converse, with the non-Arabic speaking foreigners placed together. Usually a Libyan woman will speak Italian when she is alone with a foreigner, but she naturally speaks Arabic when she is with other Libyans.

For this reason I am sitting next to Elsa, and next to me is Mrs. Chen Chi Ping, the wife of the ambassador for Nationalist China, a charming, cosmopolitan, forceful character, both gay and fierce, who speaks fluent American. Beside her is Madame Yorokuglu, wife of the Turkish ambassador and the senior diplomatic lady. Chic, sophisticated, small and plump, she speaks French, Italian and Turkish, but not Arabic.

A variety of Beshir-related children are now passing a colorful outlay of Libyan drinks and refreshments, all of which, as Elsa has said, are "horribly sweet," for excessive saccharinity is the characteristic of Libyan party foods. Our first round today is sweet tea. Traditionally, there should be three glasses served each person, but today the first two glasses have been deliberately omitted in order to give us the real delicacy which is the third glass of tea, three-quarters full of peeled, fresh almonds. It requires practice to drink the almonds with the tea, and not to leave them behind in the glass when the tea has drained off. Elsa, who looks utterly bored, has quickly drained her tea — saying something like uuuugh! — and is now plucking the almonds out of the glass with her fingers.

"Almonds are the only thing I like at these parties!"

"What do you eat at home? Libyan food or American?" I ask.

"Oh, American! Ali prefers it, and so do the children. I can't stand Libyan stuff!"

"What language do the children speak?"

"Well, they can speak a little Arabic, and some Italian, but mostly English. Ali and I always talk to them in English."

"Do you speak any Arabic?"

"*Me* speak Arabic! Oh, no! Why would I? Ali speaks English."

"How does your husband feel about your not trying to learn Arabic? And not speaking it to the children?"

"How does *Ali* feel about that? I'm sure I don't know; I never asked him!"

Although it seems slightly ungracious to make no attempt to conform, I am wondering if Elsa isn't right. She is determined to remain just what she was when her alien Libyan husband married her — an American. That's what he fell in love with, and that is what he must live with. If she were a more imaginative person, and more malleable, less determined and self-assured, less of an extrovert, she would by now have been made miserable by the forces of Ali's family and Ali's filial need to accede to them. She might even be in the harem. At best, she would be one more foreign wife who was making her own embassy miserable by her attempts to go home. Instead of which she has produced four children (three sons!), keeps a tidy house, and enjoys life in her own American way. Malesh! that she doesn't like Libyan teas!

With this in mind, I look at Elsa with considerable admiration for her coolness and strength, and her obtuseness which may be wisdom. Perhaps this is a wife that Libya needs — one with the courage *not* to be Libyanized.

I, for instance, would do the country no good, as I would be always seeing the reasons for Libyan mistakes, instead of trying to prevent them. A reformer must be blind!

"Look at that blouse!" Elsa prods me to turn as a large-bosomed lady passes us, in a blouse of silver-threaded-with-turquoise cloth, which descends to a deep V in front between generous breasts. "What's the use of hiding one eye, when they dress like that in the house!"

"But there are no men here to see."

"Well, there ought to be; they'd enjoy it!"

The V neck is the accepted blouse style, and given the average Libyan bust, it is very effective. Throats and bosoms are partially covered with numerous gold chains and hanging pendants which consist of tiny golden horns to ward off evil, Fatima's hands to protect from harm, hearts and keys and other gilded symbols of happiness and prosperity, as well as charms for protection from calamities and sorrows. The effect of all the ornaments en masse is almost like a solid-gold chest plate. As the ladies also wear heavy gold earrings, and weighty gold bracelets on wrists and ankles, their appearance is that of being somebody's good investment, which they are, as Libyan family resources are often held in deposit in the gold of the Libyan wife.

"Well, that's one thing the baracan is good for!" Elsa prods me again, as a very pregnant lady, who looks to be carrying babies both in front and behind, passes us.

"Their faces are really beautiful, though!"

"Maybe. But too fat!"

The Libyan ladies' heads are nearly all tied about with silk kerchiefs of turquoise or rose, banded with silver or gold. Each lady has a heavy swatch of hair pulled forward to show in front under the kerchief, and below the headdress and down her back swing two plaits of hair interbraided with silver ribbon. A few years ago these plaits were the lady's own hair and permanently attached to her head, but today so many young Libyans have cut their hair short that the plaits are often only pinned to their heads under the kerchief, and kept solely for use with the Libyan costume. Saha, our hostess, has very short hair with a wave.

As the silk kerchiefs are tied loosely and worn above the ears, they always seem to be slipping from the wearer's head, and the repeated graceful retying of the silk tissue with a flutter of bejeweled and beautifully shaped hands becomes a characteristic and unforgettable gesture of elegant Libyan women.

Mrs. Yorokuglu, on the other side of me, urgently nudges me to look around, saying, "Who *is* that girl! She is a perfect Turkish type!"

She is pointing out my dear friend Badria, Hammet's wife, and headmistress of a girls school. She has just entered and is immediately the most outstanding woman in the room because of her remarkable coloring. Beneath a pale blue kerchief, blonde hair the color of ripe corn escapes in shining strands across her forehead and below her cheekbones — such shimmering corn-silk hair is hers alone in all of Tripoli. Her oval, hazel eyes with yellow lights glow with excitement, as if she knows herself to be the most beautiful woman present. Her skin is pale and fine, and always looks to have been just bathed with fresh, cool water. Her large teeth in her wide mouth are very white, and now the gold tooth in the middle, which used to disturb me, seems only to enhance the beauty of her hair and eyes.

"She's lovely," breathes Mrs. Yorokuglu. "A pure Turkish type!"

"Her husband wants to divorce, I hear," hisses Elsa in my other ear.

I look at Elsa with horror. "Oh, no!" But I think back over other rumors I have heard . . .

Shimmering, corn-silk hair.

As Badria comes over to greet us, she is a mixture of dignity, gentleness and merriment. I look in her golden eyes to see if there is a ghost behind them. Who can tell? The warmth of our kisses is real, first one cheek, then the other, then we begin again. I introduce Mrs. Yorokuglu, and Badria pulls over a chair to sit near us, and answer her impatient questions.

"What is your family name?"

Badria tells her.

"It is a Turkish name!" says my delighted friend.

"Yes, my family is of Turkish origin, three hundred years ago."

"So you are a true Turk; I was right! Your name is even one form of my own family name. Your husband's name?"

"Hammet ———" and Badria gives the well-known name.

"Also a Turk!"

"Yes, for a hundred years his family supplied the Pasha rulers in Libya."

"Yes, yes, and wicked ones, too," says Mrs. Yorokuglu approvingly. "You are beautiful, my dear, a true Turk. How many children have you?"

"Two, a boy and a girl."

Apparently it takes a Turk to know a Turk, because as Badria leaves to speak with the hostess, my Turkish friend whispers to me, "Married to that family! Fierce rulers, but bad husbands!"

Now, from tall frosted tumblers, we are drinking iced almond-and-rose water, a true harem drink. Elsa hastily pushes hers away from her and leans over and ruminates in my ear, "Gosh, I wonder how Saha ever came to have this baby? She had seven babies in seven years, then seven years without any — guess she and Sadik really thought they had the secret!"

Now come orange fizz and Kitty-Kolas, accompanied by honey cakes, almond pastries, almond macaroons, chocolate eclairs, cream puffs, chocolate creams, caramels and sugar-coated almonds. Elsa piles hers in a heap and says, "I'll take these home to the kids!" I surreptitiously wrap up the dry types in Kleenex and put them in my handbag, while the gramophone plays classic Arab records at full blast.

Nafisa, Badreddin's wife, now comes to greet me. She is extremely handsome, in the classic Arab style, with long, dark plaits of her own hair, brilliant dark eyes and clear, creamy skin. She carries her first baby in her arms. After exchanging greetings she asks me if I have seen the newest bride at the party, Mrs. Hameda Zliteny?

Elsa not having alerted me on this matter, I have no idea which is the bride. To my surprise Nafisa points out a dainty, girlish figure in a pale-green tailored linen suit, with upswept chestnut hair combed in the Italian mode, a girl whom I had noticed and assumed to be Italian. She is very young and looks completely European — but she is speaking Arabic, and undoubtedly she arrived wrapped up in a baracan, with her face hidden. She is still very slim. Not ready yet for the pregnant baracan!

We have been here two hours, and it is time to say goodbye. Elsa leaves first, with a handful of sweets for the kids, a swish of her skirts, and a whisper to me, "Well, I've had enough!" As she stands in the doorway saying goodbye to Saha the two are in roars of laughter together; she's probably asking Saha how she got pregnant again. Everybody accepts Elsa; she's obviously here to stay.

Mrs. Chen Chi Ping agitates her dainty hand to get her diamond wristwatch into view, while Mrs. Yorokuglu gazes out over rooftops wondering if help is at hand. But as we say our goodbyes, the Libyan ladies are just settling down . . .

33. "Say Not the Good Man Dies"

CALLIMACHUS

THAT morning of what was to be their last day out, driving in the early morning mist on the Sirtic Desert road, Mohamed said something to Peter, his boss, that Peter will never forget. They were on their way home after a three weeks' trip in the Sahara. Like many hard trips, one of its greatest joys was to be returning home, especially so for Mohamed, whose first voyage it was outside of Tripolitania.

"Why, my friends in Suk el Juma," he boasted excitedly, "will never believe the things that I have seen! Even I never knew such places existed. These city boys know nothing about the desert in our own country! But I shall explain to them everything about the Sahara!" he said rather patronizingly. Then, suddenly overcome by his own naïve enjoyment of his new experience, he said, "I never had such a wonderful trip in all my life before! Now, today I am very happy!"

Peter, a tolerant and sympathetic young man, grinned kindly, and said, "And you have a lot of fine souvenirs to take home, too."

"Yes, yes," purred Mohamed, "I have arm daggers from Gatrun, and arrowheads from Derj, and glass beads from Ghat, and some putrified wood . . ."

"Petrified," suggested Peter.

"Yes, putrified wood," agreed Mohamed, "and volcanic rocks, and Fezzan slippers, and woven food covers . . ." he itemized, roaring along in the Land Rover.

"Yes, but watch the road a bit, old boy. The mist is still very heavy, and there are a lot of oil trucks now using this road. Better slow down."

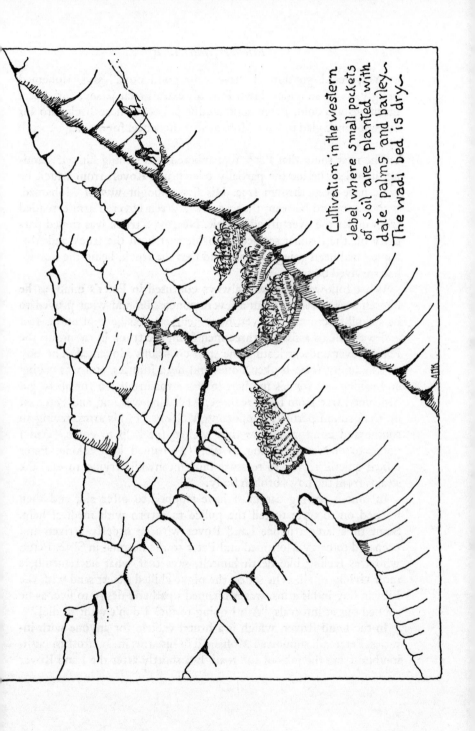

Cultivation in the western Jebel where small pockets of soil are planted with date palms and barley. The wadi bed is dry~

"Yes, yes, I go slow. I drive very good now," says Mohamed smugly, as he snuggles down into his extra green jersey, for desert mornings are cold. Peter contentedly pokes his nose back into his Swiss journal, glad to have Mohamed at the wheel for a time.

The next thing that Peter remembered was finding himself standing in a daze beside the partially overturned Rover, from which he must have been thrown free. His first thought was of Mohamed, who was not to be seen; then he saw a green-covered arm extended from under the overturned vehicle. Nearby, a truck was tipped partially off the road. It seemed probable that both the truck and Mohamed had been going too fast, and that the truck, being the heavier had survived better.

What followed then was always confused in Peter's mind, as he himself was suffering from a severe concussion and what proved to be a skull fracture. However, he remembers that he kept on his feet and was able to assist the three men from the truck in easing up the Land Rover and extricating the semi-conscious Mohamed. The boy was in agony from broken bones and head injuries, and was crying and calling out for his mother. It was a torturing job for all to get Mohamed free from the wreckage. At last he was out, and Peter sat on the ground partially supporting Mohamed in his arms, trying to soothe and comfort him as they waited for help to come. "Am I going to die? Am I going to die?" Mohamed kept asking. Peter talked quietly trying to reassure him, meanwhile trying to ease the strains from the boy's broken body.

In time a passing car must have stopped to offer aid, and then hurried on to Sirte to tell the police to return with medical help. Some time later a police Land Rover with an orderly arrived and prepared to carry Mohamed and Peter to the hospital in Sirte. Peter, who was feeling like death himself, says that what he remembers most vividly of all, as he sat on the night-chilled desert sand with the Libyan boy in his arms, was Mohamed's pathetic desire to live, as he sobbed out at intervals, "Am I going to die? I don't want to die!"

In the Land Rover, which is a brutal vehicle for anyone with injuries, Peter still supported Mohamed in his arms in an effort to cushion him from the jolts of the road. But shortly after the Land Rover started, Mohamed, with his round black head lying against Peter's shoulder and supported in Peter's arms, gave a final feeble groan, and died. Peter, uncertain whether or not Mohamed was dead or had just lost consciousness, continued to hold the boy until he was lifted from his arms at the hospital at Sirte. Then Peter himself lost consciousness.

The first we in Tripoli knew of the accident was at eleven A.M. when the Sirte police telephoned to FAO that one of its Land Rovers had been in an accident and one man had been killed and another injured. They did not name which was the fatality. Harry tried to call Sirte back to find out, but was unable to get the line through again.

Meanwhile, he telephoned to me to go immediately and find Peter's wife, Margaret, and break the news of the accident, and ask her to be ready to go to Sirte to Peter, assuming that he might be the survivor. I found Margaret, an impressively beautiful young Swiss woman, the mother of five handsome blond sons and pregnant again at the time, in her apartment just preparing to go to Tripoli College to collect the children for lunch.

There was no easy way to break the news that I was bringing, but Margaret remained wonderfully calm and strong, thinking only of what she might take to help Peter. She earned my deep admiration and gratitude, and I thanked God silently for a nonhysterical woman, more sure than ever that hysterical women have no business away from home. We collected the children from school, then asked their Swiss nanny to be fully responsible for them until Margaret was able to return, and Margaret was ready to leave.

The question had arisen at the same time of what to do about Mohamed's wife — or widow, whichever it turned out to be. As in any case Lutfeyah could not leave her house to go to Mohamed, we decided it was kinder to warn her merely that Mohamed had been involved in an accident of some sort, but that no details were known.

By two o'clock the FAO Land Rover was on the way to Sirte, carrying Margaret and Jock Wylie, who is a man of iron to lean on in time of trouble. It was an oversize Rover with rear seats running lengthwise and capable of being used as emergency beds, as Harry felt sure the police ambulance would be in dilapidated condition.

Meanwhile, Harry had made contact with the Sirte police, who had promised to start their ambulance towards Tripoli with its one injured and one dead, whom now they identified as being a Libyan.

About eight o'clock Margaret's vehicle met the ambulance on the road halfway between Sirte and Tripoli. Peter was semi-conscious on a stretcher, his many bandages soaked with blood from the jolting of the badly sprung vehicle on the rough road. Mohamed's dead body was on the adjacent stretcher. Margaret crawled into the ambulance and took Peter in her arms, determined to shield him as much as possible from the violence of the road, even as Peter had tried to shield Mohamed.

The FAO Rover with Jock and the driver then proceeded slowly ahead of the ambulance along the road towards Tripoli. Sometimes Jock would try to take Margaret's place with Peter in order to ease her arms, but Margaret refused to move. When it was midnight and Peter was still bleeding badly, they decided to stop at the British military post at Homs and ask for emergency treatment. Here a British orderly promptly replaced Peter's bandages with fresh ones, and gave him another pain-killer, while another anxious orderly brought hot, strong tea to Margaret, Jock and the drivers. Slightly more comfortable then, the miserable caravan crawled slowly onward.

It was nearly three A.M. when they arrived in Tripoli, and the problem of where to take Peter faced them. If they took him to the municipal hospital it was doubtful if a bed could be found, and equally doubtful if he would receive any attention before nine A.M., when the doctors ordinarily arrived.

As Peter was not entitled to treatment at the British military hospital, his entry would have to be arranged with the officer in charge and various hospital officials, a formality which might take some time. Meanwhile, Peter himself wanted only to escape from the hideous jolting of the broken-down ambulance and the close proximity with poor Mohamed's dead body. In the end, Jock and Margaret took Peter to his own apartment and put him to bed there. Mohamed was taken to the morgue. Jock ended up at our house at four A.M. to tell us the result of his trip.

Later that morning we moved Peter to the British military hospital, where examinations and X rays proved that he had suffered a skull fracture, a brain concussion, and a serious back injury, as well as minor cuts and abrasions. Mohamed, with a crushed skull, internal hemorrhages, and many broken bones, could never have survived. The wonder was that either of them had regained a measure of consciousness after the accident. Months later were to find Peter still hospitalized with his injured back.

The most distressing part for me came the next morning with the need to communicate with Mohamed's wife and mother. Up until now, the knowledge that Mohamed himself was past all help, the practical need to assist the survivor of the crash, plus the shock of sudden calamity had made me almost numb to emotion. Now I knew that I must go to mourn with those who were suffering the most from the tragedy, a visit which I dreaded as it would release in myself my own sorrow and loss for "my son Mohamed."

Word of Mohamed's death had been sent to his home the day before through the sheik of his tribe, whose responsibility it was to notify and assist the family in its loss. This morning I asked Hammet to go with me to the house, dreading what I should find and anticipating that I might need an interpreter. Hammet has great natural dignity, and always commands respect. We drove to Suk el Juma, and walked up the narrow lane to the blue painted door, which I had entered first for Mohamed's wedding. The house was now surrounded by curious or mourning young men and children. Hammet waited outside, while I went into the house to join the women assembled there — cousins, in-laws, and friends, all wailing and ululating. There was such a crowd of tear-stained, runny-nosed children and infants among them, weeping and sniffling, that I could not recognize for certain Mohamed's own two boys.

I made the rounds with kisses and embraces, until I came to Mohamed's blind mother, who was sobbing violently in a state of semi-collapse. She recognized me immediately by my voice and started saying over and over in English, "One son! One son, Mohamed! Mohamed dead! Mohamed dead!" Then, switching over into Arabic, "Two babies, no food! Two babies, no food! Ayeh, ayeh, ayeh!" She was almost demented, and I could not blame her. The horror of their total dependence on one young boy, now dead, was beyond expression. Again, as many times before, I was overwhelmed by the responsibility which Mohamed's life had forced him to carry.

I knew that in time the mother and Lutfeyah would receive insurance money and social security compensation for the dead wage earner, but this I could not explain in Arabic. I would ask Hammet to explain the money aspect to the male relatives who were hanging around outside the house. In any case, this could not replace the shoulders of the boy on whom they all leaned.

I had brought with me large packages of sugar and tea to help out with the ritual funeral entertaining, which had to be done out of respect to the dead person. I had also gifts of money, one sum for the mother and another for Lutfeyah. I found Lutfeyah sitting apart in her little alcove, the same small alcove in which I had met her for the first time before her wedding, and which the wedding money had fitted out with a door.

Unlike those about her, she was neither weeping nor wailing but sitting on the floor cross-legged and as motionless as if in a trance. I recalled the little bride I had seen a few years before, sitting immobile in the center of hilarity, as she tried to hide her joy. Today she sat transfixed, as if the blow had been too great, the emotion too intense, and all her instincts were stunned. Even now, as a widow and the mother of two sons, she was little more than a child in years, but her face had gone gray and pinched and ageless and looked grotesquely misplaced above her childish body, her tiny wrists and hands.

There was nothing I could say to her, no comfort I could give her. Her life now would be one of unrelieved drudgery. Her young lover, her man who had valued her, who had laughed with her and loved her, was gone. Her door to the world was closed; her reason for being was ended. Only her sons remained, and they already belonged more to the old matriarch, and to their tribe, than to her, their mother. Now, still in her teens, Lutfeyah was nothing more than the vessel which once had been used.

Mohamed, coming home from the desert yesterday morning with his young eyes filled with the wonder of the great Sahara, his heart singing out at the marvels of the Libyan world which he was finding, was at the moment of his death rich with his greatest contentment. Dear son Mohamed, for you to live was to die. Poor Lutfeyah, you must die without living. Bismi-llahi r-Rahmani r-Rahim. In the name of God, the Compassionate, the Merciful.

A few months later in Switzerland Margaret gave birth to a beautiful, much-desired baby girl. Peter was sent to a sanatorium there for treatment for his injured back, and shortly after left Libya for good. He could never forget Mohamed, who had wanted so much to live.

Nor could I forget Mohamed; I who loved him in a strange way, so that even while I rejoiced at his passing joys and triumphs I seemed to see always behind him the shadow of obstacles too great to be overcome. As we are all born to die, perhaps this was a child who died in time.

34. Alien Marriage Beds

LITTLE Gertrude, who came from Nebraska seven years ago as the wife of a Libyan Arab husband, is an encyclopedia of information on the subject of mixed marriages. Perhaps the problems of a mixed marriage are like the symptoms of a strange ailment: you never know until you have the symptoms yourself how many other people have the ailment.

When Gertrude was nineteen years old she and Fadl Wahya were students at the same Midwestern university. Fadl was much older than Gertrude, came from a prominent Libyan family, and was attending the university on a foreign grant scholarship, one of the first Libyans to do so. The government had promised him the prospect of a diplomatic post when he finished.

Gertrude was an extremely attractive girl with ultra-feminine appearance and gentle manners, and Fadl immediately became enamored of her. Her transparent skin, pale blue eyes, silky blonde hair and delicate figure were his dreams fulfilled. Gertrude found Fadl cultivated and kindly, an urgent suitor, and perhaps an escape from her own environment, and the two were married in America. If they could have remained abroad, all might have been well.

Although when he left Libya Fadl had been promised a diplomatic post, after the government discovered his marriage to a foreigner, it forced Fadl to refuse the prospective post. No Libyan with a foreign-born wife may hold a diplomatic position, even though the wife becomes a Libyan citizen by her marriage — so strictly does Libya discourage marriage with foreigners, especially non-Moslems.*

The lost diplomatic post was only the first of many blows which the young couple had to face. Although today Fadl holds a position

* Like all Arab rules, there are many exceptions to this.

of responsibility in the government, which ultimately, although it took years for it to do so, came to realize that it could not afford to waste an educated man. Meanwhile, Fadl had returned to Libya an unemployed husband and a lost hope to his family, and as such he had to introduce his Western wife into his parents' Arab household.

Gertrude never discusses her own experiences in her husband's Libyan home, but one can draw certain conclusions about them from the generalizations she volunteers about the problems of mixed marriages and foreign wives. When Gertrude says to me unequivocally, "Libyan-foreign marriages cannot work!" I feel that she speaks with some experience.

"But surely there are exceptions to this?" I ask.

"I do not think in any case such a marriage can possibly be happy!" Her voice is soft and her manner is gentle, but obviously there is tough fiber inside this fragile figure.

"But look at yourself, Gertrude. You have two sons and a daughter, whom you and Fadl adore. You keep an attractive home of your own, and you do a great deal to help Fadl in his work. You say yourself that Fadl is good to you. You also hold a well-paid secretarial position with an oil company, so you certainly haven't gone into seclusion. Is this a marriage that doesn't work?"

"I am fortunate because I have an excellent earning capacity. A woman's ability to make money has a great influence of her freedom."

"My point exactly about money, Gertrude! The combination of female pelvis plus the almighty dollar is stronger than the first alone."

"Also — husbands differ, even in Libya."

"That's what I mean. It all depends on the husband."

"No! It depends on the husband's family, and his ability to hold out against them. You have no idea of the strength of the old ladies in the background! They can make life hell for everybody about them until they get their own way. If a husband once abandons his foreign wife to the women's quarters — the harem, if you like — she becomes the property of the old ladies of the family as much as that of her husband!"

"Well, why take a foreign wife, if you only want her for the harem? Anyway, I often hear young Libyans say that they want a wife who can go out with them and take more part in their life than most Libyan women can do."

"Yes," Gertrude agreed. "They often *say* that. And one of the first modern demands they make is to see their wife before they marry her. And what does it come to? If they do see her and like her, they immediately fall into the old Libyan state of mind of feeling that she belongs only to them, and they expect to have complete control over her. She must accept their word about everything, and they soon hide her away in the Libyan female world for themselves alone. They forget all their modern resolutions, and are swamped in the jealous possessiveness of the masculine Arab world."

"But this is changing in other Arab countries, as the women emerge," I insist. "As they take a larger part in life here in Libya, the attitude will have to change."

"Maybe," says Gertrude doubtfully. "But I feel sure that today practically *all* Libyans are utterly incapable of accepting the idea for their wives of friendly contact with any man except themselves. I think Libyan women themselves are still quite unable to enter into a simple, friendly contact with any man except their husbands. At present a Western woman married to a Libyan husband and living in Libya is going to be forced, for the sake of peace and stability in her married life, to accept the same standard of docility towards her husband as a Libyan wife. One can't fight in bed!"

There seemed to be nothing to say to this.

After a minute, Gertrude asked, "Did you ever meet Joan Blank, the English girl who married the Permanent Secretary of the Ministry of Green Tea? She was a charming girl herself, and crazy about her husband, to begin with. But her closest friend here was a young Englishwoman, a secretary in the oil company where I am employed. The Libyan husband disliked this English friend of his wife's a great deal, because he felt that she was encouraging his wife to try to keep her independence. Anyway, the Libyan decided to break it up, and he told his wife that her friend had a bad reputation, and that she must cease seeing her immediately.

"Joan told her husband that the girl was her only real friend, that there was absolutely no scandal attached to her, and that she would not give up the friendship. A verbal struggle then went on with her husband for several weeks, and meanwhile Joan's female in-laws made it impossible for her to meet her friend in her own home, and reported all Joan's absences from home to her husband. Finally Joan was literally forced to give up her friendship.

"Joan recognized the motivation of the trouble as her husband's jealousy of any influence over her except his own, and she could not reconcile herself to it. The incident was not itself very vital, but it was symbolic to her of a Libyan husband's insistence on complete and unreasonable domination over his wife. In the long run, her sense of frustration and injustice began to ruin her affection for her husband, and in the end his insistence on breaking up her friendship with the English girl proved to be the first step in breaking his own marriage."

"Where is she now?"

"She's still here in Libya, in his house. You see, she's his wife! She can't get an exit visa to leave without his permission, and he won't give his permission for her to go."

"Can't she appeal to the British consul's office?"

"Not very well. She is a Libyan citizen now and, of course, she had to give up her British passport."

Gertrude, speaking now with unequaled frankness, continues, "Believe me, the Libyan man is complete master of his home! If his wife dares to go against him in any way, he can either beat her up or divorce her, and be considered fully justified in his actions. Not that I am suggesting that the average Libyan husband does this, but only that he *can* do so — and he wouldn't lose the approval of his neighbors by so doing. One young Libyan I know got drunk one evening and, being out of sorts with his wife for the moment, said before some friends, 'I divorce my wife; I divorce my wife; I divorce my wife.' As he had made the statement three times before witnesses, it became a fact, and his wife was thereby divorced.

"Of course, the practical details of divorce are *not* so easily settled. If a man becomes annoyed with his wife and sends her home to her family, the family may find her too much of a liability and send her back, or just throw her out of the household. As marriage settlements differ greatly according to the wealth and status of the two families, and also by the personal agreements made between the bridegroom and the bride's family, the return of the settlement is a matter for everlasting argument when a divorce comes up. Usually, the girl's family is required to return the equivalent of what the man paid her family before the marriage. This sum was supposed to have been spent on the girl's bridal preparations, her gold jewelry, and trousseau — but it often went into Papa's pocket!

"Anyway, by the time a divorce arises, the money or property has frequently vanished into thin air, and it has to be whistled back in some form or other — livestock, jewelry, home furnishings, or cash, before the ex-husband is content. By this time the girl is as unwelcome at her own home as she was in her husband's."

"I read in the paper," I interrupt, "that young Libyans are agitating now for a lower Libyan bride price. They say that the high price of Libyan brides is one reason why so many Libyans are marrying foreign girls."

"Yes, that is true. The government itself advises that the families of eligible girls should ask for smaller compensation, and so encourage all Libyans to marry at home."

Gertrude told me the story of a Libyan friend of hers in Tripoli who was expecting to be married, and whose family had made elaborate preparations for the usual week of celebrations. On the fourth night, as tradition demands, the expectant husband took his bride to his home and established her there, having the first peek at her himself before he left.

The following night is the crucial time, when the marital act must take place while the guests are celebrating in the other rooms of the house. Then the ultimate proof of union, and of the bride's virginity, must be shown to the guests in the form of the bloodstained sheet or sheepskin. This night the bridegroom, after an interval alone with the girl, emerged in a terrific rage and said that the marriage was off — there was something wrong with the girl! He left the house in a disappointed tantrum, as one can imagine.

The next day he returned with a doctor who was to give the girl a medical examination. This resulted in the discovery that not only was she not a virgin, but she had recently given birth to an infant.

This discovery automatically canceled the wedding contract, as virginity is the essential factor in a Libyan marriage agreement, and without this the marriage is void. The exception to this is if the girl is known and accepted to be a divorcée. The girl was returned to her parents. The father had known nothing about the girl's previous experience, and he was furious. But the mother had known the truth and had helped the girl to conceal the birth of the infant.

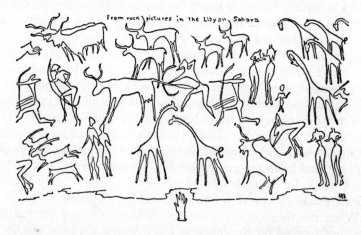

From rock pictures in the Libyan Sahara

"What happened to the baby?" I asked.

"Nobody knows. I imagine it was done away with."

The possibility of completely concealing the birth of an infant is not difficult to imagine in Libya, where women are secluded in their homes. Full term pregnancy would be almost impossible to conceal in Western costume, but it is easy to conceal it in Libyan dress, where the draped baracan folds voluminously several times over the stomach and hips. In any case, I have often noticed that my Libyan friends look much the same both before and after giving birth. The majority of Libyan women are decidedly fat by our standards, and as this is (or has been) the popular shape, they make no effort to control their posture or stomach muscles.

Gertrude described another instance of a young girl whom I shall call Lilah. Lilah lived in Benghazi where, under the Bedawi influence, girls sometimes gain more freedom to come and go than they have in Tripoli. Nevertheless Lilah, at eighteen years, was assumed never to have been out of her mother's sight nor to have been out of doors unaccompanied. Lilah, however, had managed to meet, fall in love with, and be intimate with a Libyan boy. Without admitting to her family the closeness of her relationship with this boy, Lilah asked her family to arrange a marriage for her with him.

Her family, who had already partially arranged what they considered a materially favorable match for her, refused to consider Lilah's boyfriend as husband. Alarmed, however, by realizing Lilah's sudden awareness of the masculine world, the parents made hasty arrangements for the wedding which they themselves favored to take place in the near future. Meanwhile, Lilah continued to find a way for clandestine meetings with her lover, and became pregnant.

The date approached for her marriage to the other man. Shortly before the ceremonies were to begin, she went to him and told him that she was pregnant by a lover. He shouted indignantly, demanded his money back and called off the marriage. The parents of the girl beat her, and Lilah ran away from her home in a pitiable state. She was taken in by a female relative who lived nearby, chiefly because this relative had a spite to work out against Lilah's parents.

When the time came for the baby's birth, the girl entered the Benghazi hospital for the delivery. The day after the baby was born, Lilah's brother came to see her in the hospital. As she lay unsuspecting and helpless in her bed, he stabbed her to death.

He ran from the hospital and hid himself in the house of friends while the police made token gestures of searching for him. Meanwhile, he stayed out of public view for a few weeks and then, supposedly with the connivance of the police, left Libya to go to Egypt, where he has since remained. Libyan sympathy was entirely with the brother, who was felt to be quite within his rights in avenging with death the family dishonor which his sister had brought on them.

"If Libyan girls can get into so much mischief," I comment, "when they are literally almost under 'house arrest,' there may be good reason why the men do not wish them to go out more! Generally speaking, one feels that Libyan husbands do not trust their wives, and if a Libyan goes away overnight on business he leaves a regular bodyguard of mamas, grandmas, and sisters to watch his wife's security!"

Gertrude looks doubtful and says, "I don't know if this is basically caused by lack of confidence in his wife's fidelity, or because his womenfolk insist on it. But I do agree that there is little trust between husband and wife, and neither one tells the other one the truth — except by coincidence.

"Fadl's cousin Sami," she continues, "is leaving Libya on a scholarship to the United States for a year, and the family is terrified that he'll make Fadl's mistake," Gertrude gives a rather mirthless laugh, "and marry over there. Sami thinks quite well of himself, and he said to Fadl that he wants a 'better rounded' wife than the present Libyan woman!"

"And did Fadl give him any advice?" I ask curiously.

"He told him he should first get his education, then come home and get a job, and then marry a Libyan woman, and change *her* situation for her. Let him take *her* out, and gradually mold her into the wife he wants, not bring home a Western wife and try to force her into the Libyan mold. Fadl knows as well as I do that it can't be done. Anyway, Sami may think now that he wants a modern wife, but he'll change his ideas fast enough after he marries her. He'll leave her behind in the harem; it's the easier way."

"Then you don't think the Libyan girls are nearing a change?"

"I don't know; it's more difficult than *you* think. Suppose the husband agrees to his wife going out without her baracan, the first step, and then to leaving off the black veil, the second step. Still, her father, mother and brothers must also be consulted. Granted they do agree, there is sure to be at least one antique relic on the family tree who raises hell. Then for the sake of peace and family pride, the girl stays in the harem. It's easier — and she's only a female!"

"When Sami says he wants a 'well rounded' woman, what does he mean? What changes does a Libyan himself think are desirable for the women here?"

"The Libyans I know are more certain of what they don't want their women to be than what they do want. They don't want Libyan girls to behave like some of the American wives who dash about in tight pants or bikinis. They don't want them to be included in all the husbands' invitations. They don't intend to give up their own free evenings in masculine company in the coffee shops or playing cards. They don't intend to push the baby in his carriage, nor baby-sit while the wife goes out, nor wipe the dishes, nor help about the house. They think American husbands are beaten down and emasculated, and that American women are careless of their morals, and that they all have 'boyfriends.' They see American marriage as a failure because of the high divorce rate. In fact, they want continued complete social freedom for themselves."

"So what does that leave for the women?"

"Exactly!"

"Well, forget the social aspect, and think what practical advantages there would be for the husbands if the women had more freedom. Surely a husband would be glad to have his wife take the baby to the doctor, if the child were ill? And take more responsibility for the children's health and care?"

"Yes. And he might like her to do the marketing — only that would entail letting the money out of his hands! The one thing that it is really respectable for a wife to do at present is to teach school — and bring home the monthly paycheck! All the wives I know like to teach if they can, because it is an escape from home. Even after her baby is born, the wife hurries back as soon as possible to teaching, quite lonely for her gossipy contacts again. Then Granny gets the infant to care for, and that isn't always desirable. Anyway, *I* always took care of my own kids!" says Gertrude with satisfaction.

"I went to the telephone exchange the other day," I say, "and saw a number of Libyan girls working the exchange: a few were Arabs, but most of them were Fezzani or Jewish. The girls are excellent at the work, so the supervisor says. The exchange runs a bus to pick them up at their homes. There are a number of women working at the tuna canning factory, too, because the women will come for less money than men, but they're all in the lowest social category. There are twelve girls at the nursing school this year, but almost all have Negro blood. It's just not the thing for the Arab women to work. I guess that public service, in general, is not condemned, only — 'It's not for *my* wife!' "

Gertrude is silent a moment, then says, "It's not *just* narrow-mindedness on the husband's part. Several years ago the wives of a few senior government officials got together and agreed that they would go out in public with their faces uncovered. News of their intention leaked to the prime minister. He called up the officials and told them that if their wives proceeded with their intention the husbands would be fired."

"I guess I know who that was! Nobody ever saw *his* wife! What was his reason?"

"Political. He was very popular at the time. The Arab press always called him the 'Abraham Lincoln of Libya,' because he promised everything to everybody. A chicken in every pot, and two for himself. They say that he arrived in Tripoli barefoot from the Fezzan a few years before, and after two years as PM he built himself a hundred-thousand-dollar house and hung the walls with original Picassos and Gauguins! He found the goose that lays the golden eggs. Well, you don't win friends and influence people by promoting women's rights in *this* country!"

"But there is legislation now to give the Libyan women the vote!" I remind her.

"Yes; it's already been passed. How many women do you think will go out to vote? And there is a new postage stamp coming out to celebrate woman's advanced status in Libya. Only the advanced Libyan woman can't go to the post office to buy her own stamps!"

To feed the sparrows one feeds the horses.
Arab Proverb

35. "Thy Pleasant Voices"

"WE MIGHT go to Ghirza this weekend," Harry suggested unexpectedly, having just vetoed a trip to the Tunisian island of Jerba a few days before. "I want to see Wadi Sofegin again on the way. There's some of the best barley land in the world there, Mazzocchi says. And you and George might like to see the old Romano-Berber fortified farms at Sofegin and Ghirza."

"There are some Roman temple tombs at Ghirza, too, according to the antiquities book," I contribute. "Might as well include a bit of culture with our fresh air. How long will the trip take?"

"We can drive through in a day, if we start early. Then we'll sleep at Ghirza, and have the next day or two there. Then sleep one night on the way home, stopping wherever we like. We'll take the Gypsy."

"I'd certainly like to get some use out of her besides just churning up the dust in Giorgimpopoli. But by the time we have all the travel junk loaded into the back, she'll only take two persons."

"Imperatore is coming with Land Rover No. 11, and Hammet with No. 37. I want Hammet to become familiar with the agricultural part of the country further inland. Left to himself, he never gets outside of the city limits."

"A real Tripolino!"

"Hi, Ma! Hi, Pa!" George, who is on his Easter holiday, is already brown and salty.

"George! Well, hamdu li'llah you got home at last. I thought you'd drowned!"

"There you go again, Ma — old worrywart! What's this about the weekend?"

"We're all going to Ghirza."

"Ghirza — where's that? Well, I'm O.K. for any place — only let's take Don and Digby along to liven things up."

"Why not?" agrees Harry. "There's space, I think."

"Gosh, Pa, what a shame that Mohamed isn't here! He'd have loved to go!" says George, suddenly sad. This is his first visit to Tripoli since Mohamed's death.

Yes, Mohamed would have loved to go, I agree silently. He'd have been in his element, giving us all advice, packing all the wrong things, dropping the delicate ones in his anxiety to help, getting in Harry's way in his efforts to be indispensable, and glowing with delight when he succeeded. So filled with fine intentions, and so fettered by his own realities, Mohamed is still a subject of sorrowful questioning with me. Why had it to be Mohamed? Or should one ask? Allah's will is done.

"Whom the gods love, die young," I said uncertainly, not sure if I was trying to console George, or myself.

"Do you really believe that, Ma?"

"Well . . . no . . . I don't, really. I think we would all gladly take a chance on survival — if given a choice. Philosophical statements about death are not written for young people. Yet, death is the only way one can retain youth. Mohamed will always be young for us."

"Yeah . . . but I'd rather he was alive. And he'd rather, too," said George firmly.

"One never has a choice," said Harry.

The name *Limes Tripolitanus* refers to the strategically located series of ancient fortified farmhouses which mark the furthest extent inland, the frontier zone, of Roman penetration during the third and fourth centuries A.D., by the army of soldier-farmers who were known as the *limitanei*. The fortified farm settlements were always established on the upper slopes of fertile wadi beds, or hills. South of this zone of outposts stretched the unbridled Sahara, which, from here on, the Romans were content to leave to the original desert peoples.

The most southern desert line was established at Bu Ngem, then ran east to Ghirza, east to Wadi Sofegin, east to Ghadames; farmhouse forts were constructed along this line. Ultimately, only these inland farms survived the decline of the Roman Empire in Libya. The reasons for their survival were obvious: the farmer-soldiers, as agriculturalists, were independent of coastal city life; secondly, they married locally with Berber women, a fact which gave them an indisputable foothold in the country. Although this Romano-Berber mixing resulted in so-called "debased" Roman architecture, it produced a lustier racial stock.

Ghirza, where we are heading now, is the site of what was once the largest *limes* settlement in Tripolitania, where partial remains of some thirty farmhouses, probably dating back to the fourth century A.D., still exist.

It is April, and we are midway to Beni Ulid, via Tarhuna, and traveling through waves of blowing asphodel like a pearly sea. This is the extravagant display of a grudging nature which does not glorify every spring, but only one which follows a lavish winter. Yes, we *had* rain last winter.

Harry and I are in the Gypsy with the food and cooking utensils. George and Hammet travel together with sleeping bags for all and canvas ground sheets. Imperatore drives No. 11 with plant presses, sample bags and water containers. With him in the front seat are Don and Digby, friends of George's age, who are in Libya from England for the Easter holidays. Unaccountably, everyone seems contented with his travel post, his companions, with the weather which is bright, dry and gusty, and with the objective.

The Arab village of Beni Ulid perches high on the crest of a hill on the east side of Wadi Merdum. The wadi below is filled with dusty, silvery-green olive trees, ancient, distorted and gnarled, the offspring of Roman stock, and bearing olives still. Date palms also flourish in the wadi, and the bed itself is criss-crossed with rock wall dikes to prevent soil erosion, and retain any precipitation. On the west side of the wadi on low hills lie three old towns only partially occupied; these again tell the story of migration away from the countryside and into the cities. The houses are built of rock and mud, and the tenanted ones have neat wooden doors in carved, arched doorways; the vacant ones have dark, staring doorways, open and empty.

Harry and Hammet locate the Commissioner of Beni Ulid, a handsome, dark Arab from Tripoli, for this is a political appointment, and ask him to find us a guide for Ghirza, as there is no road from here on. Meanwhile, the boys head for the town bakery where they buy a dozen loaves of crisp Arab bread to take with us, and then to the market where they buy literally a bucketful of dates which they start to eat immediately.

While we stand chewing dates and looking off across the wadi, Harry and Hammet join us with their report. The Commissioner asked a man to guide us, offering him 75 cents a day and his food, and the man refused. Harry then offered him $4.50 for three days, which the man jumped at, but the annoyed Commissioner refused to let him take. Now he has sent a police Land Rover to bring someone from the other side of the wadi who presumably will come at the lower rate.

Half an hour later our guide, Nuri, has arrived, and we are in the cars ready to start. Hammet mentions that Nuri has been instructed by the Commissioner to bring a gazelle back to him, as his friends in Tripoli want one. Although to capture a gazelle is breaking the law, which the Commissioner is supposedly here to enforce, this does not seem to attract anybody's attention except Harry's.

It is already midday. Soon after leaving Beni Ulid both road and track disappear, and the only sign of direction is an occasional stone cairn. It's not plains, nor desert, nor dunes, but more like a wide, meandering valley, and I am glad we have a guide to choose the way. In an hour we stop for food, sardines or salami, and cheese, and that wonderful, tasteful, honest-to-Allah bread.

We are soon on the way again, screaming along a bare, flat plain studded with black, volcanic rocks. The driving is violent, as the rocks tear at the wheels, and jolt the steering. I try to drive for a few minutes, but find that I can't hold the wheel securely. Imperatore always drives steadily and reliably. Hammet, who has the guide with him and George, has a good excuse now to lead, and he does so like lightning. We are all dust-coated and hot.

Now we are in Wadi Sofegin, and we cross and recross the wadi bed. There are deep ruts in many places, and three-foot nose dives cut by last winter's flood water, and crossing is sometimes almost impossible, yet heavy growths of batum trees on first one side, then the other, make it necessary. The batum trees give the wadi its name, as sofegin is Berber for betume, or *Pistacia atlantica*, the wood of which is widely used in Libya for making hand plows, and house beams.

All along the hilly top we can see ruins of the old fortified farmhouses, possibly fifteen centuries old. These are apparently always located at the highest possible point, for the sake of security. There are acres of waving, jade green or golden barley, as the lowest course of the wadi bed is barley-planted wherever possible. One can really believe that these acres helped to feed the Roman Empire! We also pass flocks of sheep and goats with lazy shepherds dawdling behind them, and on the skyline black tents are dotted along.

It is late afternoon now, hot and sandy, and I shall be glad to get out of this wadi while the Gypsy still holds together. We must be nearly out of it, to feel the dry, sandy wind so strongly. And suddenly we emerge onto a great stretch of stony desert and serir, across which I know that we are *all* going to *speed!*

When we finally strike another large wadi, Zemzem by name, we careen madly up it in a southwest direction to outrun the dusk, hoping to find Ghirza before dark. Just as darkness drifts along the wadi bed, and the sky above still shines pale and bright, Zemzem makes a junction with Wadi Ghirza. As we continue along Ghirza, we see on our right hand, in profile on the hills above us, crumbling stone edifices and tumbling temples outlined against the palish turquoise of the after sunset sky.

It is seven P.M., and we make camp by driving the three vehicles into the wadi bottom to escape that hot, dry wind which has now turned cold. Just above us, within a stone's throw, even with me throwing, are three temple tombs, as we appear to have chosen the cemetery to camp in. Although referred to as examples of "debased" Roman architecture, these temples are delicately lovely with their pinkish limestone columns standing against the blue-green, sand-dimmed sky.

But beautiful views do not fill hungry stomachs, and I prepare my regular camp meal of deluxe spaghetti. Although the wind blows the flame away from my primus, while Nuri's little charcoal and twig fire burns perfectly, everything is finally accomplished, and an impossibly large saucepan full of spaghetti is ready — every bite of which is quickly consumed.

Nobody debates the idea of lights out and bed. I am the first one down and into my sleeping bag, as I crawl in with my clothes all on, a bad habit I am acquiring from the chill of desert nights more than from sleeping in mixed company. I almost close the waterproof cover of my bag over my head, only leaving a small air tunnel leading to my nose, and a one-eye peek hole through which I can just see a crumbling tomb above me.

My last thoughts are of Mohamed, and how he used to admire these sleeping bags! Harry and I had always intended to order one for him from England for a gift some time. George, who has his sentimental moments, must have been thinking of Mohamed, too, for suddenly a tall figure looms against the sky and bends down to whisper to me, "Did you ever do anything for Mohamed's wife, Lutfeyah?"

"Yes, I gave her a little money. But no one can really help her. She's practically buried alive . . . unless she marries again."

"Mohamed always said that he'd take me to meet her sometime. You know — he was really a great kid!"

"Yes. A great kid. A good man."

"Well . . . good night, Ma."

While waiting for sleep, I am still searching in my mind for the answer, which does not seem to exist, to the death of a young person.

We spent two days discovering fortified farmhouses, and we found on the interior plaster walls some remarkable paintings which depicted the same scenes as the Stone Age ones in the Fezzan. These must have been copied from the originals at a much later period. The colors were still quite strong, mostly henna and bright blue. The temple tombs, which were probably family burial places, seemed good proof of a funeral ritual, and a cult of the dead. Although the Romano-Berber families may not have actually worshiped the dead, they obviously took great care not to offend them.

Packed up and ready to leave on the third day, we found our

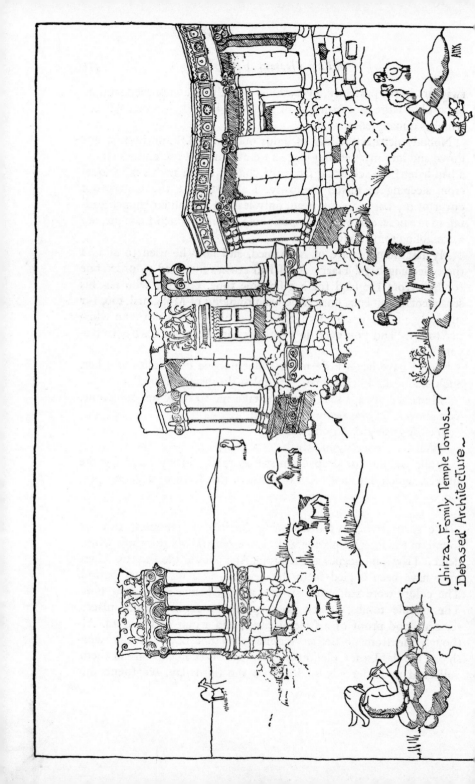

Ghirza – Family Temple Tombs.
'Debased' Architecture.

luggage was augmented by a number of new plant specimens, while our passengers were increased by one small, beautiful gazelle, acquired by Nuri for the Commissioner to give to his Tripoli friend. Hammet, and Nuri and George, with the timid gazelle, now named Little Effendi, lying with his dainty legs folded under him, in George's lap, traveled together. George fell for the lovely little creature immediately, and wanted us to keep him. Seeing him with the gazelle put me in mind once again of Mohamed, who was always urging me to get a gazelle for a pet.

When we were driving back across the stony plain Hammet, who was in front, suddenly stopped the car, while Nuri leaped out and pounced on something a few yards distant. This proved to be a lizard, one foot long and five inches wide, sand-colored, and called a dug by Nuri, who captured it in his bare hands, grabbing it behind the jaw and by the tail. The dug is eaten by desert dwellers, Nuri says. Harry intends to take it to the Sidi Mesri Zoo. Travel resumes, with Hammet driving, Nuri next to him holding the dug in his hands, and George on the outside holding the gazelle, until a sudden bump sends the dug onto Hammet. This is too much for Hammet, who stops the car and banishes the lizard to an empty provision crate.

We make a night stop in Wadi Mimum near a shepherd and his flock, from which Nuri promptly enlists a nursing goat to wet-nurse the little gazelle, who leeches to the goat's teat with instant enthusiasm. The afternoon has been terribly hot, and our drinking water is almost finished, and the cold water from the Wadi Mimum into which we lower our bucket tastes wonderful.

The next morning, I am awakened by a persistent yanking at my sleeping bag. I indignantly uncover my head and look out into a bucket full of fresh, clotted sheep's milk which is being held under my nose by the shepherd and Nuri. As the custom is that everybody drinks from the general utensil, I drink — and it is really good.

Harry receives the bucket next, and after muttering, "Good God, I shall be sick!" he hastily swallows a large amount, then turns to me and says, "Well, really, I could quite like that stuff — if it wasn't so early in the morning!"

Meanwhile, the gazelle is being suckled, and the boys are up and making coffee. And there again in my mind is Mohamed — who had always said, "Mother if you take me with you, I can make your coffee for you!"

For the last fifty kilometers of the road before Tripoli, Mohamed was with me all the time, as I thought of the eager questions he would have asked when we arrived home, of the excitement he would have felt for the dug, of his regret at our not bringing home the gazelle, of his pleasure that George should have this trip, and his near tears to miss it himself.

I tried to recall some lines that were floating vaguely in my mind from a Greek poem by Callimachus on the death of a friend. They came to me at last —

Still are thy pleasant voices, thy nightingales, awake,
For Death, he taketh all away, but them he cannot take.

36. Ramadan Disaster

ONCE AGAIN the month of Ramadan is almost ended. Soon the boom of the castle guns will tell that the Holy Man on the plateau at Garian sees the silver crescent arising in the eastern sky. Then, by the Prophet's word, the feast of Id el-Fitr may begin.

It is three days before the feast in the small town of Barce (el Merj) on the Jebel el Akhdar in Cyrenaica. All the good Moslems in their little mud and stone huts are sitting down to the first meal of the day, after a fourteen-hour fast.

In the house of Mahmood Nedjib there is an air of happiness and well-being. I have visited in this small hut several times when we used to drive up from Benghazi, for Mahmood was a friend of our friend Abdullah from the Fuihat plains. There are three sons here: Mohamed, six years, Ali, four, and Mustapha, two, and their mother, Zenabia, is pregnant again. Mahmood knows he has been blessed with the birth of three sons, and he earnestly hopes that they will stay with him through their youth and maturity to help him with his wheatland on the plain. Many of the town inhabitants here are shopkeepers or middlemen for the plains farmers, for Barce is the market center for this large agricultural district. Mahmood, however, goes daily to his own farm acres two miles away and returns at night to his little hut. That is all it is, a little stone hut glued together with mud, but it's all he has, and it's home.

His wife, only twenty-two years old, is also content. She carries water and helps in the field, although she grows tired very fast now that she is pregnant again; still, it may be another son, in sha'Allah! And this is her life by the Prophet's will: to give sons to make fertile and profit her husband's land.

Tonight they are all happy that the long period of daytime fasting is almost over, and grateful to Allah for the prospect of a three-day holiday soon. The little boys' new yellow cotton jellabias are ready for the great day, although Zenabia has nothing new for herself. Still, no one sees her, so malesh!

They have just drunk their soup, which comes first, to mark the end of the hours of fasting, and they are ready to dip into the vegetable stew. A lamb will be slaughtered tomorrow in market, and Zenabia promises them lamb shishkbab for the feast.

The hour is exactly seven-twenty, when something quite beyond this family's mortal experience takes place. The earth floor of the hut trembles slightly, Zenabia thinks she is dreaming, and Mahmood looks up nervously. Then it comes with a crashing and rumbling, as the earth shakes and jolts violently under them in three separate tremendous upheavals. When danger appears, one runs from it; but when the earth rocks and cracks, there is no place to run!

Mahmood, Zenabia and the three small sons stare at each other, powerless to move. With the first jolt, the walls of the unreinforced mud hut began to crumble; now as the earth grinds again the heavy mud and scrap metal roof collapses on them with a roar, and the family goes down under rubble and mud.

Now the torrential rains which make Barce plains fertile and the howling winds for which the Jebel is notorious roar down on the trembling, shaking ruins of Mahmood and Zenabia's family, of five hundred other families, of more than a thousand people partially buried alive in the once prosperous market town of Barce.

The town's electric plant has crumbled, the hospital is destroyed, and sixty per cent of the homes are rubble and trash. The mud and stone masonry of the houses, which are built without reinforcements, is the worst possible construction to resist an earthquake.

Within an hour Libyan soldiers from a plains camp, aroused by the tremors, are in Barce and digging in the rubble to find victims. An hour later, British soldiers and RAF men from Benghazi and el Adam arrive to assist. Rescue goes on in darkness and drenching rain, while small tremors spread terror to the survivors. Before midnight the Wheelus Field helicopters are bringing in Air Force doctors and nurses, who set up a mobile field hospital. Fresh blood is flown up from Wheelus, but although it is badly needed it is refused by Libyan authorities because of the possibility that some may have come from Jewish donors.

Among the small tumbled huts, many adults have escaped death although the rubble which reaches only waist high has completely buried their children. Mahmood is first to escape from his own sad ruin, and he manages to get Zenabia free. All three children are still buried from sight. Mahmood digs frantically until a soldier passes, and he calls for help. The two burrow and dig in the steaming wreckage. Zenabia, who is too shocked even to cry, now begins to feel premature birth pains.

It is the soldier who first reaches the body of Mohamed, the six-year-old, quite dead. Beside him lies Mustapha, age two, dead. Mahmood, digging in the opposite corner, touches a small hand, then finds the limp body of Ali, age four, dead. Although perhaps injured by the falling roof, the children probably died from suffocation in the rubble and mud. Mahmood turns in desperation to Zenabia, who collapses over their children's bodies, first weeping in sorrow, then, as the birth pains become stronger, screaming in pain. Mahmood and the soldier help her away from the sodden ruins and into a military Land Rover, and drive her to a small military hospital a mile away. Here before morning her baby is born — a son, el hamdu li'llah! Three other premature babies are born that night.

All through the night and the following day the Libyan army works furiously, side by side with American and British soldiers and airmen, to dig out the victims. American Air Force planes and helicopters fly the seriously injured persons to various hospitals. Within twenty-four hours a camp for six thousand refugees is set up with tents, blankets and food. Soon the appropriate Libyan ministers of state will arrive to speak the appropriate words of consolation and make the appropriate political promises for a rebuilt Barce, bigger and better — but preferably not on an earthquake fault!

Kings, potentates and prime ministers cable sympathy and offers of assistance to King Idris. President Nasser is reported to have cabled, saying "My brothers, ask me for what you need," but sending nothing. But help had already arrived from the Western "brothers," and the people of Barce were turning with gratitude to their fellow rescuers who worked with them through night and day. Next

morning Radio Cairo broadcasts that the British and Americans are
making use of "a small catastrophe" in Libya to "recolonize the Libyan people!" The dead in Barce now number three hundred and the
injured are more than a thousand, while ten thousand persons are
homeless.

The moon decides to reveal itself to the proper Moslem officials
on Saturday night, contrary to the almanac prediction that it will
first appear at two o'clock on Sunday. Id el-Fitr has come. The feast
which was to be three days of rejoicing is now proclaimed by King
Idris to be a period of country-wide mourning.

In normal circumstances most of us with limited means do not
actually wish to give our money away. But a sudden disaster which
forces on our attention a group of people who have suddenly lost
everything, including their children, and who are suffering through
no fault of their own arouses sympathy and a genuine desire to help.

At the time of the quake I had in my possession, as treasurer of the
UN women's group, about fifty-five dollars. This had been contributed to buy sewing materials for a charitable sewing project which
had failed to get under way. When I learned of the earthquake, the
money began to burn my pocket.

When Kathleen called me to discuss what the UN women could
do towards earthquake relief, I suggested we start a fund with the
fifty-five dollars.

"Fifty-five dollars is nothing!" says Kathleen, who is miles ahead
of me. "I think we should wire immediately to the UN in Benghazi
to buy one hundred and fifty dollars worth of blankets for Barce.
You and I will go out now and collect the cash!"

"Well, I suppose we'll have to," I answer rather doubtfully, "but
what I hate most of all is asking anybody for money! I'd rather give
myself."

"Yes, yes!" says Kathleen enthusiastically. "We will! And put our
names and the sums on the top of an open list, and that will push
them!"

"Well . . . an open list is blackmail," I say, quoting Harry.

"Never mind, it's in a good cause," Kathleen assures me.

By the time I arrived at Kathleen's house, two other UN wives had had the same idea, and soon we were all four on the road with the list of UN women in hand.

It was just twelve o'clock midday, a bad time for calling, as the Ramadan fast was still being observed and the Moslem wives would be sleeping. Mrs. N. was our first, and she arose pink and smiling when awakened by her pink and smiling ten-year-old daughter. She welcomed us as warmly as if we had been invited, insisted that we stay long enough for glasses of fruit juice and cookies, of which she could not partake, and made a substantial financial contribution to our fund. We left with our morale greatly strengthened by her generous and gracious response.

We visited five other Moslem homes, awaking them all from rest and being received in each home with the same open-hearted courtesy and generous response.

Next, we went to the home of an Englishwoman, a newcomer to the Libyan Mission. Her first words were, "Oh, I am so glad you came. I am so pleased to be able to do something. I am glad that you are gathering this fund!" She gave generously and we hurried on.

The list was used shamelessly, I fear, and thrust under people's noses just as they were wondering how much to give, and what other people were giving. Although everybody wished to give something, the list undoubtedly set a standard. Each one was interested in the other ones' comparative generosity!

By nighttime we had collected enough money so that this sum, plus our original fifty-five dollars, enabled us to authorize by telephone the immediate expenditure of three hundred dollars on behalf of the United Nations women for assistance of the earthquake victims. Ours was one of the first gestures of nonorganized aid to be received by the disaster area.

Daily, now, the Arab press repeats its thanks to all the countries who have sent help for the earthquake victims. The list usually starts with Great Britain and the USA, who were first on the spot and arrived in person. Then come the names of Morocco, Tunisia, Greece, the United Nations, Italy, Germany, France and many others, all of whom donated generously and sent blankets, food and drugs. The Arab press sometimes comments on the fact that Egypt is missing from the list.

An aftermath of the earthquake is that Barce, which had only ten thousand inhabitants before the quake, now has a public aid list for twenty thousand inhabitants! This does not include the several thousand enterprising nomads of the plains vicinity who turn up regularly for distributions of blankets, food rations, and most especially for tents.

37. Other Side of the Coin

THIS is George's last summer in Libya. It is also a summer for heat; I lie sleepless in bed many nights, but not for the heat alone.

George is studying. He always is, on holidays, because he doesn't study in term time. He sits in his bedroom in Giorgimpopoli with his bare, brown feet up on his desk. The math book is propped open almost out of eye range, and his favorite Belafonte calypso is playing full blast beside him, as he lovingly polishes his underwater fish gun. A drained coffee cup stands back on the desk, a cigarette smolders in the ash tray, and a half empty beer bottle rests beside George.

"Hi, Ma, what do you think of this gun? Good, eh? The only one in Tripoli. Vince gave it to me."

"I thought you were supposed to be studying."

"I am studying. There's my math book."

"Does the math just jump into your head?"

"Oh, good idea, that! Wish it did!"

"You'll never pass your second-year university exams like this!"

"I know, Ma, but this hot weather just isn't for studying!"

"Was London too hot for it, too?"

George groans, puts his bare feet on the floor with a smack, drains the beer bottle, flips off the record player, reaches for his math book, and says, "Run along, Ma. I can't study with you here talking! And will you ask Lena to bring me another cup of coffee, please?"

"She's busy with lunch. I'll bring you one."

Back in a couple of minutes with coffee, I find George tilted far back in his wobbly-legged chair, his bare feet up again, his gaze contentedly transfixed on the blue sky beyond the pomegranate tree, his fingers tapping in time to the trumpet record just turning.

"You know, Ma, what I was thinking? I'd like to play the trumpet just like Satchmo. He really talks with that old horn!" says George, going through imaginary motions of playing his imaginary trumpet with his long, brown hands.

I put the coffee cup down and give up attempts at moralizing except to say, "You won't have any appetite for lunch after all this coffee and beer."

"Oh, sure, Ma, sure I will. Ma, I'd like to take the Austin Gypsy this afternoon, please? We're going to Kilo twenty to try the fish gun on the reef out there."

"All right, but do be careful. I hate those reefs. Who's going?"

"Oh, Vince and Alan, I guess."

And Kitty and Liz and Mary and Ellen and . . . I thought.

An hour later as I sit reading the London *Times*, too hot to move, George comes in and crosses the living room towards me. As I look up at this tall, slender young man, he seems to me to be quite handsome, with his smooth, tanned skin and gray-blue eyes and an artless smile. He leans down and kisses me warmly on the cheek.

"Thanks a lot for the Gypsy, Ma. I'll be back in time for dinner. Now don't worry about me, Ma." He winds the blue towel around his throat, grips the bathing trunks, fish gun, and flippers, and clumps out in his desert boots, ready for sand, sea and sun.

"George pretends that it is ridiculous," I tell Harry, "but there is danger here, and especially among the coral reefs, for divers. I wish he wouldn't go bathing from those isolated rocks and beaches. The paper is always warning people not to, telling them only to bathe from the beaches where there are lifeguards."

"You worry too much, dear. Seems to me I remember swimming around the end of a long pier with you once where swimmers were forbidden! Not to mention Strawberry Pool on the campus at midnight."

"We must have been foolish!"

"We were!"

That night as I pass George's open door he is lying on his stomach, shirtless, on the bed, and reading. There are long, bloody, coral reef scratches torn across his back.

"George! What happened to you?"

"Oh, nothing much, Ma. Just got caught under the rocks. Vince pulled me out O.K. Don't fuss, Ma. Night-night."

Later: "You should see his back, Harry!"

"But he got loose all right, dear."

For Ma, there are many long nights this summer of pretending to sleep, while I listen for the sound of the homing motorcar, which returns later and later as the summer goes. One night George and the beautiful Dutch blonde are stuck in the sand and have to walk home from the club at four A.M., leaving the car behind. Good luck we had two cars, then; in Libya one needs two cars, one to haul the other one out of the sand.

"But George, it isn't because I'm worried about your driving, or any of that. It's because if certain Libyans find a parked car with a girl and a man alone in it, it infuriates them. They have such different standards for right conduct for women. They assume a girl who stays out alone with a man is bad. You must remember that there were some terrible incidents that occurred in Benghazi when Western girls and men were found in cars by Libyans!"

"Well, Ma, I'm strong, and I'm a good boxer!"

Sometimes in the night the thought comes to me — when I was young, did I keep my mother awake to all hours awaiting for my safe return? The thought comes that probably I did.

When we lived here before, the city of Tripoli consisted of two separate cities, and two distinct living centers; now there is a third living (or dying) center made up of the many Bidonvilles which camp on the skirts of the Tripolis, old and new. These Bidonvilles represent the wrong side of the coin of anticipated prosperity.

The name Bidonville comes from the French *bidon*, meaning a tin or oil drum, and it perfectly describes the hastily thrown together shelters made from discarded tins and old waste. These teeming centers of population exist without a drop of running water or a septic tank or a sewer. These are the homes of the displaced persons who come to the city to get rich on the oil dream.

Here live the unemployed and the unemployable, the oasis boy who left his oasis for an oil rig and the rig moved on; the shepherd who exchanged his sheep for an oil job and the job ran out; the

Bedawi farmer who lost his crops in the drought and hopes that oil is the answer; the nomad who has made his last move and is broke and can't retreat. Here are the maimed and the blind and the syphilitic, the half-wit, the delinquent and the criminal. All those who once were scattered throughout the whole kingdom of Libya are gathered here today on the fringe of its great luxury city, drawn by the story, the dream, and the odor of oil. They have one pastime only — they breed.

The Libyan government has a problem: it wishes to discourage migration away from the land. Yet, if the government betters conditions in the Bidonvilles, more people will come.

We have stretches of summer here which are like an inferno. The day before this, the shade temperature had reached one hundred and twelve degrees, and this day I thought it was worse. It was midday, and I was returning from an errand of mercy, or so I had thought it to be when I left home. I suppose that kindness is not without self-interest if it shows you in the mirror the person you would like to think you are.

Anyway, when Harry said later, "Why did you go out on a day like this?" I couldn't make my motive sound reasonable. One's own stone house with the shutters drawn and the fans going is the only place to stay in such weather.

I had accomplished my errand, wise or unwise, at Sidi Mesri, and I was halfway home on a road, between Sidi Mesri and our house. For the trip home I had a choice between two parallel roads a mile apart which both lead towards the coast and Giorgimpopoli. One is narrow and overcrowded with truck traffic, with a cemetery on one side and Bidonvilles on the other. I had gone out by this latter road, but decided to escape the Bidonvilles by returning on the other road, which leads across a deserted stretch of semi-dune land.

The sand was smoldering with heat, the air was shimmering above it, the steering wheel burned my hands, the car seat was like a grill, and the metal gas pedal scorched my sandal-clad foot. I was tearing along with just one thought — home and a long, cold drink, when I saw a roadblock on the road in front of me, and a detour sign pointing to the right over a sand track. I didn't like the idea of leaving the

The buried Treasure
is water —

Sahara Oasis —

ANK

surfaced road in my small car to pursue a sand track which might even lead to a Bidonville, but I liked even less the idea of returning to Sidi Mesri in order to pick up the other road home.

So I started on the detour. There was not a car in sight — who but a fool goes out at noon on a day like this! I got over the first sandy stretch, and by giving the car all the gas possible got past several more bad soft stretches. The important thing in sand driving is never to stop or go slow, and I was so miserable in the heat that I couldn't go fast enough. I topped one bad rise, then another rise, then a third — and suddenly a Bidonville spread out before me!

For just one second I had the impression that the village was completely deserted: its scrap-metal shacks lay simmering and silent in the sun, with only the flies moving. Then the second passed, and Bidonville suddenly teemed with children of all ages, bursting, creeping, and tumbling out from their sizzling shacks in the hope of making life hell for a passerby. My sand road here was the village street, now overrun with children; I topped one more rise pursued by the kids, who tried to jump on behind — I think some did — then I made an acute turn to avoid a brat — and bogged down. As the car stopped, the mob climbed on the radiator and the bumpers, jumping up and down on them to make the car sink further in.

I know enough not to race my engine in sand, in fact to do nothing until I can determine how deep in sand the car is. Holding my pocketbook tightly, I got out of the car and looked at the wheels which were not yet up to the axles. The car wasn't past help, if I could pull out in reverse. As I turned to get back in the car, I saw my seat was occupied by a young man of about twenty, who, seeing my ignition key still in place, started to race the engine as fast as possible so that the wheels spun madly and dug in, while the delinquents of all ages applauded happily.

"Stop it! You're making it worse! Get out, you!" I shouted. "Oh, damn! I'll never get the car out now!" which was just what he wanted. I got the oaf out of my seat, more by strong language than kindness, the children all roaring with laughter and dancing about me, and pinching my bare arms which my sleeveless dress exposed. I took a second look at the rear wheels and saw that the car was now quite unable to help itself.

Still holding my pocketbook tightly, I got back in the car, rolled up the windows, and thought. The delinquents, large and small, were leaping and prancing with joy, and kicking and whacking the car. I knew it was possible for me to walk to the main road towards which I had been heading and probably pick up help there from a passing car, as the average Libyan on the road is always ready to help. But I knew that by the time I returned, my car would have been cannibalized out of existence, for each small part has a very good secondhand market value here. Meanwhile, I was surrounded by a carnivorous mob of hungry cannibals anxiously waiting for me to leave.

I rolled down the window a bit (Phew, it was hot!) and waited for a proposal. The young man who had jumped in and raced the engine spoke first. "Your car no go now, lady."

"It will go if you all help me to dig it out."

"No, lady. Very hard work."

"Well, I can walk to Sidi Mesri and bring my Libyan friends back to help me." But I knew I couldn't without losing my car.

"You got friends at Sidi Mesri?"

"Certainly. I have Libyan friends in the Forest Department." This required explaining to the crowd, who temporarily stopped banging the car. Their energy, despite the heat, was remarkable!

"You got cigarette, lady?"

"No." Distributing cigarettes was one of the things I did not feel like doing at this moment. I sat and waited, sizzling and sweating.

Now the young man who has made himself the spokesman has a chat in Arabic with the crowd around me. Then, "How much money you got, lady?"

I knew I had with me in small change in a change purse about six dollars. I also had two five-pound notes (about thirty dollars) in another small purse in my pocketbook. But these five-pound notes I was determined not to give.

I took out my change purse where the crowd could see it (through the glass!) and counted it out; there was just over six dollars. "I will give it *all* to you if you boys get together and dig me out," I said.

The young man shook his head. "Not enough, lady."

"Well, too bad. That is all I have."

The spokesman chats again with the gang, who haven't had so much fun since the last time somebody got run over, I expect.

"Not enough, lady."

I sat it out, wondering, knowing that six dollars was a lot to them. Meanwhile *I* sweated and scorched. But I don't think it ever occurred to any of *them* that it was hot and uncomfortable out in the sun; perhaps it was just as bad in their shacks. They certainly had plenty of time to spend. I tried to adopt the same attitude, as I sat and wondered at what hour they would miss me at home.

Finally the young man spoke, "Well, O.K., lady. You give money first."

"No, you get car out first."

Another conference; they looked rather glum — probably thought they could get the cash without moving the car. I was dying for a cigarette, but didn't want to smoke when I had refused them cigarettes. Then suddenly, before I could believe it, they enveloped the car like ants, lifted it up bodily, swiveled it around, and placed it on semi-sound ground again. I pushed down the window, poured the cash into the spokesman's outstretched hands, from which it was eagerly snatched by his friends, started the engine, and shouted, "Push!" The next moment the young man had dodged around the car, and jumped in the front seat beside me.

The car was under way now, and nothing was going to stop me until I hit the surfaced road. The young man at my side was shifting about, either casing the joint, or just feeling hot. I stuck my pocketbook on the side by the door, and shoved it down. I wasn't sure what the fellow's idea was, but I knew what mine was — keep going! With the wheels turning, I felt powerful.

We struck the surfaced road, and I tore along, as my companion said, "I got no money! You give me some money!"

"No, I gave you all I had," I lied, feeling victorious. "Why are you in my motorcar? I don't want you."

"I want money."

"I no give you money."

"I want your pocketbook."

"No." I pushed it further down beside the door, confident now that I was on a traveled road.

"I want money."

But I could feel his indecision; he had started something he couldn't finish. He didn't have the nerve to knock me out, or to grab the wheel, or to make me stop. All he could say was, "I want money!"

"I not give you money." Even as I said it, I felt sorry for the boy, and might have given him five pounds, except for his threatening way. What a miserable life; what a horrible future; what chance lay ahead? I didn't want to think about it — in this heat!

"I stop now, and you get out," I said.

"I no get out. I want money."

I said no more. When we struck the Tunis road I turned in the opposite direction from that of my house, and drove directly to the center of Tripoli. I stopped the car at Piazza Castello near a policeman. "You get out here," I said.

The boy looked at me, and at the policeman, and he slid out and disappeared like a bad dream. And I felt very sorry indeed for him, and hurried home to my cool villa to slake my thirst in a long, cold drink such as the boy and the whole of Bidonville would never have.

I never told my Libyan friends of this incident. They would have been indignant for me, and apologetic to me, and anxious that I shouldn't think of it as a typical Libyan incident. I don't. I think it is more symptomatic of the intrusion of the Western way of life — only less violent; of the arrival of a world to be bought with cash, or lost without. And in the crimes of Western life, who hesitates to knock someone out?

When I was describing this incident at home later, George wanted to know why I was always worrying about *his* getting into some trouble! I had to explain to him that I was two completely different women; one was me, the other was Ma!

It takes a home some time to recover from a separation with its young folk. Our sunstruck, white-walled villa is not so resilient this time, and it is filled with ghosts, with the wailing strains of trumpet and sax, with the saltwater marks of wet bare feet, with the clink of ice in glasses and of beer bottles tipped over, and the contagious chortle of young men telling jokes.

The cigarette burns on the desk reproach me for reproaching the burner: Come back, and burn them again! The ash still smolders — and what difference does it make? Meals are eaten on time, there's no one to wait for. Lights are turned out; there's no one to listen for coming home late. What shall we eat tonight? George always liked crepe suzettes. . . . But for us, what difference does it make?

Well, the house will have to forget, and so shall I . . . I'll concentrate on collecting more of those dwarf cactuses for the veranda, the only plant that will stand the reflected sunlight from the cement. There's that great pulpy orange cactus blooming now that George always liked . . . and the jasmine was never so sweet as tonight . . . how he loved that smell! . . .

And, recalls Lena, he liked an egg to shampoo his hair! I always ask, George, your hair eat the egg?

There stands the Gypsy covered with dust, its love life over, its future prosaic. With dusty silence, it rebukes me for all the nights of saying, Don't be late!

All things pass; the house will forget. But not Ma.

V

Oil for Allah

38. Under the Veil

When I arrived the two old Bedawi grandmothers were sitting cross-legged on the hall floor firing up the blue enamel teapots over a small charcoal brazier. They both had rather sweet, but very deeply wrinkled, brown faces with indigo tattoos, and heavy wisps of red-black, hennaed hair. Their bodies were hidden under the rust-red striped Bedawi baracans, and they looked more like permanent hall fixtures than mobile human beings; it was hard to visualize them with regular legs which could be used if need be, hidden away in the garment's folds. Actually, they can hardly walk, Abdul told me, as their legs are "bad" from a lifetime of folding them up and sitting on them. Certainly now they must have rheumatism from squatting on the cold tiled floor.

An Arab house is sacred to its women, and I would never have thought of invading my neighbor's had I had not been especially asked to do so by Abdul, who said his wife was lonely in Giorgimpopoli. He is badly rushed in his government work, so he says, and has little time at home. Government still isn't straightened out from its move here; it never will be before it's time for the next move. Records are misplaced, files are lost, scandals are leaking out, ministers are falling, and everybody has ulcers once more! Seems that they don't have too much to learn from the Western world now that prosperity is near. Which comes first, I wonder, the money or the ulcer?

Abdul himself is a charming person, tall and blondish, with hazel eyes (a Berber, I think) and a good physique. He speaks excellent English, having served some time in the British forces in desert fighting in the war, and he is perfectly at home in Western company. He is one of the pleasantest people I know.

So when Abdul said, as if he meant it, "Call on my wife" — I called. To my great surprise, I found Abdul at home. I learned later that he had been having trouble with his minister, who had fired him! Only Abdul refuses to be fired, and goes daily to his job — but no longer works overtime.

As their house is constructed on the same plan as ours and was new at the same time, it is impossible not to compare our abode with Abdul's, which already looks dilapidated. In good weather, our house is thrown open, curtains pulled far apart and green shutters hooked back so that breeze and sunshine can enter. In extreme heat, we close the windows and shutters completely, so that anyone entering the house feels a comforting sense of dark coolness, a welcome escape from both heat and glare.

Abdul's house is always the same, never completely open to welcome good weather, nor closed to exclude bad. There it stands, a temporary shelter, a brief stopping place until the tribe migrates once more. Our house is a refuge at all times, and in all weathers; Abdul's is a great black tent, outspread for the moment, but by tomorrow ready to run.

Abdul's furniture, supplied by the government, is mostly collapsing; no wonder, with five kids, two goats, a sheep, a gazelle, a dog, chickens and rabbits, who all come and go. But there is an excellent radio, and an oversize cabinet TV, although it is afflicted with snowstorms with its programs, Abdul complains.

His wife, whom I came to visit today, charms me immediately, as Abdul, who opened the door to me, leads her in from the kitchen, stepping carefully around the two old ladies on the floor, who have already hand-kissed and saluted me. "This is my wife, Rabiaa," Abdul says. "She will speak Italian with you."

She is, of course, plump, with a beautiful neck and bosom and a youthful, almost innocent, oval face with pale skin, brilliant dark eyes, and indigo tribal tattoos on nose and chin. Her expression is one of shy delight — at seeing anyone, I imagine, who can break the monotony of her exile in Giorgimpopoli, far away from Benghazi and the red plains, and far, far from Tripoli city — at least ten minutes' drive away!

We kiss each other, and by now the family is alerted to my presence and they all arrive, one by one, from behind the flowered curtain which closes off the back of the hall. The two teen-age twin girls, Fatima and Fujra, are pure Arab with curly black hair, black eyes, and beige skins. They grasp my hand warmly, and we carry out the kissing schedule. Then comes the third girl, Laila, a fragile-looking, Alice-in-Wonderland child, with fine, fair skin and silky, straight, chestnut hair and light eyes exactly like her father. More kissing.

Now comes Muhamed (a boy at last, hamdu li'llah! and just born in time to save his mother from the disgrace of producing only girls!) and we need only shake hands. "My son," says Abdul proudly, and then, "He has a hard head, his teacher says, but malesh!" A hard head, an Italian phrase, means the head of a person rather lacking in intelligence. But the boy looks bright enough, and is quite handsome — and he is a male! The fifth child is another boy, Baderi, perhaps six years old, nice looking but very dark.

But where are the babies, I wonder? Six years without a child? Can it be that Abdul has ideas about population control? Or that Rabiaa isn't very fertile?

Abdul seats me in a battered camel's hide chair, and Rabiaa sits beside me in another, and the children perch on wobble-legged seats, chewing gum madly and eyeing me with warm pleasure as a moment's entertainment. The old ladies continue their tea-making, while Rabiaa says that she hopes I like Arab tea and hurries to the kitchen to bring the glasses. Her feet are bare and brown, with hennaed soles. Abdul excuses himself to go out and water the garden and clean out the pen where the sheep and goats live, leaving us females to entertain ourselves in proper Arab fashion.

Rabiaa pads back with the glasses. Now we can get down to it. How many children do I have? Where are they? How many years have I been married? Then why don't I have more children? Don't I want any more? Or do I understand the "secret" of not having them? Do I know how to *not* have children?

Although in past years Libyan women have universally welcomed pregnancy as giving them a hold on their husbands, times are changing now for some husbands and wives. Today, I am often asked by Libyan women the "secret" of not having children, but I have never

thought it my business to go into details. If a husband wishes birth
control, he can help his wife to achieve it, and if he doesn't, then she
is looking for trouble to employ it.

The children are all listening, also the old ladies, wide-eared. They
don't speak Italian, but they know what the talk is about. Now the
mother of Abdul, a forceful type, starts talking excitedly in Arabic
to Rabiaa and Rabiaa's mama, and I can tell from Rabiaa's face that
she is not pleased with the conversation.

Rabiaa

When the old lady quiets down, Rabiaa says to me, "The mama of
Abdul tells me I should have more sons. If I have no more sons, then
she says Abdul should get a new wife!" She gives a chagrined laugh,
obviously not liking the idea. Still, she accepts it as being Moslem
law, and Abdul's right, supposing that he wants it.

The old ladies are pouring the tea from pot to pot to make it foam,
and meanwhile Laila has shelled a plateful of green almonds to use
in it. Muhamed is sent to call Abdul to come for tea. There are four
tiny glasses like liqueur glasses. These are filled, the top half being
white foam, and Abdul, his mama, Rabiaa and I each have one. Abdul tosses his down quickly and hands the glass back to Rabiaa, who
dips it into the bowl of water beside her, then fills it with tea for
her own mama. The children must wait.

I ask Abdul what he thinks about the recent revolution in Iraq. He answers with a philosophical statement: "Evolutions come from nature, and revolutions come from people."

"But the Iraq revolution was imposed on the people by the military," I say.

"No," he says. "The military element who wish to have a coup merely watch the sentiments of the people, and then strike with the popular sentiment. So long as some people are on top, and some people are on the bottom, there will always be evolution and revolution. From revolutions arise strong men and dictators. There is always *somebody* on top! It is only human nature for the top man to take something extra for himself."

This is a sentiment which I hear expressed constantly in Libya. When a case of corruption is discussed, the reaction generally is, "Well, wouldn't you do the same yourself, if you had the chance?"

Abdul receives his second cup of tea and continues: "Whether the rule of a dictator, or a government, is good or bad depends on how much the dictator takes for himself. If he takes ten per cent for himself, and distributes wisely ninety per cent to benefit all the country, then he is good. If he keeps ninety per cent for himself, gives ten per cent to his special friends, and gives nothing to the people in general, then he is bad." Abdul scoops up a handful of almonds, and leaves us for his sheep and goats.

As I am leaving for home, I ask Rabiaa, "Will you come to my house for tea some day? I shall invite some other Libyan ladies, and you can all talk together."

Rabiaa looks pleased at the idea, but uncertain. "Ask Abdul," she says.

I do so as I stop in the garden to tell him goodbye. He answers, "My wife never goes out. But . . . we shall see . . . we shall see . . ."

We saw — and it ended with Rabiaa, the two mamas, and the children all coming to tea.

At five-thirty I drove to the house to collect them. I had temporarily banished Harry and Pucci to the study at the rear of the house, in order to give the ladies their freedom. I knew it was a great

responsibility to be entrusted with transporting three secluded females; I hoped I'd be worthy!

At Abdul's house I find the old ladies ready and waiting, but Rabiaa is still beautifying. The mamas are truly breathtaking, when I
recall the two old Bedawi whom I saw the other day crouched over
the teapots! Now one is in a blue-flowered white satin blouse worn
with a turquoise and silver baracan, and her chest is heavily adorned
with gold jewelry; the other mama wears a purple silk blouse accompanied by a purple and gold baracan, plus many tinkling gold chains
and earrings. It is indeed true that a Bedawi's wealth — if any — is in
her jewelry.

When Rabiaa finally emerges, her basic garment is a silver-
flowered white chiffon Mother Hubbard, probably conceived as a
compromise between Arab and Western dress, and her bosom is
covered with heavy, gold Libyan necklaces of varying lengths and
designs, and her pretty, plump hands and arms are weighted with
gold bracelets. I am dressed in a cashmere sweater and skirt. Before
the ladies leave their house each one covers herself completely, including her face, with the clean white baracan.

It is a problem to get the mamas down the front steps and into the
car. The twins and I together take them one at a time and almost
carry them, and it is only sheer physical pushing which gets them
into the car, backside first. They both have "bad" legs, they remind
me; and I have bad arms myself, by now. We go back then for
Rabiaa, who is nimble enough but can see almost nothing, encased in
her baracan. Hamdu li'llah that we aren't escaping from a house on
fire!

Getting them into our house isn't so bad, as the old ladies just
tumble out of the car and into our arms, and with Lena to help we
chair them up the steps. Meanwhile, Rabiaa, once out of sight of her
own home, drops the baracan from her face, and has a good look up
and down the street and all around before she enters the garden. By
now the children have arrived, having run all the way from their
house to ours. The twins are dressed in high-waisted, pink satin
dresses, but Laila is in a neat sweater and skirt, with her soft hair
hanging on her shoulders like silken floss. The boys are in clean, gray
flannel trousers and sport shirts.

Once inside the house all formality is abandoned, baracans are thrown aside, and ladies and children either sit quietly or move curiously about the room looking at everything, not rudely, but with a simple interest in things that are new to them. Our children's photographs and one of the house in Victoria surrounded by tall trees, a lalique crystal bowl filled with fresh wild flowers, small ceramic ashtrays shaped like the conventionalized Fatima's hand, and the vivid striped baracans from the suk hung up at my windows for curtains, and a large pastel portrait of a Bedawi mother and child, both fierce-eyed, hungry, and fearless, drawn by Pahlivani, a young Turkish artist. All these interest my Libyan friends and, I think, they are surprised that I value the local workmanship for decoration. Meanwhile, the old ladies sit barefoot, feet folded under them on their chairs, their slippers on the floor beside them.

Saha and Nafisa, Badreddin's wife, arrive in Saha's chauffeur-driven car and discard their baracans with a sigh of pleasure. Now Hammet himself delivers Badria to the door, and she alone enters without a baracan, her black veil tucked in her pocket, and her lovely, pale face and golden hair uncovered.

The Libyan ladies all know, or know of, each other, and now comes a barrage of Arabic which I cannot follow, but I am content to watch their faces and the accompanying gestures, which mean so much in the language of these beautiful, Eastern hands. The content of the discussion is certain to be the wives of friends, delivery of new babies, reported pregnancies, rumored divorces, misbehavior of husbands, and predicted engagements. The old ladies haven't had so much fun since they attended the last funeral, I expect.

Nafisa has just produced a second child, Samira, a daughter this time. But she refuses to be condoled with about the baby's sex, and says defiantly that they already had Osama, a son, and Badreddin wanted a girl!

But today there is a new note in the conversation, perhaps precipitated by Badria's unveiled arrival. The ladies are discussing their desire to discard their baracans, if not their veils! Badria interprets this discussion for me in Italian. This is the first time I have ever heard this general desire expressed in a group.

In serving tea for my Libyan friends, I serve all the things that I care least for myself, and everything must be very sweet. Today, I have small honey cakes from the Damascus sweet shop, sticky cakes stuffed with shredded coconut and sweet cakes filled with chopped almonds, and Lena has made a three-layer cake with thick fillings and icing. We have tea, English fashion, with sugar and milk, and sugared almonds and caramels.

After eating, the children are restless, and they soon dash off home, except for Laila, who sits dreamily on the edge of the largest chair, gently running her fingers through her long, silky hair and listening silently to gossip.

Now Rabiaa gets up and wanders into the dining room to look about, and is soon followed by the others. I suggest that they may enjoy looking over my house, and this is exactly what they are hoping for, as my way of life interests them as much as their way of life interests me. We inspect the kitchen, look inside the electric refrigerator, inside the gas oven, inside the cupboards, go into the bathroom and admire the inset fish tiles, go into the bedrooms and find one of George's old paperbacks lying open on the bed with a cover picture of a naked lady. The ladies laugh appreciatively. In the other bedroom, they admire my bright, flowered cretonne hangings. When we stop in the hall to look in the full-length mirror, Saha notices the closed door of the study.

"What's in there?" she asks.

"My husband — and the dog," I admit.

The ladies discuss this in Arabic, then start giggling and nodding their heads, and Saha says, "We all wish to see your husband. Please open the door."

I try the door, but Harry has locked it. He wants privacy, even if the ladies don't! The ladies giggle even more, and Saha says persuasively, "*Please* tell him we wish to meet him!"

I communicate through the door with Harry, who reluctantly opens it. The ladies are all happy now, everybody shakes hands with him, looks with interest at the shelves in the study filled with books, at the two typewriters, at the plant presses stacked high with dried specimens; then they say goodbye to Harry, and retreat content.

The party is over, and baracans are requested. Saha, Nafisa and

Badria are to go together in Saha's car. As tall, handsome, young Nafisa winds herself into her baracan, she gives a disgruntled shrug at its many drapings and folds. Then she whispers into my ear, "Please you tell Badreddin baracan no good! I like to wear just black veil!"

As Rabiaa adjusts her baracan she says, "Well, it's dark now!" and I see that she's not going to cover her face to drive home! The two old ladies cover their faces from habit, and it only remains to get them into the car. Lena supplies extra power for the "bad" legs and helps me trundle them out and push them in. I drive them all three home, praising Allah all the way for my own "good" legs and my unveiled eyes.

I hadn't seen Rabiaa for a number of months, but Badria had told me that she heard Rabiaa was pregnant — so I guess the old ladies had their way.

Then one morning Lena was out walking with Pucci and came home with a glowing face. "Signora Rabiaa has had a big boy baby! Twelve pounds! But Abdul says she almost died. He wants you to come and see them."

That morning we went shopping to find a proper token. A tiny gold Fatima's hand to ward off the evil eye and a small gold heart for love and kindness, both hanging from a fine gold chain, pleased Lena and me immensely.

In the afternoon we went to call on Rabiaa and Abdul. We saw immediately from the tidy state of the house — no abandoned garments about, no tea puddles, no old ladies squatting — that guests were expected. It would be a party of men, of course, to celebrate with Abdul the birth of his new son, while Rabiaa and the mamas and the girls cooked them a feast.

Rabiaa took us in to see the new king of the household, asleep in a blue satin-covered crib by his parents' bed. He seems a large, handsome infant with lots of dark silky hair, and he is very, very soundly asleep. Rabiaa picks him up and twirls him about a bit, but he snores on, and I suspect he has had some efficacious soothing medicine for the night.

Rabiaa is thin, for her, and she says that she would have died had she not been in the clinic, where they took the baby from her with forceps. They also told her that she has diabetes.

Some weeks later Laila comes to our home early one morning to ask for a bowl of ice cubes, saying that the baby is sick. She returns several times during the day for more ice. That evening I go to the house to ask if I can do anything to assist. Abdul says that the baby has "brain fever," and the doctors fear that he will die.

Then comes a siege of several weeks, during which time Abdul never leaves the baby's side. He can't leave, he says, there isn't another person in that household of three adult women and three young girls who has the least idea of hygiene, of how to give medicines, or of how to care properly for a sick child, or even to whom he can trust the baby for an hour, in a household where the old ones believe in cautery. The infant has had six doctors, Egyptian, Yugoslav and Italian, and all types of injections for practically everything, and is having intravenous feedings. The poor little body, partially hidden under ice packs, is scarcely large enough for all the needle punctures. The doctors say that there is already severe brain injury.

The house is overflowing with relatives; the old ladies once more crouch over their teakettles, probably plotting another pregnancy for Rabiaa if this son dies. Rabiaa is a picture of despair, weeping, helpless, and hopeless.

I see the baby once more a few days later — lifeless. This time I feel sure that I see in the face of Abdul what he must see in mine — that it is better this way. But Rabiaa's look is different; she would have done anything to hold onto those tiny hands . . .

Abdul is always definite that his daughters will not use the baracan, nor wear the veil. All three girls, as well as the boys, are attending school. These two conditions, education and unveiling, are now beginning to go hand in hand for girls.

Fatima and Fujra attend a Libyan all-girls school in the heart of the medina. The standard of education there is the same as in the allboys school which Muhamed and Baderi attend, which is at least a step in advance of *no* school, or of a Koranic school conducted for boys only, and teaching only reading and writing of the Koran, as in the old days.

Laila, who is younger and her father's favorite, goes to Tripoli College, a school run and partly financed by the British Council. Here the enrollment includes both boys and girls, and a chartered rule is that equal numbers of Libyans and foreign students must be registered each term. The school is only a few years old, and the enrollment fee is high, and it has astonished and pleased everyone that the school always has a waiting list, both for Libyan students and for non-Libyans. Although teaching is in English, study of both Arabic and English is compulsory for every student. In an attempt at equalizing students, gray flannel tunics are worn by the girls and gray flannel suits by the boys.

Some time ago Harry asked Abdul if the girls would go on to the Teachers' Training School in Tripoli, or to the University of Libya in Benghazi. Abdul said no, it was too early in Libya for a drastic change; girls must continue to be just girls, and wives. Somehow, I think he will change his mind for Laila.

After independence, the young Libyan government, spurred on by UNESCO, became very conscious of the great need for education, for women as well as men. But the majority of Libyans disagreed with this view. The Libyan press of the early days of independence was filled with letters of protest, with such phrases as, "Coeducation is a devilish and satanic action!", "Coeducation is a great offense against the Moslem faith!" One letter I found quoted had this urbane statment, "We in Libya are not in need of education or coeducation. Rather, we are in need of learning foreign languages which will enable us to obtain important posts immediately, and gain famous reputations everyplace!"

In Abdul's family, the twins can now converse a little in English, and Laila is fluent and also writes it. But although Fatima and Fujra are not to wear baracans, or veils, I note, nevertheless, that they are no longer to be seen in the front garden, nor do they come to me on errands. Only Laila comes and goes freely, a charming messenger at all times. The girls are responsible for helping with the housework and cooking at home, and for trying to help make their own dresses, which Rabiaa masterminds from patterns which I buy for her in town. Abdul buys the materials, and he suffers with the usual male Libyan complex which consists of buying an entire bolt of material to dress the whole family.

The boys have no apparent duties. They mix with all the children of Giorgimpopoli regardless of nationalities, and play football, box with gloves, ride bicycles, play cowboys and cops and robbers, and seem always free to play.

To hear Libyan marital relationships discussed by a Libyan is quite different from hearing them described by an outsider, or reading about them. For this reason, Abdul held an audience enthralled after dinner one evening at our house. There are questions one cannot ask without being impertinent, but Abdul was answering them without their being asked.

". . . and at our weddings the guests are all present, I mean nearby, when the bridegroom goes to the bride for the first union. The guests are seated in an adjacent room from which they can watch the groom walk down the hall to the room where the bride awaits him. He disappears inside, and the guests wait tensely . . .

"They may have to wait only an hour," Abdul continues, "or they may wait five days, as it is said that they once waited at a royal wedding here! Meanwhile, they drink sweet tea and eat honey cakes until the crucial moment arrives, when the groom emerges triumphant — or so it is to be hoped — from the bridal chamber with the proof."

"But what happens," I ask, "if he doesn't emerge triumphant?"

"Then he calls a doctor to examine the girl, and decide what the problem is. If the doctor says the girl is not a virgin, the husband can annul the marriage, as the contract calls for a virgin."

"But your Libyan girls and women live in almost complete seclusion," I comment. "You have three daughters who never leave the house, except with you or their mother. How can such girls get into any trouble?"

Abdul replies with a wicked smile, "Every morning I take my daughters to school at eight-thirty, and every afternoon I call for them at one-thirty. How do I know what they do in the hours in between?"

"But they attend a school for girls only," I suggest.

"Yes, but perhaps my daughter asks her teacher for permission to go outside to the W.C. How do I know whom she meets outside? If a girl wishes to get into trouble, she can always do so!" says Abdul, who is obviously without illusions.

I remember very well the afternoon when Abdul had suggested that I take his wife for a drive for an hour to cheer her up, after the baby had died. Rabiaa and an Arab widow and Fatima and Laila all came, the two ladies, of course, in baracans. They had been living in Giorgimpopoli for almost three years, and had never been in Tripoli City. Fatima and Laila went to their schools in the medina but had never been in modern Tripoli.

They had a long list of places in their minds which they wanted me to drive them to, one being the abandoned railway station which was now filled with squatters — to whom they waved, I know not why. Anyway, we toured the city, the ladies' baracans constantly opening wider around their faces, while I kept begging them to cover up, cover up, knowing there would be trouble for all of us if they were recognized. In my imagination I saw the government requesting Harry's immediate withdrawal from Libya because his wife led Libyan ladies astray!

But Rabiaa was determined to see everything, and she had her head half out of the car much of the time. There was a ceaseless buzz of excited conversation among them all at everything we passed, new buildings and old ones, buses, limousines, camels and donkeys, automatic street signals which they loved, sidewalk cafés which they knew from reputation as man-traps for husbands, and the Italian-built federal buildings which impressed them. The beautiful sea boulevard didn't enthuse them because they had sea in Benghazi, too, they said; they liked the mosques and the marabuts, but the Roman Catholic cathedral, tall and majestic, standing in the center of the town, impressed them most. After an hour of circulating they still had as many other places to see, but I said that I had promised Abdul not to keep them out more than an hour.

Rabiaa begged me to return to Giorgimpopoli via a Libyan hotel where a friend of hers had once lived, and when we did so, and found the hotel looking run-down and dilapidated, the ladies were very content. Each one of the four had several more sights for me to visit, but I was firm and took them home, hoping earnestly that no one had recognized them in town with their baracans gaping. On the way home, they all tuned in on one wavelength, wagging fore-fingers seriously at me, and chanting, "Don't tell Abdul!"

I realized from this experience that if a Libyan lady does escape from home, she may go to unexpected lengths.

39. Queenly Influence

Two YEARS before our arrival in Libya, the Libyan Queen Fatima, cousin of the King, daughter of a powerful Arab sheik of Algerian ancestry, great granddaughter of a famous Islamic mystic, gave premature birth to an infant son and heir at the Wheelus Field hospital. The little Senusi Prince, heir to the new Kingdom of Libya and to its religio-political Moslem Brotherhood, died on his second day, as if the burden of leadership was indeed too great. Thus the monarchic dynasty, the Senusi leadership, the new Kingdom and the old Brotherhood were imperiled anew.

The King, who was born in 1889, had been married three times and had already fathered several children, all of whom had died in infancy. This was not only a great tragedy to him as a father, but as a ruling monarch he knew that as long as he remained without an heir, the throne would be a cause of Senusi family jealousy, and political contention. Now once again, after the death of his infant son, the King was being nagged and urged by political and palace advisers to take another wife.

In the summer of 1955 the King married once more in a final attempt to supply the heir. This was much against his own desire, for he was deeply devoted to his gracious and lovely wife Fatima, twenty years his junior. She was also his cousin and his dearest companion, as she had married him during his exile in Egypt.

Nevertheless, pressed by importunate advisers, Idris finally went to Cairo and married, by arrangement, a young Egyptian woman, Aliyah Lamlum, whose womb then became the last hope for the missing heir. In Libya, there was none of the usual Arab rejoicing and excitement over the wedding. Aliyah was always referred to here as the "Egyptian Queen," while Fatima was spoken of as the

"Queen," although by Libyan law each of them was officially only the "wife of the King." Each queen had her own separate palaces in the various parts of the country where the king wished to stay, and neither queen associated with the other. One can visualize a nerve-wracking vigil for the new wife and queen, as she waited in a strange country, in a lonely palace, hoping for pregnancy.

General gossip soon had it that the fact had been accomplished. Just after our arrival in Libya, gossip even went so far as to attribute pregnancy to both wives at the same time, and predict that both would be entering the Wheelus hospital together for the babies' deliveries, and that both might possibly give birth to an heir!

But gossip about pregnancy is unalterably proved true, or false, by the lapse of time. Time passed, and anxiously though people talked, waited and watched, speculated, and quoted inside persons who definitely knew — none of this came true. No other children were born to the King. The throne still lacked an heir.

Meanwhile, the King's regal role was regarded with insane jealousy by a branch of his own Senusi family, the descendants of his own first cousin, the deceased Sayyid Ahmad al-Sharif, father of Fatima. The matter was complicated by the fact that King Idris was not only the King, but in addition the Chief of the Senusi Order, holding religious authority of great influence. The son of the deceased Sayyid Ahmad was the acknowledged future successor to Idris as Chief of the Senusi Order. With this as an excuse, the House of Sayyid Ahmad claimed that one of them must also be considered the heir to the throne of the King, unless the King produced a son.

Idris did not for a moment recognize the validity of this claim to his throne, by virtue of the inherited religious Chieftainship. He said firmly and frequently that the monarchy was a separate, secular prerogative which had no connection with the Chieftainship of the Senusi Order. He was Chief of the Senusi Order as Idris, and not because he was the King; nor was he King because he was Chief of the Senusi Order!

King Idris was thoroughly convinced, and with good reason, that the establishment of a Libyan Royal House and monarchy was really due to his own astute diplomacy. Throughout two world wars Idris had deliberately associated his country with the Allies, and had come home with the winning side. This was no thanks to Idris's cousin, Sayyid Ahmad, who had himself bet on the wrong horse when he placed his country under Turkish authority in a war which the Turks had lost!

The King's closest adviser for years was Ibrahim Shalhi, a man of mixed Arab and African blood, a childhood friend of the King's, and one who came from a distinguished Algerian family. Shalhi was a devout Senusi Moslem, quiet and dignified, with excellent judgment, always unfailingly loyal to the King, a man with a strong sense of dedication to the country and to the monarchy. He had served Idris for forty years, including Idris's twenty-two years in exile in Egypt, self-imposed in 1922 as a protest against the conditions of the Italian occupation of Libya. Fatima married Idris in exile. Idris did not touch foot to Libyan soil again until 1944, when the country was under British military administration.

In 1954 Shalhi had been made Head (Nazir) of the Royal Household, and he was known to have more influence with the King than any other single person. The King had often said that in his heart Shalhi was his son. Unfortunately for Shalhi, everyone knew this, and Shalhi's influence over the King made him the target of resentment of the pretenders to the throne among the descendants of the House of Sayyid Ahmad al-Sharif.

The King was then in residence in his handsome, single-story, Italian-style palace in the center of Benghazi town. With him was his queen, Fatima.

Cousinship, in the Arab world, is believed the best possible basis for marriage, and said to make an ideal union. Fatima, handsome, intelligent and gifted, had for years been the King's chosen, devoted and loving wife in a relationship which was beyond criticism. Both were extremely religious, and arose daily at five A.M. for prayer. The sincere devotion of the royal couple made it all the more tragic that they failed to have children.

In residence with Idris in his palace were the usual large numbers of cousins, aunts, in-laws, papas and mamas, orphaned children of friends, domestics, and poor relations which every Libyan household supports, and, of course, the Nazir of the Royal Household, Ibrahim Shalhi.

It was October, the month with a clear, blazing, hot sun and chilly, indigo nights with stars afire. The summer heat was over, and the red dust lay still on the Cyrenaican desert for ghiblis seldom stir in the autumn. Benghazi streets lay baked and silent, amid the rubble of war-destroyed buildings, and only Bedawi, camels and donkeys set the pace of the little town.

It was against this tranquil setting that Shalhi, on October 5, 1954, left his adopted father's Royal Household and went to visit the office of the Prime Minister, Ben Halim. After a short talk he left Ben Halim's office to go to his car, which was parked in Cathedral Square, the Italian center. As he stepped towards his car, he was shot dead by young Al-Sharif Ben al-Sayyid Muhi al-Din al-Senusi, the grandson of the jealous Sayyid Ahmad, and a nephew of Queen Fatima herself. The one motive of the assassination, the assassin himself declared later, was to remove the King's chief adviser, Shalhi, in the hope that the King would then surrender to the demands of the House of Senusi to give them the succession to the throne.

Horrified by the murder of his dearest friend, the King, instead of acceding the succession, immediately placed all members of the House of Senusi under permanent house arrest. To exile them, as he at first proposed to do, would have been unconstitutional, he was told. The assassin was tried in the criminal courts and found guilty. He failed with his appeal, and four months after the crime he was executed. The only exceptions to house arrest in the Senusi family were the Queen herself and the three sons of Abid al-Senusi — Siddiq, Ahmad, and Abdullah Allah Abid, now known as the Black Prince. These three repudiated their cousin, the assassin, and declared their undying loyalty to the King. All the inciters or participants in this crime were blood relatives of the King and Queen. It became obvious to all that to possess too much influence with the King was dangerous business.

When we moved to Benghazi, I remember very well seeing a large house, not far from our own, which was always surrounded by uniformed military guards. This house, I was told, housed the imprisoned family, who seldom even ventured into its garden. The street which led to the house was barred with a NO ENTRY sign, and no living person was visible except the patrolling guards. The air of stealthy medieval secrecy was never breached.

In later years in Libya, I came to realize that this Royal Household murder exemplified almost the only type of crime of violence which the Libyan commits: a crime which is committed inside the family circle, or among intimates; motivated by jealousy, personal dislike, or a fancied wrong; and a crime whose object is to avenge, or to prevent, some real or imaginary injustice or disgrace. A state of righteous wrath accompanies the deed, and the murderer always feels himself fully justified.

The King, being a just man and an extremely loving husband, did not permit the connection between the Queen and the assassin to prejudice him; in any case, the King himself was a cousin to the assassin. There was never at any time any question of the complete loyalty of the "wife of the King" to her husband. Her reputation was and always has been spotless, and nothing but praise for her is ever heard.

This violent incident finished Benghazi forever for the King, who left, never to reside there again. Always with thought for the welfare and education of his people, he donated the Benghazi Manar Palace to be the home of the young national University of Libya. There, today, young Libyans study with little thought of the violent death of the Libyan intellectual which occasioned the gift of the palace. The King himself soon set up residence in Tobruk, which has now become his favorite home.

After Shalhi's murder the question of the royal succession grew even more acute, for the King had now exiled, or arrested, all the royal pretenders! In 1953 the King's brother, Muhammed al-Rida, had been named heir apparent, but when al-Rida died in July 1955 the question burned again. Once more it was suggested to the King that he take another wife, but the King refused.

Then there was discussion of transforming Libya into a republic, with Idris as President for life. The proposal was that after the death of Idris, the office of President should be filled by election, with a ten-year office tenure for each elected President. This, however, would necessitate a change in the constitution. It was also suggested to change the government from a federal to a unitary form.

Upon hearing talk bantered about on the dust-laden Cyrenaican wind of a possible republic, the famous Cyrenaican tribal chiefs once again came into their own. They rallied en masse in Tobruk, a dusty, baracan-clad mob, to make the demand that the monarchy should continue, the King should remain as King, that the constitution should stand unaltered, and the federal system should continue as before. The King again bowed to their expressions of fealty — and more crucially than ever, an heir to the throne was needed. It was then that he surrendered to state pressure, and took his Egyptian wife.

When, after several years, it became obvious that the King would have no issue, and that posterity must find another outlet, he promptly, and with considerable lightheartedness, one imagines, divorced his Egyptian queen and returned her to Egypt in January 1958, greatly to the annoyance of the Egyptian state. Now, once more, King Idris and Queen Fatima settled down to a period of true conjugal contentment, though unblessed by any offspring.

But the problem of the throne remained, and even before returning the Egyptian lady to her home, the King and his ministers had decided to appoint an heir apparent. Many of the Senusi family were still under arrest. Finally Amir Muhammad al-Rida, the son of the King's deceased brother, was named heir apparent in 1956, thus becoming Prince Hasan al-Rida. Although the Prince belongs to the House of Senusi, he is as far removed as possible from the Senusi branch which was represented by the now exiled pretenders.

Prince Hasan is in no way a man of the world. He grew up in comparative seclusion, and his education in a Senusi zawiya, a Moslem brotherhood, of the Sufi Order, in Cyrenaica, where his teaching was entirely religious, did nothing to broaden his outlook. He has such a quiet and retiring disposition that the Prince has been described by a French journalist as "Not even unpopular, he is simply ignored"!

In 1959 the Prince married a young Libyan, the daughter of a prominent Tripoli family, and now he has a son and heir five years of age, an infant son, and twin daughters. The marriage was designed to elicit loyalty for the monarchy in Tripolitania, and to unite the two antagonistic provinces. Although domestically all goes well, the union has achieved no marked diplomatic success.

When I recently received the following invitation in Arabic, I was especially interested to see Her Majesty referred to as "the Queen," and pleasantly surprised to see what activity she was undertaking:

> The Reception Committee of the International Fair has the pleasure to invite you for a visit to the Fair in the company of Her Majesty the Queen. Arrival should be before 9:30 A.M. on Saturday 9th March, and 16th March. The meeting place shall be within the Fair in front of the National Pavilion.
>
> Signed: The Reception Committee
> Admittance by card only.

This invitation was a revolutionary, epoch-making document, for one who knows Libya. It acknowledged the Queen; it acknowledged women as something beside vessels of reproduction; it sanctified the appearance of women outside of their homes. It also made it respectable for women to attend the fair, an activity which the Moslem priests had been broadcasting against.

My invitation did not arrive until after the first Saturday named on it, an incident typical of Libyan social life, which always takes place on the spur of the moment. Disappointed to miss the first day, I made up my mind that nothing should keep me from the second Saturday. Kathleen and I drove together to the fair gate in the UN car.

Although a police colonel stood outside the fair gates, the gate itself was cared for by women attendants, and once inside, the Libyan teen-age girls were there in uniform of Girl Guides. These were in the charge of my old friend Kadija, also in uniform. Kadija is famous as the first Libyan woman to broadcast, which she did under the British military administration. Today she conducts the very popular *Women's Program* on the air in Arabic, and has some twenty Libyan girls broadcasting under her tutelage. A middle-aged woman, she always travels unveiled in a government car, dressed in rather drab but utilitarian European garments, with a rose colored scarf invariably tied over her long, black hair, the only touch of gaiety that I have ever seen in conjunction with her somber face. She is a very special case, and recognized by all as such. Yet what circumstances have made her so, no one ever remembers. Perhaps it is the combination of a naturally invincible personality with the ability to grasp fearlessly at every opportunity which have combined to make her the strongest female force in Libya, and one which is greatly respected.

She has been married, but lives now as a single woman. She has studied in England and Germany, and she speaks English, German, and Italian as well as Arabic, and has access to everyone in Libya. All the advantages of her education and privileged situation she devotes wholeheartedly to furthering her country's advancement and, as tactfully as possible, to furthering the progress of her country-women.

It is almost impossible for an American woman who has grown up in the climate of approval for her freedom as a woman to appreciate an atmosphere in which any independence for a woman is a blasphemous concept. Yet somehow Kadija always manages to manipulate a fraction of progress forward for her own sex without annoying the other sex.

As we cross the space from the entrance gates to the Libyan pavilion, who should come forward to meet me with hands outstretched and the warmest of welcoming smiles but my dear friend Rabiaa, wife of Abdul, now a permant undersecretary, one of the few non-political jobs in the country.

Rabiaa is dressed in a long, handsome, heavy, brown wool coat of European cut, a memento from her holiday in Germany with Abdul, I think. Such husband-selected coats are always brown, as if to cover a wife with anonymity, instead of a baracan.

Today, the delicate structure and shape of Rabiaa's face, with its wide-apart, almond-shaped brown eyes, is especially noticeable because her hair is neatly combed and plaited and twisted high on top of her head. Her oval face is well powdered, and her tribal tattoos are almost covered up, and I suspect she may have had a tattoo removal treatment in Germany as many Libyan ladies now do.

The day is growing warm, and her coat hangs open to show a smart, simple, brown wool dress inside. Her nylon-clad ankles show above a pair of patent leather pumps with three-inch spike heels.

Behind the baracan

"You are very elegant today, Signora!" I say admiringly in Italian. She smiles happily and says, "Abdul bought it all for me in Germany!"

We are standing with a group of some forty Libyan women, the majority of whom are covered by baracans, with their faces now exposed, while at least a dozen others are dressed like Rabiaa in European clothes. All wear very high-heeled slippers. I, and many of the European women, have worn medium-heeled shoes with an eye to comfort while walking on the gravel roads of the fair. I am just wondering how the Libyan ladies can stand up to a morning on stilts, when Rabiaa whispers to me, with a pained look at her feet:

"How do you ever manage to wear these things all day?"

"I don't," I admit. "I take them off the minute I get home. I always go barefoot in the house!"

By now the wives of the ambassadors, who form a special group of sacred cows, have all arrived and are grouped near a number of Libyan women whom I recognize as the wives of prominent government officials. While we are eyeing each other with a view to placing ourselves appropriately in the hierarchy of protocol in which I come last, a long black machine drives slowly into our midst and stops.

The car door opens, and a young woman — or so it seems, for she looks very many years younger than her fifty years — steps out: Queen Fatima, a slender, dainty figure of medium height. She is followed by a young Libyan woman with henna hair, fair skin, round face and big brown eyes, who is herself followed by a tiny, spry youngster, the Queen's Palestinian secretary.

No one could look less like the falcon-eyed daughter of an Arab sheik, the favorite child of a Sahara tribal power complex, and the chosen woman of the Chief of the iron-handed, rebellious, austere and all-powerful Order than gentle Queen Fatima.

Her gracious, amiable bearing is the first quality one notices, and then the fact that her eyes are almost always lowered, a habit natural to all Libyan women when unveiled. But her smile is brilliant, and gives animation to a naturally somber, handsome face which is slightly sallow. Her brow is wide and low, her face triangular, chin pointed; her cheekbones are high, and her mouth is wide with large, white teeth. Only her nose lacks elegance, as it is broad, and full at the nostrils. Her hair is lustrous, boot-polish black, cut short and shaped to cap her head with a becoming wave.

Her figure is svelte and slender, qualities almost unknown amongst Libyan women, in their state of perpetual pregnancy. Perhaps for lack of an heir, the royal figure has stayed! She is dressed today in a two-piece, Italian-cut, lightweight tweed suit of beige, with a beige wool blouse, a small pearl choker, and an attractive brooch on the collar. The skirt is just to her knees, and her legs are straight and neat above her high-heeled beige slippers. As soon as she alights from the car, she commences to shake hands, kiss, or greet in some fashion all those around her. The ambassadors' ladies are all introduced, some curtsying and some kissing her hand. Many Libyan ladies are kissed on both cheeks by the Queen. Then Kadija takes her by the arm and the tour begins.

The Queen is followed closely by the little Palestinian secretary whose skirt is well above her knees, and who is soon staggering under the variety of presents which are presented to the Queen as she tours the pavilions. Also following the Queen, and having trouble with her high-heeled, lavender satin pumps, comes the pretty young woman with henna hair. She is the wife of the Crown Prince's brother, Rabiaa says, and a sister of the Crown Prince's wife. She wears a tailored lavender wool coat and dress.

Under way now, the royal entourage zooms along the fairgrounds with a wake of some sixty or more females hobbling behind. The first pavilion we enter is the Libyan arts and crafts, and I am delighted and surprised to see the tremendous recent improvement in the locally designed ornamental tiles. All the unstamped tiles here are imported from Italy, but the arts and crafts school now emblazons a variety of local designs on them for use in tables and in wall panels. A few years ago these designs were totally lacking in imagination, color or artistry. Today one sees the use of desert themes, camels, local vegetation, fish, and also the influence of early Roman or Greek mosaic designs such as are found all over Libya in scraps of ancient floors and pavement.

There are many articles made from local leather which now, thanks to the advice of FAO tanning experts, is being properly tanned. There are displays of local silver work. I have seen silver work in the suks all over Libya, even in small oasis markets in the Sahara, but I still think that by far the best Libyan silver work is turned out by an Italian artisan, Angelini, in Tripoli, who works with Arab designs.

In the Libyan pavilion the Queen is presented with a handsome dressing table mirror mounted in silver. As she leaves the booth she shakes hands with each attendant and thanks them all for their assistance. The pavilions are all guarded at the doors by Libyan Girl Guides.

By now we ladies-in-waiting are developing a technique, and those of us who fail to get inside the entrance in time to be near the Queen wait outside the exit to be the first after her for the next pavilion. The ladies of the diplomatic corps prove especially agile in their pursuit, and there is considerable eyeing of one another to see that the senior diplomatic ladies are holding their legitimate positions near the Queen. There is one free-lance Oriental lady who outwits all pursuit, and her bright Oriental garment may be seen floating not only abreast of the Queen, but sometimes ahead of her.

The Yugoslav pavilion is mostly machinery, but even for this the Queen has a gentle smile. The Czechoslovak and Bulgarian exhibits are more machinery, a great waste to my mind! Nations are rapidly burying their individuality and abandoning their handmade arts in the effort to turn out more and more cheap imitations of Western goods. Here sleazy nylon slips, phony blue jeans, fake typewriters and adding machines, flameless cigarette lighters, and collapsing bicycles, which are "just as good as" famous-named ones, flood the exhibits. The final blow is entering an Indian pavilion filled with bicycles, lead pipes and joints, and bathtubs and toilets, with never a sari to be seen!

Although the Queen visited the Russian pavilion last Saturday, she is going again today by special request of the Russians, who wish to present her with a gift, which proves to be a huge bouquet of red roses, accompanied by a number of handmade ties for the King. I hear critical comment about the Queen's visiting the Russians twice, but I thought it was rather clever of the Russians to arrange it.

The Moroccan exhibit turns out to be another machinery and tinned goods display, with only a few examples of the magnificent rugs which they make, and very little of their distinctive and beautiful leather work. I spent the time here limping about with Rabiaa, whose feet were hurting and who was trying to find a drink of water. The fair is arranged so that no drinking water is available, in the hope of driving people to the restaurant and drinks bar, oases which are closed today. As we pass the hydroelectric exhibit, we see a mass of various pipes with great streams of water gushing out, but never a drop to drink!

The Queen is not going to the Tunisian pavilion, as she visited it last week. I have been there before, but I want Rabiaa to see it, and together we enter the Tunisian cupola which centers around a courtyard with a fountain playing, the only pavilion which has its own individual type of architecture. Beautiful woven wool blankets in Arabic designs and vivid, barbaric colors hang from the walls, and hand-woven silk stoles, and rugs from Kairouan, and reed mats. Magnificent hand-hammered brass, silver and copper plates, huge bowls and platters are tastefully displayed, and there is a great variety of silver and gold, handmade jewelry and varicolored beads. Tunisian blue, the bright Mediterranean blue of the doors in Tunisia, the blue of its latticed windows, and blue-painted ironwork balustrades, is also freely used in the jewelry and weaving. The famous silver fretwork bird cages, which are ornamental with or without a bird, are here in all sizes. There are, I admit, some examples of machinery, and an exhibit of Tunisian tinned fruits, but these do not predominate. Tunisia's handwork is still her most exportable commodity, and Tunisians know it.

We rejoin the herd and hurry down the pasture. This time the royal group enters the pavilion of the United States of America, which as one would imagine is supermechanized, with nothing done by hand that a machine can do. I am just groaning with boredom, when a wonderful aroma comes to my nose. Coffee is being brewed in a completely mechanized kitchen by some real, alive American embassy wives! New life spreads through our weary crowd, and we push closer — not to the Queen, but to the coffee.

It is midday now, and we are all wondering if the Queen will last much longer. Barclay's Bank has a tiny, two-story exhibit, outside which waits Jan Bassett, a very persuasive power and the wife of the British bank manager. The Queen, it seems, has been advised by a Libyan friend that she mustn't miss Barclay's Bank! So, graciously as ever, she turns in here. Up the steps the party toils, while the rest of us drape ourselves on adjacent railings; down the steps the party trots. "Did Jan sign her a blank check?" everybody wonders.

Rumor has penetrated that a treat is coming: the last pavilion is temporarily occupied by the world famous Italian Fat Woman, Donna Cannone, seven hundred pounds of female pulchritude, and one of the most popular attractions of the Luna Park section of the fair. Donna Cannone, as a tribute to the Queen and to Women's Day at the fair, has offered a vision of herself free to all who wish to view her.

The Queen enters the pavilion first, but what her reactions are I do not know, as Donna Cannone proves so popular with the Libyan ladies that I cannot squeeze inside the doorway, and soon give up trying. I sit down on a patch of grass in front, and wait. After

twenty minutes of crowding, a great mass of humanity squeezes
back out of the double doors of the pavilion and flows towards the
fair exit; at the core of this fleshly tissue, so it is rumored, is Donna
Cannone herself, who, having given her all for Women's Day, is
now being escorted back to her Luna Park quarters. As the fair gates
clank behind her, the living mass flows back towards the center of
the fair, where the Queen is now ready to say goodbye. Except for
the Queen, Donna Cannone is certainly the hit of the day.

Royally gracious to the final smile, Queen Fatima shakes hands
with all about her, gives and receives kisses and blessings, embraces
sheeted figures and shrunken forms, many of whom look to be her
grandmother, her own trim figure outstanding among them. To the
ladies of the West who are curtsying, bobbing up and down and
handshaking, she gives a Western handshake and a warm smile. She
enters the long black car which waits beside her; in hop the red-
haired lady-in-waiting and the little secretary, and they drive from
the fairgrounds between two rows of saluting Girl Guides. Fatima's
hand lifts gently in the farewell of a Sahara Queen.

Did it really happen, I wonder? And what does it mean?

I look at Rabiaa drooping beside me; she gives a sigh, and mur-
murs, "My feet!" She is carrying her high-heeled slippers now, and
wearing an old pair of flat canvas ones which she borrowed from a
Guide, a friend of her daughter. Her coat is over her arm, her hair
has come down in two long, coal-colored braids which hang beside
her now pale face where the tattoos show indigo again. She struggles
into her long coat despite the heat, adjusts her heavy black veil to
hide her face, and says, "I go now. Abdul has sent the car." She
kisses me, and sighs again, whether from relief that she is going
home, pleasure at getting her shoes off, or regret at going into hiding, I do not know. "Please come and see me soon," she says.

What will the Libyan ladies talk about when they arrive home, I
wonder? About the exhibits they saw at the fair? About machinery?
About Donna Cannone? Or, Oh, how my feet hurt! Or about their
gracious Queen who walked with them and talked with them freely,
if only for a day?

40. Cold Night

"The Gypsy won't make it, Signora!" Imperatore, the Italian driver of the Land Rover, kept telling me all the time we were in the Fezzan. And always the Gypsy made it.

Ultimately, it came down to the test of the Sand Sea, one of several great sand masses in Libya. "You *must* go by the road, Signora, between Sebha and Brak, and meet us in Brak. Only a Land Rover can cross that Sand Sea!"

"But the Gypsy is as strong as a Rover," I insist. "She has gone everyplace the Rovers have gone so far. And she's going to cross the Sand Sea!"

Imperatore's smile is that of one who humors a half-wit of whom he is fond. I am quite sure that he has no intention of seeing us start off tomorrow in the Gypsy — something which we have every intention of doing!

The next morning we are up at six, the three Rovers are loaded and the Gypsy stands ready. Malcolm and Awad are in one Rover, Imperatore in another and Hammet and Badreddin in the third, and Harry and I are in the Gypsy, with Harry at the wheel.

Imperatore has checked everything for readiness in all the cars, and now he keeps an uneasy eye on Harry and me as we wait for Hammet to finish his coffee in the restaurant. As Hammet emerges, Imperatore hurries over to us and says pleadingly, "You must not take that Gypsy, please! She's not strong enough!"

"But she is, Imperatore. That's what we bought her for — sand travel. Who says she's not strong enough?"

"The police here. They say they had a couple of Gypsys last year, and they couldn't make the sand crossing to Brak."

"Oh, the police! They probably had broken-down, old second-

hand models! Anyway, they never up-keep their cars. Our Gypsy's
a different model, and in good condition, and she can make it, I
know!" The Gypsy is my special pride, as we bought her specifically so that I could accompany Harry and the FAO cars on desert
trips. "What do you say, Harry?"

"Oh, we'll try it," says Harry calmly.

But Imperatore hasn't finished, "Then let me drive, or Hammet,
Signore. You are not accustomed to desert driving . . ."

"No!" I shout. "No!" I am not going to see my modest husband
cheated out of his right to join the Sand Sea elite, or let Imperatore
undermine his confidence. "Harry's a good desert driver, Imperatore. We'll get there, you'll see!"

Imperatore shakes his head forebodingly, looks helpless, shrugs
sadly, and accepts defeat.

"Let's go," says Harry. "We'll *all* get stuck if we hang around
here arguing!" We are aiming for a strip of the Ubari Sand Sea
which must be crossed in the early morning while the nighttime
damp is still on the sand to form a crust, so we have been told.

We pick up our guide on the outskirts of Sebha, and with Imperatore leading, our four cars trundle, head to tail, through a maze of
abandoned palm gardens, making so many sharp right-angle turns
that I lose all sense of direction. We arrive at the edge of Ramla
Zelaf, the beginning of the sand area which presages the dunes ahead.
Here we stop and slightly deflate our tires in order to have more
surface traction.

Imperatore gives Harry and me one final appealing look, and we
get under way again. Imperatore leads, and as he has the guide who is
theoretically showing us the safest way, we start out in procession.
But as the important thing is not to lose momentum nor hesitate for
a moment, in no time at all the four cars are veering about on their
own, engulfed in an apricot landscape of sculptured, rolling dunes.

Brak, our goal, is north of Sebha, and the dunes here lie in general
east-west, and at first we travel northerly by zigzagging around the
ends of the dunes. Then we catch a glimpse of the guide on top of
one, evidently pursuing the system of up and over. We follow his
lead, and this proves to be much more exciting, like riding a roller
coaster, only without the assurance of coming safely to the end of

the ride: the dunes are high and steep, and you can't see the other side until you reach the crest, and this must be done at top speed, or you will sink in the sand. Often, the far side of the dune is steeper than the one you ascend, and once over the crest you roar down even faster. The bottom is the danger zone of softer sand, where you may stick in a pulpy, uncertain trough; the crest is harder, being formed from heavier grains of sand, which resist the carrying force of the wind and rest on top.

As we travel, I can feel the acute chill rising from the sand mass under our wheels, before the sun has warmed and softened it. The quality of chilled sand is not one that I used to connect with deserts, but I have learned that nighttime sand is as extreme in its chill as the sun-warmed sand is in its warmth.

The Gypsy is sighing softly as she speeds, without vibration or mechanical noise, which both seem to be absorbed by the immensity of the sand surface. The soft sounds and stifled phonetics of sand travel must be one reason for calling these masses "sand seas." The feel of our vehicle's speeding, spongy tires dragging in the sand is like the sensation of a broad, slow boat pushing gently against a tide.

Harry is driving well; we haven't been stuck, and that's the test. Who can do better than get there?

There is never a second to hesitate in decision, and no time to look about. He stays free of four-wheel drive in order to keep up the speed, which he holds at fifty miles per hour, and this seems like flying. We can't get more speed, driving with soft tires on sand. Meanwhile, our vehicles are converging and diverging — one moment all are sighted, the next moment all are lost. They are like four huge beetles going crazy.

Dunes surround us every place now without any visible difference amongst them, and we try not to lose sight of the guide, or if we do, we try to follow his wheel tracks which are fresh on the sand. But this is not successful, and we almost hit Hammet head on as we both top the same dune, Hammet also "following the guide," but from the opposite direction!

Imperatore and the guide have their own problem, as they, too, dare not slacken pace. At the bottom of dunes, they disappear from sight, but if we manage to top dunes at the same time, we find them

again. The speed of everything is what impresses me; there is no
time for second thoughts.

Once Hammet gets stuck in the trough of a dune. No one of us
dares stop to help until we can land on the top of a distant, hard
dune. Then Malcolm and Awad, Harry and I walk back to help him.
Hammet is just free of the sand when Imperatore and the guide return to find us.

After two hours of dune driving we begin to see beyond the undulating apricot sand the harsh outlines of Nubian sandstone, rust
color nearby and blue-black in the distance. Now there is the dark
blue outline of the Brak plateau, and Chatti Valley where Brak lies,
with pale hills and pale sands between the oasis and us, in the height-
ening sun.

Now Imperatore and the guide draw up triumphantly on the
gravel top of a semi-slag dune, and signal to the rest of us to stop.
The cars line up, everybody jumps out, as the guide shouts that
we're across! Everybody shakes the hand of everybody else, as this is
the first time for any of us.

Imperatore hurries over and pats the Gypsy approvingly on the
hood — in place of shaking her hand!

How cold it is! The sun is pale above us, the sand still damp beneath us and breathing out cold breaths of chill. Meanwhile, we are
all photographing, or being photographed, each one intent on preserving his own identity as a Sand Sea sailor, except for Harry, who,
having clicked his shutter once to preserve Gypsy and me for posterity, has wandered off on the usual search.

But it is no place for plant specimens. Harry, sniffing along the
crest of the gravel dune, with his nose almost lower than his knees,
has nothing to show in flora. But Harry knows that the crest is no
place to look for vegetation so he must be on the scent of something
else. If it's not plants, I tell myself, it must be artifacts! Of course!
This is the vicinity where Henri Le Houèrou from Tunisia told us
he had found Pleistocene flints.

Some distance from the rest of us, Harry has straightened up, and
is standing and polishing something with his sleeve. I hurry over to
look. He holds a brown, arrowhead-shaped piece of flint, about six
inches by four inches, and one inch thick in the center, but flatten-

ing and tapering to a sharp cutting edge all around, hand-hewn by some method. A stone hand axe, I wonder?

"Is it?" I ask.

"It is."

"How old?"

"Well, lower or middle Pleistocene, I think. About two hundred fifty thousand years before Christ. I'll have to verify at home by *Neolithic Culture*, but I think it's Acheulian type."

The others now come to look. Age does not impress Libyans, who live in a Stone Age country, as it impresses outsiders; especially myself, in whose native land a hundred years makes an antique.

However, inspired by the guide's assurance that "such things" are plentiful here, we all start searching on the gravel and sand. But perhaps there is a ration of one a day on hand axes, as no one finds anything.

"How did you find it?" I ask Harry. "Did you dig it out?"

"Not exactly. I remembered that Henri found one here, so I had my eyes open. I scooped up a handful of sand just to feel the coolness, and that exposed the edge of the flint. I suppose as the wind moves the dunes these things are gradually being uncovered."

A week follows. We have visited the oases of Murzuk, Traghen and Gatrun. Harry and Badreddin and Hammet have had satisfactory talks with the Fezzan ministers and officials, and agreements have been reached. It is the end of November now, and our last night out. I shiver all the time, except for a brief midday sweat in the pale noon sun. For once, everybody agrees with me that it is cold.

We are camping on an absolutely flat sand and gravel serir, or plain; not a hill, not a dune, not a tree or bush in sight, and the wind sweeps across us. It is a bad campsite, but as it grows dark at six, we have no choice.

We have two campfires going, one for tea and one for the lamb stew which Badreddin and I are making, and both for warmth. Badreddin bought a hunk of freshly killed lamb at the last village we passed, and we are throwing in everything of our rations that remains.

While the stew stews, fanned by a sandy wind, we retire with our drinks to our sleeping bags and cots to keep warm. The cots radiate out from the fires. Harry, Malcolm and I have whiskey, and the Libyans have hot tea. Badreddin has his transistor radio on, relaying Arabic records broadcast from Radio Cairo. There is one which I like especially that Badreddin says is a great favorite in Libya now, "Ana Lak Ala Toul." I'll try to buy the disc in Tripoli for George; he loved the Arab music here. How long ago it seems since he left Tripoli! The desert makes the other part of our lives seem like a dream; and yet in reality the desert is only a dream for me. The reality is the hackneyed, pedestrian life of a conventional, respectable Ma, who only escapes to the desert in these brief fantasies.

The stew is ready, and it is the best we have ever had. Without doubt, Badreddin is a better cook than I am. We clean the dishes ready for morning and place nearby the coffee, and the kettle filled with rather salty water from the last oasis well. It is growing colder all the time, and I have decided to sleep with all my clothes on, including my Hudson Bay reefer.

Harry has an inspiration. He gets the two heavy canvas tarpaulins out of the Gypsy, and places one flat on the desert floor, from where great gusts of frigid air are coming. Now, we line the cots up side by side as close as possible, Harry's at one end with mine next to him. The last one to get in will place the other canvas tarpaulin over the six of us! With some difficulty, because of my clothes, I struggle into my sleeping bag, having already pushed my shoes inside to avoid finding scorpions in them in the morning.

Hammet is serving tea again; clad in a smart pair of blue and white striped pajamas, worn on top his clothes, I think, he brings my glass of tea to me in bed. Awad is washing his feet; my God, I couldn't do that tonight! Badreddin has the transistor set for Radio Libya, and he suddenly lets out a roar of excitement. "My Father! The federal government has fallen!" He listens again. "My Father! The Fezzan government has fallen, too!"

"My God!" says Harry. "Then our agreements are no good! It's all to be done over again!"

"We could go back tomorrow," I suggest hopefully.

"Do you think the minister knew this was coming when we talked with him?" asks Harry.

Visitor at Murzuk

"Probably," says Hammet. "That's why he agreed with us so quickly!"

With everybody in bed now, and fires smoldering without warmth, Badreddin starts plotting another desert trip — to Kufra, he says, next time. He doesn't know yet that we will not be here.

Some bird or animal makes a night call in the distance, and another answers.

"Radio Cairo!" says Hammet.

This is a night aflame with stars and glowing with the colors of celestial bodies, a night when starlight throws long shadows on the desert sand, and makes strange Stone Age animals out of our vehicles, our cots and us; a night when the desert shares the wonder of its timeless past with those who pass.

Looking up into that cold, blazing sky, I wonder how it is possible to describe the essence of such a desert stop. It is a combination of exhaustion followed by comfort, of chill followed by warmth, of sand made edible in stew, of brackish water become drinkable, of primitive conditions (no W.C. — no bush!) made bearable for good reasons, of landscape magnificence pitted with human insignificance; and it is absolute isolation — but in good company.

I pray Allah for a gift before I sleep. I pray for the gift of remembering this night: every star with its shadow, every sound and its silence, every call and its answer, the smell of smoke and stew and sweat, even my shivering bones, and now my nicely warming feet (I think I'm sweating! Waterproofed, fleece-lined sleeping bags promote quick heat!) and every feeling, sad or gay, of this last night in the Sahara.

41. When Is a Riot?

A SEETHING group of perturbed, half-hysterical young Libyan students gathered one morning in the halls of the College of Advanced Technology in Tripoli. Speaking in loud guttural Arabic, which lends itself especially well to excitement, with their dark heads nodding and wagging, their swarthy faces somber and scowling, and hands weaving volubly as they huddled together, they were obviously incapable of settling down to study. When ordered by their supervisor and teachers to go to their classrooms and start work, they as one man shouted out one answer, more or less to this effect:

"How can we study? All over this country our relatives and loved ones and friends are being murdered! How can we study? There are sixty-five people dead here in Tripoli! Fifty people were killed in Zavia! A hundred were shot down in Tarhuna! And maybe a hundred killed in Zliten! And you tell us to study? How can we study? Walahi! Walahi! Walahi!"

The supervisor answers reassuringly that he believes these reports are all greatly exaggerated; that there is no real evidence as to the exact number of dead; that so far the government has only said there were eight deaths in the rioting.

Then comes the pupils' incredulous and unbelieving answer, "Ah, but *we* know better! We are Libyans! Our fathers, brothers, uncles, cousins, friends, all *say* so! *We* know better than you!"

And as people are usually willing to believe the worst, the young Libyan students undoubtedly believe that they do know. So, for obvious reasons the schools are now closed for a period of three weeks.

Thus, the hairsbreadth differences between nonviolent riots and violent ones was passed in Tripoli for the first time in my eight

years' experience of Libya. Today is the third day of stone throwing, stick beating, fire setting, window breaking and all around destructive action throughout Libya which has resulted in the deaths
of eight young people, and injuries of a large number of civilians and
police. Many shops and businesses have been looted or destroyed,
and at least a thousand cars have been broken up, set fire to, or overturned by rioters. Few actual facts are released for publication, and
this censorship gives rise to greater unease, and more frantic rumors.

To understand this unfamiliar violence in Libya, the least violent
of all Arab states, one must commence with the Summit Conference
of Arab States held in Cairo, where most trouble starts, three weeks
ago in January 1964. This meeting was intended to be not only a
gesture of Arab solidarity but a conference for the purpose of discussing possible action against Israel, where the government was successfully pushing ahead with her engineering project to divert a part
of the water from the Sea of Galilee to the arid Israeli Negev desert
to make it fertile and habitable.

Among the Arab chiefs of state who went in person to the Cairo
Conference were King Hussein of Jordan, who for the occasion forgot his feud with Nasser, President Sallal from the Yemen who also
buried his hatchet, King Saud of Saudi Arabia whose oil revenues are
now being courted, young King Hassan II of Morocco whose crime
of being a royal personage was temporarily forgotten and who was
soon kissing Algeria's Ahmed Ben Bella. President Bourguiba of Tunisia was also there, his crime of being plebeian and modern being totally ignored, while Premier Amin Hafeg of Syria found that his
Baathist allegiance was temporarily passed over. Also present were
President Aref of Iraq, where tumbling regimes are a habit, and last
and probably least, Hasan al-Rida, the young Crown Prince of Libya
and nephew of King Idris, escorted by Sayed Mohedin Fekini, the
Libyan Prime Minister. The King himself, at seventy-five, seldom
leaves his kingdom except for medical treatment — or such was the
press statement given at the time.

It was learned later that the Libyan security police had just uncovered the first of what was to prove a series of alleged plots in the
Libyan army in which seven Libyan officers conspired with some

Egyptian army officers and the Egyptian military attaché in Libya to give funds and arms to Libyan Nasserists who were believed to be plotting to establish a Libyan republic, which was later to be united with Egypt. The discovery of this plot, through a Libyan army officer who defected from it and informed the Prime Minister, was the real reason why King Idris did not attend the first Arab Conference in Cairo in January 1964.

At the Cairo Conference it was hard to believe that all these disputatious persons could ever get together. Given this group of forceful liberators working in unison, it was not surprising that the Cairo Conference was shortly pronounced to be a "great success" — although exactly what it did besides talk was not immediately divulged. That was to come later!

While eyes were thus on the Arab world, the young people in Libya, pushed by hidden forces they did not understand, decided to demonstrate their own Arabism and their solidarity with King Idris, who had broadcast his support of the conference. In Tripoli, on Monday, the first conference day, I was walking towards Barclay's Bank on Freedom Street when I heard young voices chanting and singing in the distance. I and other pedestrians stopped to look with interest towards the direction of the voices and clattering feet, and the next moment around the corner came running some thirty young girls all chanting an Arabic chorus in unison, and cheer-led by several of the largest girls. All were school girls of ten or twelve years, dressed in European dress, many of them waving head scarfs as they ran. Laughing, panting and shouting, it was all obviously good-natured, even if one did not understand all the Arabic words.

We onlookers smiled in sympathy with their youth and energy as the girls swept down Freedom Street and I couldn't help but think that this might be their last gasp of freedom, for most of these girls would soon be bundled into baracans and herded behind closed doors. For although many a father of a young girl now claims that his daughter will not be dressed in a baracan and hidden away, nevertheless, when the time of her womanhood comes the girl quietly disappears from sight. The next time one hears of her, one probably learns that she has been engaged, and married, sight unseen, and is just about to produce an infant. And once again comes the boast of the new young father, "My daughter shall not be hidden away," and again one hopes — but wonders and questions.

The parents of young girls fear that their daughters will lose their good names and their marriageability. In this country of unchallenged tradition, even modern leaders are afraid to emancipate their wives against public opinion. And certainly the mere father of an anonymous, undistinguished girl-child is justly terrified to allow her to show her face, and use her brains, in a country where woman's one asset has been her body.

And so, as I did my shopping this morning in Tripoli and heard in the distance the girls' chanting voices, I rather admired their initiative and energy, and hoped that in time it would bring them some reward. I later learned that many of these girls had been forced to demonstrate against their own wishes, by their Egyptian schoolmistresses; the girls themselves came from families whom their act would horrify.

The following morning as I drove into Sciara Mizran, the street which houses several secondary schools, I saw a block of stalled traffic ahead, a mob of young boys and men, a number of jeep-loads of armed police parked on the side streets, and a group of motorcycle police trying to get traffic moving. Thanks to police efficiency, we were quickly under way again, and as we rolled past the sidewalks which were laden with young men students, I saw their faces were sullen and threatening, and I guessed that I had just missed a demonstration.

The city was bristling with armed police and there were few civilian vehicles about, and I had no difficulty finding a vacant parking meter. Soon I noticed that all the Jewish shops were closed and shuttered, and I recalled, as the shopkeepers must do at such times, the Jewish massacres here in 1945 at the time of the partition of Palestine, when over a hundred Jews were murdered in the medina in Tripoli.

Today there was obvious determination on the part of the police to permit no violence. I wondered, however, whether or not it was wise to break up student demonstrations: the Libyans claim that these give the young people relief for their feelings, and an outlet for their emotions. But there is a very narrow margin between a peaceful demonstration and a violent one. Although at this time the city appeared to be peaceful, I learned later that the student mobs had formed in front of the Khuld Palace in a demonstration of protest against the fact that the King himself had not gone to the Arab Conference, an absence which had been brought to their notice by their Egyptian teachers. As the King was not in residence in the Palace, but was ten miles outside the city at Suani Ben Adem, it was a wasted gesture.

The next morning I arrived in town to find again a partially deserted city. My first errand was in an Italian shop where the Signora greeted me with the surprised exclamation of "You are in town!"

"Yes, is there any reason why I shouldn't be?"

"Haven't you heard about Benghazi?" And then in a whisper she told me the following story: The owner of her shop had a ticket to fly to Benghazi this morning, but a Libyan friend had called him the night before, and advised him not to go as there was "serious trouble" in Benghazi. It seemed that the Benghazi students had held demonstrations for two days to show their solidarity with the Arab States Conference. These demonstrations had begun peaceably, but had become violent on the second day when the students started throwing stones at the police. At this point the Cyrenaica Defence Force, a military organization which does police duties at Benghazi, attempted to break up the student mob, and the students retaliated by hurling stones and bottles at them. In the fight which followed, the police had opened fire and killed eight young people, while two or three hundred others were injured, and now in hospital.

This story seemed so extreme that although it was told in good faith, I mentally divided the casualties by ten and disbelieved completely the report of any deaths. On my way home to Giorgimpopoli, I saw that the city was still overflowing with police and security forces, but all seemed amiable enough. I recognized old traffic police friends who were looking as cheerful as ever. There were, however, many new khaki-clad figures, perhaps special security forces, and these were wearing pistols.

When Harry came home I asked if he had heard the Benghazi report, and he said that Hammet had been in to tell him the story.

According to Harry's assorted informants, the number of dead in the riots ranged from two to twelve, but everybody agreed that several hundred people including police had been injured, and that the police had fired and used bayonets. There had been a number of demonstrations in Tripoli, also, but the police here had not fired.

All news of the brutal Benghazi event was strictly censored, and not a factual breath of it has yet come on the Libyan radio, or any other locally heard radio, and nothing has appeared in the Arab daily press. As the foreign papers here are afraid to print anything controversial until after it has appeared in the Arab language press, there is no official news but many rumors about this second most brutal event in Libya's modern history, the first being the Jewish massacres almost twenty years ago.

After the fatal riot of Tuesday, it is believed that the government ministers from Benghazi and Cyrenaica went in a body to the King and handed in their resignations in protest at the police shootings, at the same time demanding that a commission be formed to make a full investigation. The ministers are quoted as asking the King how it was possible for His Majesty to condone the murder of Libyan young people who were only following the example of His Majesty himself by demonstrating their solidarity with the aims of the Arab States Conference. One can imagine the King's feelings in the light of his own knowledge of the Egyptian-Libyan plot against him. Nevertheless, the King refused to accept the resignations of the ministers, and promised a complete investigation. The chief of the Libyan police force and of internal security was in Tripoli at the time of the killings, and this may be an excuse for uncontrolled Benghazi violence.

Another story is that the chief of police had hoped to attend the Cairo Conference, and when the head of the armed forces was sent in his place, he was disgruntled, and, in a bad mood himself, gave overly severe orders to his police. One will never know the truth of it in this country of press censorship. Because there is often no accurate *factual* printed report of vital events here in Libya, one lives in a state of incredulity, believing nothing or everything, and quite frequently being fooled by the worst coming true.

My immediate reaction to the Benghazi news was disbelief of the brutality and indiscretion of the police there, perhaps because I have always been impressed by the good humor, patience, fine appearance *and* outstanding efficiency of our Tripolitania police force. I have been here in Libya through the anti-British riots at the time of the Suez crisis, the anti-French riots, which seldom cease, though one never knows why they begin, and the anti-foreign demonstrations, which constantly take place, one never knows why, but I have never seen the Tripoli police force use brutal retaliatory tactics, no matter what the provocation, and during the Suez riots, the provocation went as far as bombs. The police have always maintained a peaceful Tripoli, and they stand for the civilized enforcement of the law for all, both Libyan and foreigner.

The Cyrenaica Defence Force, whose personal responsibility is to protect the King, is tougher in its methods of law enforcement. Certain it is that the Libyan government is determined not to permit violent demonstrations to become a habit. Most people are conscious of the fear that the King's death will bring a revolution, for although everyone respects the King, his heir, the Crown Prince, has few ardent backers.

On the other hand, the Black Prince, Sayed Abdullah Allah Abid, son of the first cousin of the King, who is as black as can be and has Negro blood, probably through a maternal slave strain, has a tremendously forceful and telling personality. When he appears, he is the center of every gathering. He is naturally intelligent, and has an acute business sense which has already made him the richest man in Cyrenaica. Although he may be quite content with being a baron of commerce, rumor says that he is also willing to take on a royal role on the side.

For five days now the Jewish shops have been closed, as the Jews are "whipping boys" for trouble here. This morning I started to town again (the sixth time) in the hope of being able to retrieve a christening cup and plate from the Jewish jeweler who has been engraving it. As I arrived at the outskirts of the city, my car was held up in a slow line of traffic on Omar Mukhtar Street, and I saw that the sidewalks were solid with Libyans. I was uneasy, but I could not escape from the traffic block. Just before the line of traffic entered Piazza Spagna, a mob of young men came surging down the opposite side of Omar Mukhtar into oncoming traffic which they had halted. My traffic line progressed slowly until I was level with the crowds, and I could see that these boys were all armed with broomsticks or clubs and were pressing strongly forward.

Six traffic police in the piazza made no effort to interfere with the boys except to guide them away from the other stream of traffic so that the mob flowed through the piazza rather than into it. I entered the piazza and then turned half right into Twenty-fourth December Street, as there was no other way to go unless I steered into the crowds. As I entered Twenty-fourth December I could see ahead of me solid black objects which filled the air like a flight of birds. These dark objects proved to be stones.

Now traffic comes to a halt, and I with it, and I roll up my windows and lock the doors; now traffic moves slowly forward again, and I see that the shop windows are shuttered. The sidewalks are mobbed with ill-dressed men and young people; there must not be a single student left in any Tripoli school!

Now a police jeep filled with soldiers roars past me on the left side, traveling on the sidewalk in order to pass the stream of stalled motor traffic. I reach the crossing stop signal which is green, but the street ahead is blocked. I progress little by little, and I see that the pavement is littered with stones and rocks, three or four inches in diameter, which obviously have been carried by students for throwing. We come to a stop just behind the police jeep, out of which pour the soldiers, but their officer, a tall, handsome Libyan, is out ahead of them, and he is already facing the mob unarmed except for his little swagger stick.

He is furious with the crowd before him and harangues them fiercely, striking the palm of his hand with his swagger stick repeatedly, shaking his fist at them, striking at the air, and you can see that he would just love to shake some sense into them. In fact, his controlled violence is more impressive. Meanwhile the brave mob of youngsters and rowdies stands gaping in front of him, their jaws dropping, looking surprised and rather cowed. Now the cop clears a way for us, and I continue up Twenty-fourth December Street, which is littered with rocks all the way, until I pass out of the shop-

ping district and head for home via Garden City. Today is obviously
not the day for shopping!

When I arive home Lena is out looking anxiously for me from the
veranda, as Harry has just telephoned to tell me to stay out of the
city today.

Harry's explanation of today's trouble comes from Hammet, who
says the trouble started when the young people lined up in a fake
funeral procession with an empty coffin, to symbolize mourning for
the dead Benghazi boys. The police at first hesitated to take action
because of the nature of the procession, which soon arrived at the
Prime Minister's office and called for the Prime Minister to come
out.

Mr. Fekini emerged, and with tears flowing down his cheeks, expressed the deep regret and sorrow of the government over the Benghazi deaths. The habit of public crying is typically Middle Eastern,
and the people of this area pride themselves on it. I often hear Arabs,
especially Jordanians, describing proudly how long and bitterly
their tears have flowed at the occurrence of some sad event. I am
sure they must consider *us* as being quite without hearts, or feelings.

After the Prime Minister had stopped crying, wiped his eyes, and
addressed the crowd, the boys moved on en masse, and the police
tried to persuade them to disperse. But the boys were armed with
sticks and stones, and determined to find somebody at whom to
throw them, and in the end the police resorted to tear gas bombs to
disperse them. Hammet, who came through town just after the tear
gas bombs had been let off, was still sniffling fiercely and for the first
time appeared to be quite out of sympathy with the demonstrators,
who he usually assures me are quite harmless. I have always
thought so too, but today, when I saw the whole of Tripoli turned
into a surging young male Arab mob, I realized how helpless the
police would be against a solid city of wild young men and boys, if it
turned against them and the crowds took command. It would be
impossible then to halt bloodshed without more bloodshed.

Another Benghazi University student, one of the seriously
wounded casualties of the riot there, has just died. He had been operated on, and died less from the wound, it is said, than from lack of
sterile conditions in the Benghazi hospital.

Great dune masses
curl and spread

Eight o'clock the same evening. I have just returned from the city where I collected the newly arrived (and censored) European magazines and papers. I purposely delayed my trip until almost seven o'clock, knowing that at this hour during Ramadan all Moslems would be at home waiting eagerly for the guns to sound, and the signal from the mosque that the sun has set and they can eat. Sure enough, the city streets were deserted. A few of the shops had opened their doors but had not taken down their shutters, as shop windows were expensive. Twenty-fourth December Street had already been cleanly swept of all the rocks, stones and sticks, and signs of disturbance, and there was nothing to suggest the morning's turbulence. I collected the journals without incident. I decided that if a crowd of Moslem boys can choose between going to school or having a riot, they choose a riot; but if they must choose between having their meal or a riot, they eat.

A few days later Harry brought home the *Cyrenaica Weekly News*, published five days after the riots. To my surprise there was a brief note on the Benghazi riot, with a statement that "several" Libyan boys of fifteen and sixteen years had been shot dead, and a number of casualties had been inflicted by the Security Forces police, five of whom had now been suspended pending investigations. This quite factual statement of a tragedy, of which we all knew, was almost reassuring. Where there is no factual statement, and no official bulletin is given, rumor always gains strength. The truth, whatever it may be, is best acknowledged.

42. Mob Violence

Guns turned against children in Benghazi laid the fuse for violence; firing Prime Minister Fekini set the match to it.

It was soon generally understood that the forced resignation of the Prime Minister had been preceded by a visit to the King. During this night meeting on January 21, it is believed that Mr. Fekini demanded the retirement from office of Mahmud Buquwaytin, Commander of the Cyrenaica Defence Force and Chief of Libyan Internal Security, as Commander Buquwaytin was technically the responsible authority for the Benghazi police action in firing on the students.

This request faced the King with an almost impossible choice. Buquwaytin was a long entrenched supporter of the King who stood in a special relationship with His Majesty by virtue of being the son-in-law of Ibrahim Shalhi, the King's trusted adviser who, after serving the King for forty-one years, was assassinated by the nephew of the Queen and second cousin of the King. Buquwaytin was also the brother-in-law of the murdered man's son, Busiri Shalhi,* whose sister he had married. Busiri Shalhi was at this time the Nazir of the Royal Household, a man with a strong, subtle influence on the King through the King's feelings of obligation, an iron bond in the Arab world, and of almost paternal affection for Shalhi's murdered father.

With this internal palace set-up, it was obvious that to displace Buquwaytin would cause intense discomfort in the Royal Household to an aging, fragile, but far from senile King, who now, since the uncovering of the revolutionary army plot, had even greater reasons for valuing personal loyalty to himself. Faced with the Prime Minis-

---

* These two men, Buquwaytin and Shalhi, were both dead within the year, Shalhi in a motorcar accident, and Buquwaytin of natural causes.

ter's ultimatum, "Get rid of Buquwaytin, or accept my resignation!" the King accepted Mr. Fekini's resignation.

Soon the rumored reason for the Prime Minister's resignation leaked out. Then the crowds who, a few days before, had been shouting, "Down with Fekini!" and had demonstrated against him on his own doorstep, were shouting, "Up with Fekini! Fekini! Fekini, the martyr! We want Fekini to return!"

The following day the United Nations headquarters was given a hint that major demonstrations of unusual violence were expected on Friday and Saturday at midday. Consequently, UN dependents were warned to stay out of the city. Midday Friday is the time when great numbers of the Moslem male population leave the mosques after prayers. The mosques are the central public meeting places, and the priests have strong political influence; it appeared that riots might be dictated from the mosques. The demonstrations were to be in support of Fekini, and in support of the demand that the five army officers who were suspended in connection with the deaths of the students should be tried and sentenced in public court.

Friday, the weekly Libyan holiday, Harry was home all day, and we rested tranquilly in our suburb, although by afternoon we were hearing by telephone from friends that there was rioting in the city. Saturday morning Harry went to his office, but telephoned me as soon as he arrived there and warned me again to stay off the roads. Demonstrations Friday had been violent, and were continuing today; they had ceased to be spontaneous student demonstrations.

The mobs were now stoning everybody indiscriminately, including Libyans and police, with an impartiality which annoyed the Libyans whose former experience of riots had been those directed against foreigners only! Lena and I did our shopping uneventfully in the Giorgimpopoli supermarket, which we found overcrowded with out-of-town customers who were afraid to enter the city.

By mid-afternoon Harry arrived home, having sent the girls home from the office before midday to avoid trouble. He had avoided the mobs himself by taking a cross-country road from Sidi Mesri. Hammet had told him that the demonstrators' slogans had now changed to, "Down with the King! Fekini for President!"

This was more shocking to me than stone throwing. "Down with the King!" has never before been heard in Libya, where King Idris is regarded with great reverence, not only as King, but as the religious leader of the Libyan Moslems. To hear, "Down with the King!" must shock most Libyans, and certainly shocks all foreigners, to whom it has always been offered as the one sure security that, "While the King lives, there will be no revolution!"

We were discussing the implications of the situation, when the gate bell rang, and Hammet entered the garden looking decidedly ruffled. As he ran up the veranda stairs he said, "I come to tell you to *not* go on the roads this afternoon! You must stay in the house. To-day, very bad people make very much trouble for everybody!"

We made him sit down and tell us the details of what was happening in town. He was filled with indignation as he described his own experience. "I came through town, which is filled with police and soldiers, who throw many tear bombs at the crowds. They use over two hundred bombs yesterday, but now the men just run away from the tear gas, and then mass together some place else. The police can keep them moving out of the town, but they cannot stop trouble. I am driving on Omar Mukhtar Street just before the Lido [a bathing resort on the outskirts of town close to Giorgimpopoli] when I see many boys and men throwing stones at all the cars — even at mine!

"I stop my car and shout, 'Why you do this stupidity? Why you do this to me, a Libyan? You no careful, you break my windows!'

"They make me get out of my car, and they say, 'You like Fekini? You want Fekini come back?'

"So I say, 'Yes, I like Fekini. Fekini very good man. Hurrah for Fekini!'

"So they let me get back in my car, but say, 'You better drive with your head outside so people see you Libyan! Better you shout, "Up Fekini!"'

"I see in this same place near the Lido seven or eight cars all smashed up and abandoned, and one car is United Nations No. 57, and I do not see the driver. So I come to tell you to stay in your house today. These people very bad men. Just like to destroy everything. No good people!"

"United Nations No. 57?" says Harry. "That's an FAO car — it's

Gerry Van Hoorn's! I wonder where Gerry got to, and if he's all right?"

"I do not see him; I think he escape."

"How is this trouble going to end, Hammet?"

"I don't know. Everybody very angry now. First, because the police kill the boys in Benghazi — that's no good to kill children. Then, angry because the government not make a public trial immediately for those policemen. But now more angry, want to throw out everybody, even the King — perhaps they make a revolution. These people act stupid and bad now, because throw stones and make fires and hurt *everybody*, no matter who! The police cannot stop them now because the police and soldiers are afraid to hurt anybody."

"Tripoli has never been like this before!" Harry says.

"Because now the police can do nothing!"

We were standing in front of the house saying goodbye to Hammet, when a taxi with its windows broken drove up and Gerry jumped out.

"My Land Rover is finished!" he said cheerfully. "All broken up!"

"Hamdu li'llah you are not finished!" I said. "Come in and tell about it."

"I'll let the taxi driver go. He says all he wants is to get home and stay there!"

It seems that Gerry had been on his way to work at the tannery, when he was stopped in front of the Lido by a barrage of stones and missiles which broke all his windows. As the stones continued to pound into the Land Rover, Gerry jumped out and ran for the police post near the Lido, a couple of hundred yards from his foundered vehicle.

A traffic policeman was standing in front calmly watching the fun, when Gerry said, "That's my Land Rover! Can't you do something about it?" The policeman shrugged amiably, and said no, he was helpless. Gerry waited a few moments and saw the crowd trying with some difficulty to set fire to the cushions in the car, which didn't seem to be very combustible. Then, thinking that the crowd might turn its attention to him, and as the policeman was not prepared to interfere, Gerry started to run down the side of the road towards Giorgimpopoli. At the crossroads he saw a taxi standing with its windows broken by the rioters, and asked the driver to bring him to our house.

"Well, the Land Rover is really a Libyan government vehicle provided to me as an FAO expert, so if Libyan crowds ruin it, that's the business of the government," concluded Gerry. "But the crowds today are really vicious. They know the police dare not hurt them, and they don't mind what they do!"

Just then Werner Grumblat arrived in his Land Rover to tell Harry that he had passed Gerry's abandoned Land Rover on the road, and he thought we should start a search party for Gerry. He was greatly relieved to find Gerry with us.

Werner said that when he first entered Omar Mukhtar Street he saw crowds in the street ahead, so he turned down a side street and waited. In a few minutes the jeeps of the riot squad passed him, and unloaded their police behind the mob, which began to melt before them. The riot squads and soldiers have been stationed in the central piazzas of the town all day, and consequently the crowds were radiating farther out, and arriving in the suburbs near Giorgimpopoli.

"Do you think these people have any idea *why* they are doing this? Have they any objective? Or are they just enjoying being destructive?" I asked.

"I am sure that most of them are being paid to go out and make trouble," said Werner. "There is certainly an organizing hand behind it all!"

"Last Tuesday," said Gerry, "when they were throwing stones on Twenty-fourth December Street, I was on the sidewalk when the crowd passed me and I went along with them for a bit, and as I did so I asked several boys in Arabic, 'What are you doing this for? What is it you want?' And all anyone could say was, 'I don't know! I don't know! Rah rah rah! Rah rah rah! I don't know!' Not one of them had any real idea what he was demonstrating about!"

While we were standing on the road saying goodbye to Gerry and Werner, cars with shattered windshields were passing, driven by women with pale faces filled with a mixture of surprise, fear, and indignation. Most of the cars were American, with children and babies, as well as adults, inside. Had it not been for the comparatively unbreakable glass which most cars use, the casualties would have been very severe. The women looked shaken, and several who stopped to talk to us were hysterical. Shattered glass becomes opaque, and I don't know why more road accidents didn't occur. By now there was a general air of tension and catastrophe in Giorgim-popoli, and we could hear the hum of confusion and shouting in Tripoli.

The sky over the city was filled now with black smoke, which Harry thought must come from burning oil or a rubber tire deposit. Although we could not see flames, the smoke continued for hours, and meanwhile new jets of smoke and flame sprang up all over Trip-oli. We learned the following day that the main fire came from a Jewish-owned tire deposit, which was entirely destroyed, with a loss of $75,000. All over town, cars were overturned and burned, wher-ever the mischief-makers were able to set fire to them.

There is a ghoulish fascination in watching a skyline which tells of disaster and in hearing the distant crescendo of violence, while occa-sional victims pass close by, and you wonder when and if the forces of evil will overtake *you*. One of the most frightening qualities of mob violence is its total lack of motivation, or direction. If mobs were reasonable, even if they had special objects of vengeance, one might guess at their movements and try to escape. But the Tripoli mobs seemed only to wish to inflict discomfort on everyone possible.

The hum of confusion and the flicker of flames on the skyline continued until almost dawn, at which hour the Moslem masses has-tened home to have their last meal before the daytime fast began, as this is Ramadan. Being Ramadan may have added to the bad temper of the time, as everyone grows irascible then.

Meanwhile the streets of Giorgimpopoli were, for the first time in history, free of cars. Everyone had found some nook or cranny in which to hide the old jalopy so that it was not in the street inviting destruction!

The next day, Sunday, I decided not to go to the Garrison Church, as I would have to pass through a Bidonville to get there. Instead, Lena and Pucci and I thought we would drive around Gior-gimpopoli and see if we could pick up any news. So we turned into

Gurgi Road, which marks the rear boundary of Giorgimpopoli, the front boundary being the sea. No sooner had we entered Gurgi than Lena saw three boys standing beside the road, waiting. She pulled in Pucci's head, which always protrudes from the window, and slammed up the window, just as the stones struck, fortunately on the body of the car. I sped up and the rocks bounced off us and we escaped without breakage. I felt quite indignant that this should happen in Giorgimpopoli, and I involuntarily wanted to stop the car and scold the brats! But I remembered that an American woman had done this the day before, and was so ruthlessly stoned that she suffered a serious brain injury.

I don't believe that the worst forms of violence will continue much longer, *unless* the trouble develops into a real revolution, but I do think that it will be a long time before we can travel on the roads without fear of being stoned by boys. Stone-throwing comes naturally to boys, and after they have once seen their elders permit and sanction, even applaud, the action, it will be difficult to break them of the habit.

Harry's only comment when I told him was, "Well, I suppose you'll keep on going out until somebody breaks your window!"

The hospitals are said to be full, both with police and civilians. As the police are forbidden to use their pistols, they now carry pickaxe handles. They continue to concentrate on city protection, and violence continues to radiate further outward.

Monday was a day of quiet; no one knows why.

U Thant, the Secretary General of the UN, is about to make a tour of Africa, and was scheduled to visit Libya, arriving here on February 6. The Libyan government has today requested him not to come. Either they fear that conditions here will still be chaotic, or that a visit now might give rise to rumors that the UN has been called on for help.

After a day of dull quietude Monday, devoid of both event and rumors, Tuesday offered more variety. I have just finished reading in the local Italian-language newspaper the text of the radio broadcast given last night by Mahmud Muntasser, the new Prime Minister, not red-hot news but at least he has opened his mouth. He said, in brief, that he was appealing to the people of Libya not to shame themselves in the eyes of the world by permitting "a small, evil minority" to incite them to further violence. This must cease, or violence would be met with violence.

The Minister of Information and Guidance followed him on the radio with a quite dramatic speech in which he first praised the fact that the Libyan constitution guaranteed the right of free expression, by democratic means, even against the executive authority, so long as the expression was peaceful.

However, he continued, burning and looting of shops and motor-cars, and violence to innocent individuals including their own police force, were not peaceful nor democratic means of expression, and must stop immediately.

He believed, he said, that the first genuine student demonstrations had been quickly perverted to hide a deliberately destructive element here which sought to undermine the government. He now called on all parents to be responsible for the future lawful conduct of their children, and on all Libyans to stand with their government against the exploitation of innocent emotions, and in the fight against false propaganda.

I thought this was a sensible appeal to all the decent, self-respecting, proper-behaving people which the vast majority of Libyans are.

I feel especially sorry for the police here, whom I have always found to be kind, friendly and efficient, and so many of whom are now in the hospital as the result of facing the mobs without using violence themselves.

So much for words; now for the latest in deeds. Yesterday was market day at Zavia, a small village twenty miles from here, and the town was full. Every little village has its own market day, when the nomads from outlying vicinities bring their camels, sheep, goats, chickens, barley, red peppers and any other bargaining wares to sell and barter in the open marketplace.

Market days are usually friendly occasions, but by midday in Zavia a large, belligerent group of young men and boys had formed in the central piazza, shouting and roistering and haranguing, ostensibly to show their sad feelings for the Benghazi "boy martyrs" — in reality, to pick a fight.

Soon they were elbowing the market visitors, upsetting market goods, kicking at people's ankles, tormenting the tethered animals, and finally throwing stones at everybody in their way. At first the police tried quietly to control them, and protect market property, but the mob quickly turned its menacing attentions on the police, and showered them with stones. The police formed in front of the police station and threw tear gas bombs at the rioters, who broke up momentarily, but quickly regrouped. This time the mob advanced, throwing stones and brandishing their knives and shouting threats to break into the police armory and steal the weapons.

At this, the police opened fire. They killed outright at least two men, although most reports claim seven, and wounded about thirty others. A number of the police were wounded, and the Commandant was seriously injured.

Before the affair quieted down, several nearby houses were set on fire, one belonging to an Italian farmer who, with his wife, was injured trying to defend their home. The wife, whose leg was broken, was taken in and sheltered by an adjacent Libyan family, whose assistance probably saved her life.

We are wondering what the reaction in Tripoli will be to the police killings, which were certainly provoked by the mob. The Zavia people are known for their truculence, however, and not popular in Tripoli. A young Libyan said to me today, "Well, you know these Zavia people are always in trouble. They are the Texans of Libya!" President Kennedy's assassination has left its mark.

The King is said to have had a heart attack meanwhile, and to be in Wheelus Field hospital. I doubt it: there are not enough extra police about to suggest this.

When Harry phoned me to say that the town was quiet this morning, I took advantage of the lull to rush in and pick up our Italian journals. Although some streets were littered with stones, all disorder had apparently ceased. Few people were out, and those out were mostly Libyans. I saw many extra police with clubs. After getting the journals, Lena and I drove across the city to see how Galliano's family had fared.

Zia Maria said they had no trouble themselves, as long as they stayed inside the apartment, but there had been pandemonium about them for some days. A gas station at the corner was broken up. We stayed only a few minutes, as we wanted to be off the streets by midday.

Galliano's road in the old end of town ends in a cul de sac and I am never at ease when sitting there in my car, yet I don't dare to leave it parked, unattended. The neighboring Arab kids habitually throw stones near me, pinch the dog as they pass, jump on the rear of the car, and batter the windows, only being diverted from me in order to swing on the tailboard or bumper of other cars that pass. And when I turn my car around to leave, the kids always cluster perilously on it front and back, until in my imagination I feel the crunch of their bones under my wheels.

Today they were unusually intent on annoying me, and just as I got the car successfully turned around and sighed with relief, I glanced ahead to where the road enters the highway and saw that the intersection was completely blocked with a mass of baracan-clad men pouring out from the nearby mosque. This is it! I thought. But I had no choice except to sit there and wait for them to pass, or to do whatever they had a mind to do. After a few minutes I realized with intense relief that I was only watching a funeral cortège!

We returned through town without event. The absolute quiet of the city streets is now almost as alarming as a disturbance.

For several days the town continued to be breathlessly quiet, just as if those rioting mobs had been imaginary. Even the extra police with their wooden bats have disappeared. But there are a number of broken shop windows, and the majority of shops still have their metal shutters closed. The silence of the city is awesome.

Latest rumor is that the King is dead, and his body is being kept in deep freeze at Wheelus. I do not believe it — if only because the police have vanished from the streets.

This rumor very soon reached such proportions, and enlisted such general belief, that the American ambassador finally went to the King's personal representative and told him that he, the ambassador, was being questioned on all sides as to the truth of the rumor. People obstinately, and even indignantly, refused to believe his denial. He suggested that the King should make an appearance in person, or at least give a TV or radio address, to confirm the fact that he was still alive.

It proved impossible, however, to persuade the King to make a personal appearance, something that he abhors doing. He was finally persuaded to make some comments on the radio about irrelevant events. Although his subject matter rather furthered the Alice-in-Wonderland aspect of the local non-news, his speech did serve to resuscitate the King's person in the public mind.

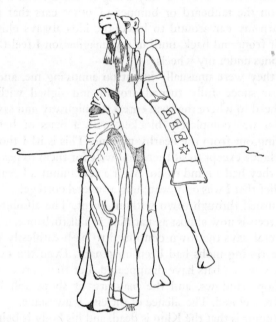

Great Warriors once— The Tuareg.

The Benghazi police officers have not yet been tried. One of them, when he was brought into court to be charged, was kidnaped from his police escort by his fellow tribesmen as they left the court. He was, however, returned after a few hours. A lot of bargaining must have gone on, out on the red Cyrenaican soil!

I think this is the end of the rioting — for this time. The deaths of the school boys in Benghazi undoubtedly brought about a genuine emotional crisis. It was known to the Security Police and the King that this crisis was being taken advantage of by Egyptian agitators and by a revolutionary Libyan group, who very nearly launched the long-talked-about revolution.

But the Tripoli police kept calm and stood firm, and in the end the new Prime Minister, with the new Council of Ministers, pulled its cohorts together, and traded its horses just in time. Meanwhile, we have learned how close revolution may come.

Thus endeth another Ramadan. The peace and joy of Id el-Fitr are with us again. Flotillas of young Libyans, looking in their feast-day garments like brilliant tropical fish, drift along the roads, hand in trusting hand. Allah is on watch Up There; and all is right down here!

The past is forgotten, the stones are swept up, the windshields are mended (government paid!), the police are out of the hospitals, and boys, large and small, are behaving in exemplary fashion.

Maybe it never happened.

43. Two Strong Men

The master of a nation is he who serves it.

Arab Proverb

HERE in Libya, what with Radio Cairo haranguing, thousands of impassioned young Egyptian school teachers ranting, and all channels of publicity eulogizing, it is not surprising that Gamal Abdel Nasser, President of the United Arab Republic, is a hero. Throughout the Arab world, he is the idol of its youth, and the dictator of its politics. And in justice, he deserves it. He has never failed: his image has never cracked.

Here, Nasser's portrait is frequently hung beside that of the Libyan King. The great Egyptian, his magnetic eyes glowing, his white teeth flashing, his tremendous nose overhanging, his heavy jaw jutting belligerently forward, looks to be what he is — a man of driving personality — an easy man to idolize. He makes a strange, vital contrast to the gentle, aristocratic visage of the Libyan King.

In every building and office, airport and coffee shop, in villa and mud hut and tent, deep in the desert, and in every oasis, the King's dignified portrait keeps strange company with Nasser's swamping smile. Nevertheless, the ascetic countenance of Idris, austere, fastidious and patrician, gives an otherworldly impression which is far from justified in this very shrewd diplomat, religious leader, dictator, and king.

It was a surprise to no one when, on United Arab Republic Day, February 22, 1964, Nasser made a florid and fiery speech in Cairo. The day called for fireworks, and Nasser found a popular theme: he said that the foreign bases in Libya were a threat to all Arab peace, and he demanded their immediate liquidation.

Had any other being, human or inhuman, talked like this to Libya, she would have been furious. In fact, she was — but Big Brother Nasser gets by.

Nasser had two talking points. First, he said that foreign bases would attract retaliatory bombing in any war. Second, he said that Libyan bases would be turned against the Arabs in a war with Israel, if the US and Great Britain "continued to support and to assist Israel"! It was easy to ignore the fact that Libyan British bases had already been proved useless against another Arab state during the Suez crisis, when Great Britain, at Libya's request, had inactivated her bases here. But Nasser knew he was singing a sympathetic tune, for no country can possibly like to see foreign soldiers on its soil. Nothing, he said, short of a demand for immediate base liquidation would keep the Arab brothers feeling like brothers!

In summing up what the bases meant to Libya, however, Nasser neglected to include the fact that it was these same foreign bases which had given Libya security all the years of her short life: a) against internal strife, or revolution, and b) against outside covetous eyes of neighbors. Now that Libya is one of the wealthiest of the Arab states, this last reason is especially vital.

Probably the secret of Nasser's demand for base liquidation in Libya is spelled o-i-l. At the end of 1963, Libya, for the first time in her history, had a favorable balance of trade, with more exports to report them imports, thanks to her large oil revenue, which promises to increase in years to come. Although her future oil revenues will make Libya financially independent from her foreign base agreements, they make her need for the guarantee of security for her borders, and for internal calm, greater than ever before.

To understand the base agreements one must go back to 1951 when Mahmud Muntasser was in office for the first time and making Libyan history as the first Prime Minister of the independent Kingdom. Mahmud Muntasser continued in office until April 1954, and during this period he negotiated the British Military Base Agreement under the Treaty of Friendship and Alliance between Great Britain and Libya, which was ultimately signed in 1953. Incidentally, this treaty limited, for the first time since the war, the British forces which had been scattered throughout all Libya during the British military occupation.

By this treaty financial aid was promised to Libya in exchange for the establishment of military bases here, but the treaty was not entirely a matter of money. It was also designed to fortify and protect the independence of the newly emerged kingdom against possible aggression from overneighborly neighbors, and to assist in preserving internal security in a sovereign state which had been synthetically created out of three mutually antagonistic communities, Tripolitania, Cyrenaica and the Fezzan.

Libya's first national problem was to quell the purely provincial ambitions of the three separate but now legally united provinces. Tripolitania, formerly an Italian colony, was considerably advanced and somewhat Europeanized. The Fezzan, which was entirely Sahara, was still under French military administration. Cyrenaica, although superficially Italian-occupied, was more Bedawi than Arab. This province had always been a battleground for its many diverse Bedawi tribes who said of themselves: "We hear without obeying" — and continued to do so.

King Idris, as Emir of Cyrenaica, the one individual with any control over the tribesmen there, had spent twenty-one years in exile in Egypt, waiting for his country to achieve independence. As the vision slowly became a fact, and Libya finally emerged as a nation, there was no other possible contender who could hold the three provinces together — but Idris al-Mahdi al-Senusi, the supreme spiritual leader of all Libyan Moslems. This was an overbearing position which entailed extreme autocratic religious authority, for Islam is a way of secular life, as well as spiritual. Thus King Idris epitomized every unleashed force in Libya, both spiritual and material, a combination of powers which is the basic secret of Islamic potency.

The history of the American Air Base Agreement, by which Wheelus Field is maintained in Libya as the largest US air base outside of the United States, ties in indirectly with the British agreement. The British, while still engaged in the Second World War and occupying Libyan territory, had granted to their ally, the United

States, the right to use a military air base near Tripoli at Mellaha, which later became the site of Wheelus Field.

After the war's end, when British military authority was transferred to an idependent Libyan nation, the United States, because of the Soviet threat to Tripolitania, asked Libya for a continuation of the base agreement. Negotiations for the US treaty were conducted for Libya by Prime Minister Muntasser, at the same time as negotiations for the British treaty, but the Libyan-American treaty was not concluded until 1954, under Ben Halim, the second Libyan prime minister. In exchange for air base rights, this treaty pledged the US to give financial assistance to Libya for the next eighteen years, or until 1972. Its existence also added to the internal and external security of Libya. Such, in brief, were the British and American base agreements with Libya, which in 1964 were under threat of being liquidated and abolished by the Libyan government, under pressure from Egypt.

At various times the British and US military families have each occupied about a thousand houses and apartments in Tripoli. British bases employed several thousand Libyan civilian employees, and the US base employed as many more. In addition, a large number of Libyan boys and young men are employed in domestic service with British and US base families.

Harry's Libyan driver, Hammad, made a practical comment on the proposed abolition of the bases here. Hammad is the father of seven, and a taxi driver after office hours. Hammad simply says, "Who gives me eat, he my father! I want the bases to stay!"

United Arab Republic Day, the so-called sixth anniversary of Egypt's union with Syria, tactfully disregarded the fact that for the last three years Syria had been *dis*-united from Egypt. With this beam in its own eye, the UAR was delighted to attack the mote in the eye of Libya, and demand her liquidation of foreign bases. Nasser's speech came to Libya over Radio Cairo, and instantly aroused two slices of Libyan population, the young men, and the Libyan politicians, who are always ready to exploit the moment. Overnight, there sprang up here a "popular demand" for immediate liquidation of the bases.

The local Arab press, generally severely censored, was for this event quite unbridled, and emitted hysterical screams. "The foreign oppressors, exploiters, abusers, war mongers, bullies, rapists — *get out!*"

Such was the popular outcry. But amongst our personal Libyan friends, we found none to say quite the same. In contacts with ministers and permanent secretaries, Harry found no one ranting. It is true that every Libyan would be happy (and so, I am certain, would every American in the same situation) *not* to see foreign soldiers on his soil — but informed opinions here appreciated the stability that the base treaties had given to Libya. Whether she could hold her own entirely by herself was a matter for hope as much as for credence.

Meanwhile, temperatures rose or cooled off as fanned or neglected by Cairo and her cohorts, until the Libyan parliament met in the summer capital of el Beida. Here the "Five Dissident Deputies," as they were called, a political lobby, became violently active in carrying the cause of liquidation into parliament. Here for two days, the case was hotly debated, although what was said and by whom will probably never be known in the Western world. It is generally believed that the cabinet and the more responsible representatives in both the Senate and the House had no wish to demand immediate liquidation of the bases, but that they did not dare to take a public stand for a middle way in this country which, as a monarchy, is an unprotected target for new-thought Arab revolutions. In the face of the propagandistic demands of Nasser, it could easily be made to seem that a vote against immediate liquidation of bases was a vote to betray Arab brotherhood.

Nevertheless, Prime Minister Muntasser himself, courageously and without thought for his own popularity, made two separate protests against demands for immediate liquidation. Each time he proposed to compromise with a more diplomatic undertaking to "open negotiations to discuss the future of the bases." But this did not satisfy the politicians. A unanimous vote was demanded, and executed, in both House and Senate, to force the government to ask for "immediate liquidation" of the bases. At the same time, the houses presented an ultimatum to the government: the government could have one to three months in which to complete the demands for liquidation of the bases. After this, the House would act on its own. What an ultimatum to hand to a king! After this action, the Prime Minister agreed to ask for immediate consideration of liquidation.

These activities took place at el Beida, now the summer capital of Libya, which was until a few years ago a tiny village scarcely noticeable as one drove by on the road. In 1946 this village had been the scene of a remarkable spectacle when Idris, who was still domiciled in Egypt where he was carrying on diplomatic bargaining with the British for Cyrenaica's complete independence as an emirate, had returned to el Beida for a short visit. As soon as his arrival was known, his small limestone villa was immediately surrounded by clamoring, pleading Cyrenaican tribal chiefs who begged him to remain in Cyrenaica as their leader, and never return to Egypt. Idris, however, who was already an artful dealer in politics, returned to Egypt to strengthen his bargaining hand with the Allies. When in 1947 he came back to Cyrenaica as a resident, it was only after assurance by Great Britain that Cyrenaica should have its independence. In 1949 Cyrenaica became a fully independent emirate with Idris as emir, and this was the first step towards independence for the whole of Libya.

Stirrings of nationalism were instantly seething in favor of unity with Tripolitania, and independence for the combine of Cyrenaica-Tripolitania. At the same time the Fezzan, still under French rule, began to bubble with rebellion, and local patriots there secretly started to negotiate with the Cyrenaica-Tripolitania combine for a three-province federated independent state. In due time, after passing through the meat grinder of the United Nations trusteeship, and escaping from the Circe of Soviet wooing, the independent Kingdom of Libya emerged. Independence was declared on December 24, 1951.

On March 23, 1952, Idris as King took the constitutional oath of loyalty to the independent Kingdom of Libya.

Idris has always been an enlightened monarch, but he is also very much an Oriental potentate. His consciousness of his own power and rightness show in his every utterance. He is The Power in

Libya, in spite of his age and frail physical being, for both by his doctrine and by his desert-wide Senusi missionary heritage he is the Strong Man here. His character is unassailable, and his nature is incorruptible — except by such bargainings as might benefit his country, for he is completely devoted to the concept of national Libya.

Looking back over the last twenty years, one sees this one man as the diviner, creator, life force, and builder of the independence of Libya. It is accepted by all that no individual but Idris, who rules as Moslem chieftain, tribesman, and King, could have held the three provinces together. But today, a few modern young men with revolutionary ideas would like to step in and utilize for other purposes the incipient unity which Idris has brought to his country. The King, however, has a subtle political sense which makes him difficult to outmaneuver — when, in addition, he symbolizes the complete devotion of the Libyan tribesmen.

The existence of Libya with continuing dignity, with growing vitality, self-respect, and increasing self-confidence, is a tribute to the force of this Sahara personality. His gift to Libya today is his survival.

In the light of the recent discovery by Libyan security police of a revolutionary plot to change the Kingdom of Libya into a republic, with a view to uniting it with Egypt, it is not surprising that the sagacious patriot King Idris was alert to tones of criticism. He undoubtedly experienced severe twinges of annoyance when he listened to the rabid orations in the parliament against foreign military bases. After several days of fanatical ranting, with no one speaking truth or common sense except the Prime Minister, the King, who has a reputation for keeping his promises, is reported to have called his cabinet to him and spoken with heat:

"This country doesn't deserve to have a good ruler, or a decent government! This criticism includes also the House of Senusi [the King's own tribe]! I have had enough of it! I am tired to death of all this foolishness! I am going to abdicate!" He is then quoted as adding tactfully, "For reasons of health, and old age!"

His Majesty made no comment about not caring to be dicated to by Brother Nasser, nor about internal subversive activities, but the King is well known to be patriotically very jealous of Libya's national prerogatives. Immediately after his decisive statement, he gathered the members of the Royal Household about him, piled them into the assembled royal motorcars, and they rolled out of Beida headed for Tobruk, the seat of his best-loved dwelling, the Dar-es Salam (Abode of Peace) Palace.

How much of the King's action was bluff, how much was patience tried too far, how much political intuition and sophisticated knowledge of his tribesmen, and how much a burning necessity for furious action on the part of a man who has for many years controlled his furies — we will never know. For in very fact, we *are* faced with a King who *is* old and tired . . .

Tobruk is a small seaside village about fifty miles from the Egyptian border, and once the scene of the Second World War's most bloody North African battles, and now chiefly known for being the favorite residence of the King. Within a few hours the tiny village teemed and bulged with tribesmen from all over Cyrenaica, and visiting VIPs brought by chartered plane from Tripolitania and the Fezzan. Soon every tiny hotel, rooming house, shack, restaurant, and school was filled to bursting with humanity, and thousands of people slept in their motorcars or on the Cyrenaican soil outside the Palace Royal, where they waited anxiously hoping to hear that the rumors of the King's abdication were false. Or, if true, to try to persuade the King to reconsider.

Meanwhile, the King and his household move hastily out of his palace home into his own small, privately owned residence nearby, Bab ez Zeytun. This move gives even greater credence to the reports that he has abdicated. Now for several days, the people of Cyrenaica believe that they are truly without a chief of state. Possibly the country itself is saved from active violence by the very thing I often deplore — news censorship — which prevents the abdication gesture from being known throughout the country until after the crisis.

Saturday morning, following the King's hasty exit from the capital, the Prime Minister, accompanied by the cabinet, the leaders of the Army and the Security Force, and practically everybody of any importance in parliament, arrives in a madly careening motorcade of cars at the palace gates, and thence to the doors of the cottage itself. Soon it is known that a critical conference is in session.

Meanwhile, always-growing crowds of Libyans — city folk, desert people, nomads, shepherds, farmers, old men and young, clad in baracan or in trousers — are massing outside both the palace and the cottage, where the King is in reality staying, shouting out pledges of their allegiance to the King, mixing their loyal promises with supplications not to abdicate, and prayers to Allah to preserve the King. Never before in the history of Libya has such a demonstration of devotion and loyalty been given to any human being.

We all have in us greater strength than we know. We all have a capacity beyond the physical which seems born to us on the wings of angels, when we call to our God for help. When a whole nation prays to Allah, the force of the prayers must shake heaven and earth.

King Idris I
From an official likeness.

Perhaps, in the great tradition, King Idris also prayed, "Take this cup from me," and in the reverberations of his people's prayers he finds his answer. There on his native steppe, he does something this night that he has almost never done before — he makes a personal appearance before his massed countrymen. He stills the wild roars of the cheering crowds with a slight gesture of his uplifted hands, as he stands before them, the symbol of their religion, their tribal brotherhood and their Sahara land.

"Fellow citizens and followers of Islam," he speaks. "My only concern is for you, my people. It had been my intention to abdicate the throne immediately — because of my ill health and old age, for I had feared that I was unable to give you complete service. However," he pauses and looks sternly out at them, before he adds the truly kingly touch, "however, it is not and never was because We are at odds with Our government. Our government is loyal to Us . . . and had We thought otherwise, We would have dismissed it! Our Chamber of Deputies is likewise loyal . . . and had We thought otherwise, We would have dissolved it!"

It is, he assures them again, only his old age which makes him seek rest. Nevertheless now, after seeing this tremendous demonstration of the people's loyalty, affection, and intense desire for him to remain as King, he has changed his mind. He has decided to remain on the throne, regardless of his age and tiredness, and he promises them now to dedicate the remaining years of his life to them.

The King's dignified statement is made in a clear, decisive voice. This is not oratory; these are the words of a brave and very astute old patriot who offers himself, his soul and body, to the service of his land. He makes no mention of the heir apparent, Prince Hasan al-Rida.

A great sigh of relief passes through the crowd — Hamdu li'llah! Hamdu li'llah! The will of Allah is done! The men of the desert, of the scorching winds and the desiccated crops and the hungry flocks, know only one way to meet this; now thousands of Arab throats, raw and hoarse with emotion, give thunderous thanks to Allah, Lord of the Worlds, the Compassionate, the Beneficent, the Merciful, who has answered their prayers.

This night, Radio Cairo is silenced.

And the military bases? They are still in Libya — awaiting another UAR anniversary speech, I expect.

44. Prosperity in Barbary

It was Allah the Compassionate who in eons past endowed the Libyan desert with its buried sea sediments. Today, these are the priceless sources of Libyan oil.

Now the problem of mere survival, which has been the antagonist of this land through all history, is to be removed from Libya between dusk and dawn. Libyans who have held their heads high on crusts, have fought their battles barefoot, have remembered their Prophet, and worshiped Allah in rags in the desert, are now to become fabulously rich overnight.

Allah is All, but money helps when rightly used. Can they use it? Can Libyans survive prosperity? They are making a colossal effort.

The Libyan oil story is fantastic. Granted that Allah began it eons ago, man first looked with intensive interest at the Libyan desert in 1947 — and then passed on. It wasn't until 1955, after oil had been found in the Algerian Sahara, that oil exploration in Libya began in earnest.

Just four years later, in 1959, Esso Libya struck a prodigious oil flow at Bir Zelten in the Sirtic Desert, and from this time on new companies arrived, explored, drilled, and made new strikes. Great fortunes for Libya were now being safely predicted, and her future was written anew.

With the opening of the Marsa el Brega oil pipeline, 104 miles long, in the Sirtic Desert, in October 1961, the first crude oil started to flow from the Libyan desert to foreign markets, and the dream of riches became a reality. From being a chronic debtor, Libya will soon be fabulously wealthy in cash. In February 1965, Libya approved the construction of a fifth oil pipeline. When all pipelines are working, she will have a capacity for daily crude oil export of two and a half million barrels.

Here today everybody participates in future great expectations. Hotels are always full, and new ones are being built, and modern office buildings are going up for oil company occupation. New houses and apartments go up, rents, food prices and wages go up. City populations increase, and oases are partially deserted, and gardens go untended.

With hearty-eating oil families and foreigners about, Libya does not begin to produce enough meat or vegetables to feed them; in fact, with an increasing demand for food, Libya is now producing decreasing food supplies because her shepherds and farmers wish to be oil men! Highly taxed foodstuffs are imported profitably for foreign tastes. Oil machinery, pipes, and oil company supplies are coming in, and businesses are being built on their sales and distribution. Fortunes are being made on desert trucking, the trucks meanwhile tearing the roads to ribbons, and making highway driving a peril. Texas accents are everyplace. The majority of foreigners now are only interested in bringing their way of life to Libya, rather than in seeing Libya's life.

King Idris and the Libyan government, which changes overnight, showing an instability which is the greatest detrimental factor in a promising picture, have taken a firm stand, in principle at least. Seventy per cent of the oil income,* they promise, is to be spent on a long-range national development program. The King pledges that the people must benefit. As oil employment dwindles, there must be other employment ready for the people. But other employment requires the development of new skills among the Libyans, and this takes time. Nevertheless, the first step is taken in that the King and the government (but which government?) have dedicated the money to the people. It only remains for the people to get it!

Harry, also, is involved in this wave of anticipated prosperity. The Five Year Plan for the national spending of millions is underway. The planners consist of ministers of state, permanent secretaries, and

* The oil agreement is for a fifty-fifty division of future profits, in addition to high royalties.

their various advisers, of which latter Harry is one. The fact that he has traveled all over Libya, border to border, as few Libyans have, gives him insight now into the country's problems, and gives his advice considerable weight. Meetings take place three times a week and last for several hours at least. After each one Harry comes home in a state of controlled insanity. The planners have now been at work for many months, and the plan is about ready. There is little choice in what to develop as every department needs to be developed: health, education, roads, transport, new industries, agriculture, forestry, electrical power, tourist trade; every aspect of Libyan life needs assistance.

Harry foresees that by the time the plan is submitted to the parliament, government will fall again, and the incoming ministers will demand a new plan. The new plan will have to be approximately the same, as the same needs continue, but each government wishes to appear to be responsible for producing a plan, even if it is identical. By this time the new government will fall, and the incoming one will demand another plan, and so on . . .

Meanwhile, Harry comes home late every night in a frustrated frenzy, much aggravated by heartburn from strong Libyan tea. Still, he feels that the meetings are successful because they are forcing the planners to study the needs of the country, and to formulate their own ideas. Indigestible though the tea may be, verbose though the discussions, inexhaustible though the arguments, the fact is that the end result is going to be a very sound Five Year Plan. The problem is to keep a government in office long enough to get the plan passed and pursued.

There is another danger. Libyans are alerted now to being rich. Yet when each man feels in his pocket, he still finds no money; he is rich, and he continues to be undernourished and poorly dressed; he is rich, while Bidonvilles grow larger, oasis gardens die without water, dates are not picked, and wells are not cleaned. He is rich, but he must work harder, for government working hours are lengthened.

So where is this money? In the pants pockets of the government? So throw out the government, and bring in another one that will put a pack of cigarettes in every pocket, Kitty-Kolas in the well, a TV set in every house and tent, and a beautiful blonde in every bed, while everybody spends his unearned profits!

Giorgimpopoli is no longer a ghetto, but a suburban shopping center, USA.

American housewives are busy all about me doing their housework in flowered slacks, cerise pants, cotton breeches, Bermuda shorts, striped pajamas, and fluttering housecoats, with hair in curlers and faces not yet applied, but with movements sure and purposeful.

Their children are off to school, and the object is to get the housework under control and be on the road by nine o'clock, their infants with them, babies of every age and shape, in strollers, carriers, cots, shoulder slings and bread baskets, and under their arms. By nine-thirty at worst, the trousered Amazons, hair still in curlers, are on the prowl — for a cup of coffee, a word of advice either given or taken, a ration of gossip exchanged, a companion for shopping, a sick person to take to the doctor, for something to do for someone, or someone to do something for them. Either relationship is equally welcome if it saves them from being alone. These are the kindest hearts in the world, and the most gregarious. The American housewife has tremendous talents: she can bake her own bread, make her own clothes, play poker, paint houses, give parties, attend lectures; she can do everything — except stay at home alone.

Giorgimpopoli shopkeepers do their best to make us all happy here. There are two supermarkets now with frozen foods, three fresh meat butcher shops, a fish and poultry shop, four vegetable merchants, three beauty shops, two notions stores, a branch post office, three gas filling stations, and two hamburger stands. They all flourish. Even as the oil begins to flow from the desert sands, several thousand oil technicians and people of allied professions and their families are in the land, and eating, drinking, living heartily. Happy days are here for the shopkeepers of Giorgimpopoli.

Giorgimpopoli is no longer exclusively American, for Libyan families occupy a number of houses which are rented by the government and allocated to its senior officers. But the extra suburban living space at which Americans rejoice is not welcome to the secluded

Libyan woman. Chained to her house, she prefers it to be in a crowded vicinity where other Libyan wives are close to her. This is especially true now that there is a gradual relaxation of tradition, and more fortunate Libyan wives are sometimes permitted to visit nearby friends.

Much Giorgimpopoli land is now Libyan owned; although foreign owned land has not been confiscated, it may only be sold to Libyans. The Libyan landholder builds his houses to rent to foreigners, but seldom to live in himself. He builds without cash, still living, as he has done for decades, on next month's credit. Only his credit is bigger now that prosperity is near, so he lives better!

"An hour or two from Tripoli, near Gargaresh, are curious caves which might once have sheltered an army of Troglodytes. Camels were decidedly the best conveyance to go by, but one time we had excellent donkeys for the trip . . ."

This is a description of what is now Giorgimpopoli, written about 1905 by an American woman, Mabel Loomis Todd, in *Tripoli the Mysterious.*

In Mabel's day there was no road to the Giorgimpopoli area (known then as Gargaresh). The route Mabel followed was the sands of the Tripoli shoreline, wandering among the tombs of Moslem holy men, where her camel lazily picked his way. She was able to pluck twenty-six different kinds of wild flowers en route, mounting and remounting the camel each time, no doubt!

She passed an ancient, crumbling Turkish fort still occupied by bored Turkish soldiers with faded sashes tied over their rags, and she studied with interest a pre-Moslem ruin, dating back to the days of Leo Africanus, which lay quietly disintegrating in the blazing sun. Tripoli itself, she said, was a city devoid of tourists!

Mabel came to Libya with her astronomer husband to study the total eclipse of the sun in 1900, and again in 1905. Their telescopes were set up on the British consulate roof terrace in the medina inside the city walls. This consulate building, constructed in 1744, still exists today as medina housing.

Mabel loved Tripoli extravagantly. She exulted in its Oriental enchantment, in the Roman arches and ruins, the Moslem funerals and

Murzuk — The old Turkish fort

weddings, the mosques and minarets, the caravans, the desert wilderness, the scorching heat of the sun, the "limpid purity" of the days, the black, star-shining nights, in everything that made it different from her home in Massachusetts. At the end of her stay she wrote of Tripoli, "It did remain quiescent in the sense of world progress, but its charm . . . was never to be resisted. A city of enchantment, white as dreams of Paradise."

Mabel dear, I love you!

Tell me, Mabel, did you suffer from lack of frozen pork chops? From no ice cream? No toilet paper? No fresh milk? No electric lights? No white bread? Did you suffer when you had to eat local lamb, kus kus, and dates? When you rode a camel instead of a taxi? Did you mope for your exile to end? And pine for your civilized friends? Did you long to go back to "God's country," and communicate again with God, instead of His local representative, Allah?

Or did you, as I will soon, look back with deepest love to the spicy shores of Araby the Blest?

Nevertheless, there are little nuisances in modern Tripoli life which Mabel didn't have to put up with.

I used to be able to drive to the large central market in Tripoli, and park my car in front. Today, I must drive around several square blocks many times to find space.

A few days ago Lena and I returned from market to my car, and as I slid into the driver's seat, I saw in my rear-view mirror a horse in my back seat, his amiable, melancholy face peering gently at me over my shoulder. Investigation proved that the horse was not actually in the back seat, but had been driven so close to my small car that his chest rested on the trunk while his nose rubbed the rear window and his breath fogged it. A car was parked in front of me, bumper to bumper, and I had no way out.

I was not surprised to see that the horse belonged to a dray which belonged to an Arab driver who stood nearby with a group of other drivers laughing heartily at my predicament. I asked the driver to move the horse, but this amused him even more, as he had placed the horse there on purpose. This is a favorite spot for horse-drawn drays which require double car space, as the drivers are always hoping that some foreign housewife, when parking her car, will become impatient and nick the horse, and the driver can claim compensation. Most foreign drivers will settle any claim on the spot sooner than spend time in court where the burden of proof is on the foreigner.

I was determined not to start my car until I had space between the horse and myself. I liked the horse, whose expression of disillusioned resignation must have been like my own that day, and I didn't reckon to buy either a leg or a head of him at a high price. I sat and waited.

Lena is not one to sit and wait — no Italian is. She jumped out of the car, grabbed the horse's head and backed him and the dray out into the middle of the main street, flouncing her skirts and talking fluent Arabic as she did so.

The drivers understood her action perfectly; she had won. If they saw her again, they'd give her a space. They never would have understood my sitting and waiting.

Many bicycles in Tripoli are in a dilapidated state. All that their owners pray for is a touch from a foreigner's car that will collapse them.

I saw the spindly, bread-carrying tricycle parked in front of my car, at right angles, but I thought I could pull safely out. Its owner had double-parked it in my meter space and disappeared. I'm sure I scarcely touched his front wheel, for I heard no noise — until a passing Arab shouted at me. Then I stopped the car and got out to look; I saw to my disgust that the wire network of the front tricycle wheel was completely mangled.

While staring at the wheel with annoyance, I was promptly surrounded by a group of Libyans who looked at me reproachfully and angrily, while one dashed off to find the owner. A miserable little man turned up and started to cry. He was backed up in principle by all the onlookers, who joined in a tremendous powwow in Arabic, and those who where not ready for tears were growing indignant. It was a bad time in Tripoli then, as the young men were proving their democracy with riots, and I could feel their quickly aroused sentiments against me.

At last one of the young men said to me in English, "He wants you to buy him a new tricycle. You have broken his."

"I won't buy him a new tricycle. That one wheel can be fixed," I said as a bargaining stand, but with little hope.

Everybody studied the broken wheel again, and the conversation grew hotter and louder, while the owner continued to weep and shake his head. Now the young man repeated in English, "He wants a new tricycle!"

"No," I said firmly, "I will not buy him a new tricycle — maybe a new wheel, though. But never mind, I think I call a policeman, because he should not park double in my parking space."

Another conference, and then, "He says if you buy him a new wheel, and pay him for this day's work which he must miss, that is O.K. Is better for you, too. If police come, it just makes more trouble."

I knew he was right. I settled immediately for the cost of the wheel, twelve dollars, and two dollars for the day's work. The sight of cash changing hands reversed the entire temper of the crowd. They were happy then, and they all came over to my side; the capitalist had been bled, and the poor man had been fed! The little fellow dried his tears and trundled his tricycle away, and I drove off amid everybody's friendly waves and cheers.

To me, who remembers the old days, the city of Tripoli now bulges with foreign intruders. Yet, here is the latest count: 170,000 Libyans, 27,000 Italians, 6000 Jews and 5000 "others." The "others" are the intruders, the latest come.

Here jewel shops blaze. There are green emeralds, fiery rubies, and dazzling diamonds in Neechamal's huge bazaar windows, and in Santanucita's tiny jewel shop there are treasures in gold and jade. In Buoncorso's small popular arcade corner hides a fortune in high carat gold, while yellow gold bangles and long dangling gold chains line the lanes of the suk.

The prosperous modern shopping district is gay and tempting with imports from Italy, France, England and West Germany, and a fortune may be spent on toilet goods, female beautifiers, lingerie, gowns and shoes. Along the arcade-covered walks stroll individuals of every faith, color, race, and political conviction. Sidewalk cafés are crowded with a galaxy of races, and mostly men, who sip espressos, suck sweet lemon sodas, dandle cigarettes between fingers which glint with heavy rings, and ogle svelte signorinas who saunter smartly by.

The essence of Tripoli is unchanged; it is still the Tripolino, a man who feels himself more a part of his city than of his native land. He is a town man, and a Mediterranean. He likes his comforts and his own form of civilized living which his womenfolk, who have spoiled him outrageously all his life, see to it that he to some extent has, no matter how poor he may be.

For in his home he is king. All his life there has been a woman waiting on him, and for him. As a baby, his mother adored his masculinity, and his sisters kissed, toted and overfed him; as a boy he ruled the roost; as an adolescent he may have had conflicts with Papa but mother and sisters were always near to soothe; as a young married man, his wife took over the spoiling, under mother's instructions. Now as a successful man-about-Tripoli he is self-confident, sophisticated, a little lazy, suave, often good-looking, usually now well-groomed, and always very susceptible to good-looking girls of all races. He has in addition an admirable last-ditch courage, a Boccaccian sense of humor, natural gaiety and exceptional charm.

The female Tripolino fills a different role in life, and has a different aspect. Beauty is hers, unseen by the world though she is, and feminine submissiveness. Not Asian submissiveness, but a wily Arab one: if pushed too far she has her own weapons for boudoir use — sobbing and screaming and all states of hysteria, simulated pregnancies, dietetic whims and fancies, deliberate neglect of children, and the ultimate method of defense and revenge in the formula of *A Thousand Nights and a Night* — just a little something popped into hubby's tea.

She is excluded from mixed social life, yet she knows better what goes on there than her husband does (he claims!). She has very limited rights, but manages quite frequently to get her own way by making the alternative completely unbearable. Her tears are her natural weapon, and she has an unlimited supply.

She isn't expected to use her mind, nor powers of reason, but experience shows that she has both. Her latent possibilities command respect, and possibly apprehension on the part of her men, who see that the old status is changing.

This is Tripoli, the city of hidden squalor, unknown wealth, and endless promise.

Today, the educated adult Libyan is self-critical and ambitious. First of all, he sees that there is work to do, and that in order to accomplish it, Libyans must work harder.

The government workday has been increased from six hours to eight hours. The increase in work hours was preceded by a substantial salary increase.

Today, there *is* an educated Libyan. In 1951 there was no educated class.

Now, about seventy per cent of Libyan primary age children of both sexes attend primary schools, a high attendance percentage for a developing country.

Libyan public school education provides for six years of primary instruction, from the ages of six to twelve; three years of preparatory school, from twelve to fifteen years; and three years of secondary school, from fifteen to eighteen years. There is a College of Advanced Technology for young men, a Teachers Training School for young women, and the University of Libya which is open to both sexes. There is the Islamic Arts and Crafts School with two hundred students, mostly orphans. There are a large number of adult education classes all over the country.

There is an excellent School of Nursing for Women in Tripoli which graduates fully qualified nurses, but its students are almost exclusively of Fezzani parentage. In the Libyan Arab point of view nursing is "dirty work," and not suitable for an Arab girl; to study this profession would ruin her chances for marriage.

The greatest educational problem is the lack of trained Libyan teachers. Except for the primary schools, almost all the teachers are Egyptian. This is because 1) Egyptians are Arabic speaking, and Moslems, and 2) Nasser is content to rent his teachers to Libya for the sake of their propaganda value and political influence. In the university, too, the professors and teachers are non-Libyan and largely Egyptian.

The University of Libya is unique. It grants free tuition, free maintenance, free books, and in addition gives a special monthly allowance to every enrolled student, sixty-six dollars a month to a student living outside his home, and thirty dollars monthly to a student at home. I have never before heard of a university which not only supports its students, but also pays them wages for attending — *when* they attend! For in spite of the apparent bed of roses on which the students lie, they go on strike for bigger allowances, on strike in protest against their teachers' severities, against their teachers' personalities, on strike to show their political sympathies, and on strike for shorter hours. Literally, they refuse to let the government support and educate them, except on their own terms — an odd concept of a dedicated student.

Libya is to some extent the creation of the United Nations, and this organization is correct in feeling an obligation to the country. Yet I see in my memory a long procession of UN Technical Experts, at intervals arriving optimistically — and at intervals departing pessimistically, disappointed because they have been unable to accomplish what they in their expertise had hoped.

I think the only fault lies in the past, and every year of education is lessening it. One cannot step from primary school into a doctorate.

A modest forest policy is now accepted by the government in principle; in fact, it has been accepted by government after government, as they fly by in the night! The problem is to stabilize a government long enough to get the policy supported by legislation.

Tribal lands claims continue to be an obstinate problem, and one which all tribal countries have: there is good reason why the adjective "dissident" is almost invariably connected with tribesmen! Today a team of eight experienced advisers is at work in an attempt to bring about a settlement of tribal claims so that a survey may be completed. Meanwhile, time itself is stengthening Libyan national loyalties, which must ultimately supersede tribal ones if the nation is to continue. Nine years ago Libyans themselves spoke with doubt of the survival as a nation of the three provinces; today, they speak with determination that the nation shall survive.

The national government now has a forest department staffed with some enthusiastic, well-trained men. The provincial departments have been amalgamated under the national one, and a singularity of purpose has developed.

The Sahara is not yet stopped on its seaward march — but its advance has been greatly slowed. This is perhaps the greatest single Libyan step forward. A large amount of dune fixation is being done in all areas, and increased Libyan wealth will be of great help here.

At least eight million seedlings, mostly eucalyptus because they best survive the climate and the aridity, are now being planted every year for permanent forests, dune stabilization, and for firewood.

About now, as I round up steps forward, Harry always says, "No thanks to me!" — which I quote, without crediting.

Nine years ago Harry complained at not finding enough interested Libyans to whom to give advice. Today they come to him and ask for advice, and are well enough informed to have an opinion, and sometimes to argue about it.

Next to the need for teachers, the most acute shortage in Libya is that of qualified artisans, and skilled agricultural workers. In the education plan, these should ideally receive six to nine years of general education, followed by at least two years, preferably four, of specialized training.

A good civil service is not a beanstalk which sprouts overnight. I remember hearing the Libyan civil service described by two ministers of state in the following terms, when I first came to Libya.

One said, "Our civil service takes care of the heroes of the Resistance!"

The other one said, "In Great Britain you maintain a welfare state, with the dole, and old age benefits. Here we have only the civil service!" It is safe to say notable progress has now been made away from those two concepts.

For a country of only one and a half million persons, Libya has a noticeably elaborate and expensive system of government. Until April 1963, Libya was a federation of three provinces, with a fully developed federal form of government, and in addition three separate provincial governments, each one of which was a duplicate of the federal government. This was a costly and controversial machine. The provincial governments were autonomous, and spent their energies on a) unnecessarily duplicating the decisions of the federal government, or b) defiantly nullifying them, or c) ignoring them.

In April 1963, a bill was approved by the houses of parliament to terminate the federal form of government, and to make Libya "an hereditary monarchical State with a representative government." The system of provinces was abolished, and the Kingdom was divided into ten administrative districts.

Despite the considerable administrative simplification which this change brought, the government of Libya is still the most costly in the world, per capita of population. There is a Prime Minister, with fifteen ministries, with many separate departments under each one. Little attempt is made to appoint ministers to work which they understand, or in which they have experience, as the appointments are usually political rewards. When a minister is once "in," he joins the Mad Hatter's tea party where every so often everybody moves up one place. Ministers are constantly being reshuffled and turning up in new offices, behind new signs, which the minister himself has to hurry out and read before he knows what he is representing, and what hat to put on.

The maintenance of two official capital cities, and a third one, el Beida, which the King favors and hopes will become the permanent capital, is both costly and inefficient. The transportation of government files and personnel with their belongings is expensive, and weeks of work time are wasted with each move.

In the Arab tradition each individual family, or the tribe, is considered responsible for giving assistance to its own needy ones, an obligation which in the West is allocated to organized charity and social welfare. Libya, however, seems to have acknowledged a social conscience as well, as more than fifty thousand persons a year here receive assistance from social welfare.

Libya is the only country in the world which financially assists its people to make a pilgrimage to Mecca. This is a hard trip, and costly, and it is the goal of every devout Moslem. Many go more than once, as each trip adds status, both religious and social, to the pilgrim. Old men spend a life's savings to go, and young men indebt themselves for life to make the Hajj. Many old people die on the homeward journey, fulfilled and happy, and ready to enter directly into Paradise. Women also may go. Libya awards a considerable number of free tickets to those who are considered most worthy. I have heard it said by an official who had to do with awarding the tickets that numbers of would-be pilgrims gathered nightly outside his house, weeping and begging for tickets.

Libya now has a nationwide school feeding program to feed 180,000 school children, supplying one supplementary free meal every day. This is paid for by an additional five per cent customs duty on Libya's imports.

It is my belief that Libya needs her womanpower even more than she needs UN experts, or gushing oil. I especially emphasize the vital need of Libya to exploit her untouched asset, the women, because in Libya the females are usually easier to teach than are the men and boys. I have been told this repeatedly by foreign male teachers who say that in general the girls learn more quickly than the boys simply because they do not suffer with the need to always prove themselves right — often an obsessive need of the young Libyan male. He will argue tirelessly on the very subject the teacher is teaching, to try to prove to the teacher that he, the student, knows more about it than the teacher. As he starts with the premise that he knows everything he often finds it difficult to learn. The girls, however, have no false face to preserve, and are quick and anxious to learn.

If one were to judge entirely by Libyan news items, one might visualize Libyan women as making a sudden spectacular leap forward. For instance, one reads that in 1964 Libyan women were given the vote. Just how they will get to the polls, and how many will actually vote, we shall see. The Libyan woman has already been the subject matter of a postage stamp, although pictured still half-blinded in her baracan. The police force, I have also read in the news, is now hoping to have women members.

A few years ago lectures were given in the United States by a Libyan, Mrs. Mohedin Fekini, on "The Progress of Libyan Women." Mrs. Fekini spent some years in the United States as the wife of the Libyan ambassador to the United States, who was at the time Libya's permanent representative to the United Nations. Mrs. Fekini was extremely active on the UN women's committees. She and her husband returned to Libya in 1963 when Mr. Fekini became the sixth Libyan Prime Minister. Mrs. Fekini sponsored a previously unheard of action here when she appeared in public and without a veil, to act as her husband's hostess for all social events while he was in office.

I know one young Libyan woman (of Libyanized Jordanian parents) who is studying to be a lawyer, and another one of like parentage who is hoping to become a doctor. The new principalship of the Teachers Training School, a position which was held for years by an excellent Egyptian headmistress, is now filled by a brilliant young Libyan woman.

A child welfare clinic at Suk el Juma in Tripoli is a center for training young Libyan women in child welfare, in order to send them to other centers, sixty of which are being established in Libya.

There are three women's clubs in Tripoli, one of which is a cultural club. The members of the club, mostly schoolteachers, meet monthly, arriving in baracans and veils, which they hastily discard.

Both the International Girl Guides and the Boy Scouts are extremely popular here, and both have large bodies of enthusiastic Libyan members. The Scouts appear regularly in uniform to assist police in traffic control work on parade days.

So there is a change. It is nothing dramatic, except in a few individual cases. Perhaps it really depends on the individual, as it did in the case of Najia . . .

I recognized her immediately when she sat down beside me in the hairdresser's; she was the first Libyan airlines hostess, and the only one for over a year. I had often watched her ushering groups of passengers to the planes with all the jauntiness of one born to the job. She had a true hostess' figure, and looked better than neat in her Prussian blue suit, short skirt drawn tightly across her gyrating bottom, eyes rolling mischievously, and hair piled high in Italian style. She was evidently a ground hostess, as I always saw her at the airport.

Today she chatters in Italian to the hairdresser, an old-timer here who speaks **excellent** Arabic — but she chooses to speak Italian. He is giving her the works in hair improvement — a shampoo, a bleach, a henna tint, then a hair straightener to get the kink out, and now at last a back-combing, and the bird's nest pile-up.

She and I have been smiling at each other in the mirror which we face, as I think she recognizes me from my frequent visits to the airport.

"I hear the plane could not come in yesterday because of the ghibli," I comment.

"Yesterday was very bad, Signora. The planes returned to Malta."

"Do you like your work at the airport?"

"Oh, yes, very nice. But I like to go in the air, now. Next week perhaps I go to Rome."

"You'll like Rome, I'm sure. All Libyans do. Is your home in Tripoli?"

"My mama and papa are from Fezzan, but I live in Tripoli now."

"How did you happen to start this work as air hostess?"

"My boyfriend works at the airport. He tells me that Libiavia wants a Libyan girl to learn hostess work."

The following week we meet on Freedom Street. As always, she is outstanding because of her slender figure, her stylish hairdo, her happy air of cheerfulness and vitality, the bright smile on her dark-skinned face. This day she is stomping gaily along in a pair of ultra-styled, high-heeled, very tall kid boots.

"Those are beautiful boots, Najia," I comment. "I saw pictures of some like that in *Grazia* this week. We can't buy them in Tripoli."

"Thank you, Signora. My friend brings them from Rome."

Najia has the increased freedom which in Libya goes with not being white. In the United States dark blood has been a handicap; here in Libya, where women of Semitic blood are hemmed in by stringent restrictions, dark blood can add stature to woman's estate. Yet this girl's very freedom shows Arab racial prejudice, implying, as it does, that it matters less what an African girl does for she is a less valued household possession.

Some time later I read in the Tripoli newspaper that another Libyan girl, Fatima Etuate, of seventeen years, was training to be an airlines agent and hostess. She had been flown to London where, like any other female, she did some hasty shopping for dresses and a sweater.

She was from Benghazi. A Bedawi, perhaps?

Outside the new Giorgimpopoli Pharmacy hangs a tradition-breaking sign — NAHDU PHARMACY, OWNED AND MANAGED BY MRS. AREF BEN MUSA.

Every morning at nine o'clock a little, battered red car driven by a small, bright-eyed woman, without either baracan or veil, drives up and parks outside the pharmacy. She jumps from the car, hurries to the adjacent vegetable stand, returns with her arms full of cauli-flower, cabbage or beans, which she dumps into her car. Now she searches her large handbag for a key, opens the pharmacy door, and enters. This is the owner-proprietor, Mrs. Ben Musa, the wife of a Libyan ambassador to a nearby country, a woman who has lived abroad and is now determined to put her time to good use.

Here she is to be found every day except Friday, smiling behind the neatest and best kept of pharmacy counters, handing out cough mixtures, cold remedies, eyedrops, painkillers, liniments, ointments, paper tissues, fruit salts, and feeding bottles to any who come — and many do. A licensed Italian woman prescription clerk works with her. Both have teen-age children, and the children often help in the shop, as they speak and read English as well as Italian and Arabic, while neither mother speaks English. Mrs. Ben Musa does not fit in at all with what I have said about the shackles of Libyan women — but she proves their capacity to throw them off.

The pharmacy was inaugurated some time ago by a cocktail party given by Essayed Aref Ben Musa on behalf of his wife. It was offi-cially opened that night by the Nazir of Health on behalf of the Governor of Tripolitania. Many foreigners of both sexes attended the cocktail party in the pharmacy premises. Mrs. Ben Musa herself did not attend. I suppose this was a fine point of some sort which I don't understand: the journey forward has many steps backward. But never mind, Mrs. Ben Musa was there bright and early the next morning at work.

The pharmacy may well make a million, but it isn't for the money alone that Mrs. Ben Musa does it. She likes her pharmacy, and she loves her work. I can see it in her interested, speculative face every time she sells me toothpaste, and asks about my last week's pain. This is her life.

It is the only pharmacy in Giorgimpopoli, and the situation is worth a fortune across from the largest supermarket, beside a vegetable stand, around the corner from the beauty shop, and almost beside the police station. There are always several policemen inside, busily buying babies' cough mixtures, powdered milk, pacifiers, dusting powders, feeding bottles and so on, with obvious family devotion.

The expectant father does the shopping here, and it is astonishing to see the kinds of infant supplies and baby equipment which were at one time stocked only for the local American mothers, and are now going out over the counter to Libyan fathers for Libyan homes. Mrs. Ben Musa serves everyone equally with a smile, but she takes especial care in explaining directions and dosage to Libyan customers, even wrapping daily doses in separate daily packets. Although not everyone would like to run a pharmacy, I think it compares favorably to life in a harem.

That little red car is a great assurance to me. Every time I see it on the road, busy and battered and bulging with bundles and children,

Business as usual at Traghen in Fezzan

its driver unveiled, energetic and cheery, looking freely to right and to left — I know that it can be done.

Here on the fourth shore of what was once the Roman Empire I hear the lost greatness of that Empire mourned. Here were its granaries, there its olive orchards; here its dams survive, there its cisterns; here were its roads, its monuments, its cities and temples and theaters. But gone is the glory of Rome.

Today on Roman ruins stands Libya, a land that is ancient and a kingdom that is new; a desert denuded, a country once impoverished, becomes prosperous today on its fossil endowments — but not on these alone. The Roman Empire was made great by the Romans. Only the Libyans will make Libya great, and only the women will make her strong.

45. Last Handful of Sand

A VEILED Libyan woman traveling alone to Rome to meet her husband? Such a thing was unbelievable eight years ago; today it happens.

Nafisa is dressed in a long brown coat which Badreddin has sent to her from the United States, where he has been studying for a year on a scholarship grant at Missoula University in Montana. He sent also the small brown hat she wears, the high-heeled slippers, and a handsome shopping bag in which she carries all her credentials. The only Libyan touch is the opaque black veil which Nafisa, after kissing four-year-old Osama and baby Samira goodbye, and before emerging from the house, drapes securely over her head and face.

How would I feel, I wonder, if for the first time in my life I prepared to travel alone, to leave my homeland, to go up in an airplane, and to show my face in public? I think I might be more perturbed than Nafisa, and she is nervous enough. No astronaut going into outer space could face a more grueling test.

To make matters worse, there is a crisis about her reservation, which is still not certain. Unused to the popularity of air travel, Badreddin's brother, Najmedin, whom Badreddin has entrusted to buy Nafisa's ticket, has not applied for the reservation in time. For three days now, he and I and Harry have been applying what pressure we can to Alitalia to get Nafisa a seat. My pressure consists only of talking pathetically to the manager about the tragedy of the Libyan husband meeting the plane to greet his wife — and no wife; about the first-ever trip of the wife — and no trip; about the psychological effect on Libyan-Italian relations, et cetera. I know that they *do* have a seat — planes always do — but you have to know the right threat to make to get it!

This morning we are driving to the airport in hopes. Najmedin, a gentle, well-educated, Italian-speaking young teacher, who was badly lamed by an Allied bomb in the war, is with us. Nafisa and I sit together in the back, and he sits in front with Imperatore. Nafisa's hands are like ice, but considering the circumstances I think she is composed.

I tell her that if she doesn't get a seat on today's plane, we will come to the airport again tomorrow, by which time we will surely have succeeded in getting a reservation. As we do not have Badreddin's hotel address, we will ask Alitalia to find him at the airport, where he will be looking for her.

But Nafisa shakes her head vigorously, and says, No! If she doesn't get on the plane today, she is not going! If Allah wills her to go to Rome, he will get her a seat!

I personally am urging Allah very earnestly in my prayers, as we travel towards the airport, to get her that seat. I couldn't bear not to see this trip go through.

Arrived at the airport, we visit the reservations desk immediately, and there is still no seat. The office is seething with people who have reservations, and quite a few like us, I hear, who are waiting for that one extra seat! I call Najmedin's attention to this, and say, "She may not be first on the list! We'll have to *do* something! Whom do you know?"

He thinks soberly — and an idea comes: he will phone the chief of police, an old friend of Badreddin's, and a distant relative.

"Good, good! Why didn't we think of it before! But hurry!"

Nafisa and I sit and wait; she doesn't realize, I hope, that all this row of people is waiting for that one seat. Nafisa whispers through her veil, Thank you for helping me. I squeeze her hands, and hold them with my own cold hands. Finally Najmedin returns. The police chief is out of his office; Najmedin must call again. We glance at the clock. Less than half an hour to flight time. "Are her documents all passed, and her exit permit ready, in case she goes?"

"Yes, we have everything — except the seat."

Now I spot a young man in the crowd, one of George's friends, who is returning to London to his university. I grasp the opportunity, and hurry over to him and tell him our trouble. I describe Badreddin carefully to him, and say, Now you see that young Libyan woman over there? If she doesn't get on the plane, please find her husband at the Rome airport and tell him that she will come tomorrow; for him to meet tomorrow's plane. He agrees.

Now we learn that the plane will touch down in Sicily before going on to Rome. Again I approach the young man, who must by now regret our acquaintance, but remains amiable. I say, Please, if this young Libyan woman *does* get on the plane, please watch her when it comes down in Catania, and be sure that she gets back on the plane when it leaves Catania. Again he agrees, and grins understandingly. I think even young foreigners in Libya are sympathetic with the problems of the veiled Libyan woman.

Najmedin leaves us to phone once more. Nafisa seems calm, no doubt trusting in Allah — but I am watching the clock.

Najmedin is away some time; it is almost the scheduled hour for the plane to depart. At last I see him coming, and his face speaks. Hamdu li'llah! Nepotism has won, Nafisa has the seat, and God bless the chief of police!

The hour and the moment are here. This Nafisa is remarkable! Her pocketbook in hand, her documents out, her veil down, she and we work our way through the ticket door, and then, given sanctuary by our veiled woman, we ignore the policeman and go with her to the plane, and inside to her seat. She settles down quite calmly, in Allah's care. We fasten her seat belt, and leave, as she lifts her veil . . .

Tonight the scene is in reverse, and Nafisa with Badreddin is about to return triumphant; the astronaut comes back to earth after ten days in orbit!

Three of Badreddin's brothers, many of his friends, and many others from the Forest Department, are at the airport to meet him, as he returns from his year in the United States. I alone am there to meet Nafisa, as only a female may meet her, and obviously not a Libyan one.

Badreddin's brothers are an astonishing group, all good looking and capable. The youngest is a Libyan Army colonel, one of six Libyan military experts who last year made an around the world tour of foreign defense installations. He is very young, and extraordinarily handsome, with an air of supreme self-confidence. My favorite, however is Najmedin, with whom I shared the problems of getting Nafisa airborne.

Hammet is there, looking very smart and swagger in a military style overcoat and, as always, well groomed. The members of the Forest Department all look fairly prosperous, neat and well dressed. It is impossible to exaggerate the difference in appearance between the young civil service men of today and those of nine years ago, when a public gathering seldom produced a single neatly dressed young man. It is not primarily the difference in the money they spend on dress, but the fact that they are now conscious of the value and desirability of a neat, well-shaven, well-groomed appearance. One clean shirt, for instance, is not expected to last the season!

Harry is here, also, and we are listening to the young Libyans discuss the changes in government which were announced this afternoon. At last there is a change they can approve of, as a great favorite, Mohamed Bey Derna, a fine agriculturalist, who is loved and respected by all the young men with whom he has worked, has just been named the federal Minister of Agriculture.

The Alitalia plane touches down, and rolls in. The young colonel picks up Osama, Badreddin's young son, and walks across the tarmac to the plane, conscious that his uniform need follow no airport rules. I go with him, to be there when Nafisa descends.

We wait, while all the passengers disembark. At last, black-veiled and carefully assisted down the landing steps by the hostess, comes the single Libyan woman passenger, Nafisa, almost blinded by the veil and the dusk, and battling with paper bags and parcels. Just behind her is Badreddin.

The colonel thrusts Osama into Nafisa's arms to compete with the tumbling bundles, and then he hurls himself on Badreddin in brotherly embrace in true Libyan fashion, with kisses and hugs. After welcoming Badreddin, I take Nafisa by the arm, with Osama and paper bags, and lead her across the tarmac to where our car is parked. Thus she escapes both Immigration and Customs, which will be handled by her husband, as is customary with veiled Libyan ladies, who can't be spied upon.

Nafisa seems quite unchanged until, inside the motorcar, she lifts her veil, and I see that her hair is cut short and waved. I ask if she was happy in Rome, and she smiles and points at all the parcels she has brought. I imagine that shopping was the greatest of her pleasures, although I am sure that many of the packages are either gifts or commissioned purchases for friends and relatives.

Without waiting for Badreddin, we drive directly to his and Nafisa's home, where she rejoins once more the mass of family females: mothers, sisters, cousins, in-laws, and a dozen nubile females, as well as innumerable infants in arms and toddlers; and all are welcoming, laughing with, kissing, teasing, giggling at, admiring, and squeezing Nafisa, who looks much gayer now than the day when she said goodbye to them. What a relief, perhaps, to be safe again, and out of sight?

Her short, waved hair is a modern step which delights the young ones of the family, and alarms the elders.

Has she changed at all inside, I wonder? Can she forget the other world?

I ask Badreddin later if she was able to eat the unaccustomed dishes in Rome. He said that at first she tried to eat in restaurants with him, but the sight and taste of the strange foods, and the odor of pork, nauseated her. Also, the fact that she was not used to eating with him, or with any men nearby, had made her too nervous to eat in public. In the end, he ate alone in restaurants, and then brought food that she could eat back to her in her hotel room.

Lifting the veil is less easy than we think.

Badreddin was showing us the color films he had made in Seattle of our daughter, Jean, with her husband, Harold, and their four children. In the film he shows us first, he is visiting Jean and Harold on his Thanksgiving vacation from Missoula University. The four children are mugging the screen enthusiastically.

In the second film which he shows, this one taken by Harold, Chris, who is near the age of Badreddin's own son, Osama, is cuddled up close to Badreddin. Jean has written to me of how Chris hero-worshiped Badreddin, and tagged his heels every minute of the visit.

When I first see this family film group, I say, "But where are you, Badreddin?" seeing only an unknown young American sprawled out in a big chair in American male fashion, dressed in a colored wool sport shirt and heavy slacks.

"That's me," says Badreddin, putting his finger on the unknown American.

I look again in perplexity. "But you look so American! Yet, when you are in the desert and wear that Arab headcloth, you look like a perfect Arab sheik!"

Badreddin laughs, and quotes, "Clothes make the man."

"Jean said that the children were at you all the time to tell them everything about Libya," I say, "the desert, the camels, the people, what you eat, and wear, and everything you could think of!"

"Yes," says Badreddin. "But most of all they liked me to talk about Ramadan. And when I tell them that we do not eat or drink at all during the day, for a month, they think it is very cruel, and that we must suffer terribly! Chris was very worried, and cannot understand how we can become accustomed to it."

"Did you make Jean any lamb stew, or kus kus?" I ask.

"Jean is an excellent cook," says Badreddin seriously. "She did not need me to help her. Also, she is a good mother, and wife."

"Do you think you would like to live in the United States?"

"Oh, no!" he says in a horrified tone.

I already know what he thinks of the Missoula climate, where he had icicles hanging from his nose all winter!

"Why not, Badreddin?"

"Well," he hesitates, not wishing to be tactless, I think. "Well, it is not my country."

"What did you think of American women at home?"

"But they are never at home!"

I laugh. "I really mean, what do you think of American women in America?"

"They all have boyfriends! It surprises me. The wives have boyfriends, the husbands have girlfriends. That is all they talk about at Missoula — my boyfriend, my girlfriend!"

It surprises me, too! I used to think of Americans as being rather puritanical. Perhaps I do not know Americans any more.

"Of course," he continues, "the United States is not a Moslem country."

"No, but there is religious freedom. You can believe as you wish."

"Well, yes, maybe," he laughs. "One day some young men come to call on me, and ask me what is my religion. When I say I am Moslem, they say they like me to go to their church with them, and learn another religion."

"What a nerve!" says Harry. "What religion were they promoting? Not Judaism, I hope!"

"I really forget. I think perhaps Mormon, or Adventist, or Witnesses, but I forget. I say, No, thank you very much, I do not wish to learn a new religion. I like very much to remain Moslem. Then they say they wish to help me find God. I tell them that I did find God, and Allah is God. They say, but you do not understand! I say, you do not understand Islam! So I explain. But they just shake their heads and say, We wish to help you! If you change your mind, you telephone us, and we come any time!"

"But, Badreddin, do they do that to all foreign students?"

"I think so, because I have a Pakistani friend there, and he told me that they want him to find God, too."

"They'd have a problem with a Hindu!" says Harry.

This is a farewell party for us, who came to Libya for a year, and who now after almost nine years are leaving, because Harry is retiring from FAO.

"But why do you go?" asks Badreddin. "We would like you to stay here forever. Our climate is good, no icicles hang on your nose, and you have good friends here. You shall become Libyans!"

"But we have no house here, and we do have one in Victoria."

"You buy a house here. Hammet sells you one of his."

"Yes, my father," says Hammet promptly. "For small price, too!"

"Foreigners can't own land in Libya," Harry reminds them.

"Ah, do not worry! All that shall be arranged!" reassure Badreddin and Hammet.

"I suppose," says Harry seriously, "that our answer is the same as yours, Badreddin. This is not our country."

We have eaten a large Libyan dinner, cooked by an invisible Nafisa, and served to us by Badreddin. There was sherba, a rich soup, kus kus with lamb and red pumpkin and chick peas, also kafta, a Libyan speciality of tiny meat balls, then cornstarch pudding, fresh apples and oranges, and Libyan tea. Although we were all slightly torpid afterward, the films have awakened us.

Badreddin turns on Radio Libya for the news in Arabic. It is principally politics. Oddly enough, the government has not fallen! And the Five Year Plan is going through.

Now Badreddin rises, clears his throat, looks very impressive, and makes a gracious speech to Harry on behalf of the Libyan foresters. He presents him with a very beautiful, large, silver plate, hand-hammered in Libyan designs, and engraved in the center in both English and Arabic, as follows: PRESENTED TO MR. H. G. KEITH BY FORESTERS IN LIBYA FOR SINCERE FRIENDSHIP.

Before we leave I go back to Nafisa's bedroom to thank her, and say goodbye. Large-eyed, smiling, vivid and beautiful, she glows with the success of the evening, even though she was not present with the guests. She is a warm-blooded girl, filled with love and affection, and the need to give it to those about her.

Her hair is recovering now from its Roman clip and hangs down to her shoulders, on top of the rose satin dressing gown that Badreddin brought from the States. She is very happy now that he is back, she says. She hopes that he never, never goes away again! A woman needs her husband all the time.

Lena and I paid a farewell visit to Rabiaa a few days before we left. Rabiaa and Abdul and their children all love Lena; Lena, who hates kus kus, honey cakes, rancid oil, fat meat, Arabic radio, and many things Arabic, loves Abdul and Rabiaa and their family.

Abdul, after a long separation (with pay) from government because of his defiance of the minister above him, has just been appointed by the King as a minister himself, a most unusual reward for political independence.

The family has moved to a larger house in the neighborhood, having worn out the one they were in. The moving was accomplished quite simply, as goods and furniture were carried on foot by houseboy, driver and children; chickens and rabbits were carried in arms, and ladies and girls were transported in the government Volkswagen. The only real problem was the goats, who entered the Volkswagen when their turn came, without complaint, but refused to get out of it. It soon appeared that either the vehicle door or the goats would have to be sacrificed, so the door was removed.

"More suitable to a Minister's wife" Rabiaa

We went on our farewell visit at ten A.M., having sent word the night before of our coming. Rabiaa received us dressed in a cloth-of-silver, high-waisted, Empire-line dress (suitable, I expect, to a minister's wife), with her jet hair piled high on her head, arranged by twin Fatima, she says. Her tattoos look paler, and I think she covers them with the flesh greasepaint I sent her. Except for tattoos, she has a marvelous skin of creamy perfection. She is a beautiful woman, as

I see her now — and yet nine years ago, would I have thought so? Or would I have seen just a plump, tattooed dame? I can't see clearly any more, because my eyes are filmed with love.

I knew we had to have tea, even though I felt I couldn't bear it; not because I don't like sweet Arab tea (although I don't), but because I know I'll never again see a tiny blue enamel teapot steaming on a charcoal brazier in a living room!

But I didn't have to bear it: we had weak tea served in English cups, suitable to a minister's establishment! Only the old ladies, sitting barefoot and cross-legged on chairs, shook their heads at such stuff.

I try to describe to Rabiaa the distance we are going, our route through the Panama Canal, the climate of Canada, and I show her snapshots of our Victoria home. She shakes her head at all those gloomy trees around the house. She asks Lena if she thinks she will like it in Canada.

Lena answers, "The Signora and the Signor are like my mama and papa; I go to live with them because they are my family now."

"But why do you want to leave Libya?" Rabiaa asks me. "Why don't you *stay* in Libya? Don't you like it here?" She looks at me, mystified.

I know there is only one way for her to understand. "Our married daughter and our son cannot live in Libya. To see them, we must go to North America," I say.

The old ladies nod, Rabiaa concedes, and the point is made.

"But you will come back some time to see us all again?" Rabiaa insists.

"I don't think so," I have to say.

To Rabiaa, this is a new idea, I see. Suddenly her eyes fill with tears. "But you have always been in Giorgimpopoli with me," she says. "I have no other friends in Giorgimpopoli!" She sniffs and wipes at her eyes.

Oh, dear! I don't want my tears to start yet. And this is the country to which I came, determined not to become emotionally involved!

"But you have your family, Rabiaa — and I have mine."

She nods, but continues to cry. Tears do not follow reasoning.

We kiss all around, including the old ladies. As I see them today, they are all very dear. We kiss again, Lena and I go out the door and down the walk. We look back at Rabiaa standing in her silver dress, with her hair once more falling down in a black river around her face, her jet black eyes wet with tears, her face distorted, her hands clasping and unclasping in an empty gesture — for something we have both lost — and we are not sure what.

Oh, dear. Oh, dear. Oh, dear.

Naturally, Hammet's farewell party was as different from Badreddin's as the two men are from each other. Hammet's was a cocktail party, most unusual for a Libyan host.

His apartment is elegantly furnished in gold-lacquered, tapestry-upholstered Louis Quinze furniture, manufactured in Egypt and imported to Libya by Hammet. Everything is authentic, or so it appears to me, who know nothing about gold Louis Quinze furniture except that Hammet likes it. Ornate-legged gold chairs, scroll-backed gold divans, magnificent, ornate gold-framed mirrors, crystal and gilt-trimmed ashtrays, vases and lamps, and glistening, tinkling crystal chandeliers overhead, and a many-colored, many-flowered carpet underfoot: it is a complete incarnation of Louise Quinze *siècle* influenced by *A Thousand Nights and a Night.*

There is no other abode like it in Libya. Hammet and Badria are proud of it, and somehow it suits them. Only the gold silken hair of Badria could compete with the furnishings about her. Yet her beauty seems always more delicate, the more glittering her background.

As for Hammet, one of his dearest qualities is his frank delight in his own acquisitions, of which he now has many. He is a part owner in several agencies, a transport truck owner, a landholder in Giorgimpopoli, and a professional man. Without going into detail, I can only say that Hammet is a marvelous financier!

His cocktail party was to be done in the best Western style. All the members of FAO were invited, and many of our Libyan friends, and all of the Forest Department. Hammet consulted Lena extensively for expert advice on what drinks to serve, and what quantities of each to have on hand, and how to make the preferred appetizers and hors d'oeuvres. It was to be an event in Libyan society history.

Badria was to be present as hostess, as she always is when we come to the house.

Hammet planned everything perfectly, except for one detail of timing: Badria was pregnant, and due any day for the baby. Hammet was ardently hoping that she would give prompt birth to the baby in time to hurry home and make hors d'oeuvres for the party. As for the baby, Hammet could take it or leave it, having fathered a number.

I am happy to say that it all turned out perfectly. A son was born in time, Badria made hundreds of appetizers, she was also a gracious hostess, and Hammet was a glowing, triumphant host, and everyone who was invited arrived.

The peak came when Hammet called for silence, and read a speech, written for him, I am sure, by Bill Marshall, a Scots friend. This speech eulogized Harry and was more than kind to me, and was followed by a presentation to Harry of heavy gold English sovereign cuff links, and to me of a gold brooch set with pearls and garnets.

This is my undying memory of Hammet and Badria: a house with golden furniture, with golden drapes, with a golden-haired girl, and a dark, unfathomable man under whose tapering fingers all things turn to gold, reaching out tonight with lavish hands to press gold gifts upon his friends.

This was almost the last pain I felt: as exhaustion progresses, one becomes anesthetized against suffering. Perhaps this is the best way to leave a country that you love too much.

This exhaustion is added to because I packed all last night. Harry slept soundly all night, secure in the knowledge that everything had been taken care of, arranged, and efficiently handled several weeks before — from which time on his greatest responsibility was hurrying me.

Consequently, this morning I arrive at Idris Airport half-dazed. When I see all the people there, I wonder who can be leaving to draw such a crowd! Then suddenly I know.

I can remember writing, when we first came to Libya, "My contacts with the Libyans are pleasant, but I know none of them well, and I don't think I ever shall."

Today the airport is filled with friends, and half of them are Libyans. Those whom we love the most are here — but without their wives. Abdul brings me one final "Please come back sometime," from Rabiaa, and adds, "May Allah go with you!" from himself.

Badreddin is here, literally managing everything — our luggage, Customs, Immigration, and permits — for "my father," proud that he can do it.

"And we will not forget the trees," he promises Harry. "Each year we shall plant more seedlings, to have them ready for the time when you return!" Harry smiles, and pats his arm.

Hammet stands near Harry, but to one side, looking oddly alone in the chattering crowd. It is the same look of aloneness which I remember always from the face of "my son Mohamed." Yet surely this fortunate Hammet, with his superfluity of wives and Lovely Ones, his nursery of children, his big businesses, and his golden home, is never lonely! Who knows? Are we not all — alone?

"Hammet, will you please try to keep in touch with Mohamed's wife and children? And send me word of them sometimes?" I ask. He nods absently, and smiles, and I remember our first meeting with that glowing smile.

It is a magnificent North African day, well calculated to break the hearts of departing travelers. Lena has her Italian friends near, some weeping; but not Lena; she is proud, she has already told them to stop! Maltese Pucci stands nervously beside his Alitalia air crate, afraid to lift a leg, his tranquilizers seeming only to make him more alert.

The time is here when Harry and I, Lena and Pucci, must shake off the dust and sands of Libya; abandon its seductive sea, its singeing desert winds, its lucid sky, its blazing sun, its beauty, elegance, and squalor — and its enigmatic, contradictory, prodigal, pious people whom I love.

If only I could take them all with me: Badreddin and Nafisa, Hammet and Badria, Abdul and Rabiaa, Majid and Samira, Halima, Mabruk; Mr. Abou Babba to grow my oranges, Badreddin to philosophize, Hammet to make us gay, and Badria because she is beautiful and brave, and Rabiaa because she misses me — and set them all up in "God's country," as we Westerners like to refer to our part of the globe, quite confident that God would never settle for keeps in any other!

But — the fact is that these friends don't wish to leave Allah's country, which is their home.

I would like to take with me all my United Nations friends of many nationalities: Kathleen and Harold, U Hla Maung and Khin Than Tin, Gerry, Kitty and Wym, Nine and Karst, Anita and Jock, Y.Y. and Gay, and Leonce — friends from Europe, from the UK, the Middle East and East. But they wouldn't come; all have commitments on a soil of their own. All have their God, their Allah, their own deity who suits them very well. No, God's country must get on without them, too!

I would like to take with me to Victoria, stone by stone, the white villa with its pink geraniums, its veranda with flowering cacti, its terrace on which to bake in the sun, its high stone walls to shelter behind, and its wrought iron gate to open to friends. Only — a white stone villa in Victoria! Too cold! The pink geraniums would freeze in winter, the terrace would drip with the rains of the evergreen playground, the high stone wall would offend better gardens' tradition, and the iron gate would be anti-togetherly.

I would like to take with me the Racing Camel Hotel and set it up, blue-tiled courtyard by blue-tiled courtyard, and then go there daily and sit under the great magenta flowering bougainvillea and drink tea, or gin. Only — there wouldn't be any magenta flowering bougainvillea in Victoria, or the blazing African sun in the courtyard, or a myriad sparrows in the vines, or any muezzin calling to prayers — still, there would be gin!

Every person to his destiny, under Allah, or under God. Mine is the West: that of these friends is not.

I can only say hamdu li'llah that I have known them. Thank God, and thank Allah, for friends.

We are back again in Victoria, in the same old rickety house, almost sixty years old, they say, and nothing new but the crimson front door with the brass Maltese knocker.

Upstairs in our bright dormer bedroom, things are much the same; two long Chinese brush drawings still hang over the beds, and very old Japanese prints from Kyoto hang beside the fireplace. Now there's a sunshine-filled Gauguin Tahiti reproduction I found in Rome (recent acquisition) tacked up on the closet door, the only space left.

It's a comfortable bed, I think, as I sink into it, and reach for my book. But the room is too full of memories for me to read. I am almost asleep when I hear, or perhaps I dream, heels clicking on the road outside. I listen — and the gate swings, the front door grunts, and the stairs creak; it's an old house, I said. The stairs creak as they used to do with young, stealthy steps — though I know that tonight it's only an old house creaking. The hall creaks, my door squeaks, and a beloved apparition ducks in its head and says with an artless smile, "Good night, Ma. Don't worry, don't fuss!"

Index

462

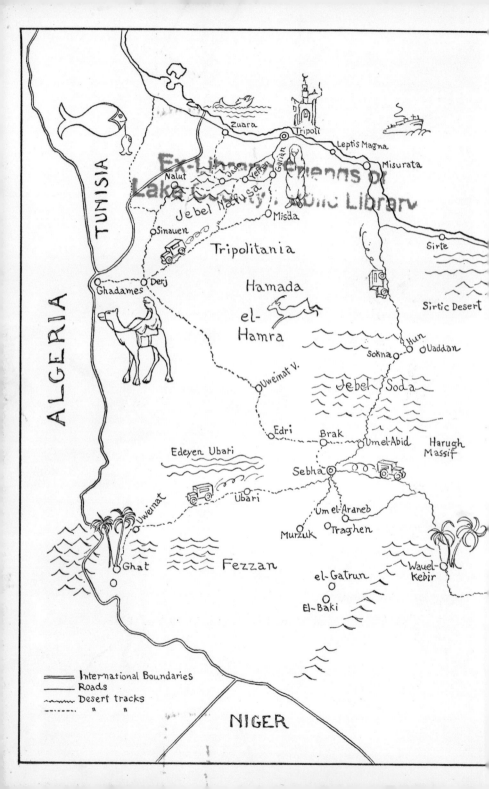

ALGERIA

TUNISIA

Zuara · Tripoli · Leptis Magna · Misurata

Nalut · Jadu · Yefren · Gharian

Jebel Nafusa

Sinauen · Misda · Sirte

Tripolitania

Ghadames · Derj

Hamada el-Hamra

Sirtic Desert

Uweinat V. · Sohna · Hun · Uaddan

Jebel Soda

Edri · Brak · Um el-Abid · Harugh Massif

Edeyen Ubari

Uweinat · Ubari · Sebha

Um el-Araneb · Traghen

Murzuk

Ghat · Fezzan

el-Gatrun · Wau el-Kebir

El-Baki

——— International Boundaries
——— Roads
∼∼∼∼ Desert tracks
-------- "   "

NIGER

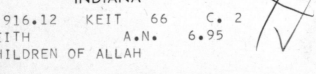